Love at Fourteen

Fuka Mizutani

1

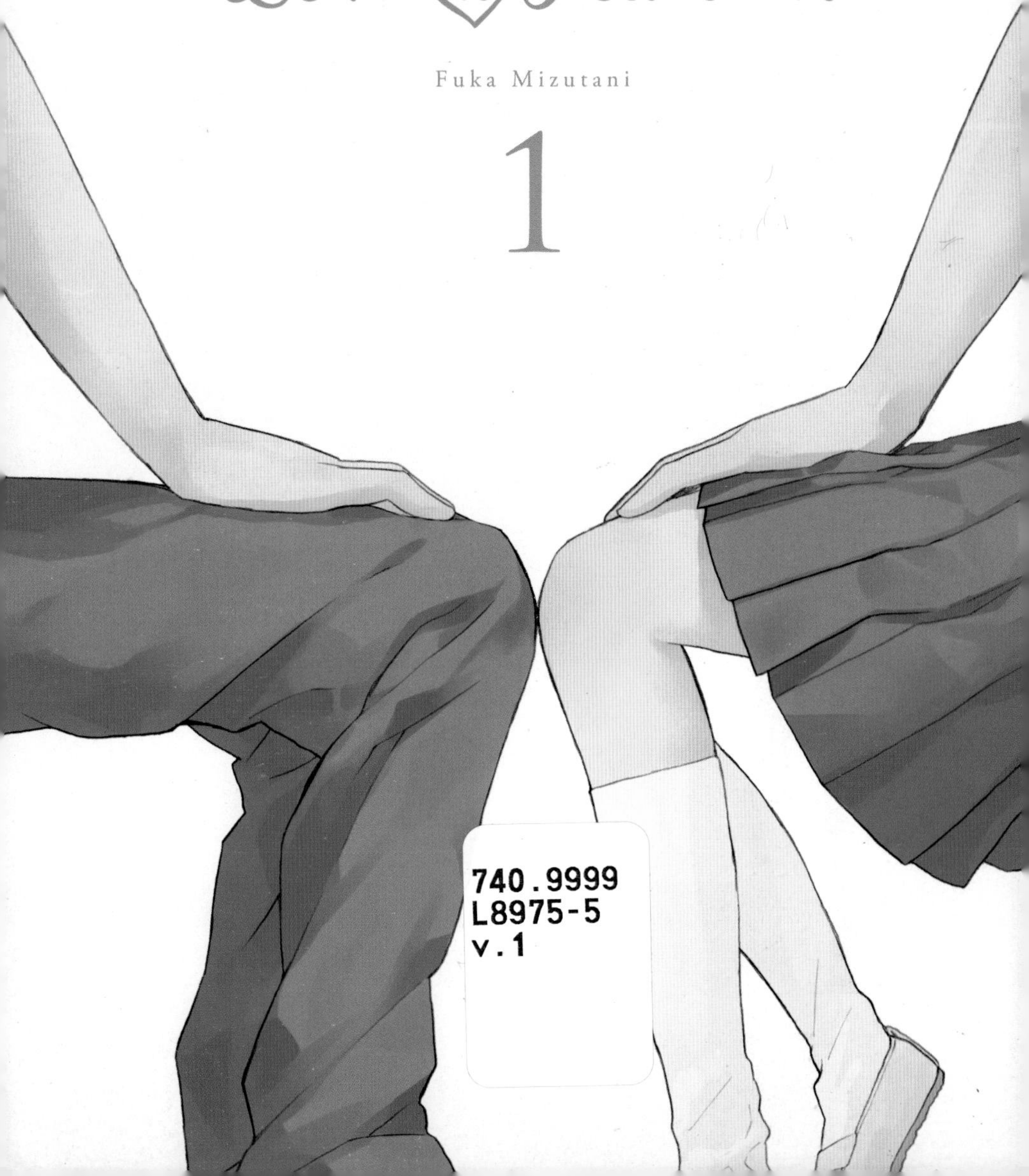

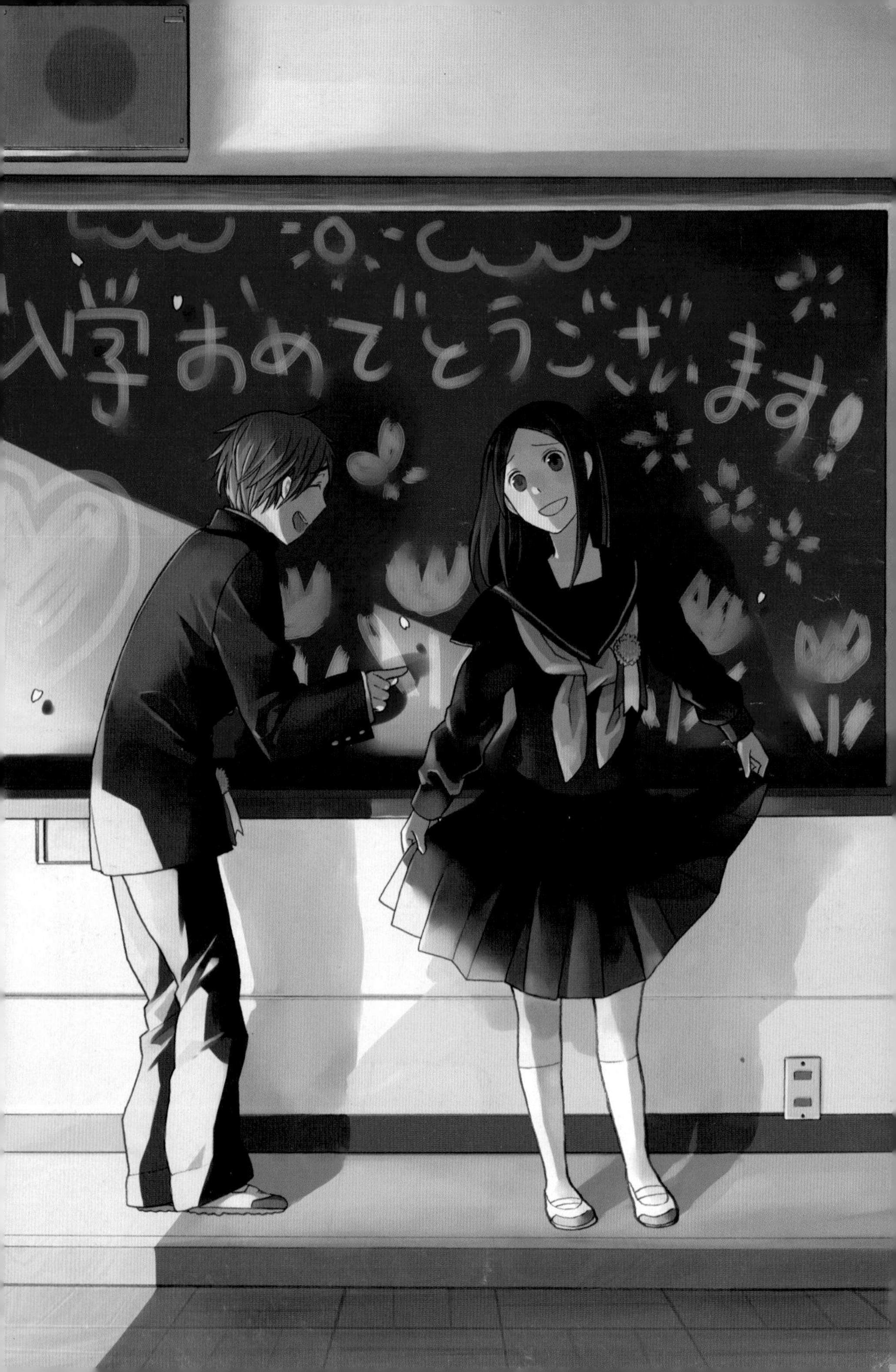
入学おめでとうございます!

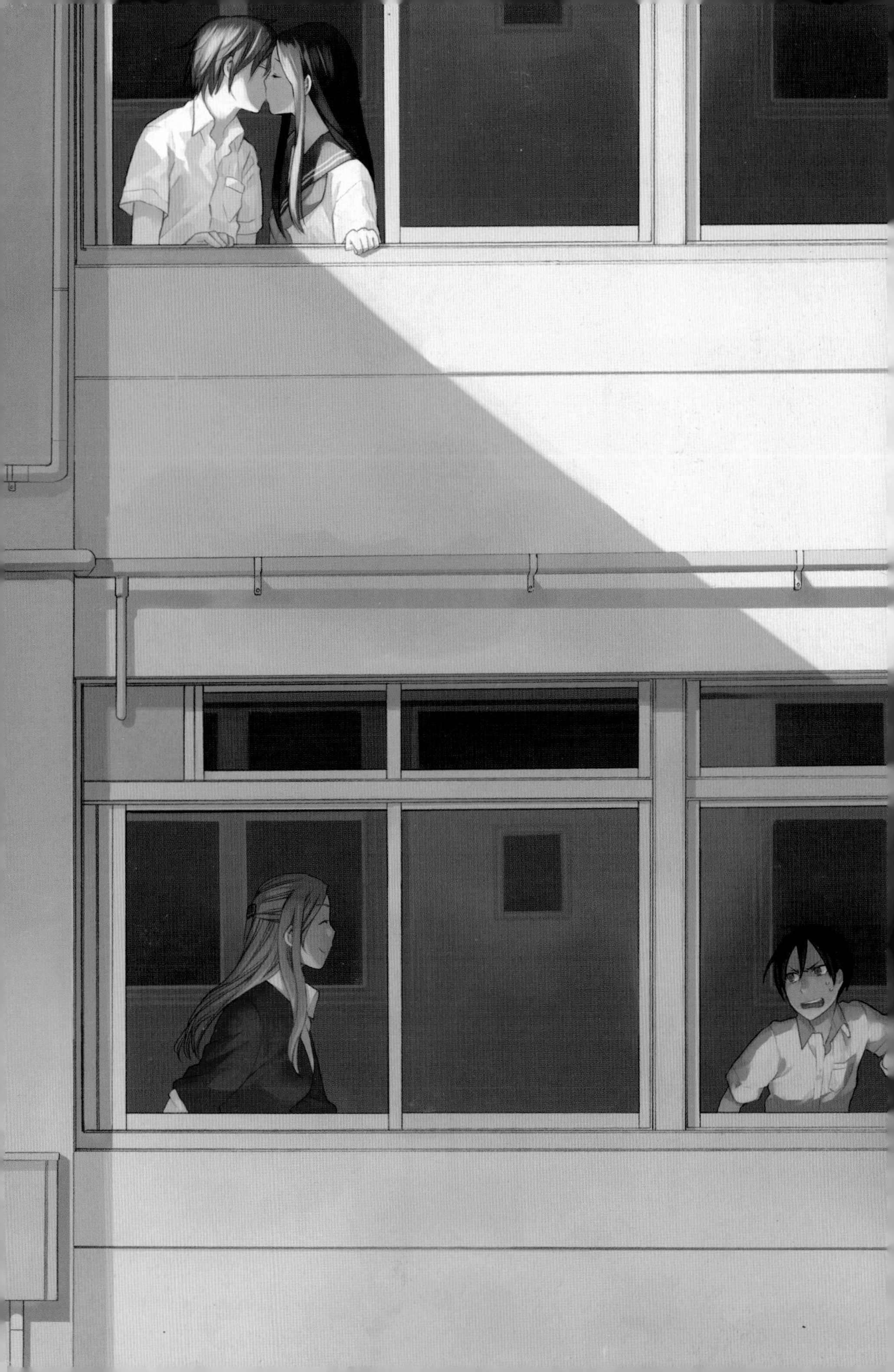

Contents

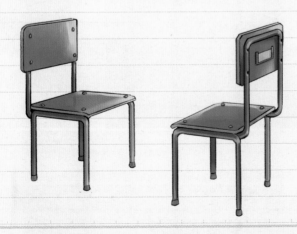

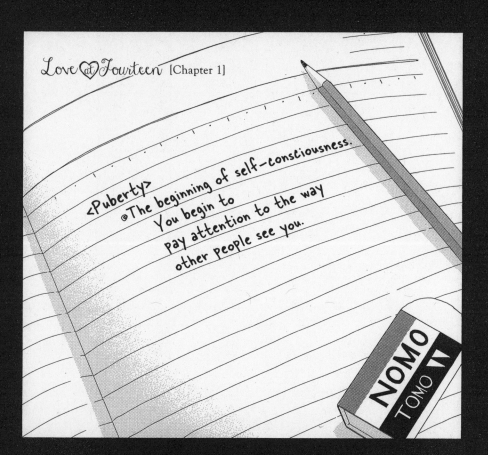

Love ♡ Fourteen [Chapter 1]

<Puberty>
◉The beginning of self-consciousness.
You begin to pay attention to the way other people see you.

NOMO
TOMO N

THESE FEW, MEAGER LINES IN A TEXTBOOK...

...ENCAPSULATED OUR FOURTEEN-YEAR-OLD SELVES.

Love ♡ at Fourteen

[Chapter 1]

CLASS 2-B'S...

...KANATA TANAKA AND KAZUKI YOSHIKAWA ARE RATHER MATURE.

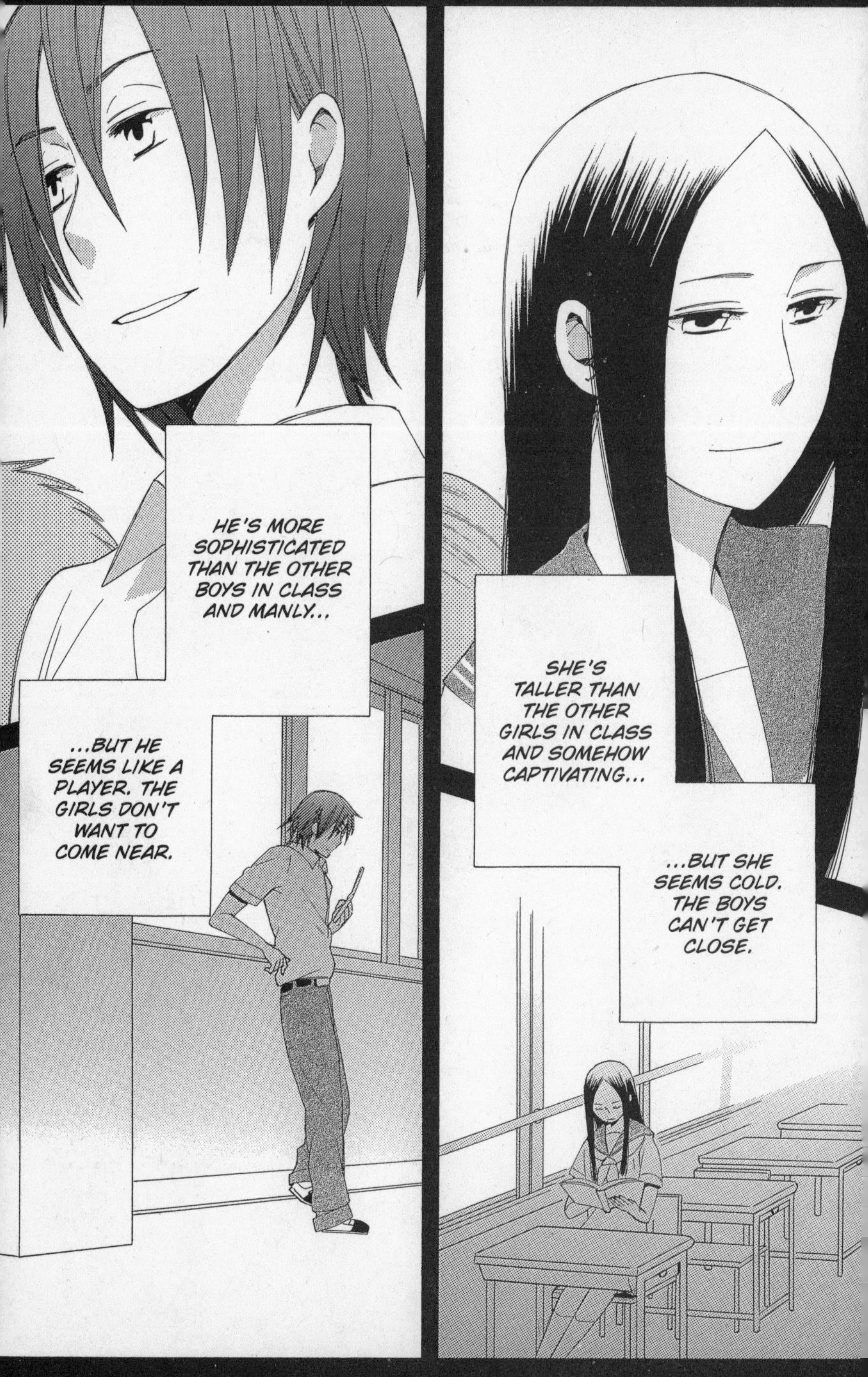
SHE'S TALLER THAN THE OTHER GIRLS IN CLASS AND SOMEHOW CAPTIVATING...
...BUT SHE SEEMS COLD. THE BOYS CAN'T GET CLOSE.
HE'S MORE SOPHISTICATED THAN THE OTHER BOYS IN CLASS AND MANLY...
...BUT HE SEEMS LIKE A PLAYER. THE GIRLS DON'T WANT TO COME NEAR.

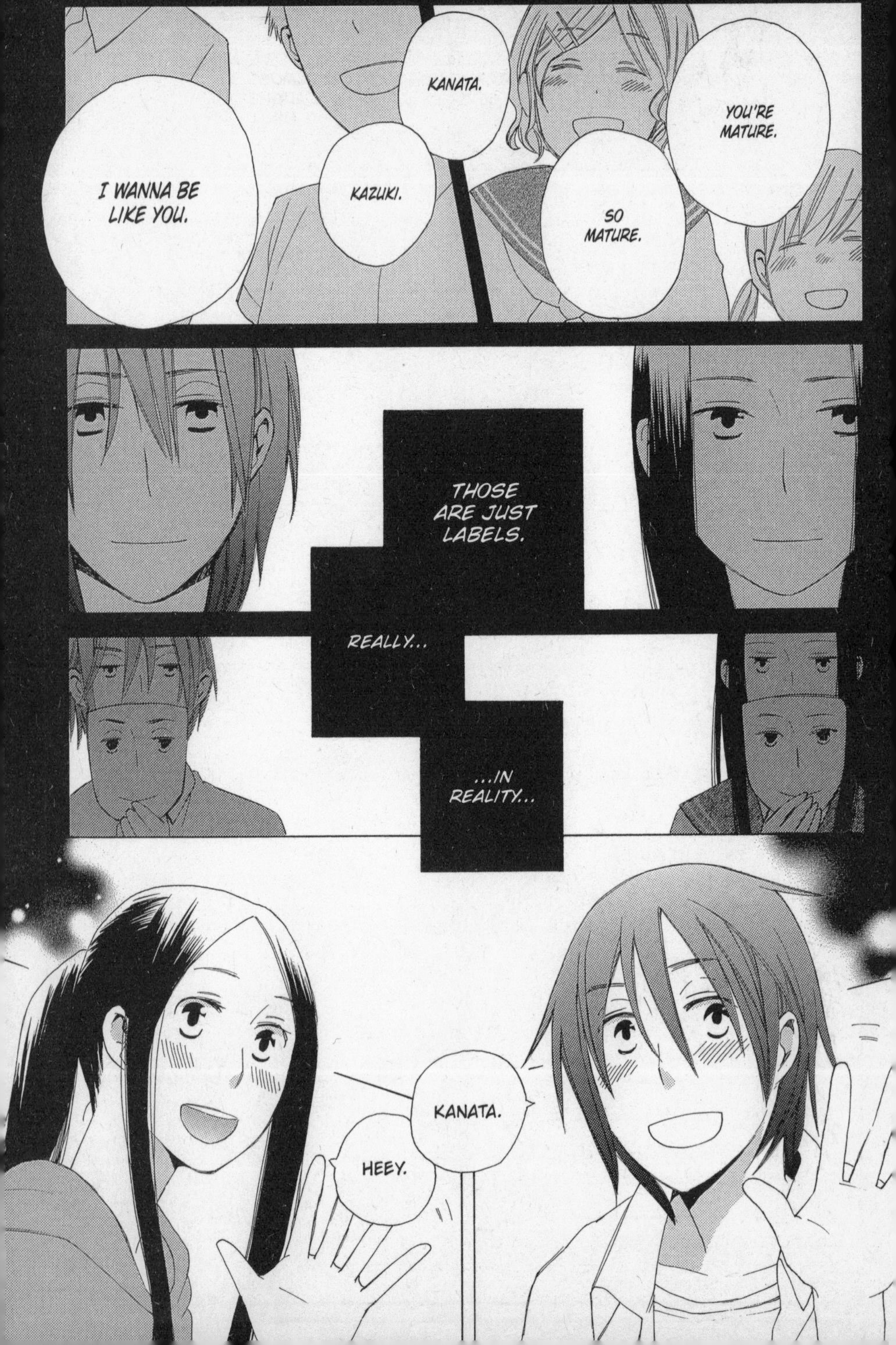
YOU'RE MATURE.
SO MATURE.
KANATA.
KAZUKI.
I WANNA BE LIKE YOU.
THOSE ARE JUST LABELS.
REALLY...
...IN REALITY...
KANATA.
HEEY.

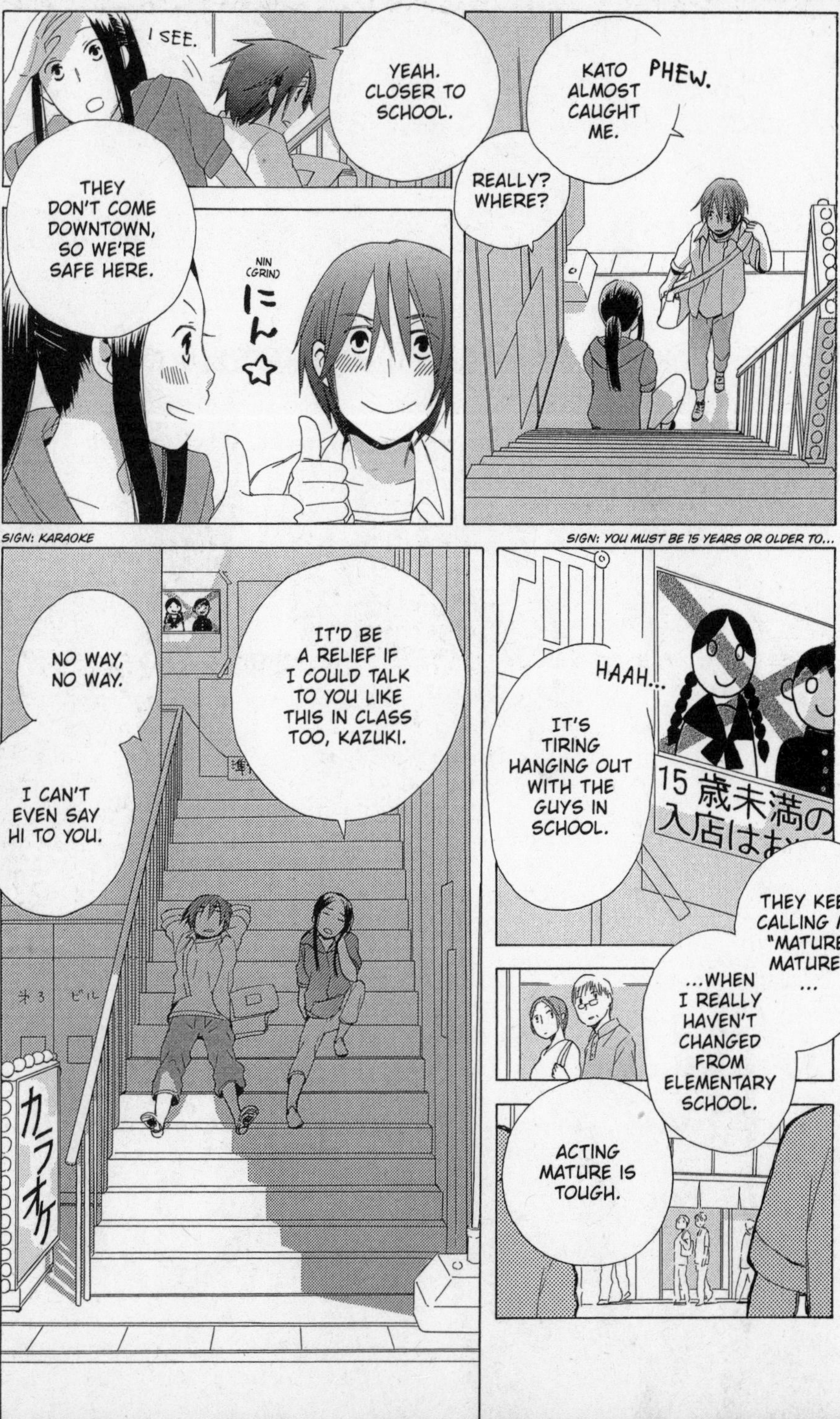
KATO ALMOST CAUGHT ME.
PHEW.
REALLY? WHERE?
YEAH. CLOSER TO SCHOOL.
I SEE.
THEY DON'T COME DOWNTOWN, SO WE'RE SAFE HERE.
NIN (GRIN)
にん☆
SIGN: YOU MUST BE 15 YEARS OR OLDER TO...
SIGN: KARAOKE
HAAH...
IT'S TIRING HANGING OUT WITH THE GUYS IN SCHOOL.
15 歳未満の
入店はお
THEY KEEP CALLING ME "MATURE, MATURE"...
...WHEN I REALLY HAVEN'T CHANGED FROM ELEMENTARY SCHOOL.
ACTING MATURE IS TOUGH.
IT'D BE A RELIEF IF I COULD TALK TO YOU LIKE THIS IN CLASS TOO, KAZUKI.
NO WAY, NO WAY.
I CAN'T EVEN SAY HI TO YOU.
カラオケ

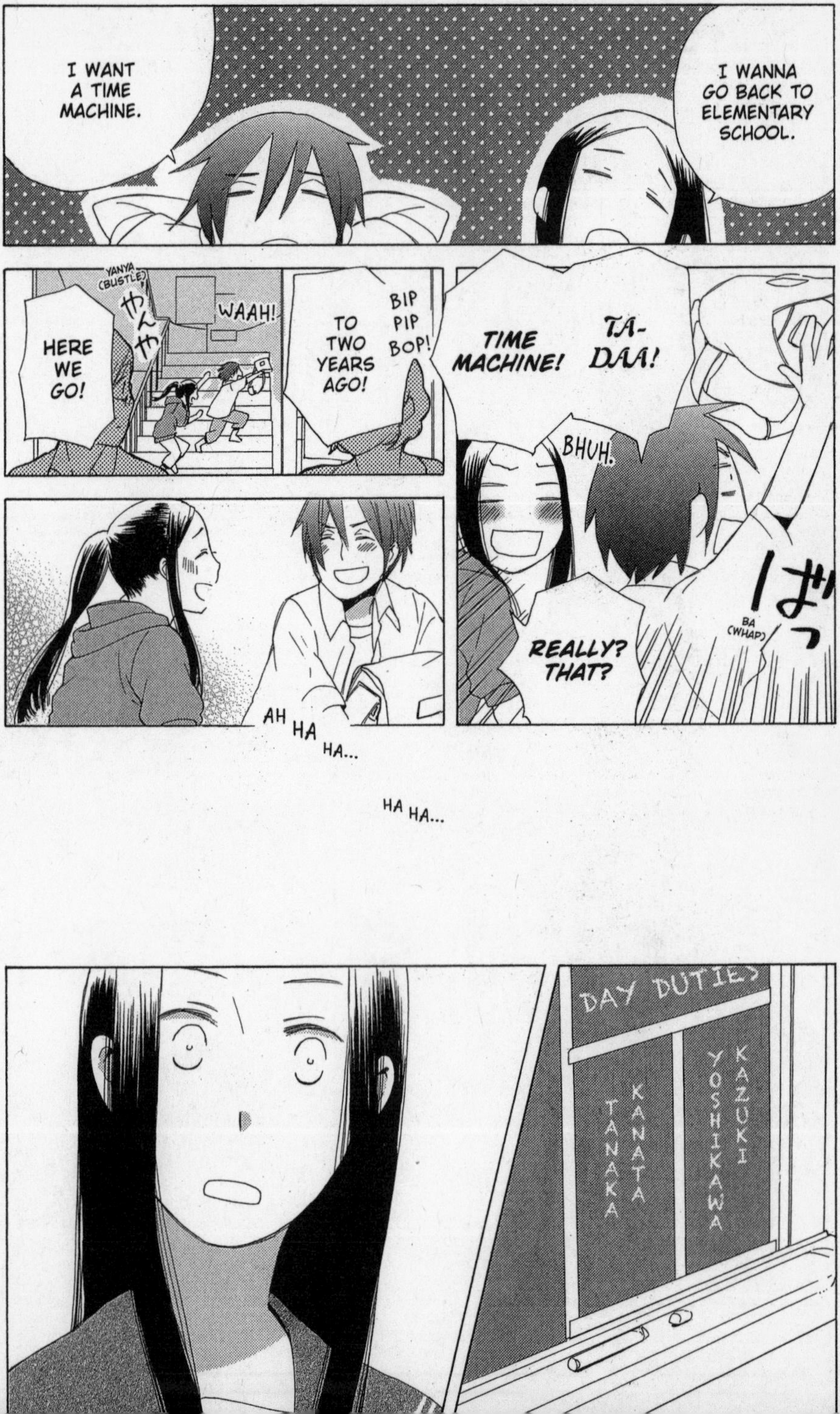
I WANNA GO BACK TO ELEMENTARY SCHOOL.
I WANT A TIME MACHINE.
TA-DAA!
TIME MACHINE!
BHUH.
BIP PIP BOP!
TO TWO YEARS AGO!
WAAH!
やんや
YANYA (BUSTLE)
HERE WE GO!
ぱっ
BA (WHAP)
REALLY? THAT?
AH HA HA...
HA HA...
DAY DUTIES
KAZUKI YOSHIKAWA
KANATA TANAKA

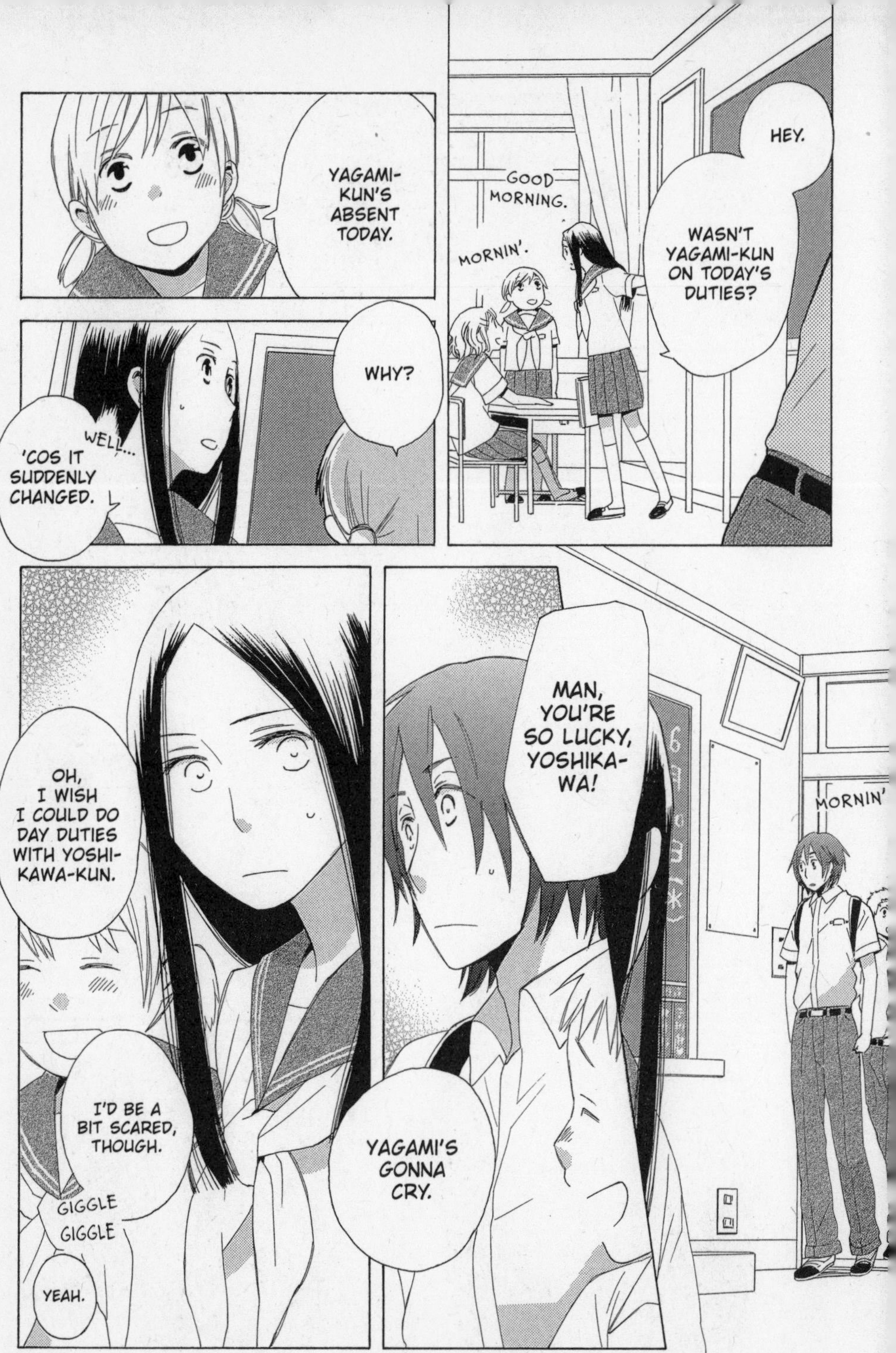

HEY.
WASN'T YAGAMI-KUN ON TODAY'S DUTIES?
GOOD MORNING.
MORNIN'.
YAGAMI-KUN'S ABSENT TODAY.
WHY?
WELL...
'COS IT SUDDENLY CHANGED.
MORNIN'
MAN, YOU'RE SO LUCKY, YOSHIKAWA!
YAGAMI'S GONNA CRY.
OH, I WISH I COULD DO DAY DUTIES WITH YOSHIKAWA-KUN.
I'D BE A BIT SCARED, THOUGH.
GIGGLE GIGGLE
YEAH.

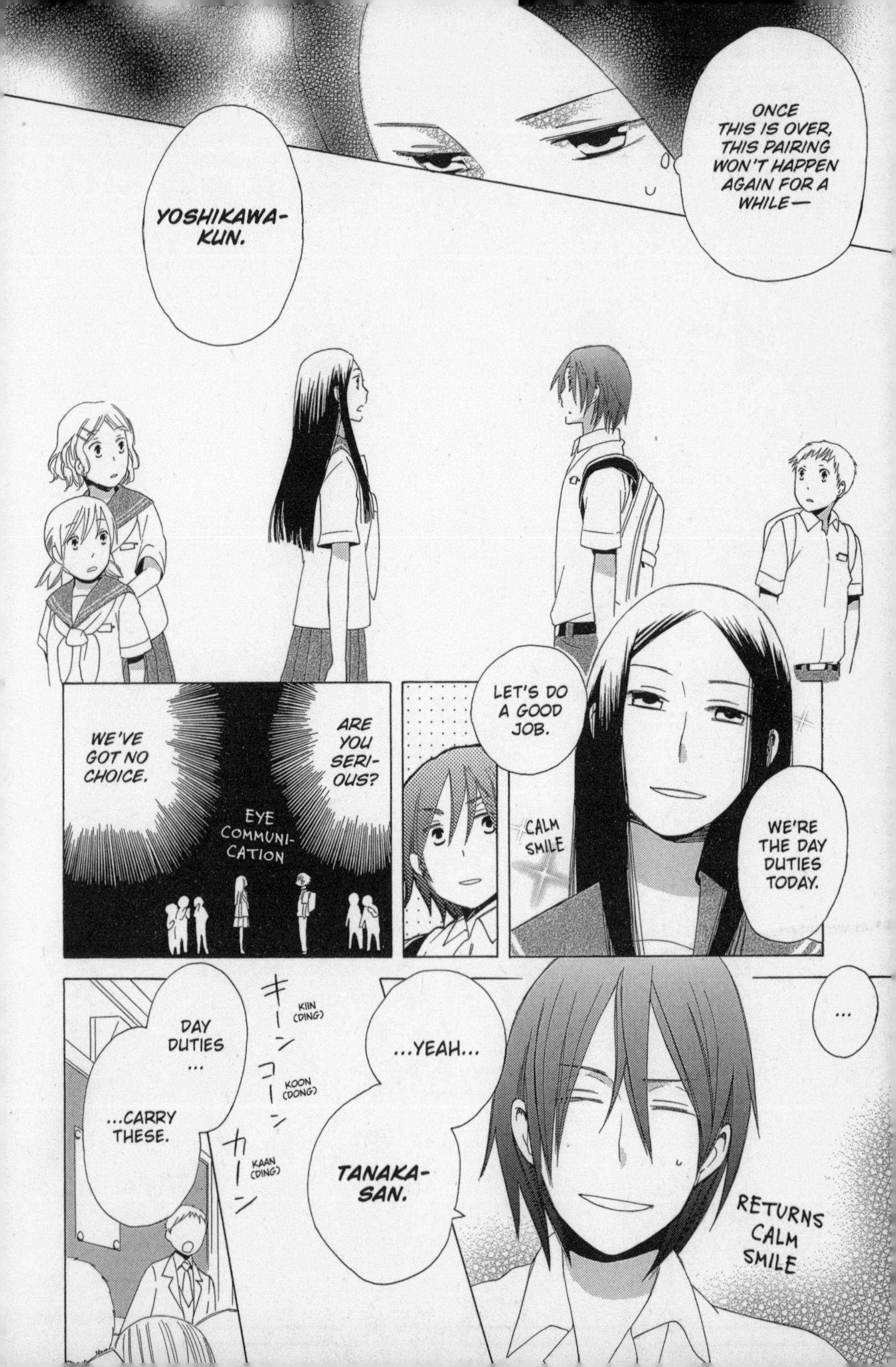
ONCE THIS IS OVER, THIS PAIRING WON'T HAPPEN AGAIN FOR A WHILE—
YOSHIKAWA-KUN.
LET'S DO A GOOD JOB.
CALM SMILE
WE'RE THE DAY DUTIES TODAY.
ARE YOU SERIOUS?
WE'VE GOT NO CHOICE.
EYE COMMUNICATION
...
...YEAH...
TANAKA-SAN.
RETURNS CALM SMILE
キーン
KIIN (DING)
コーン
KOON (DONG)
カーン
KAAN (DING)
DAY DUTIES ...
...CARRY THESE.

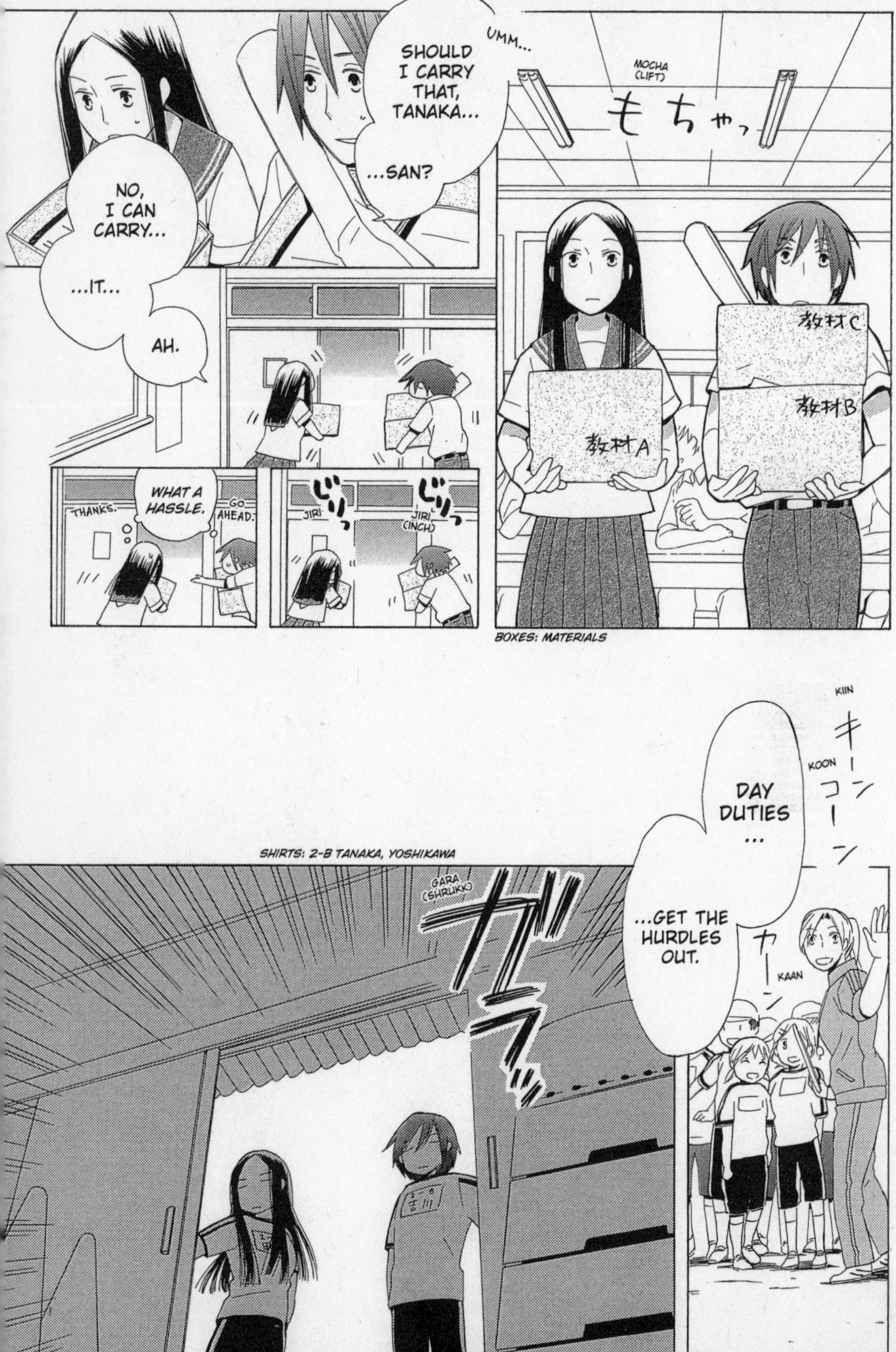
MOCHA (LIFT)
もちゃっ
教材C
教材B
教材A
BOXES: MATERIALS
UMM...
SHOULD I CARRY THAT, TANAKA...
...SAN?
NO, I CAN CARRY...
...IT...
AH.
JIRI (INCH)
じりっ
JIRI
じりっ
GO AHEAD.
THANKS.
WHAT A HASSLE.
KIIN
キーン
KOON
コーン
DAY DUTIES ...
...GET THE HURDLES OUT.
KAAN
カーン
GARA (SHRUKK)
ガラッ
SHIRTS: 2-B TANAKA, YOSHIKAWA

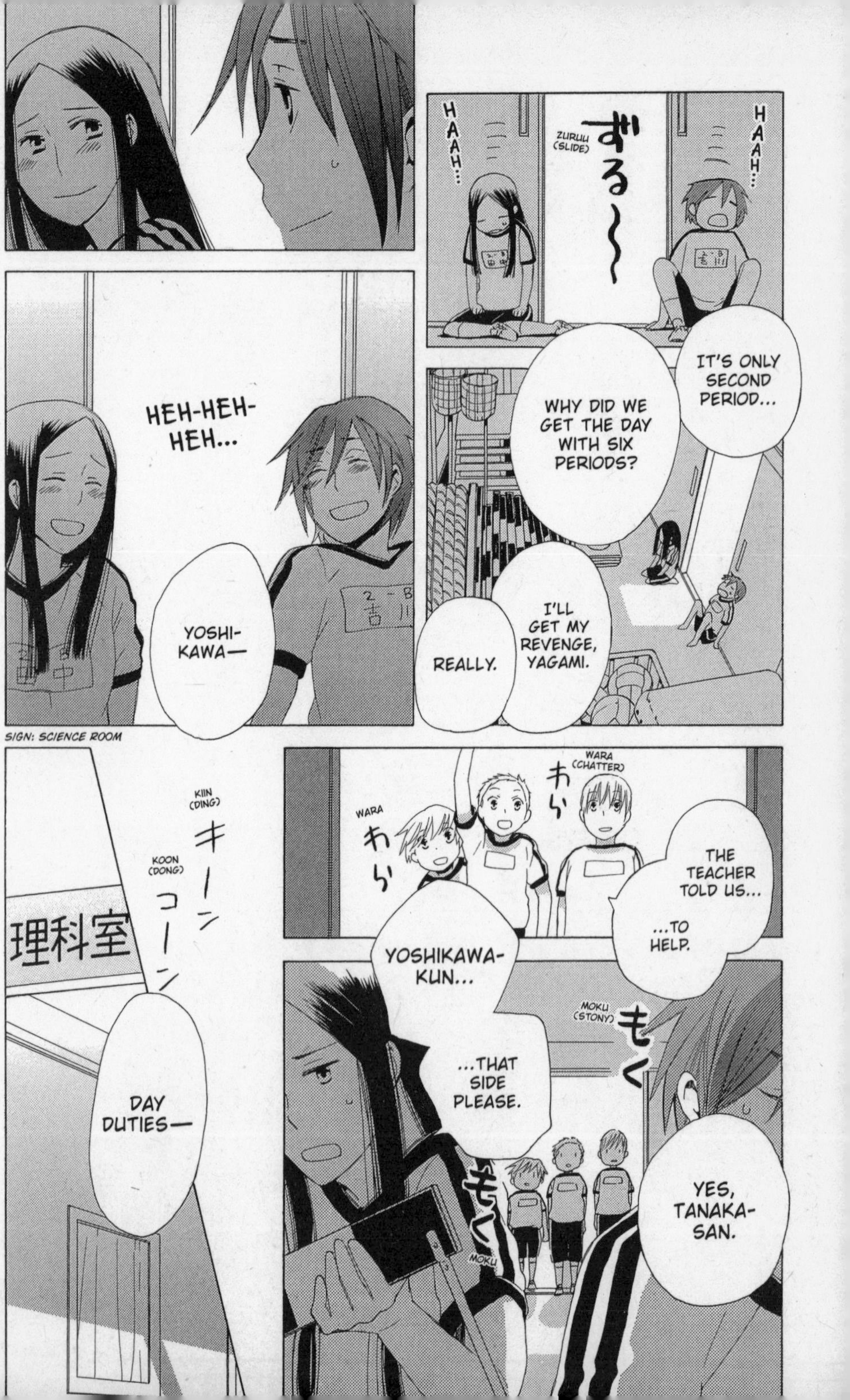
HAAH...
ZURUU (SLIDE)
ずる～～
HAAH...
IT'S ONLY SECOND PERIOD...
WHY DID WE GET THE DAY WITH SIX PERIODS?
I'LL GET MY REVENGE, YAGAMI.
REALLY.
HEH-HEH-HEH...
YOSHI-KAWA—
SIGN: SCIENCE ROOM
WARA (CHATTER)
わら
THE TEACHER TOLD US...
...TO HELP.
WARA
わら
YES, TANAKA-SAN.
MOKU (STONY)
もく
YOSHIKAWA-KUN...
...THAT SIDE PLEASE.
もく
MOKU
理科室
KIIN (DING)
キーン
KOON (DONG)
コーン
DAY DUTIES—

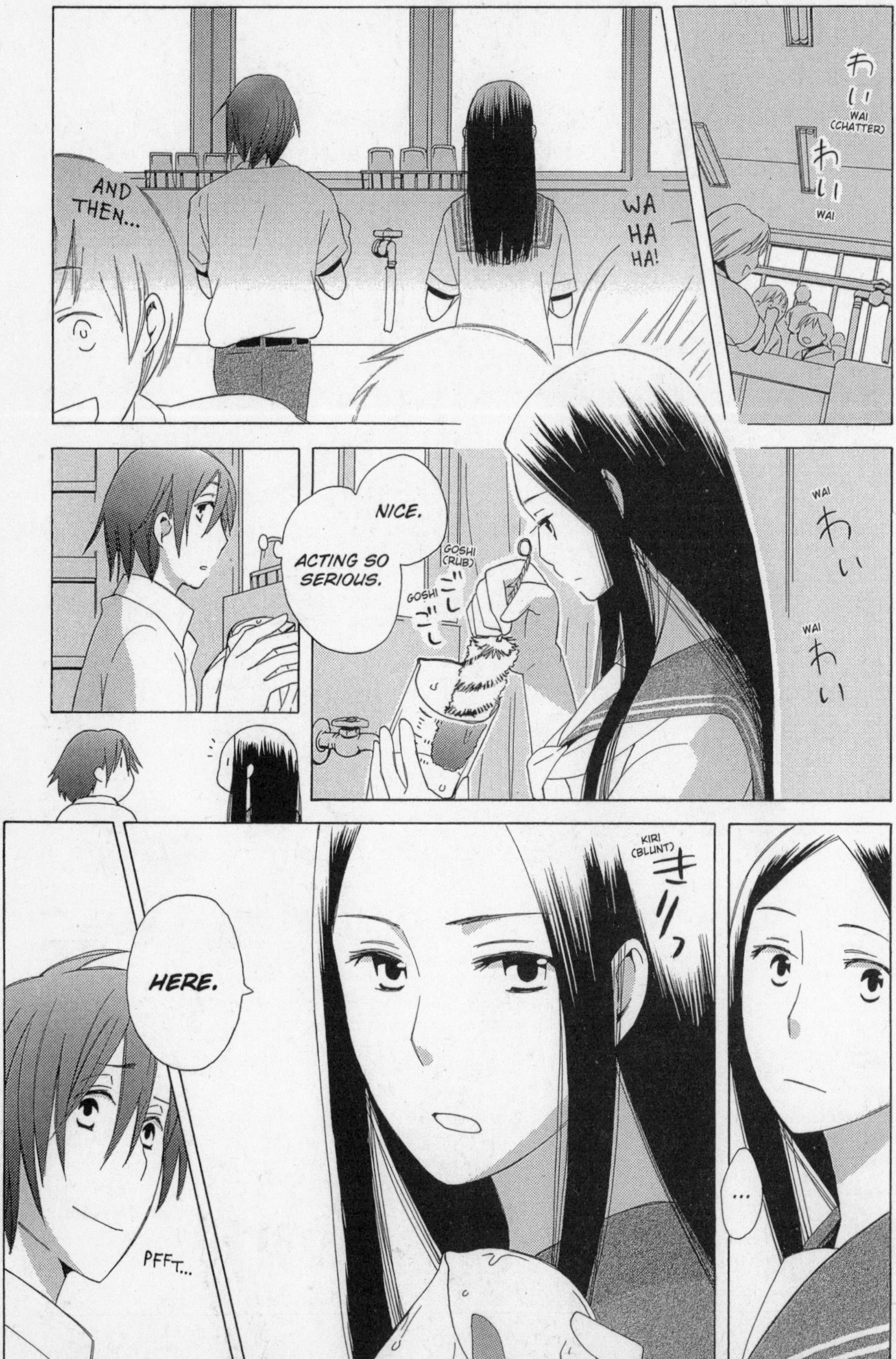
わい
WAI (CHATTER)
わい
WAI
WA HA HA!
AND THEN...
わい
WAI
わい
WAI
NICE.
ACTING SO SERIOUS.
ごし
GOSHI (RUB)
ごし
GOSHI
...
きりっ
KIRI (BLUNT)
HERE.
PFFT...

KOSO
KOSO (WHISPER)

Nice acting.

You too.

KEH HEH...

SHHH.

PFFT...

WA HA HA!

THANK YOU.

BFFT...

きりりり
KIRIRI (GLINTER)

4

HMM.

VERY MATURE.

キーン コーン
KIIN (DING) KOON (DONG)
カーン コーン
KAAN (DING) KOON

HOW'S YOSHIKAWA-KUN?

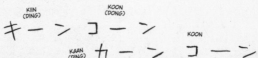

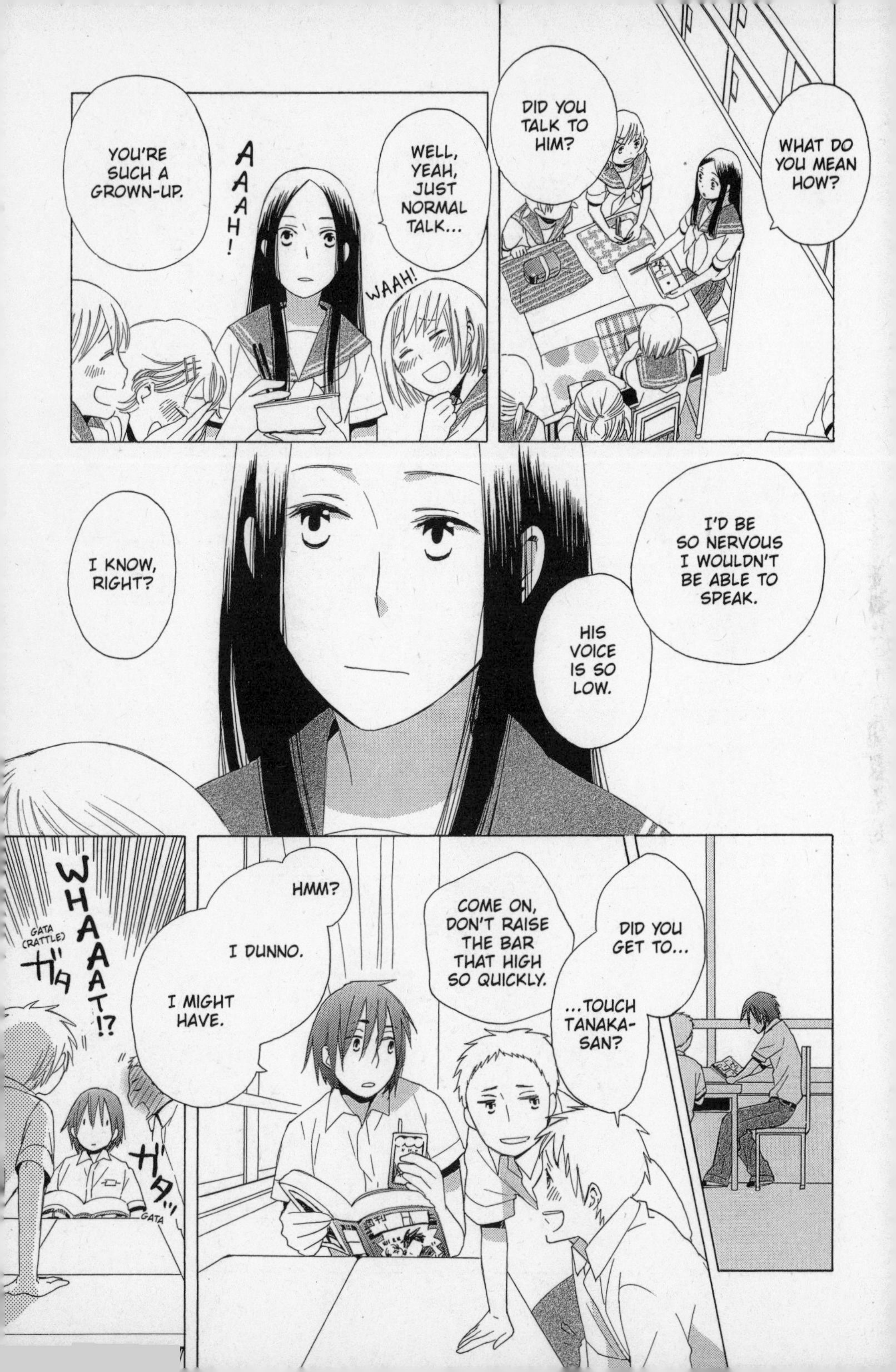
WHAT DO YOU MEAN HOW?
DID YOU TALK TO HIM?
WELL, YEAH, JUST NORMAL TALK...
AAAAH!
WAAH!
YOU'RE SUCH A GROWN-UP.
I'D BE SO NERVOUS I WOULDN'T BE ABLE TO SPEAK.
HIS VOICE IS SO LOW.
I KNOW, RIGHT?
DID YOU GET TO...
...TOUCH TANAKA-SAN?
COME ON, DON'T RAISE THE BAR THAT HIGH SO QUICKLY.
HMM?
I DUNNO.
I MIGHT HAVE.
WHAAAAT!?
ガタ
GATA (RATTLE)
ガタッ
GATA

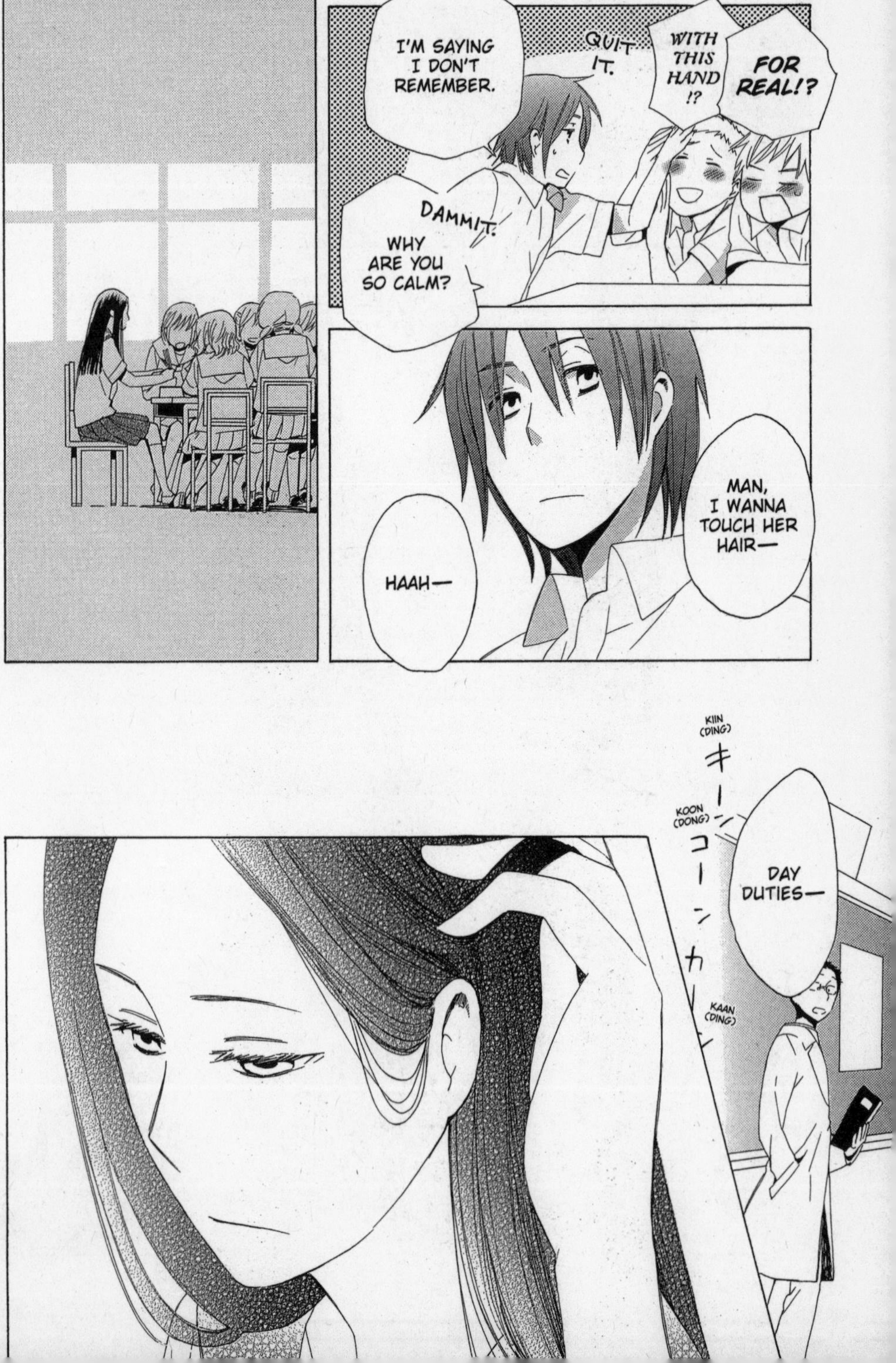
FOR REAL!?
WITH THIS HAND !?
QUIT IT.
I'M SAYING I DON'T REMEMBER.
DAMMIT.
WHY ARE YOU SO CALM?
MAN, I WANNA TOUCH HER HAIR—
HAAH—
KIIN (DING)
キーン
KOON (DONG)
コーン
DAY DUTIES—
KAAN (DING)
カーン

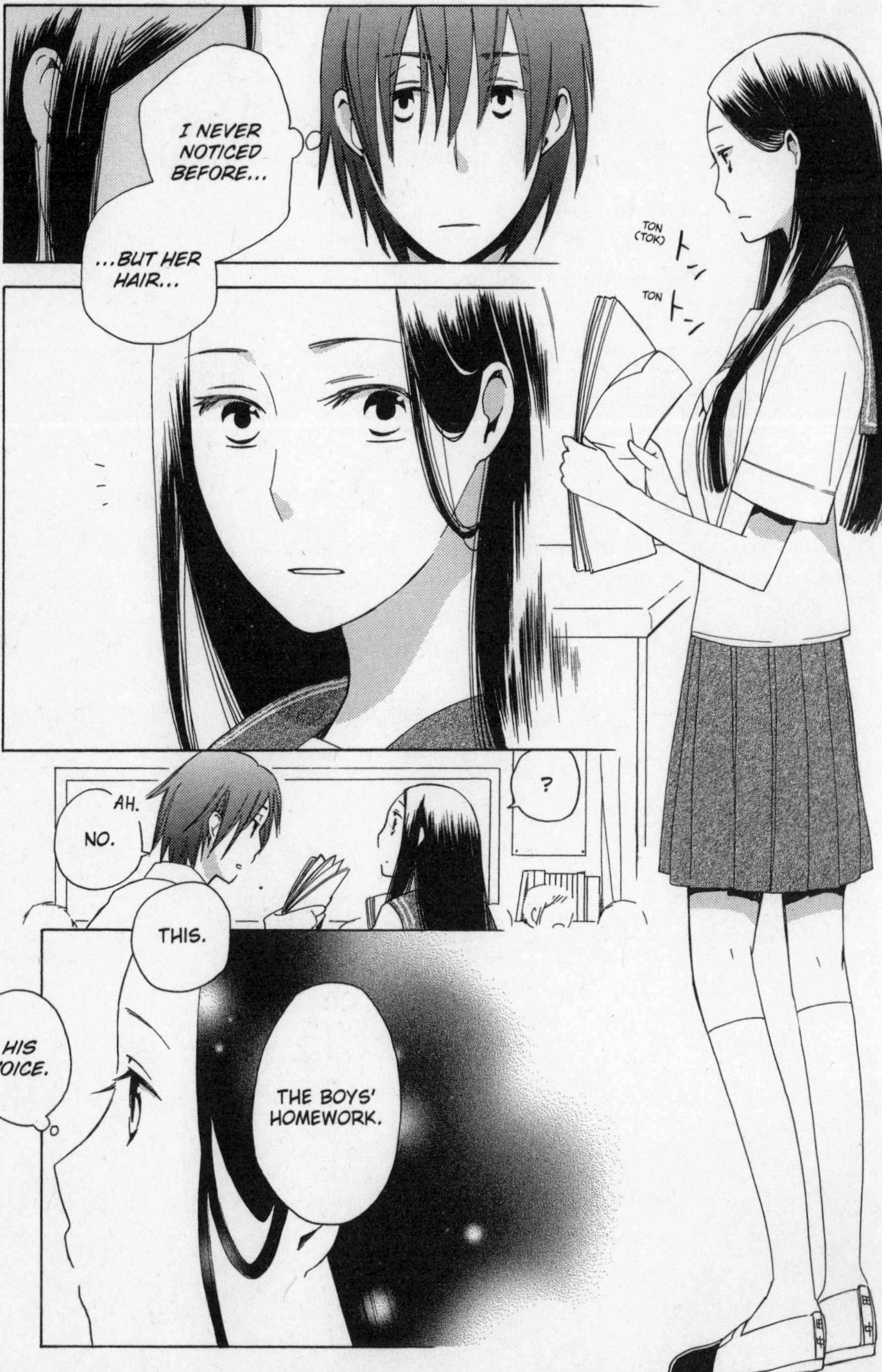
TON (TOK)
TON
I NEVER NOTICED BEFORE...
...BUT HER HAIR...
?
AH.
NO.
THIS.
THE BOYS' HOMEWORK.
HIS VOICE.

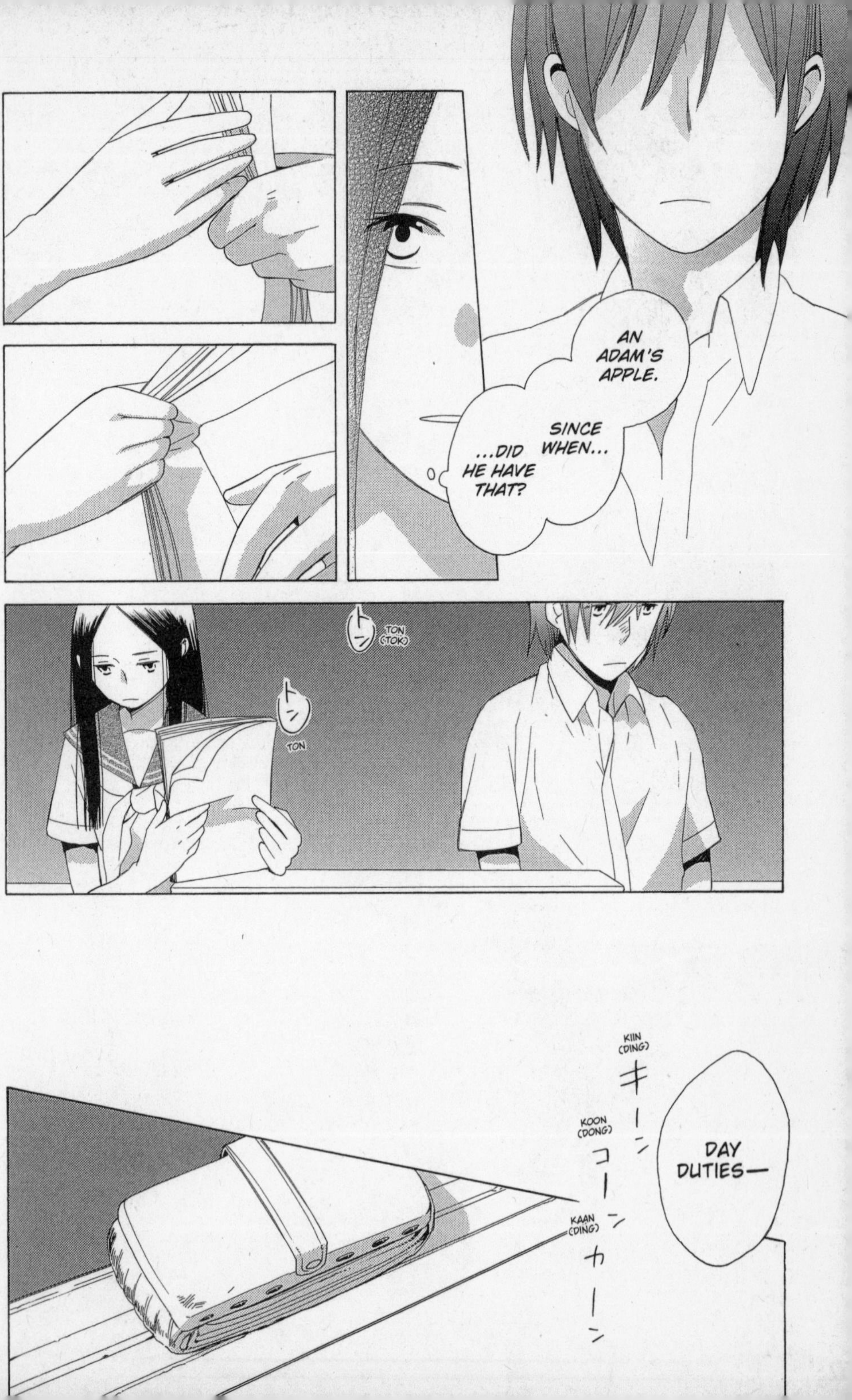
AN ADAM'S APPLE.
SINCE WHEN...
...DID HE HAVE THAT?
TON (TOK)
TON
KIIN (DING)
KOON (DONG)
KAAN (DING)
DAY DUTIES—

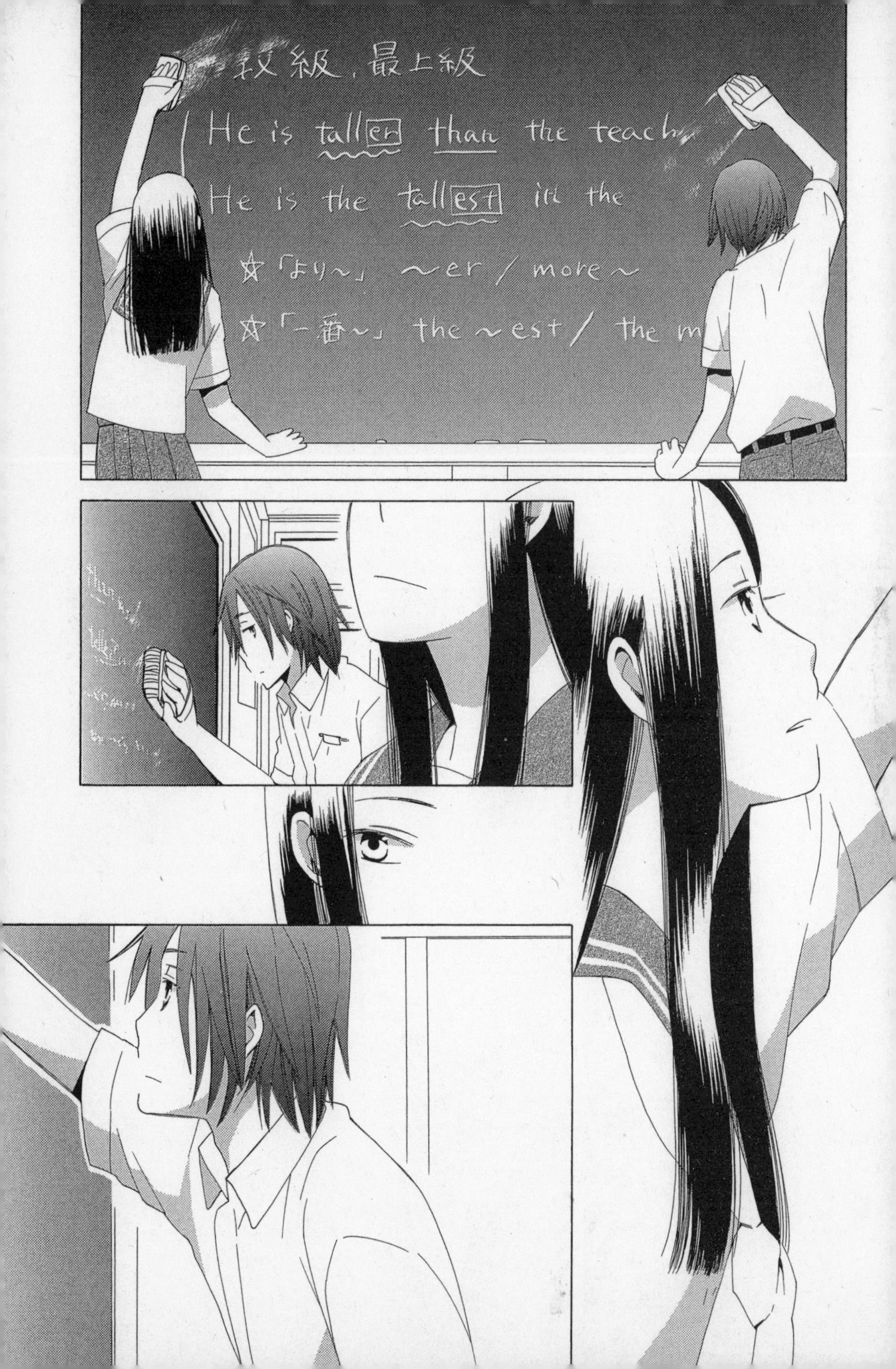

級，最上級
He is taller than the teach
He is the tallest in the
☆「より～」 ～er / more～
☆「一番～」 the～est / the m

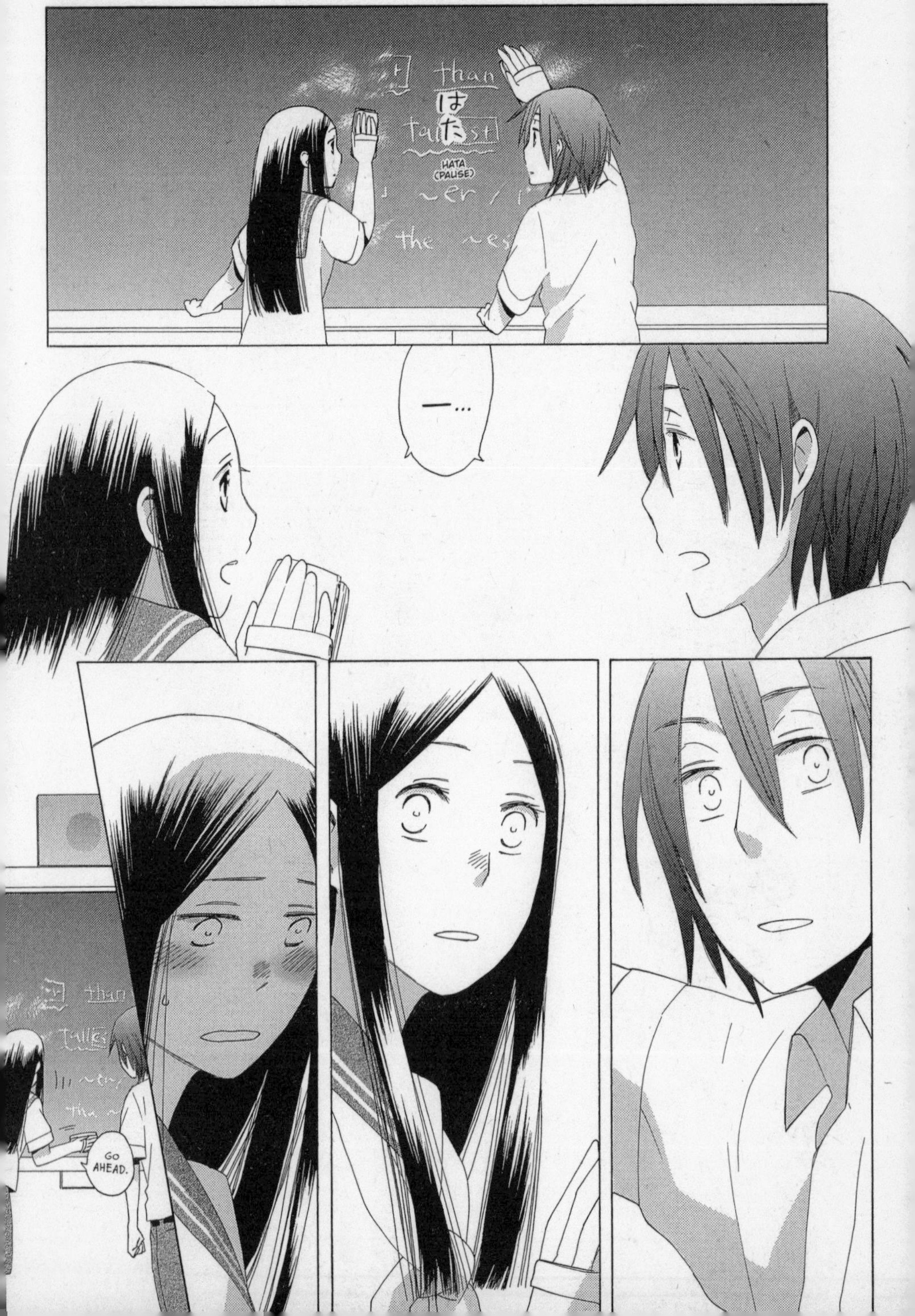
HATA (PAUSE)
—...
GO AHEAD.

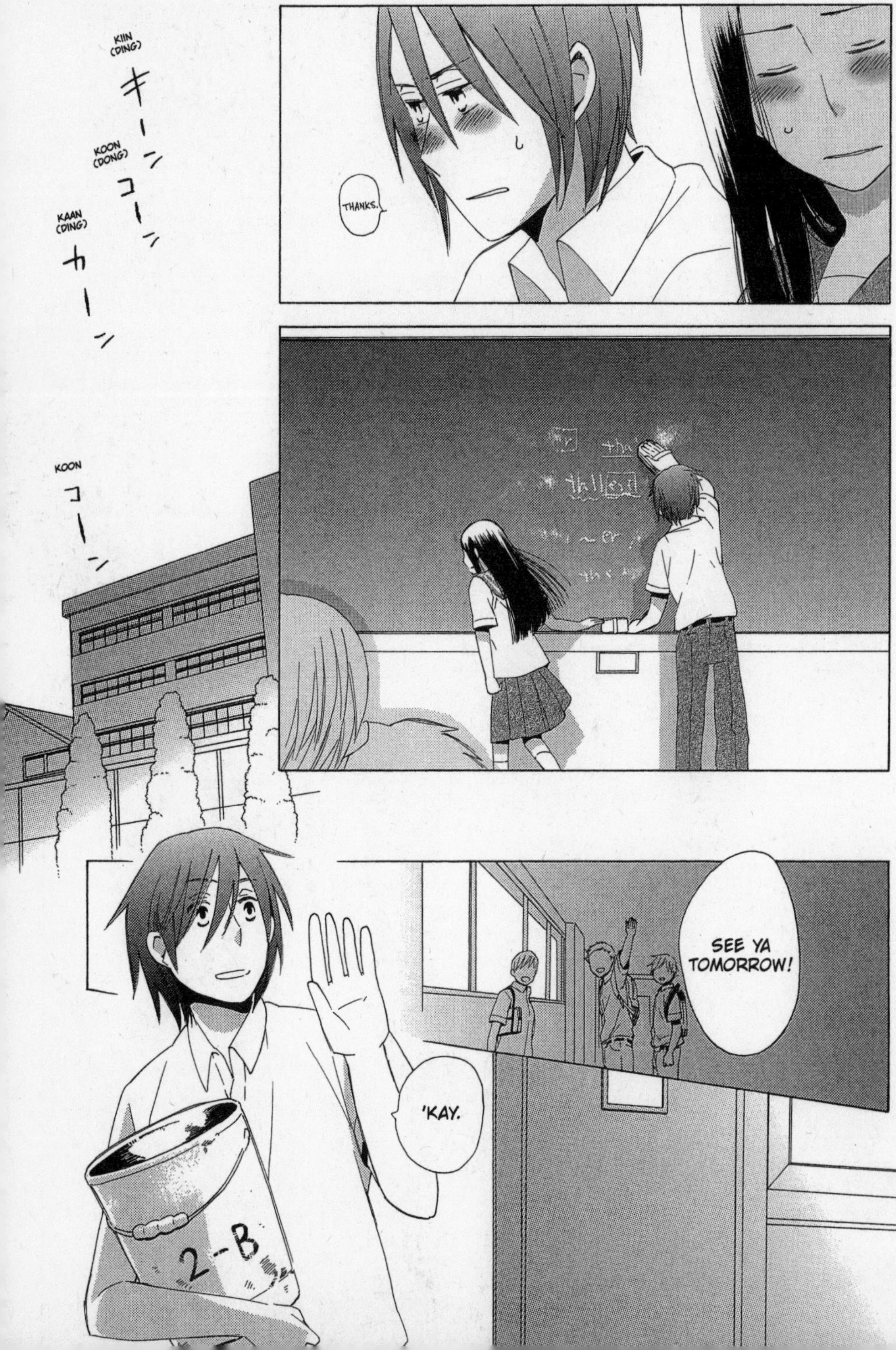
THANKS.
KIIN (DING)
キーン
KOON (DONG)
コーン
KAAN (DING)
カーン
KOON
コーン
SEE YA TOMORROW!
'KAY.
2-B

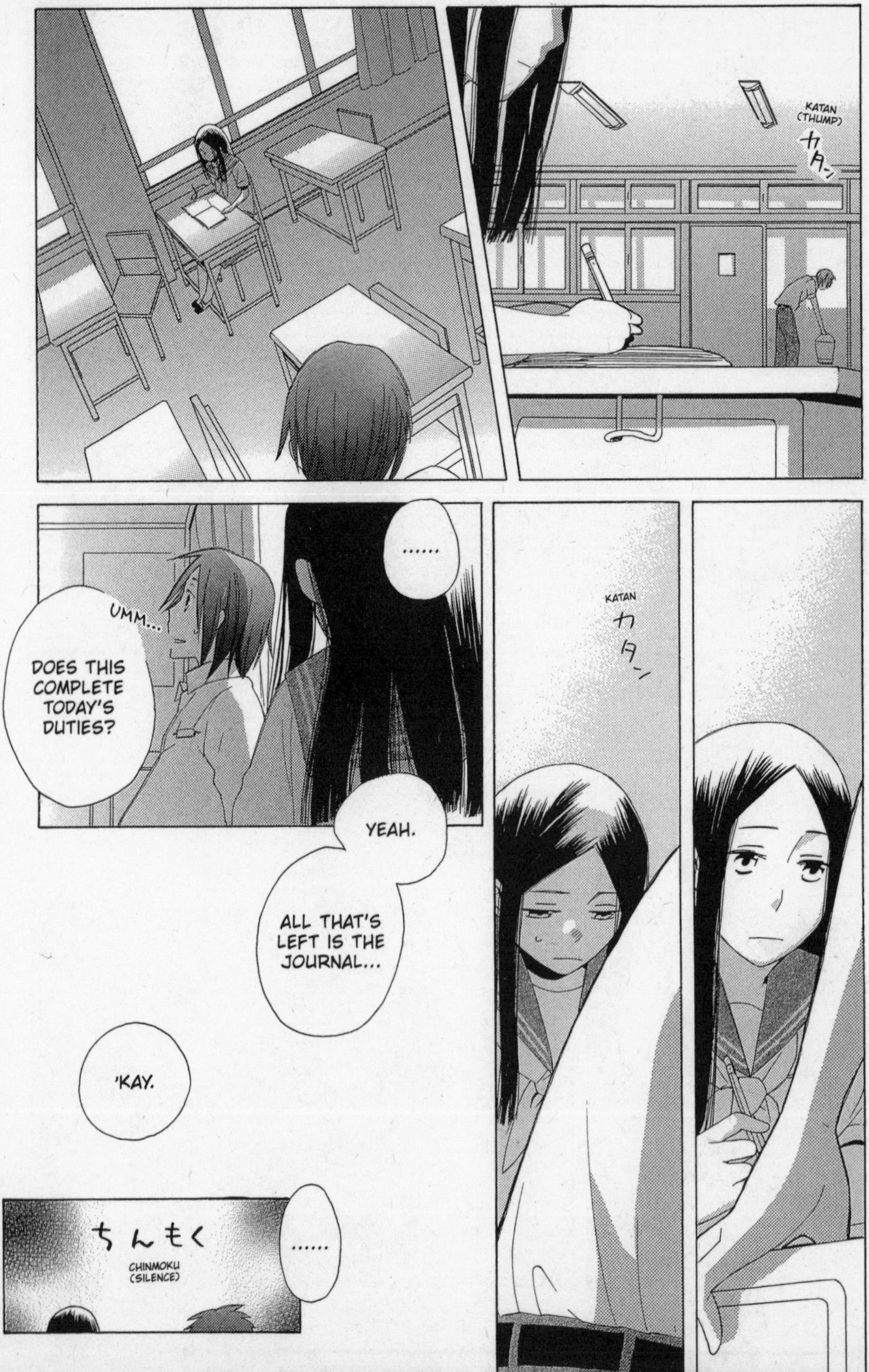
KATAN (THUMP)
カタン
KATAN
カタン
......
UMM...
DOES THIS COMPLETE TODAY'S DUTIES?
YEAH.
ALL THAT'S LEFT IS THE JOURNAL...
'KAY.
......
ちんもく
CHINMOKU (SILENCE)

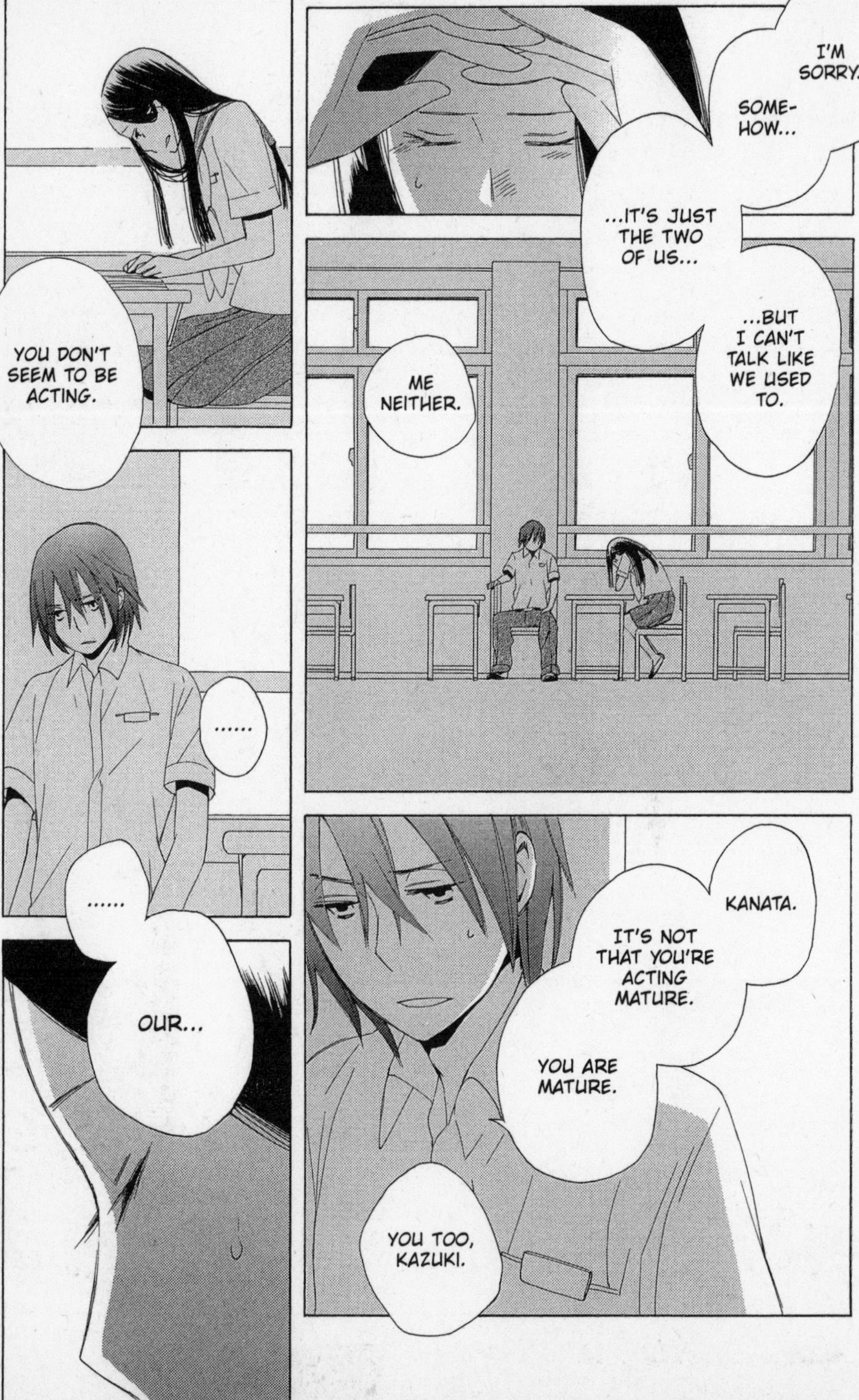
I'M SORRY.
SOME-HOW...
...IT'S JUST THE TWO OF US...
...BUT I CAN'T TALK LIKE WE USED TO.
ME NEITHER.
YOU DON'T SEEM TO BE ACTING.
......
......
KANATA.
IT'S NOT THAT YOU'RE ACTING MATURE.
YOU ARE MATURE.
YOU TOO, KAZUKI.
OUR...

...MATURE ACT...

...HAD SOMEHOW BECOME REALITY.

OUR CHILDISH FACES HAD BECOME...

...OUR FAKE SIDE.

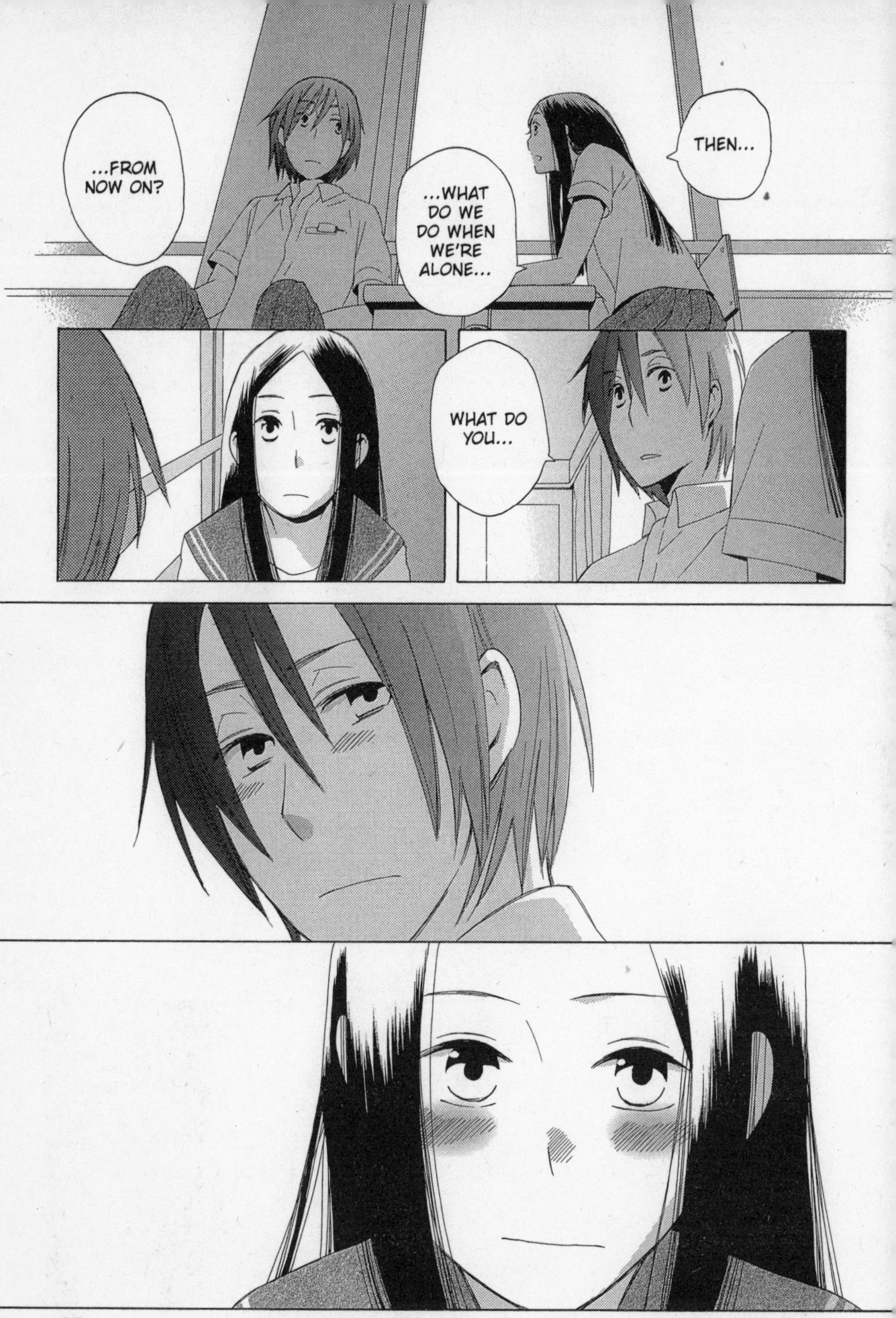
THEN...
...WHAT DO WE DO WHEN WE'RE ALONE...
...FROM NOW ON?
WHAT DO YOU...

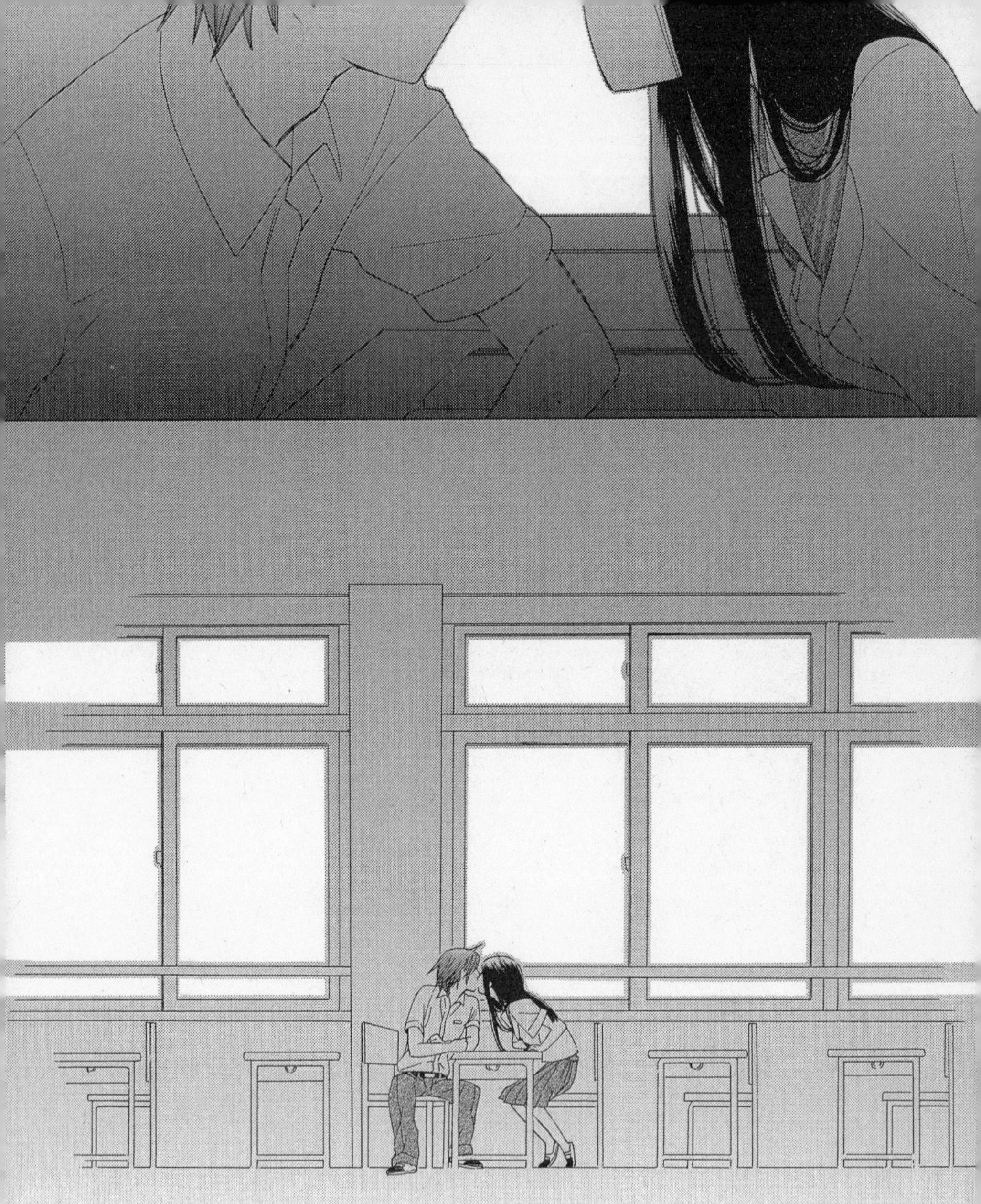

Fin

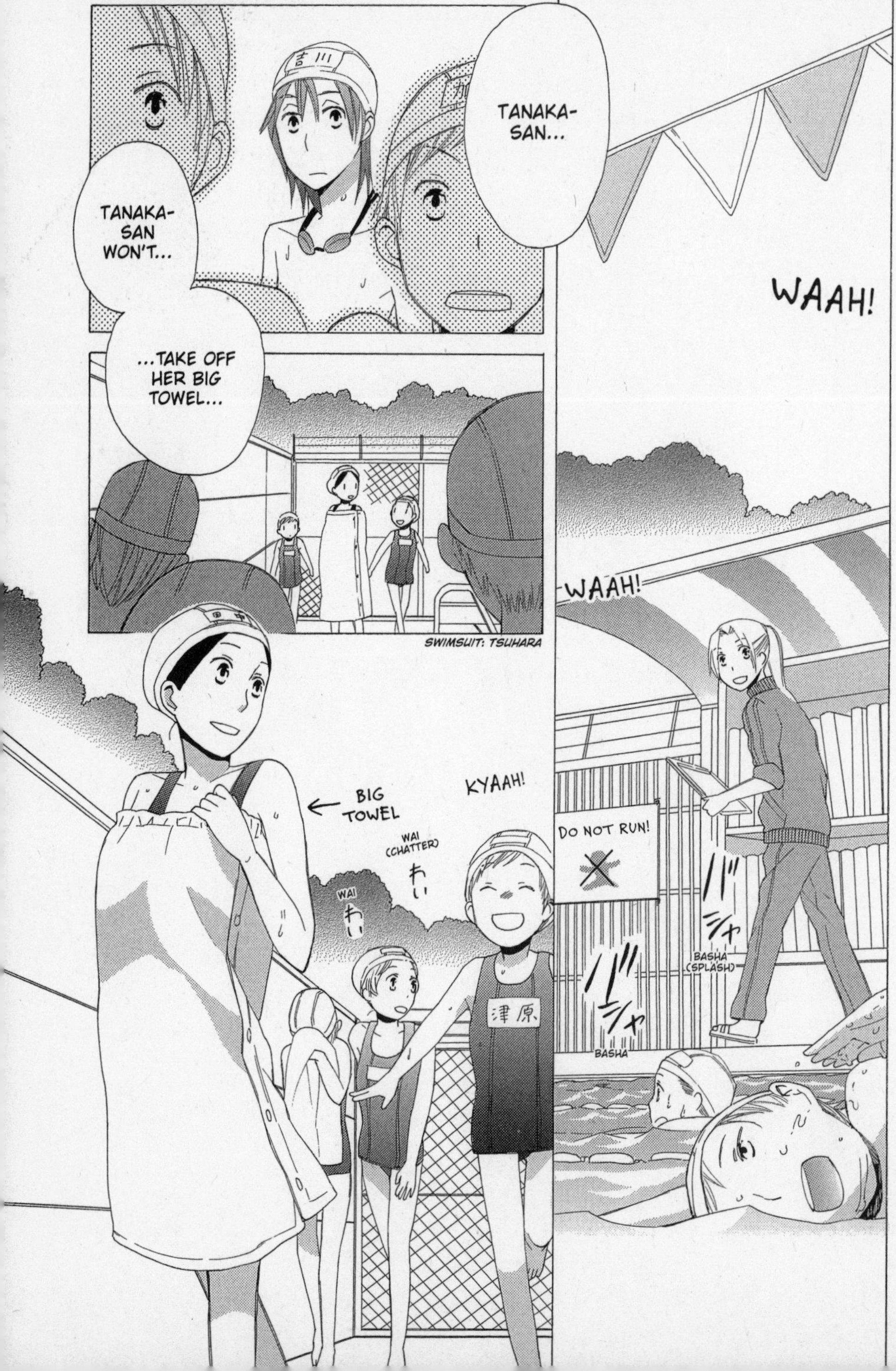
WAAH!
WAAH!
DO NOT RUN!
BASHA (SPLASH)
BASHA
TANAKA-SAN...
TANAKA-SAN WON'T...
...TAKE OFF HER BIG TOWEL...
SWIMSUIT: TSUHARA
KYAAH!
WAI (CHATTER)
WAI
BIG TOWEL
津原

Love at Fourteen [Intermission 1]

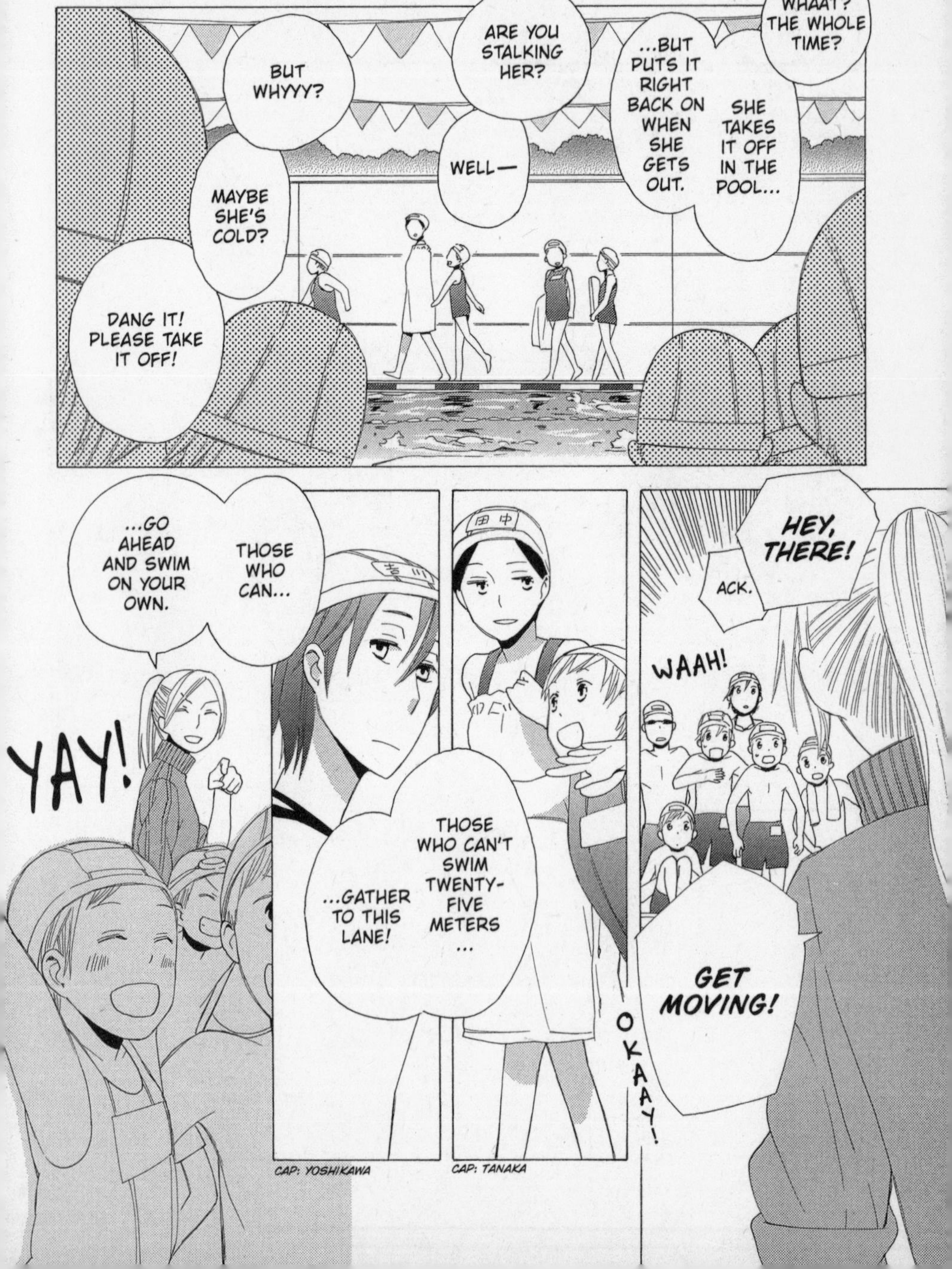
WHAAT? THE WHOLE TIME?
SHE TAKES IT OFF IN THE POOL...
...BUT PUTS IT RIGHT BACK ON WHEN SHE GETS OUT.
ARE YOU STALKING HER?
WELL—
BUT WHYYY?
MAYBE SHE'S COLD?
DANG IT! PLEASE TAKE IT OFF!
HEY, THERE!
ACK.
WAAH!
GET MOVING!
OKAAY!
THOSE WHO CAN'T SWIM TWENTY-FIVE METERS ...
...GATHER TO THIS LANE!
CAP: TANAKA
CAP: YOSHIKAWA
THOSE WHO CAN...
...GO AHEAD AND SWIM ON YOUR OWN.
YAY!

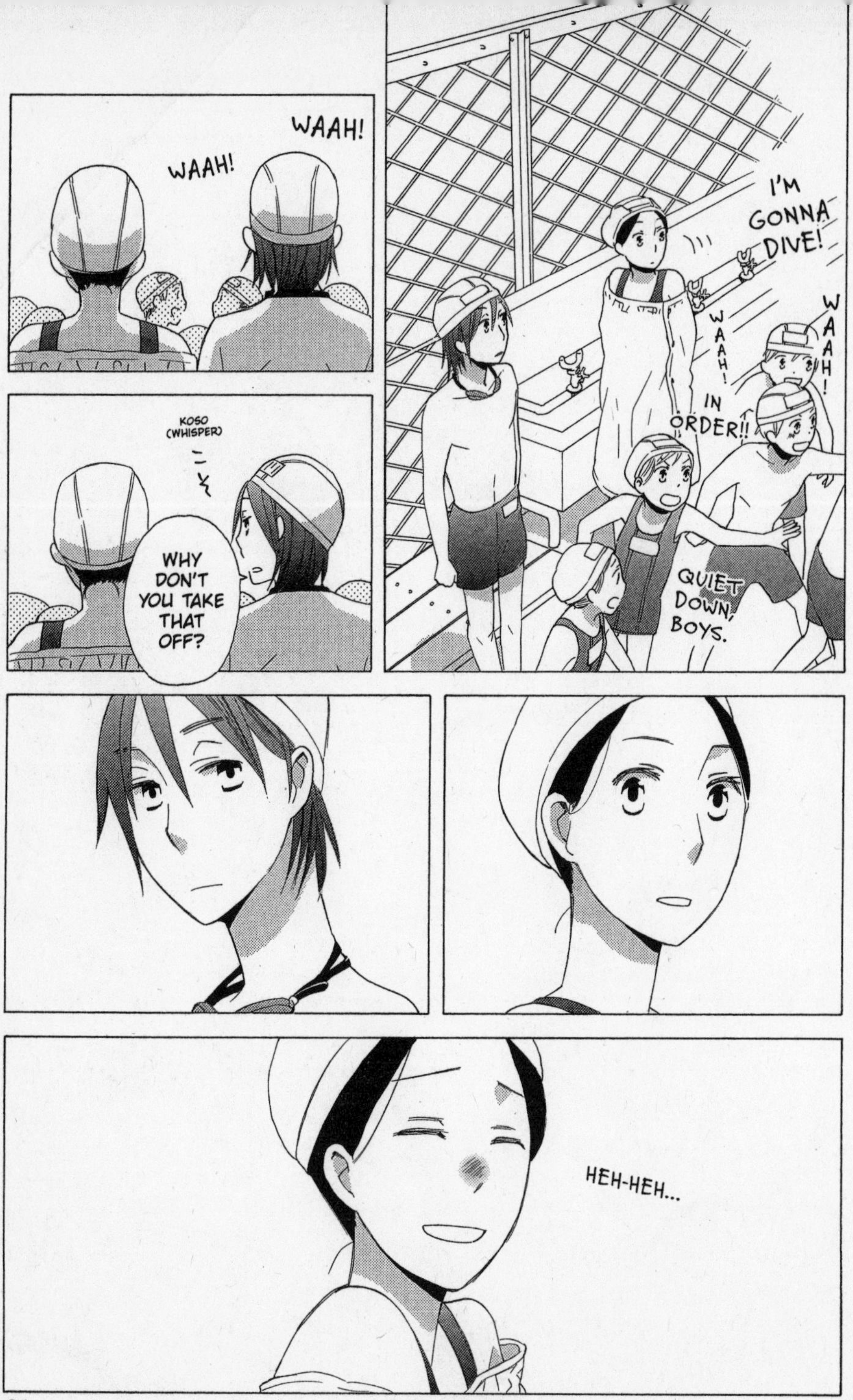
I'M GONNA DIVE!
WAAH!
WAAH!
IN ORDER!!
QUIET DOWN, BOYS.
WAAH!
WAAH!
KOSO (WHISPER)
WHY DON'T YOU TAKE THAT OFF?
HEH-HEH...

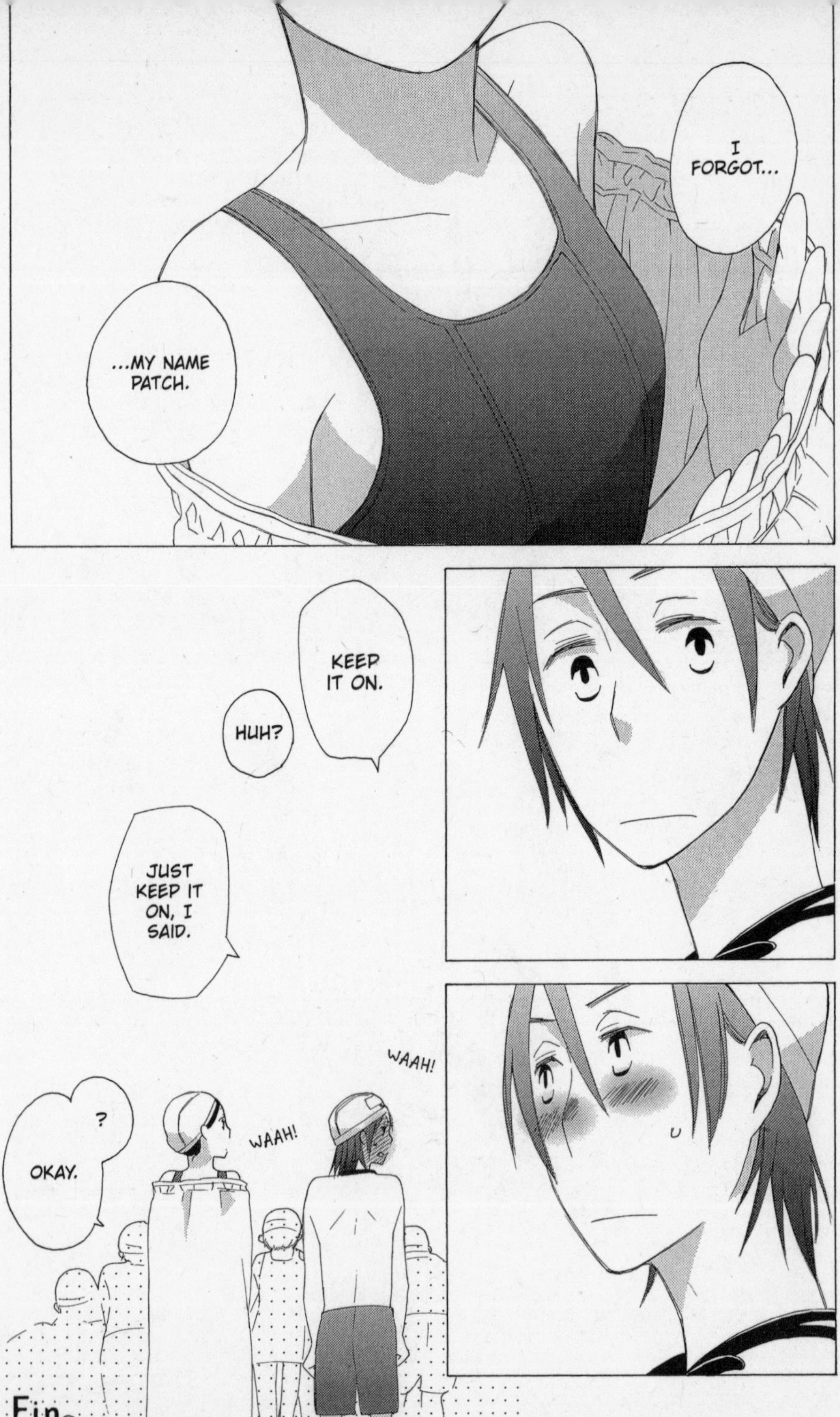

I FORGOT...
...MY NAME PATCH.
KEEP IT ON.
HUH?
JUST KEEP IT ON, I SAID.
WAAH!
WAAH!
?
OKAY.
Fin

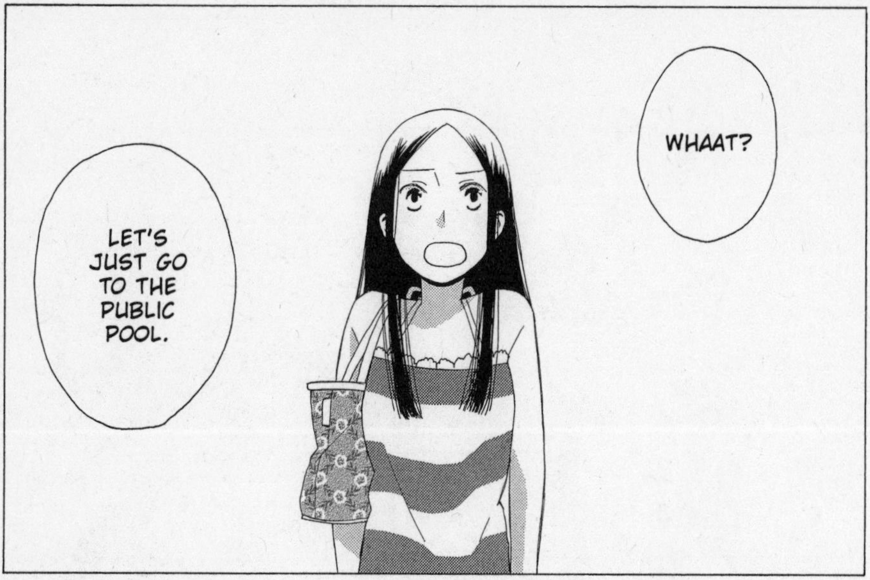
WHAAT?
LET'S JUST GO TO THE PUBLIC POOL.

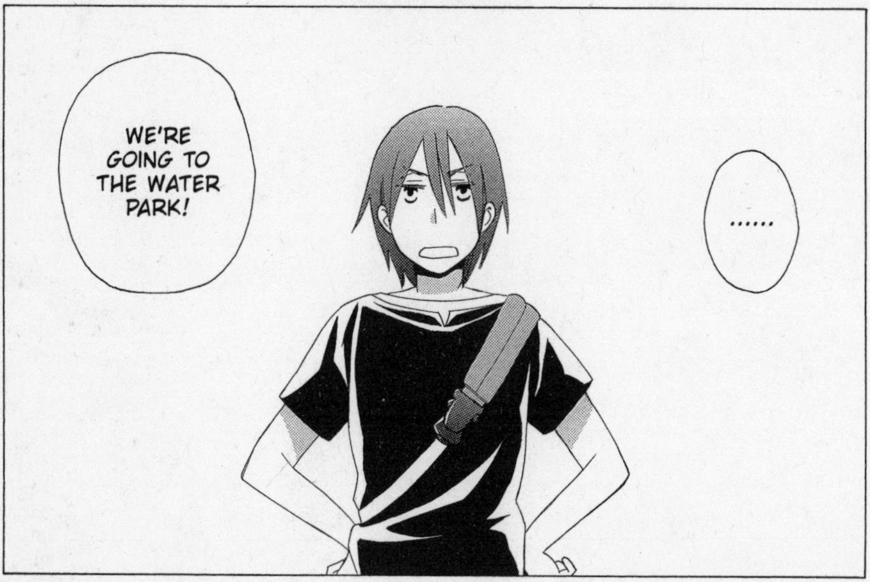
......
WE'RE GOING TO THE WATER PARK!

Love at Fourteen [Intermission 2]

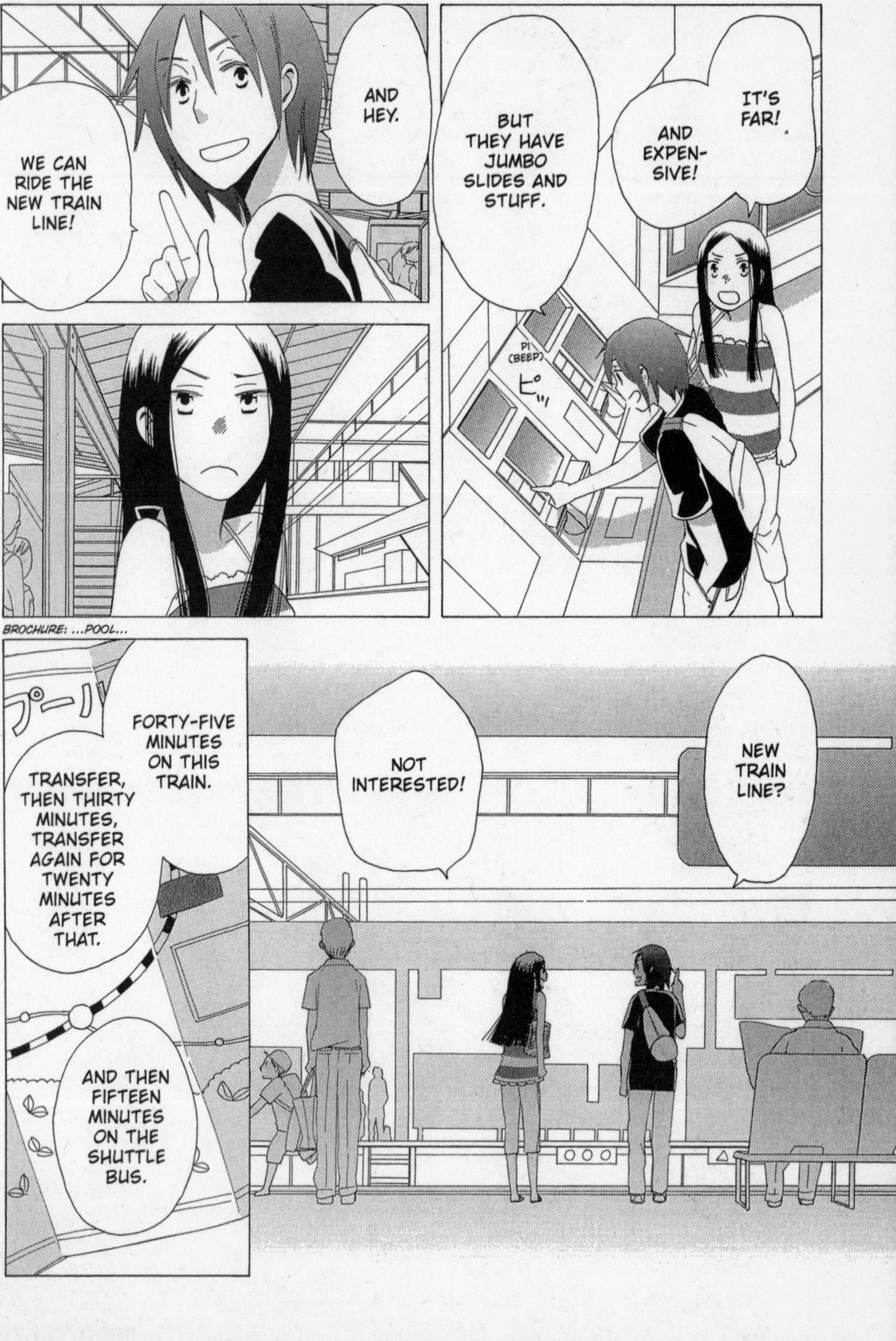
IT'S FAR!
AND EXPENSIVE!
BUT THEY HAVE JUMBO SLIDES AND STUFF.
PI (BEEP)
ピッ
AND HEY.
WE CAN RIDE THE NEW TRAIN LINE!
NEW TRAIN LINE?
NOT INTERESTED!
FORTY-FIVE MINUTES ON THIS TRAIN.
TRANSFER, THEN THIRTY MINUTES, TRANSFER AGAIN FOR TWENTY MINUTES AFTER THAT.
AND THEN FIFTEEN MINUTES ON THE SHUTTLE BUS.
プール

BROCHURE: ...POOL...

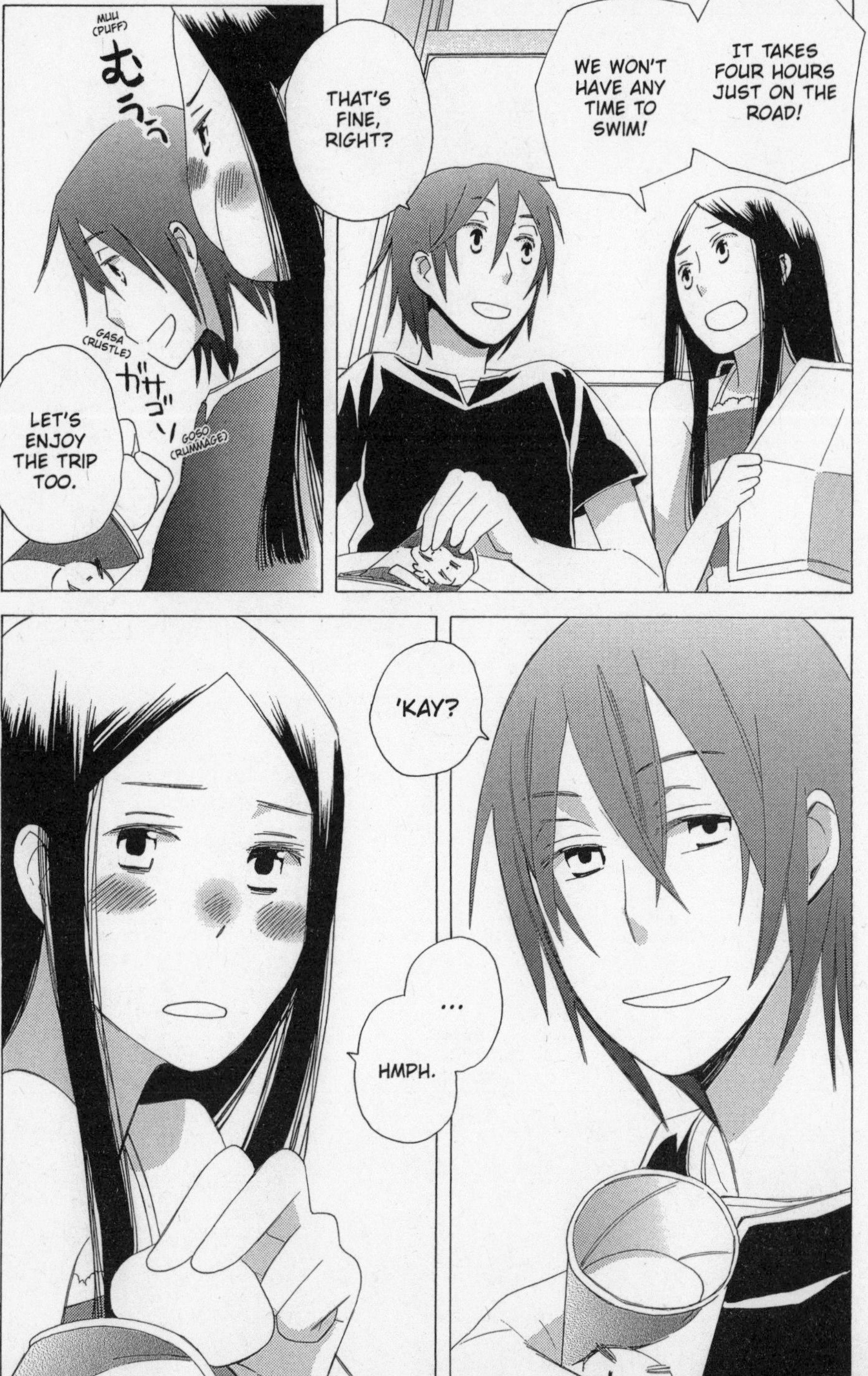
IT TAKES FOUR HOURS JUST ON THE ROAD!
WE WON'T HAVE ANY TIME TO SWIM!
THAT'S FINE, RIGHT?
MUU (PUFF)
むぅ～
LET'S ENJOY THE TRIP TOO.
GASA (RUSTLE)
ガサゴソ
GOSO (RUMMAGE)
'KAY?
...
HMPH.

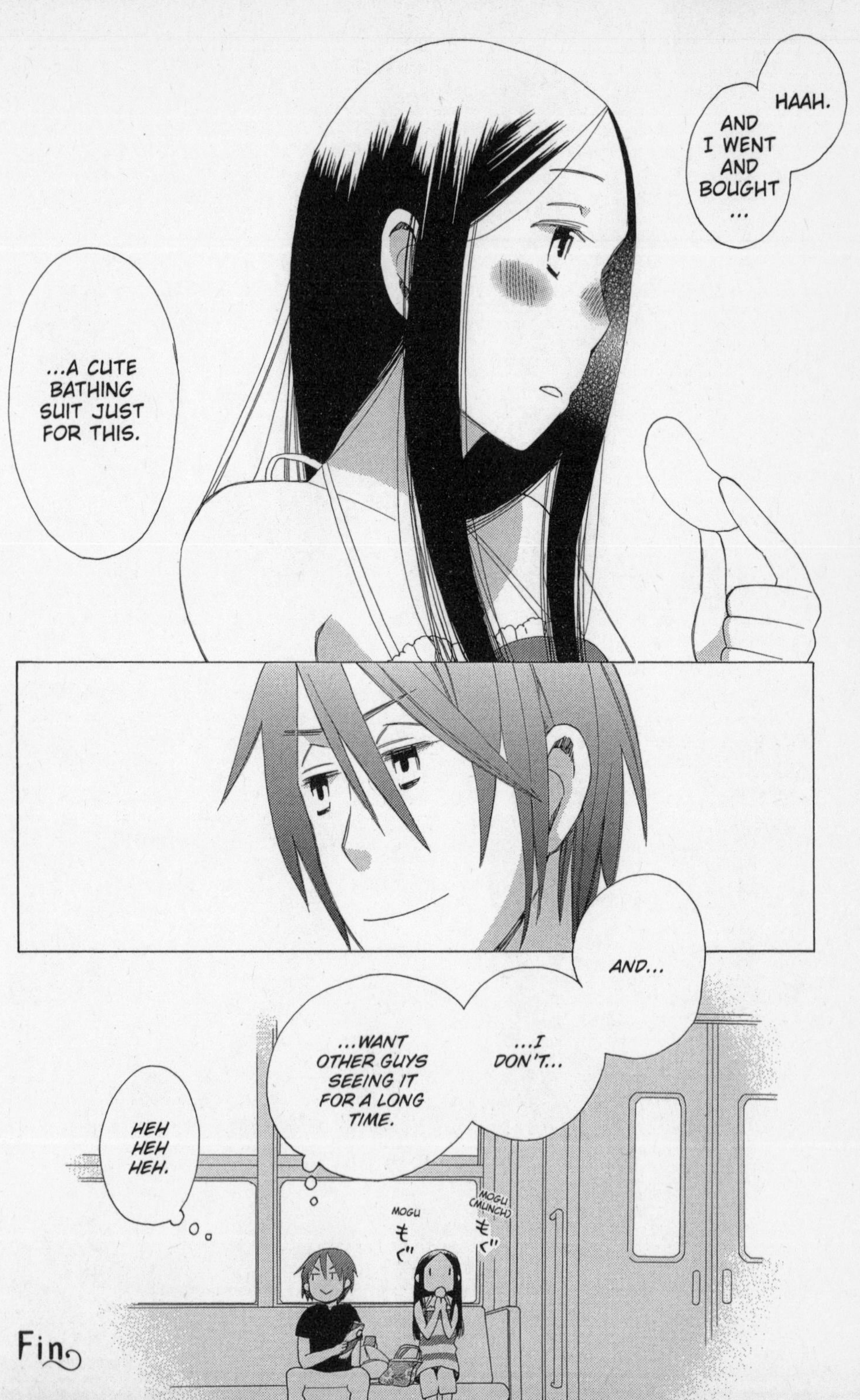
HAAH. AND I WENT AND BOUGHT ...
...A CUTE BATHING SUIT JUST FOR THIS.
AND...
...I DON'T...
...WANT OTHER GUYS SEEING IT FOR A LONG TIME.
HEH HEH HEH.
MOGU (MUNCH) もぐ
MOGU もぐ
Fin

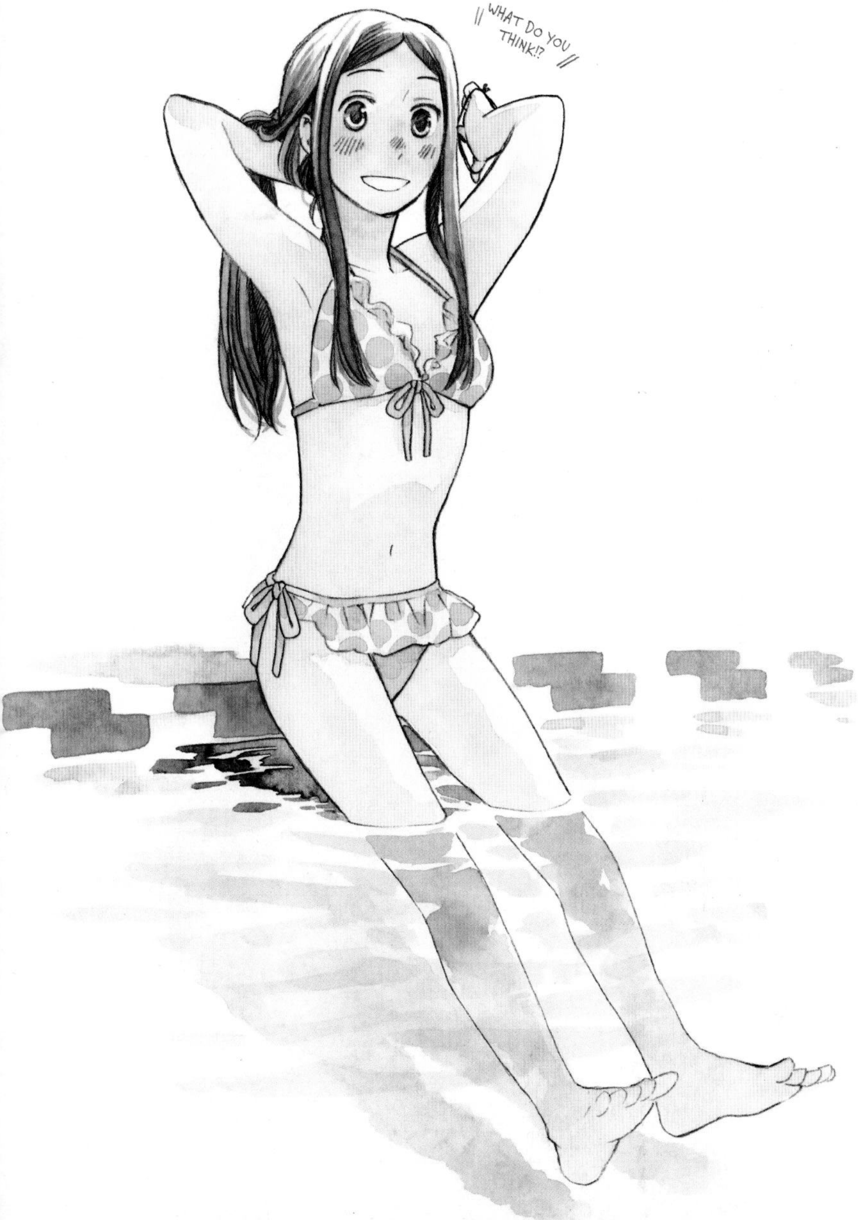
WHAT DO YOU THINK!?

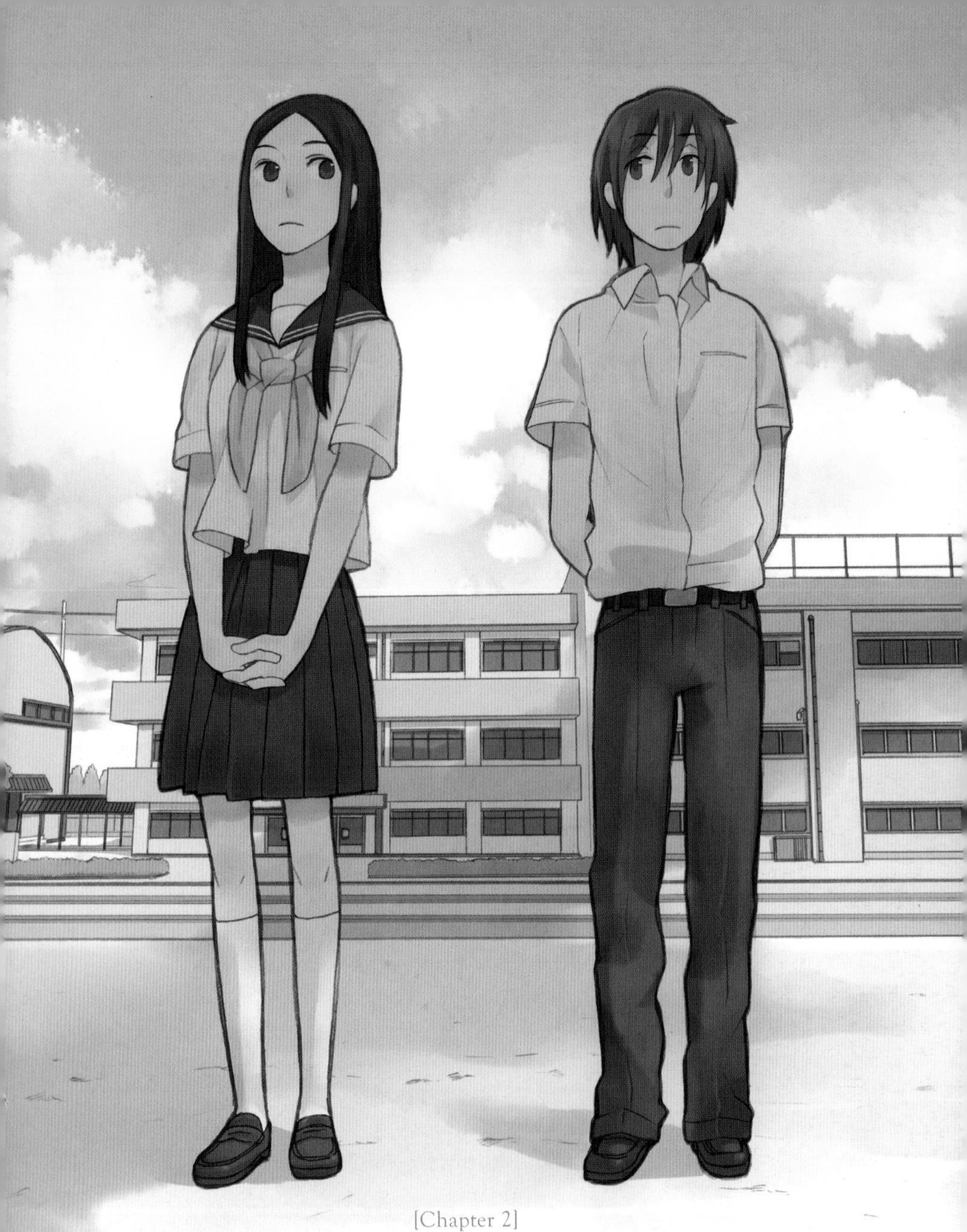

[Chapter 2]

Love at Fourteen

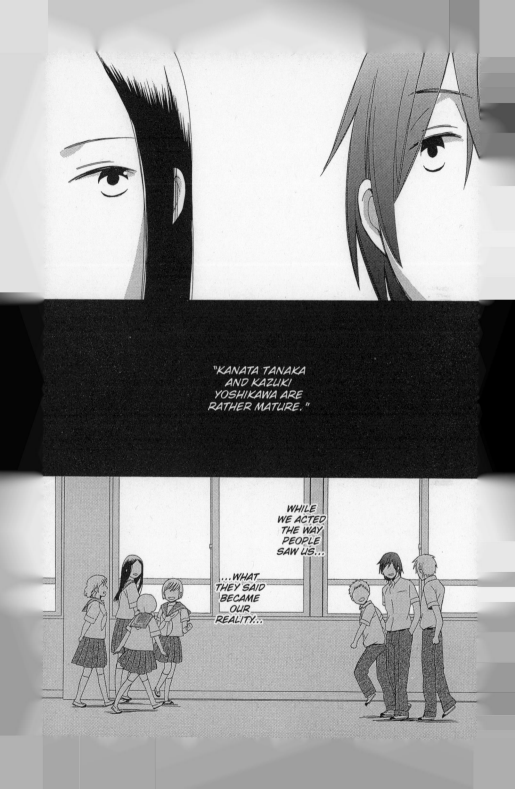

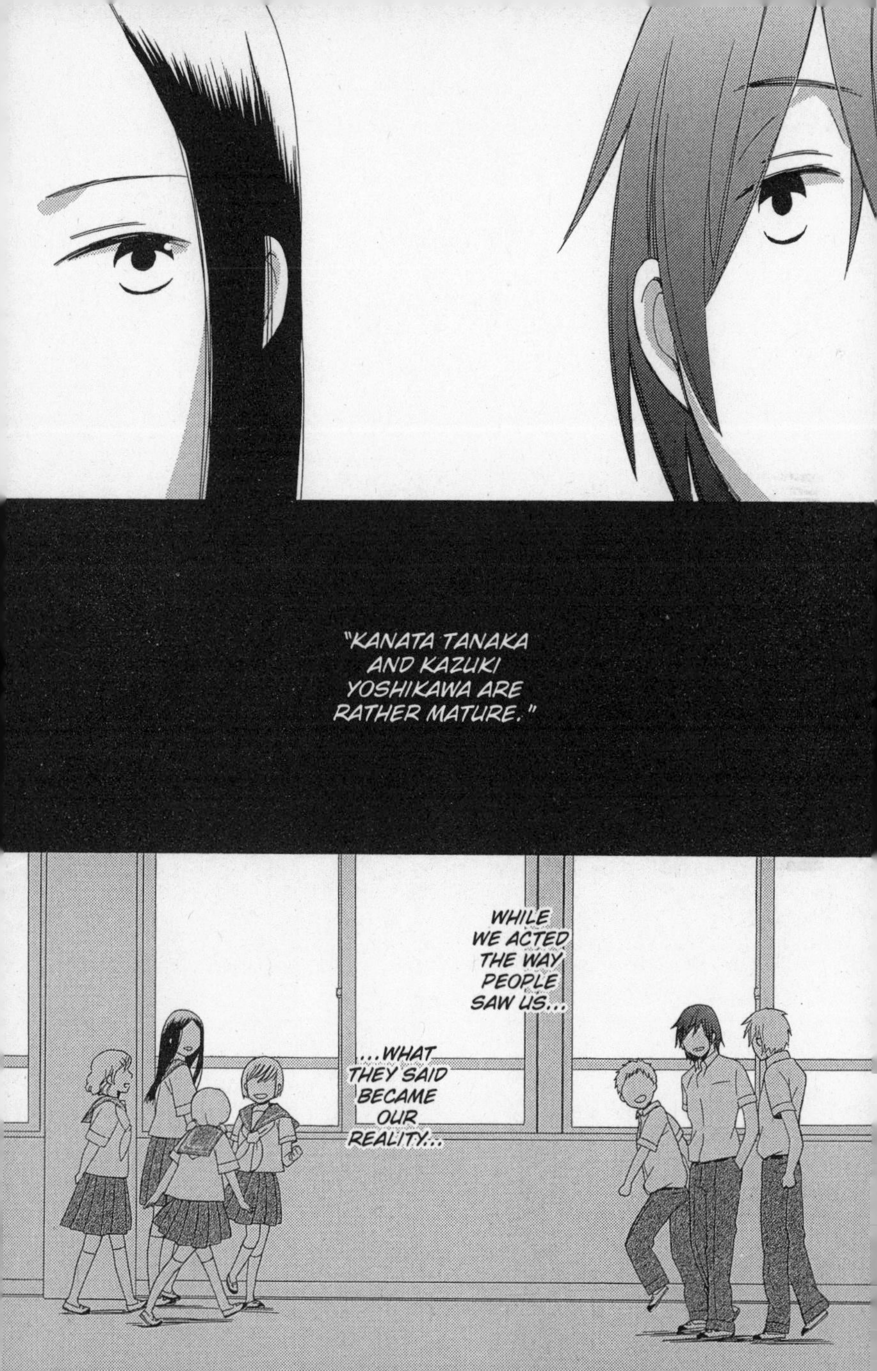
"KANATA TANAKA AND KAZUKI YOSHIKAWA ARE RATHER MATURE."
WHILE WE ACTED THE WAY PEOPLE SAW US...
...WHAT THEY SAID BECAME OUR REALITY...

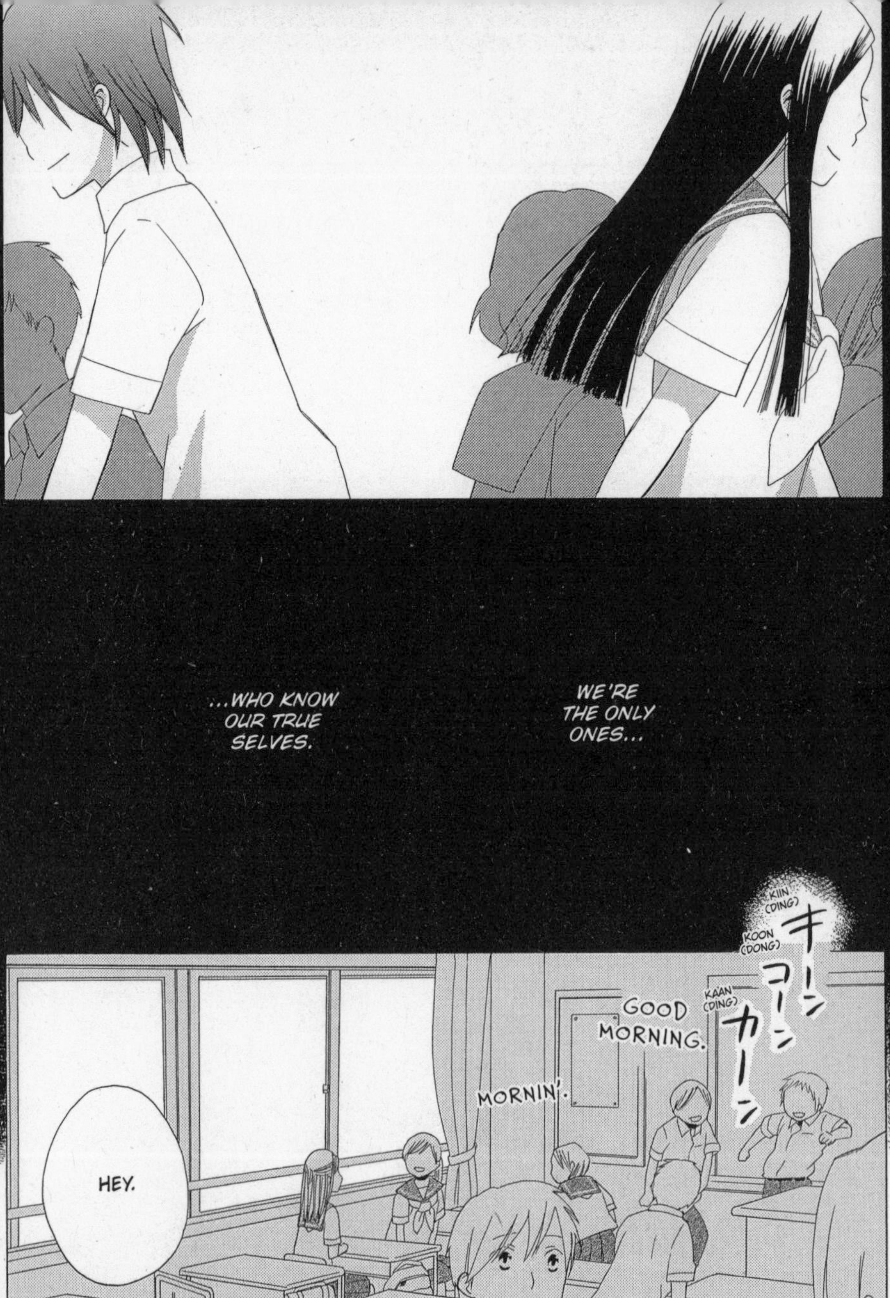
WE'RE THE ONLY ONES...
...WHO KNOW OUR TRUE SELVES.
KIIN (DING) KOON (DONG) KAAN (DING)
キーン コーン カーン
GOOD MORNING.
MORNIN'.
HEY.

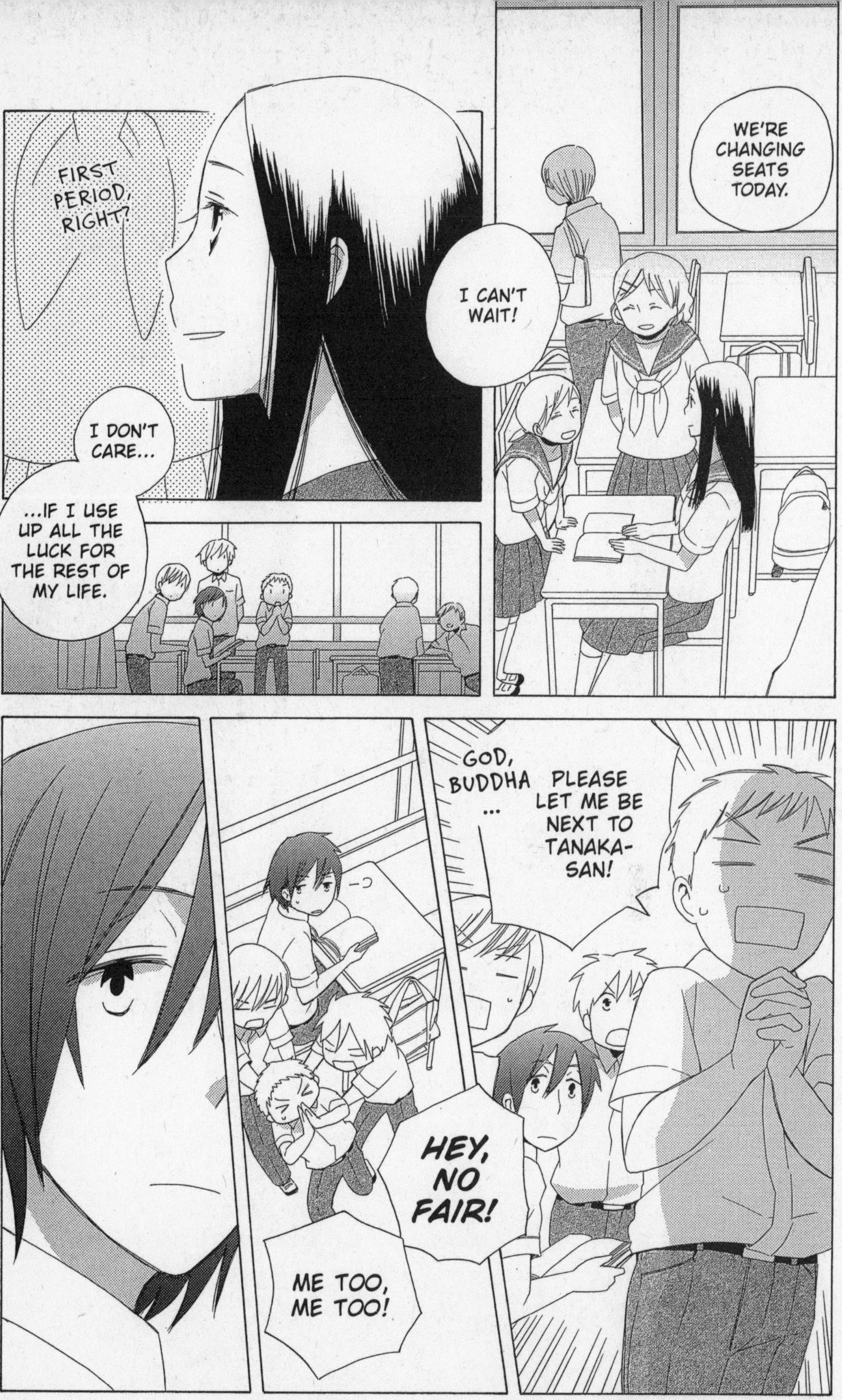
WE'RE CHANGING SEATS TODAY.
I CAN'T WAIT!
FIRST PERIOD, RIGHT?
I DON'T CARE...
...IF I USE UP ALL THE LUCK FOR THE REST OF MY LIFE.
GOD, BUDDHA... PLEASE LET ME BE NEXT TO TANAKA-SAN!
HEY, NO FAIR!
ME TOO, ME TOO!

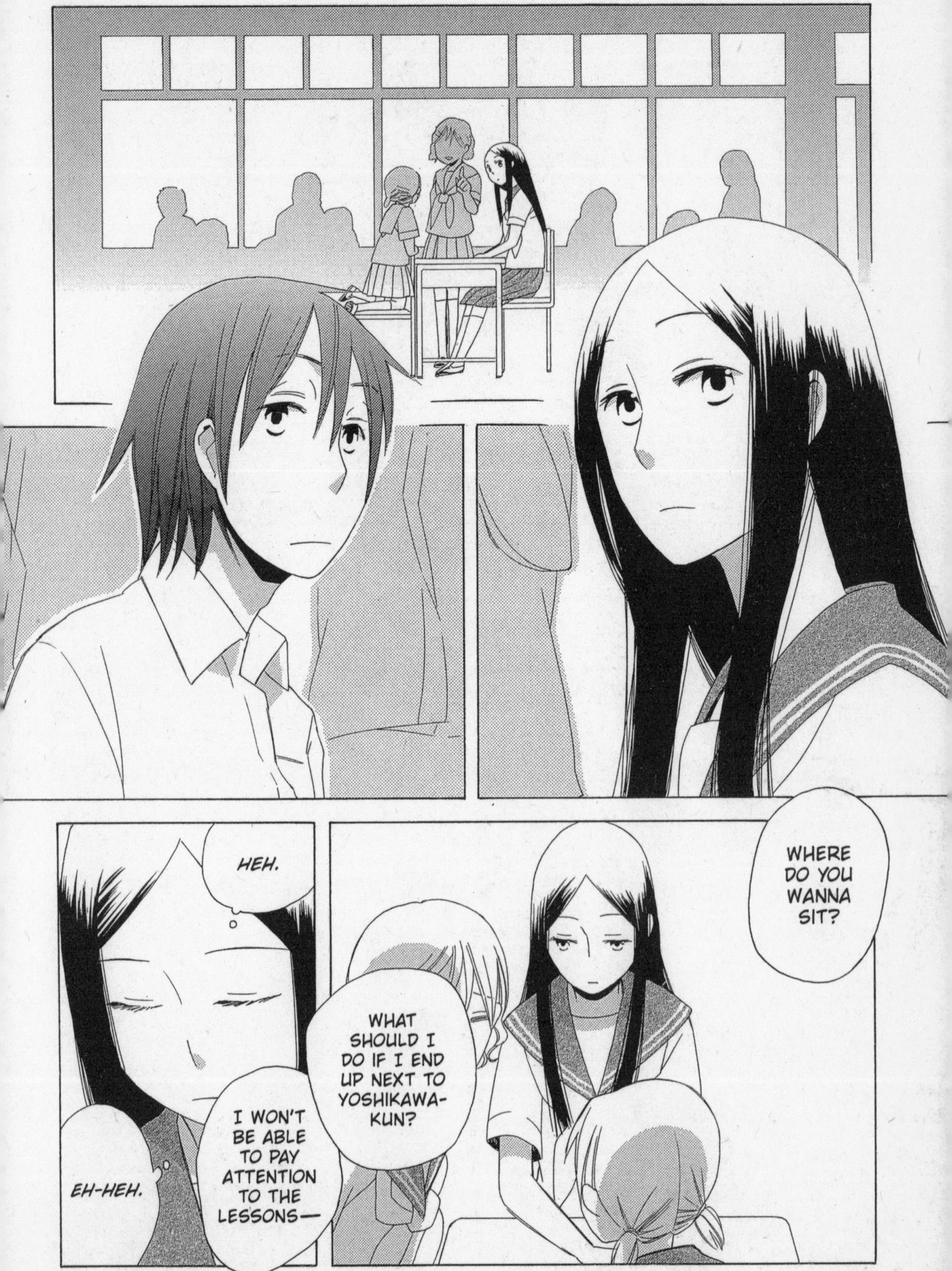
WHERE DO YOU WANNA SIT?
WHAT SHOULD I DO IF I END UP NEXT TO YOSHIKAWA-KUN?
I WON'T BE ABLE TO PAY ATTENTION TO THE LESSONS—
HEH.
EH-HEH.

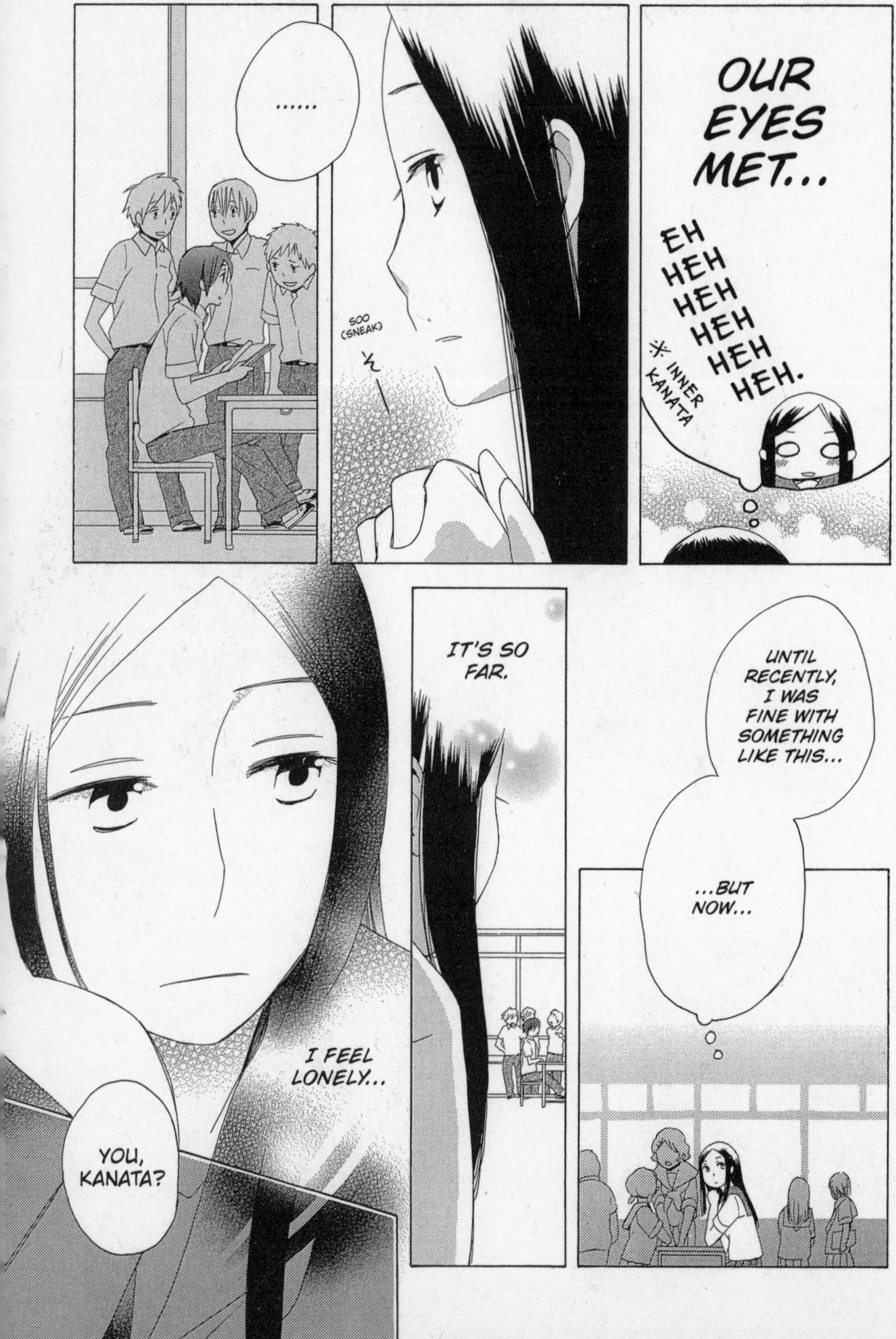
OUR EYES MET...
EH HEH HEH HEH HEH HEH.
※ INNER KANATA
SOO (SNEAK)
......
UNTIL RECENTLY, I WAS FINE WITH SOMETHING LIKE THIS...
...BUT NOW...
IT'S SO FAR.
I FEEL LONELY...
YOU, KANATA?

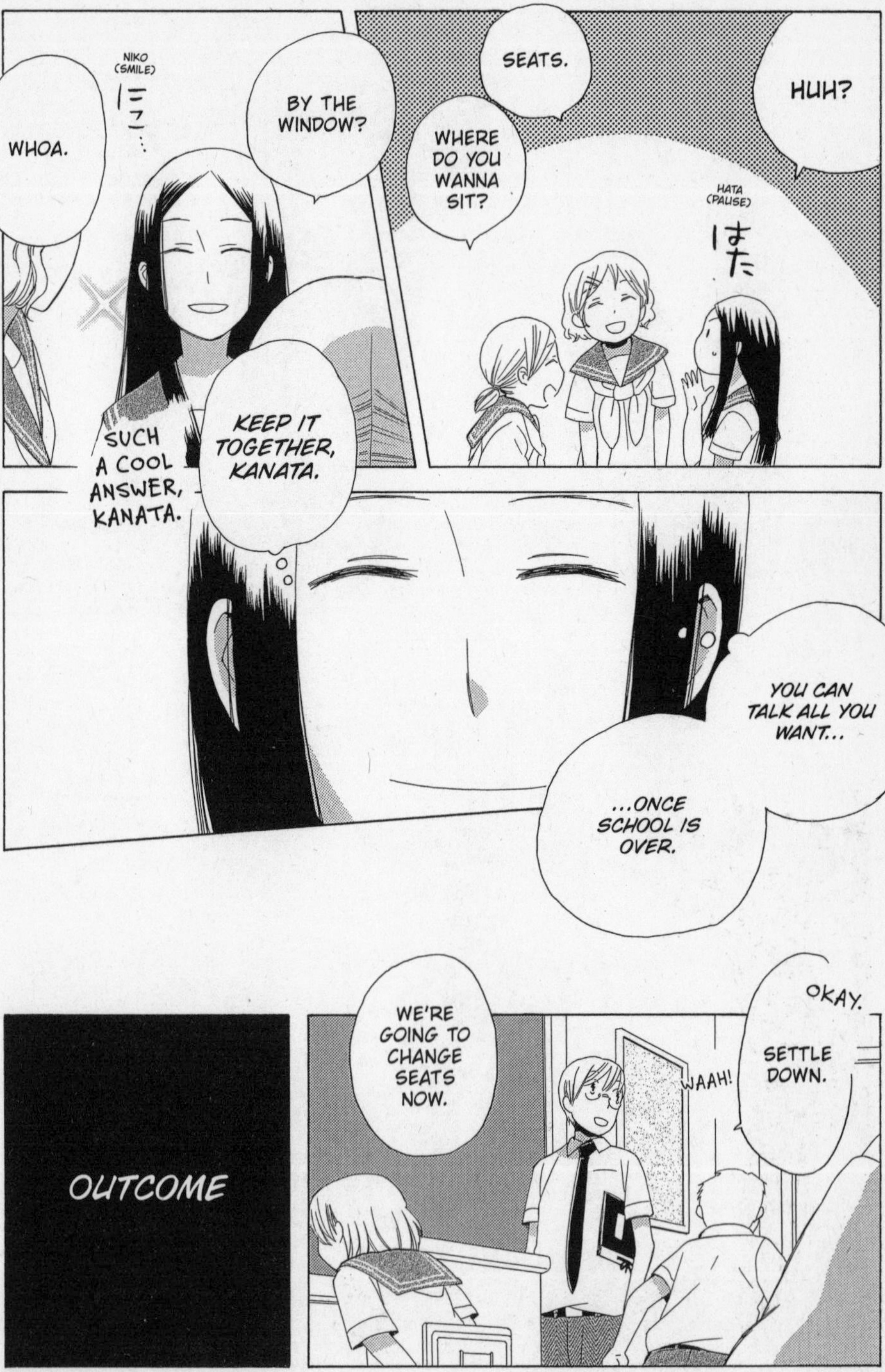
HUH?
SEATS.
WHERE DO YOU WANNA SIT?
HATA (PAUSE)
はた
BY THE WINDOW?
NIKO (SMILE)
ニコ…
WHOA.
KEEP IT TOGETHER, KANATA.
SUCH A COOL ANSWER, KANATA.
YOU CAN TALK ALL YOU WANT...
...ONCE SCHOOL IS OVER.
OKAY.
SETTLE DOWN.
WAAAH!
WE'RE GOING TO CHANGE SEATS NOW.
OUTCOME

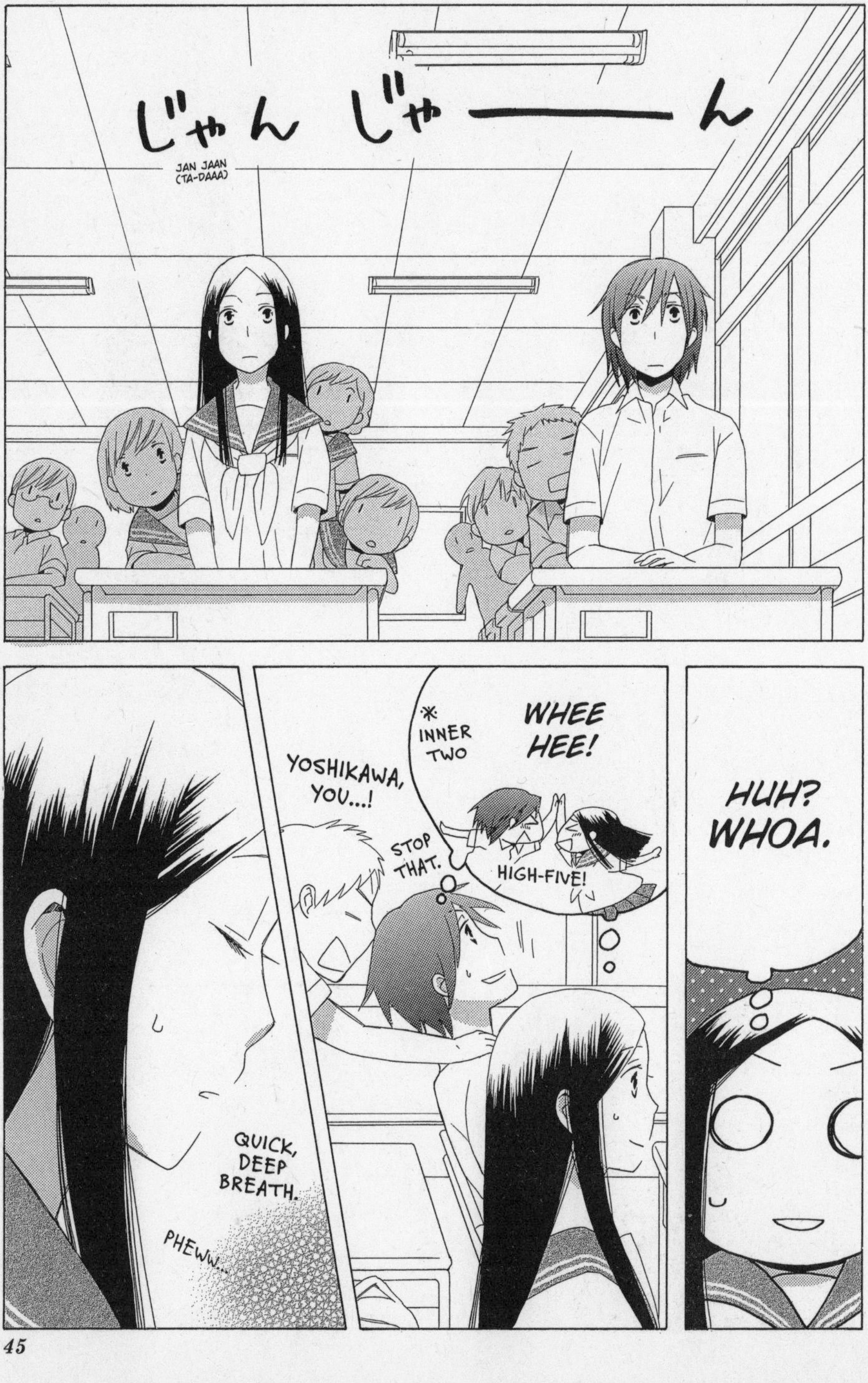
じゃん じゃーーーん
JAN JAAN (TA-DAAA)
HUH? WHOA.
WHEE HEE!
※ INNER TWO
YOSHIKAWA, YOU...!
HIGH-FIVE!
STOP THAT.
QUICK, DEEP BREATH.
PHEWW...

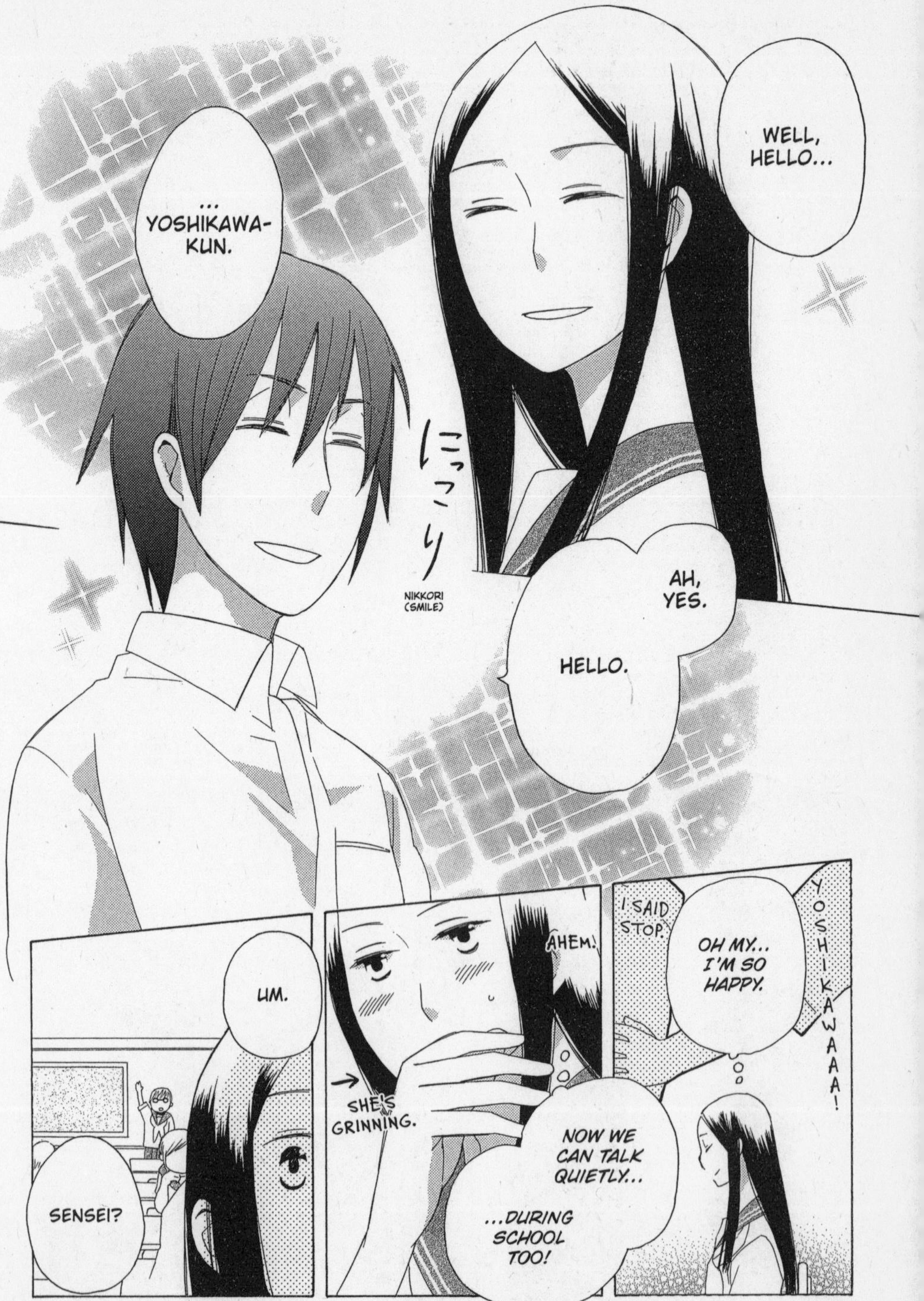
WELL, HELLO...
...YOSHIKAWA-KUN.
にっこり
NIKKORI (SMILE)
AH, YES.
HELLO.
YOSHIKAWAAAA!
I SAID STOP.
OH MY... I'M SO HAPPY.
AHEM!
SHE'S GRINNING.
NOW WE CAN TALK QUIETLY...
...DURING SCHOOL TOO!
UM.
SENSEI?

TANAKA.

YOU'RE TALL.

COULD YOU CHANGE SEATS WITH TERASHIMA?

I CAN'T SEE THE BLACK-BOARD.

YES.

SENSEI.

NO, NO.

THANK YOU. I'M SORRY.

THIS...

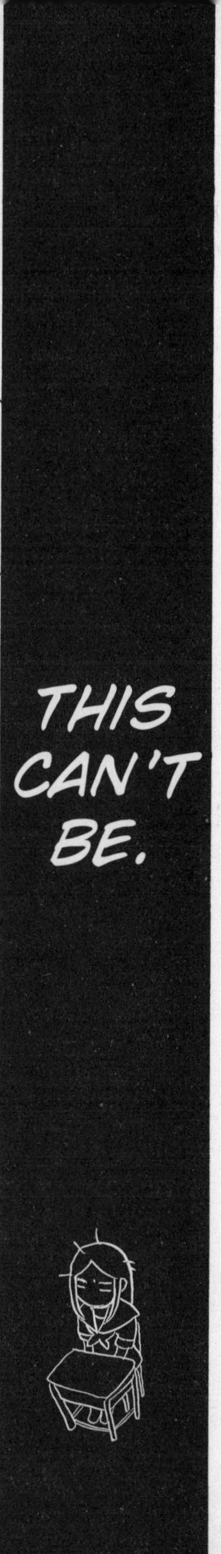
THIS CAN'T BE.

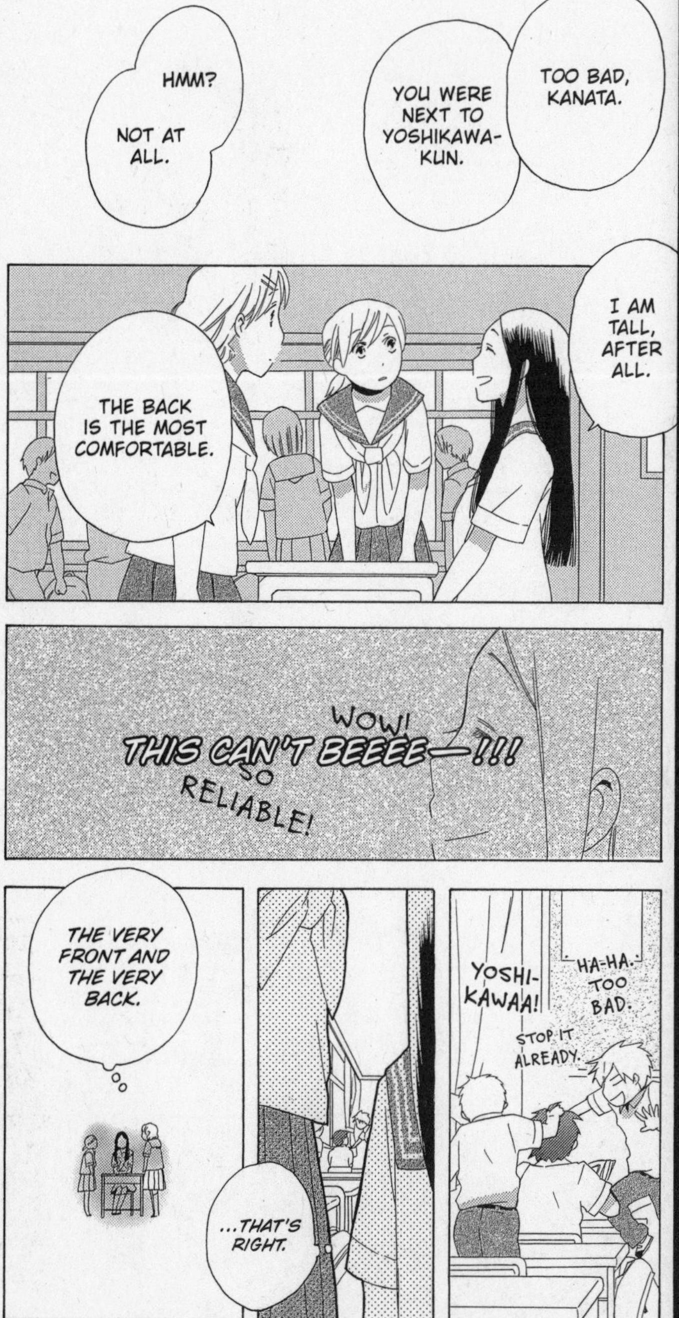
TOO BAD, KANATA.
YOU WERE NEXT TO YOSHIKAWA-KUN.
HMM?
NOT AT ALL.
I AM TALL, AFTER ALL.
THE BACK IS THE MOST COMFORTABLE.
THIS CAN'T BEEEE—!!!
WOW! SO RELIABLE!
YOSHI-KAWAA!
HA-HA. TOO BAD.
STOP IT ALREADY.
...THAT'S RIGHT.
THE VERY FRONT AND THE VERY BACK.

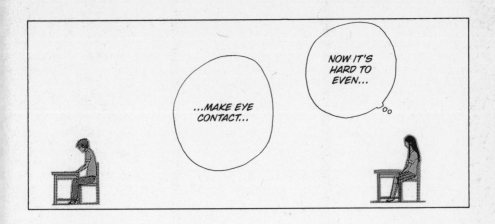

NOW IT'S HARD TO EVEN...

...MAKE EYE CONTACT...

OKAY, TAKE OUT YOUR NOTEBOOKS.

KIIN (DING)
KOON (DONG)
KAAN (DING)
KOON

SENSEI...

I FORGOT MY TEXT-BOOK.

OH WELL.

SHARE WITH THE PERSON NEXT TO YOU.

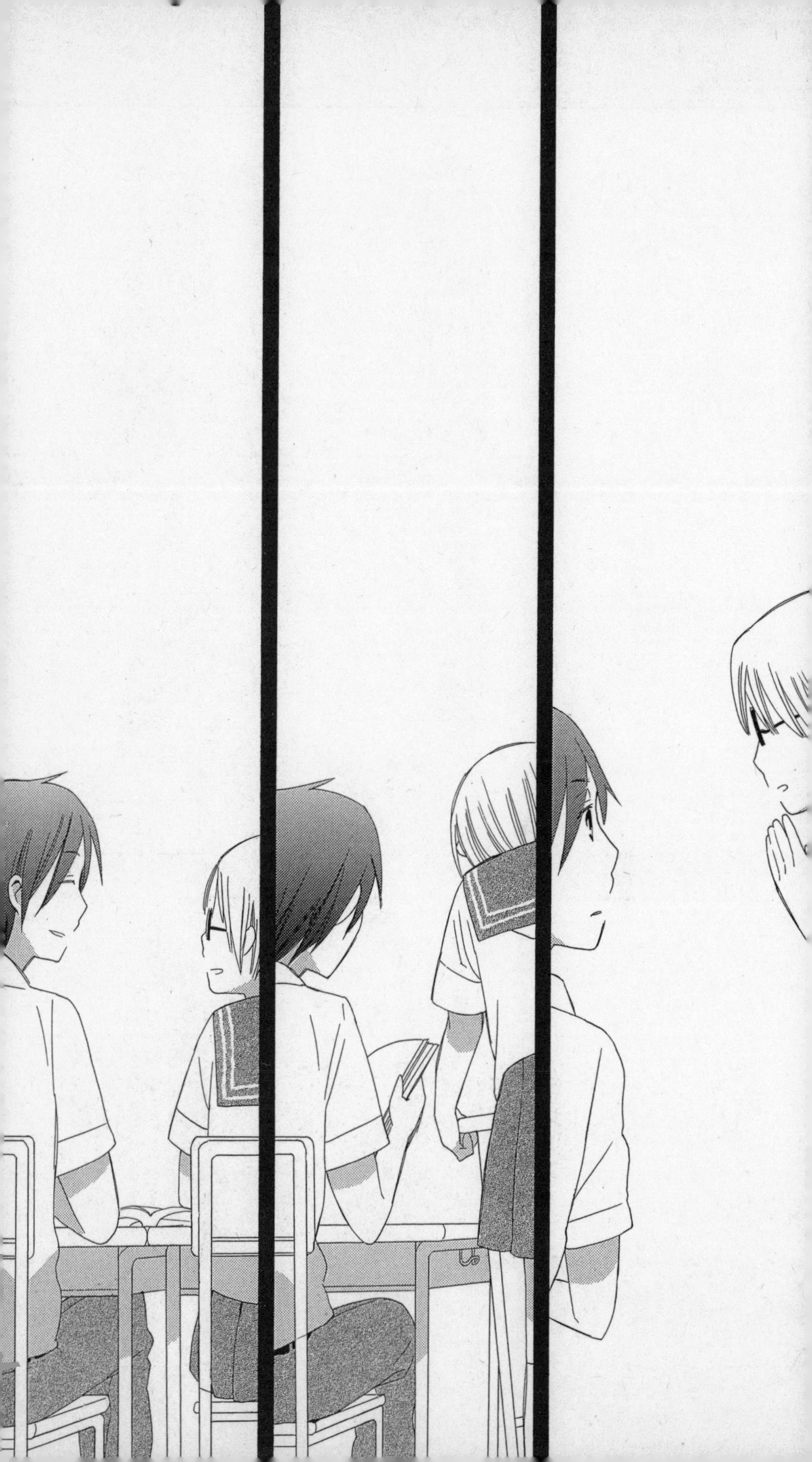

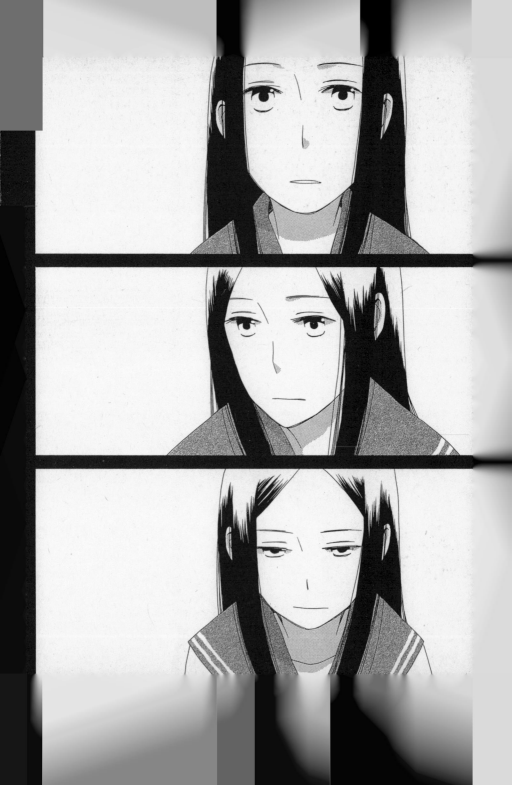

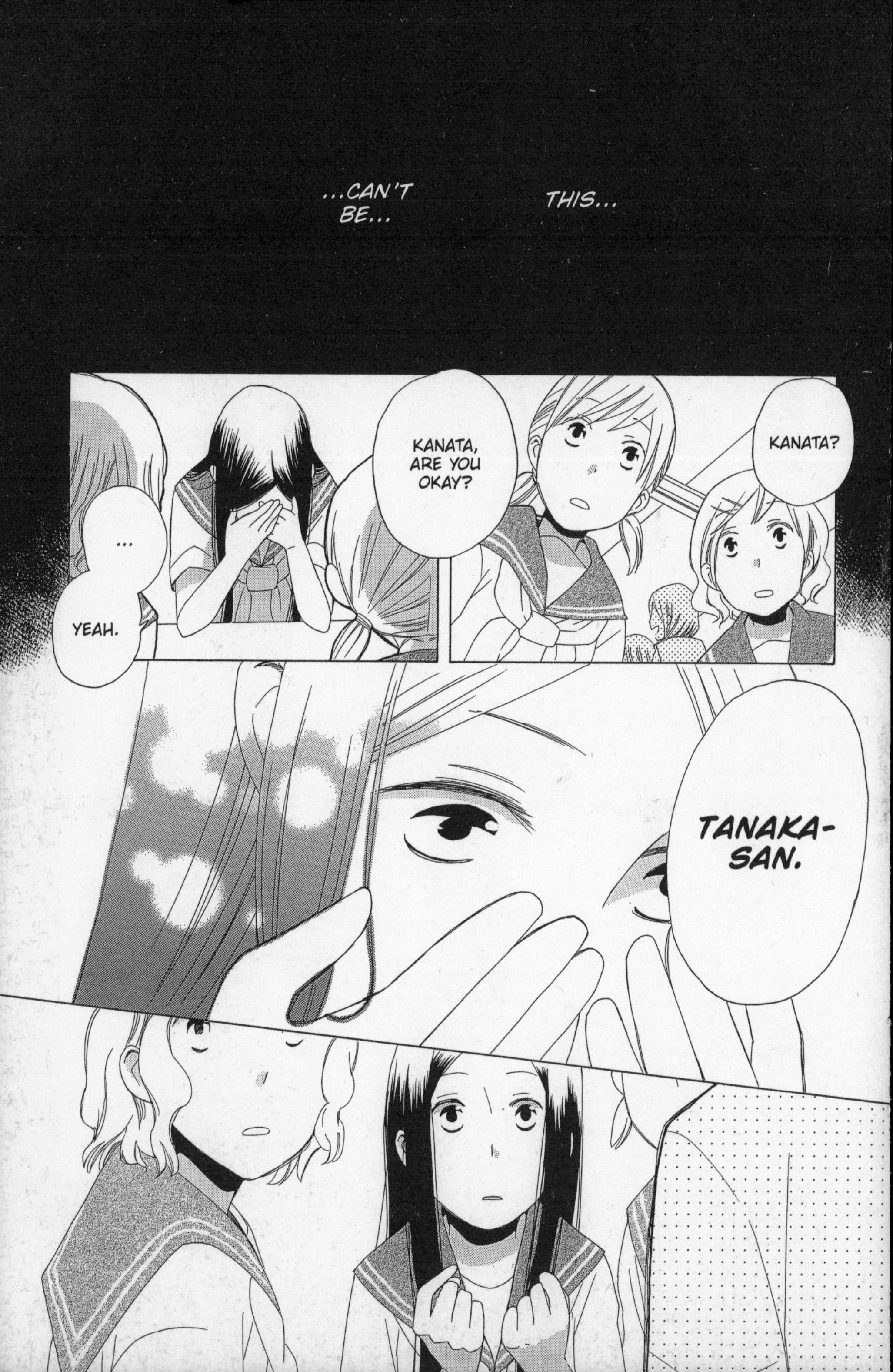
THIS...
...CAN'T BE...
KANATA?
KANATA, ARE YOU OKAY?
...
YEAH.
TANAKA-SAN.

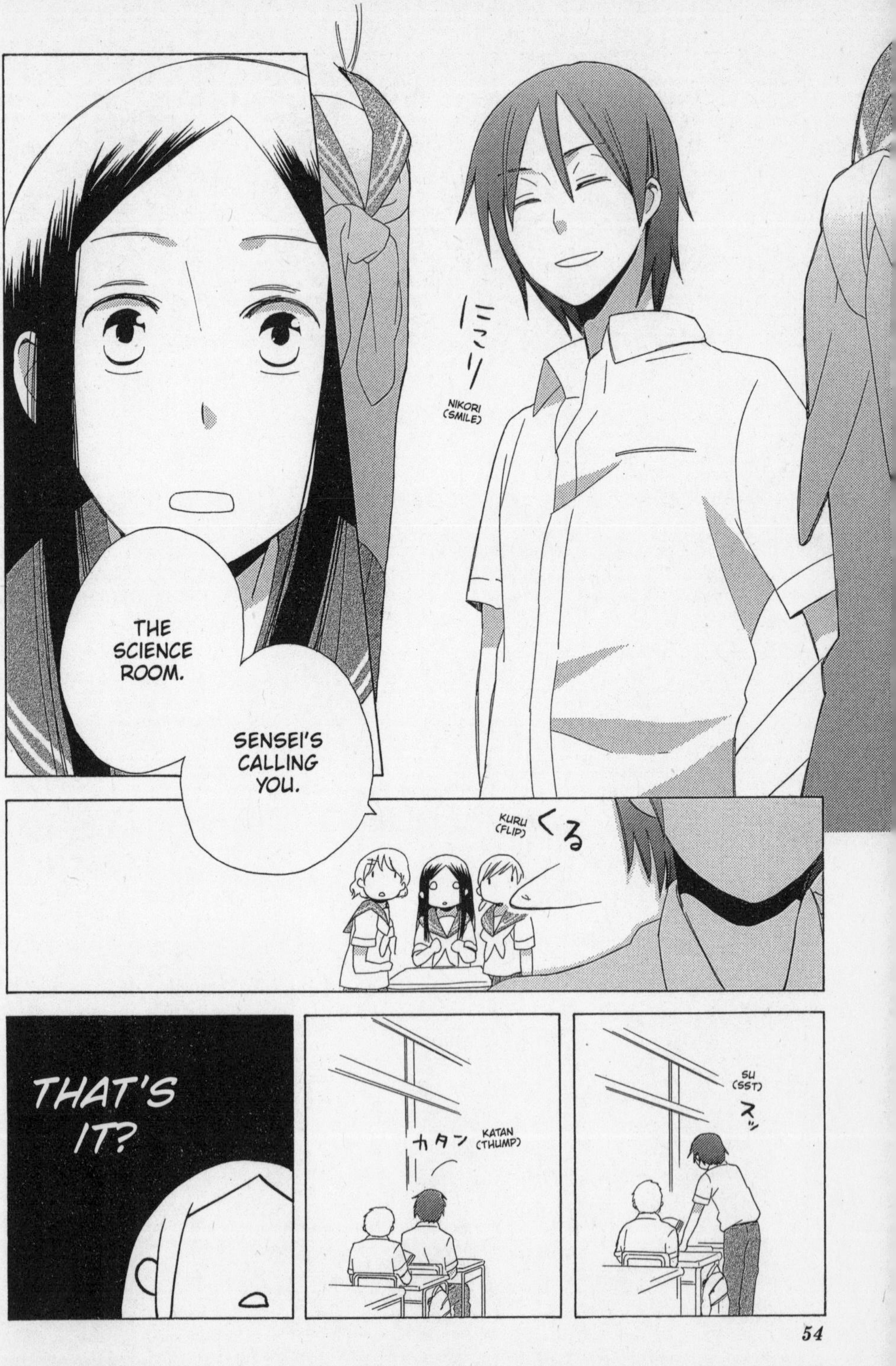
にっこり
NIKORI (SMILE)
THE SCIENCE ROOM.
SENSEI'S CALLING YOU.
KURU (FLIP)
くる
SU (SST)
スッ
カタン
KATAN (THUMP)
THAT'S IT?

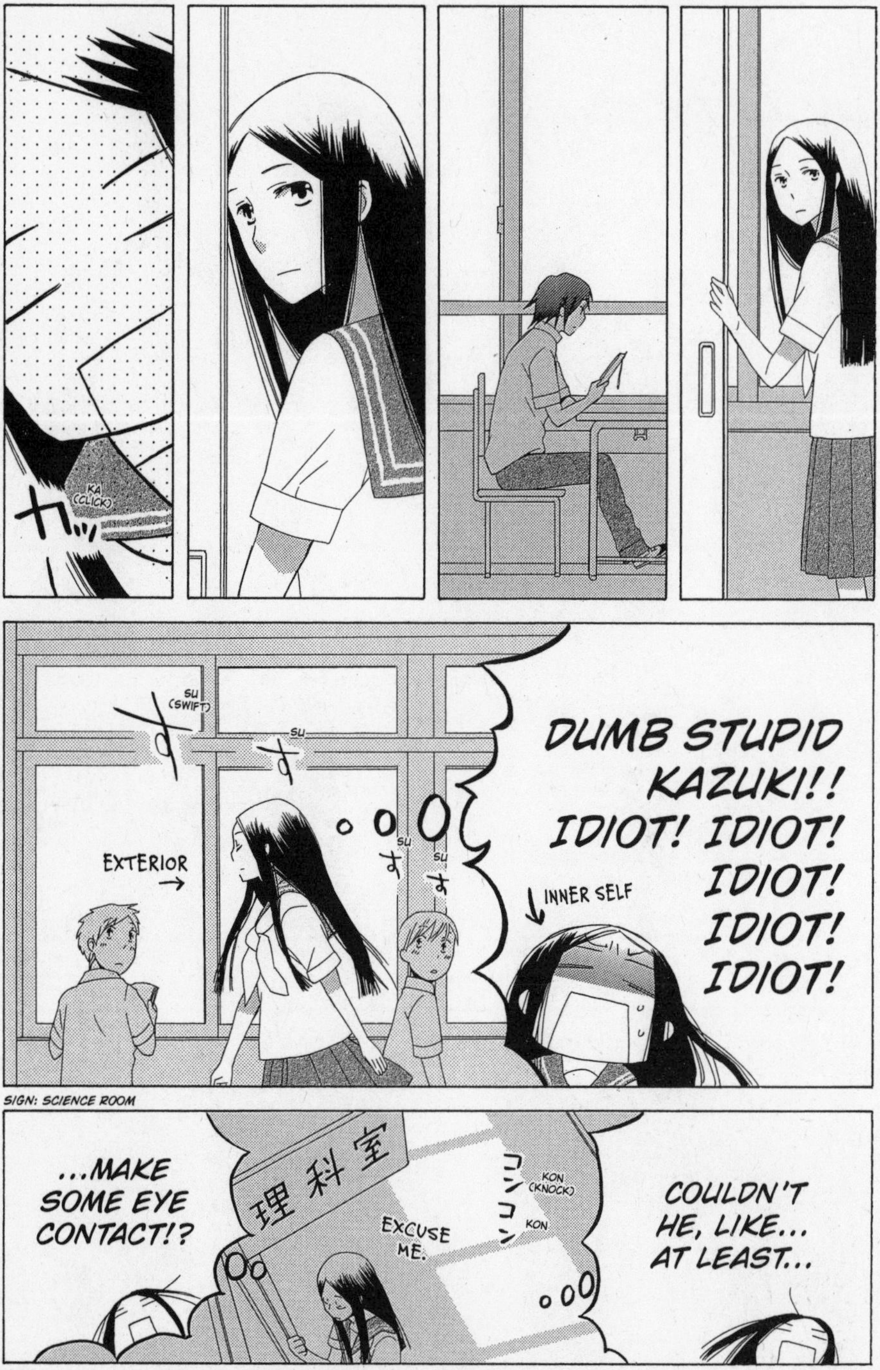
KA (CLICK)
カッ
DUMB STUPID KAZUKI!! IDIOT! IDIOT! IDIOT! IDIOT! IDIOT!
INNER SELF
SU (SWIFT)
SU
SU
SU
EXTERIOR
SIGN: SCIENCE ROOM
COULDN'T HE, LIKE... AT LEAST...
KON (KNOCK)
KON
コンコン
EXCUSE ME.
理科室
...MAKE SOME EYE CONTACT!?

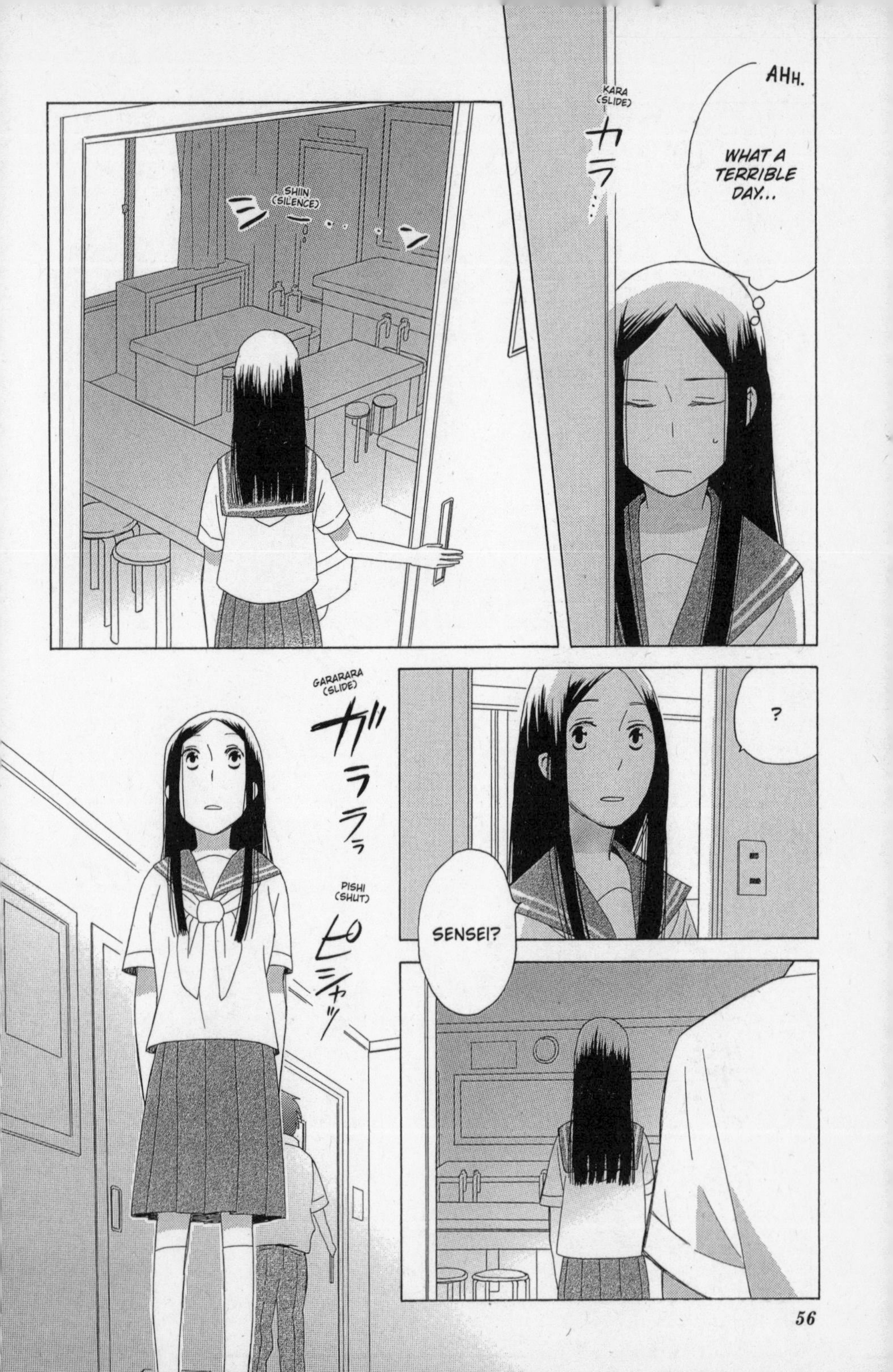
KARA (SLIDE)
カラ…
AHH.
WHAT A TERRIBLE DAY...
SHIIN (SILENCE)
シーン……
?
SENSEI?
GARARARA (SLIDE)
ガラララ
PISHI (SHUT)
ピシャッ

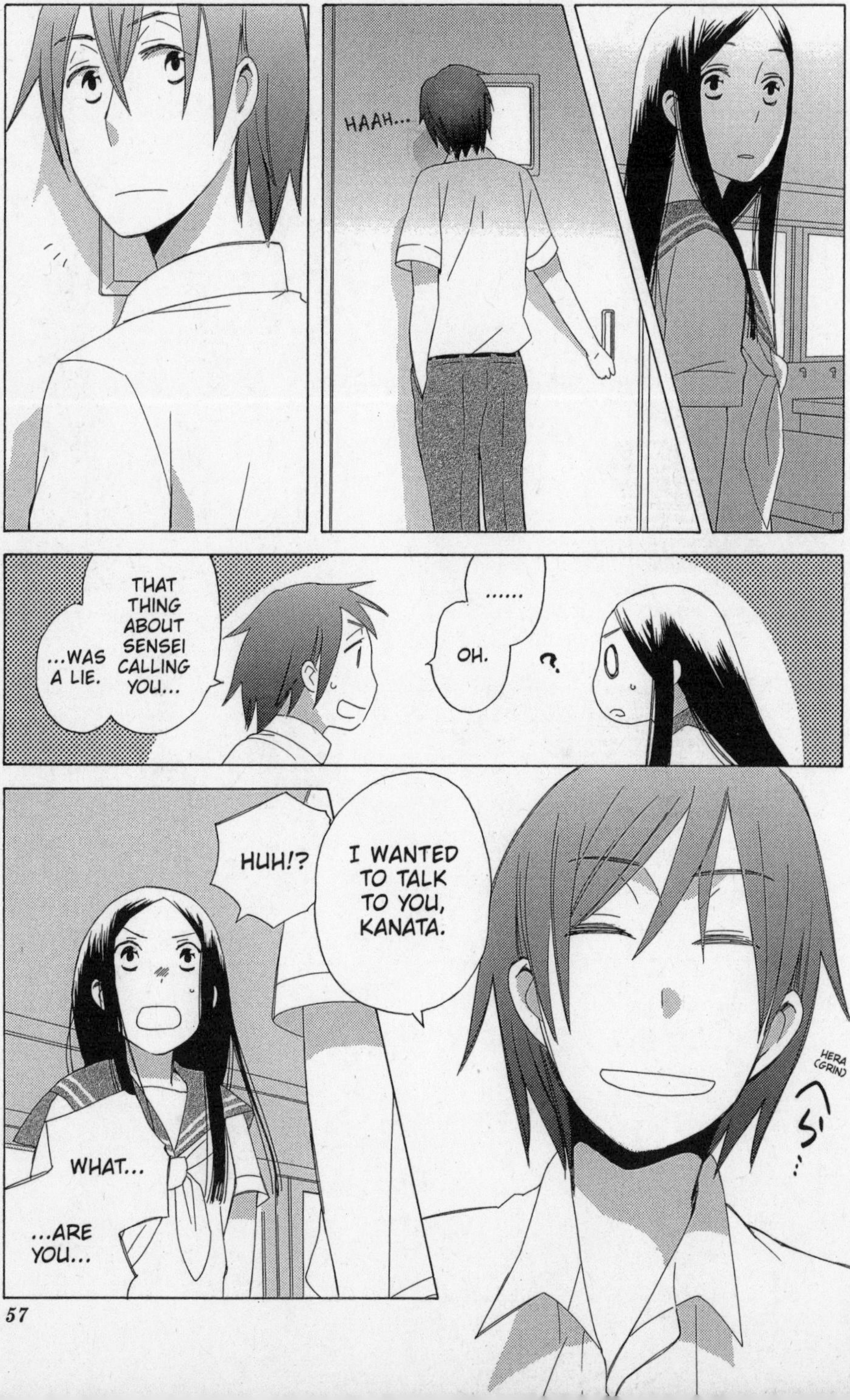
HAAH...
?
......
OH.
THAT THING ABOUT SENSEI CALLING YOU...
...WAS A LIE.
HERA (GRIN)
I WANTED TO TALK TO YOU, KANATA.
HUH!?
WHAT...
...ARE YOU...

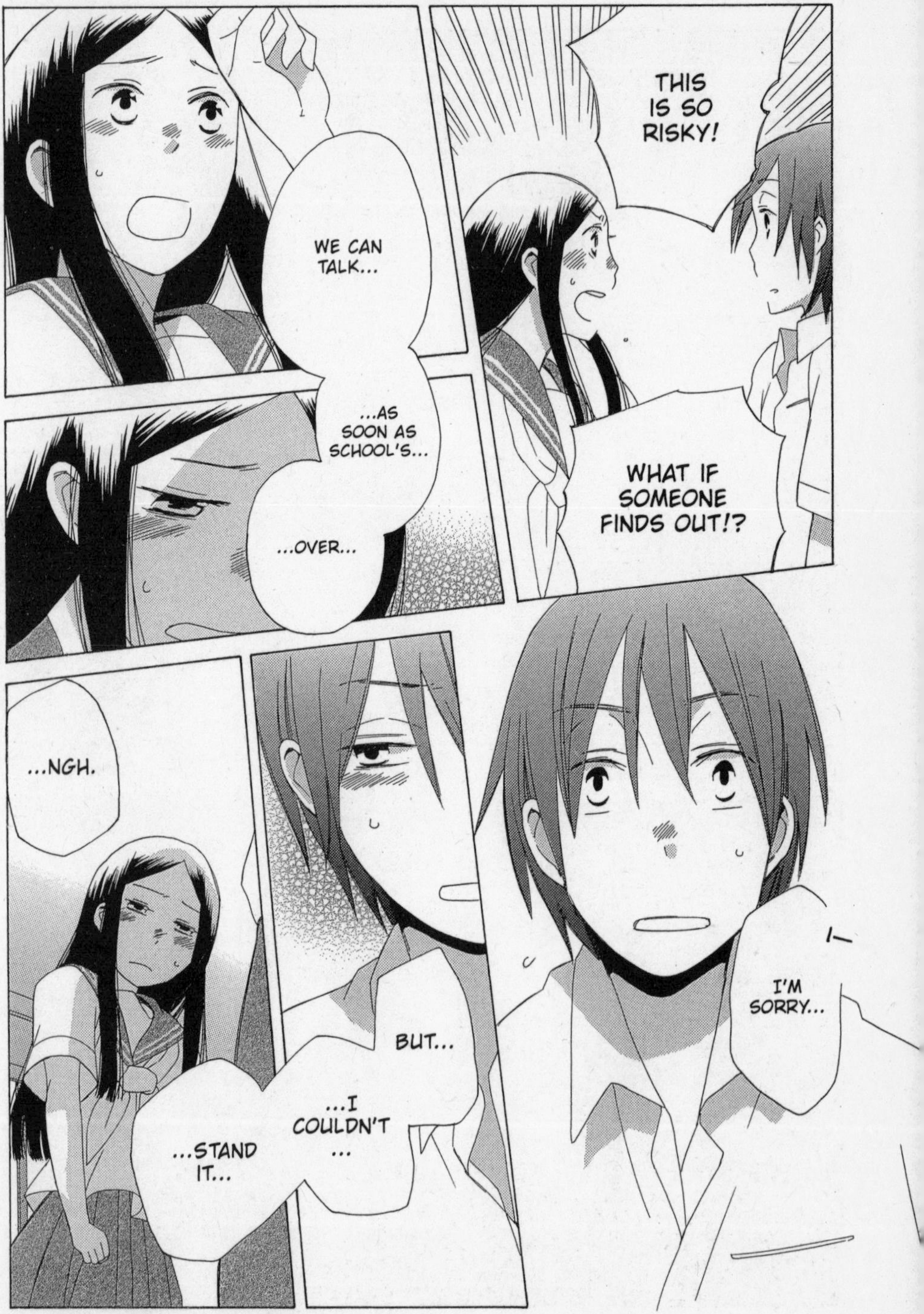
THIS IS SO RISKY!
WHAT IF SOMEONE FINDS OUT!?
WE CAN TALK...
...AS SOON AS SCHOOL'S...
...OVER...
I—
I'M SORRY...
BUT...
...I COULDN'T ...
...STAND IT...
...NGH.

...NO.

I'M SORRY TOO...

BATA (TMP)

BATA

GARA (CLATTER)

SENSEI...

WHERE'S THE THERMOMETER?

IN THE BACK CABINET.

ONE PER GROUP.

OKAY.

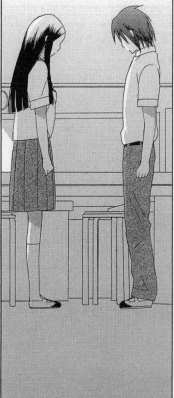

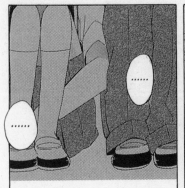

......

......

YES, THAT'S IT.

THIS, SENSEI?

ヒソ
HISO (WHISPER)

HISO
ヒソ

They're from Class A.

Their class is out on the field. They'll leave right away.

KOKU (NOD)
コク

KOKU
コク

HISO
ヒソ

KOSO (WHISPER)
コソ

OUR SEATS...

WE'RE APART NOW.

...YEAH.

OH...

...THAT'S RIGHT.

I...

...CAN'T SEE YOU AT ALL ANYMORE.

WHAT A SHOCK.

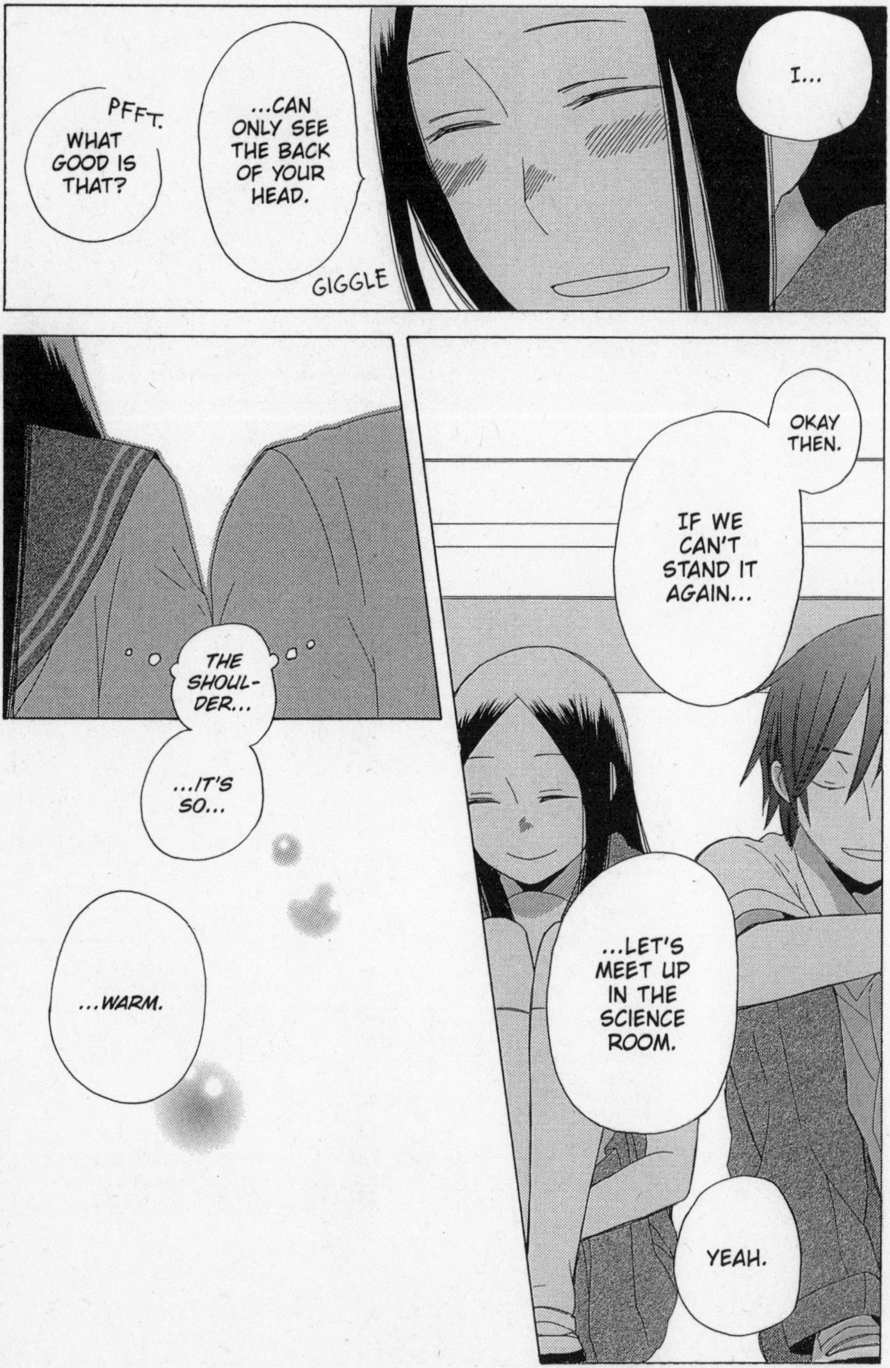
I...
...CAN ONLY SEE THE BACK OF YOUR HEAD.
GIGGLE
PFFT.
WHAT GOOD IS THAT?
OKAY THEN.
IF WE CAN'T STAND IT AGAIN...
...LET'S MEET UP IN THE SCIENCE ROOM.
YEAH.
THE SHOULDER...
...IT'S SO...
...WARM.

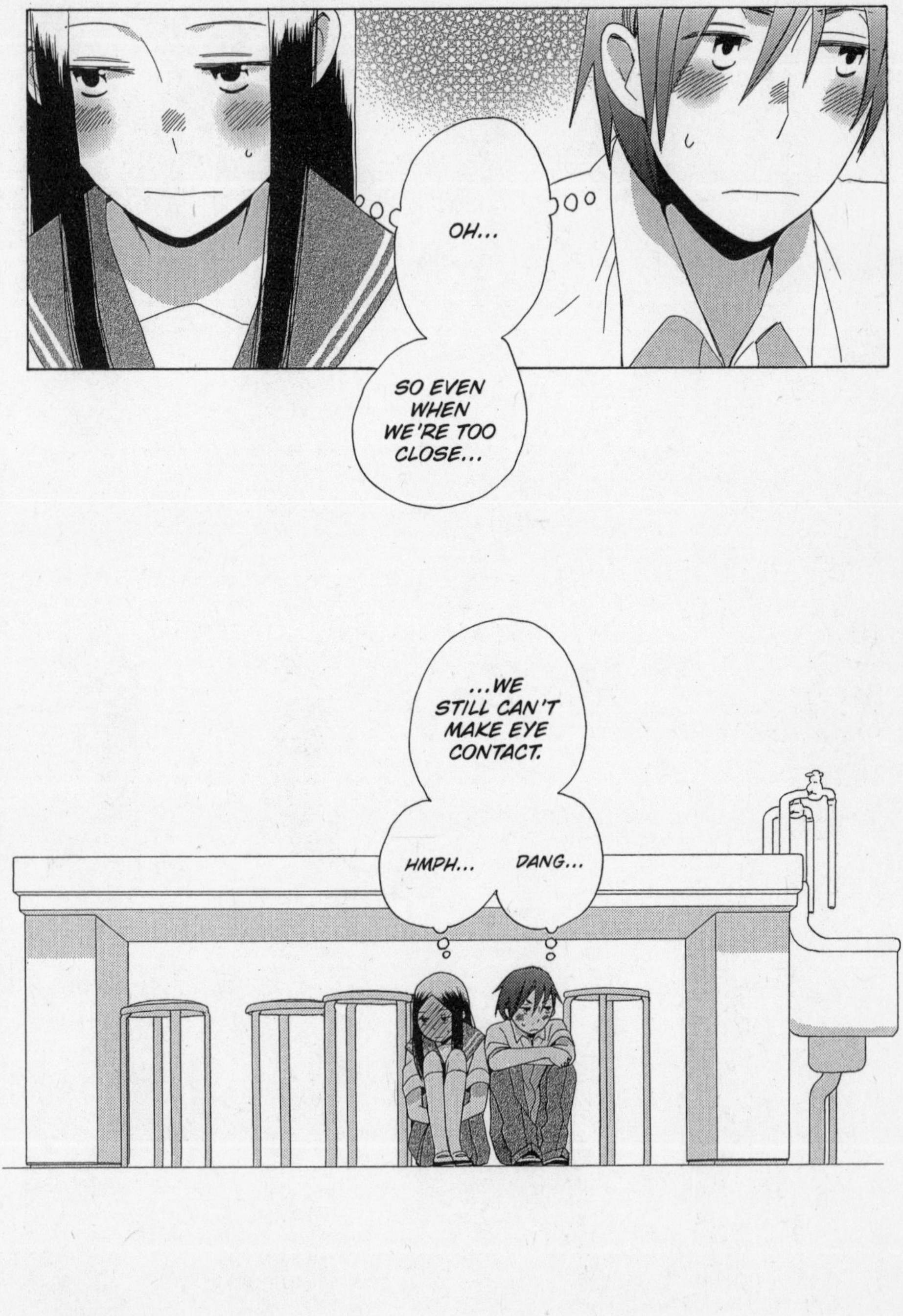
OH...
SO EVEN WHEN WE'RE TOO CLOSE...
...WE STILL CAN'T MAKE EYE CONTACT.
DANG...
HMPH...
Fin

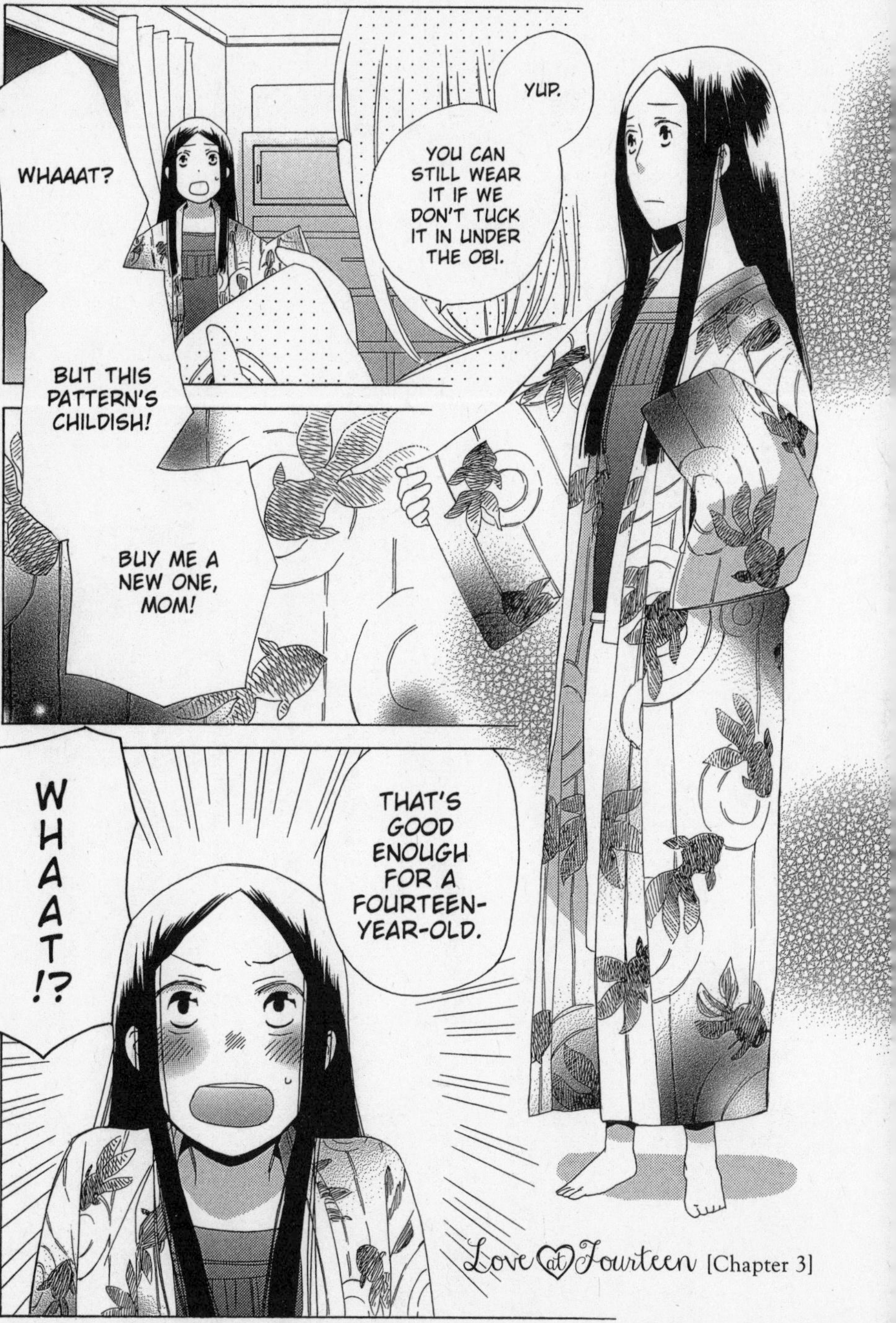
YUP.
YOU CAN STILL WEAR IT IF WE DON'T TUCK IT IN UNDER THE OBI.
WHAAAT?
BUT THIS PATTERN'S CHILDISH!
BUY ME A NEW ONE, MOM!
THAT'S GOOD ENOUGH FOR A FOURTEEN-YEAR-OLD.
WHAAAT!?

Love at Fourteen [Chapter 3]

Love at Fourteen

[Chapter 3]

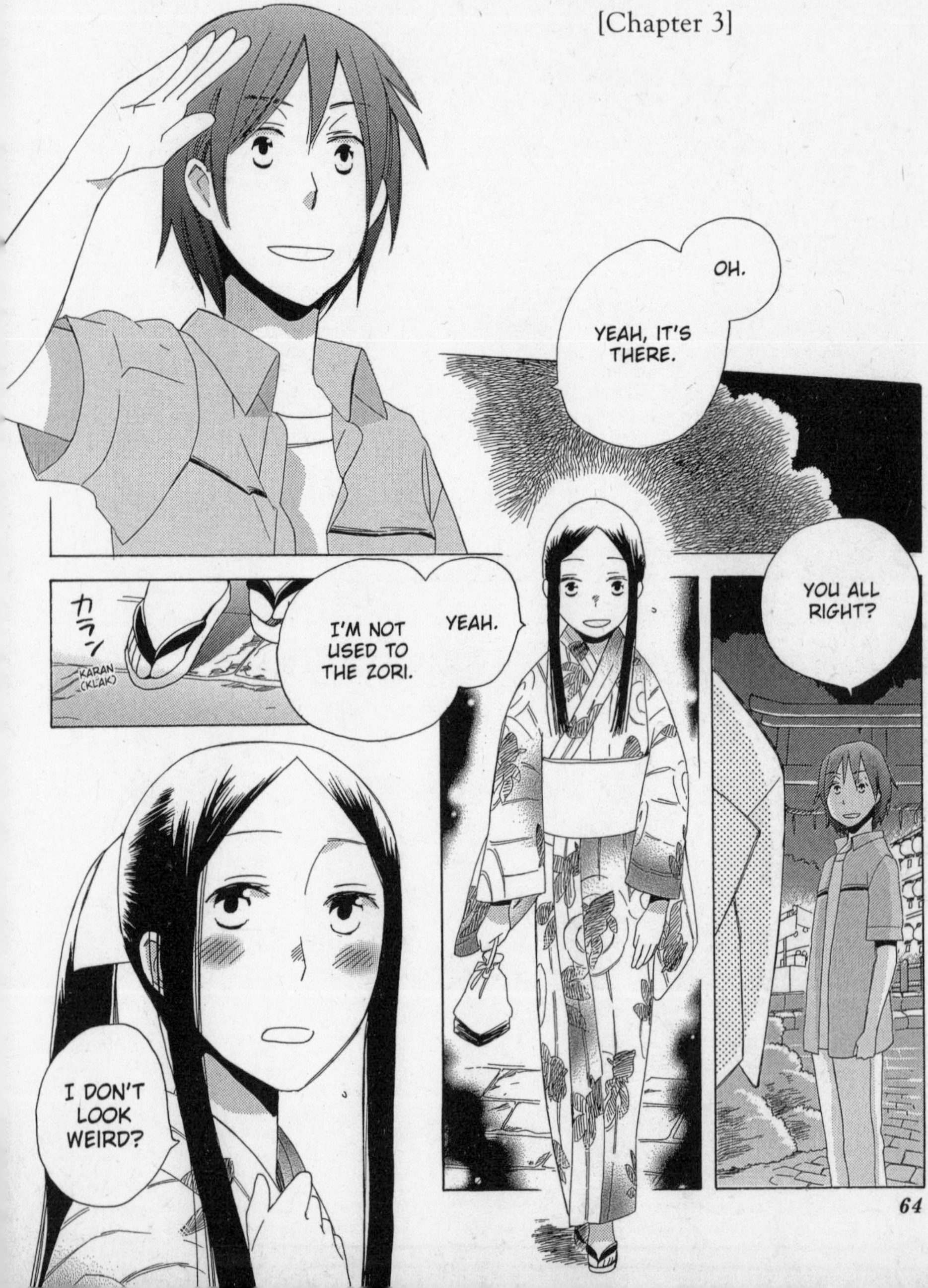
OH.
YEAH, IT'S THERE.
YOU ALL RIGHT?
YEAH.
I'M NOT USED TO THE ZORI.
カラン
KARAN (KLAK)
I DON'T LOOK WEIRD?

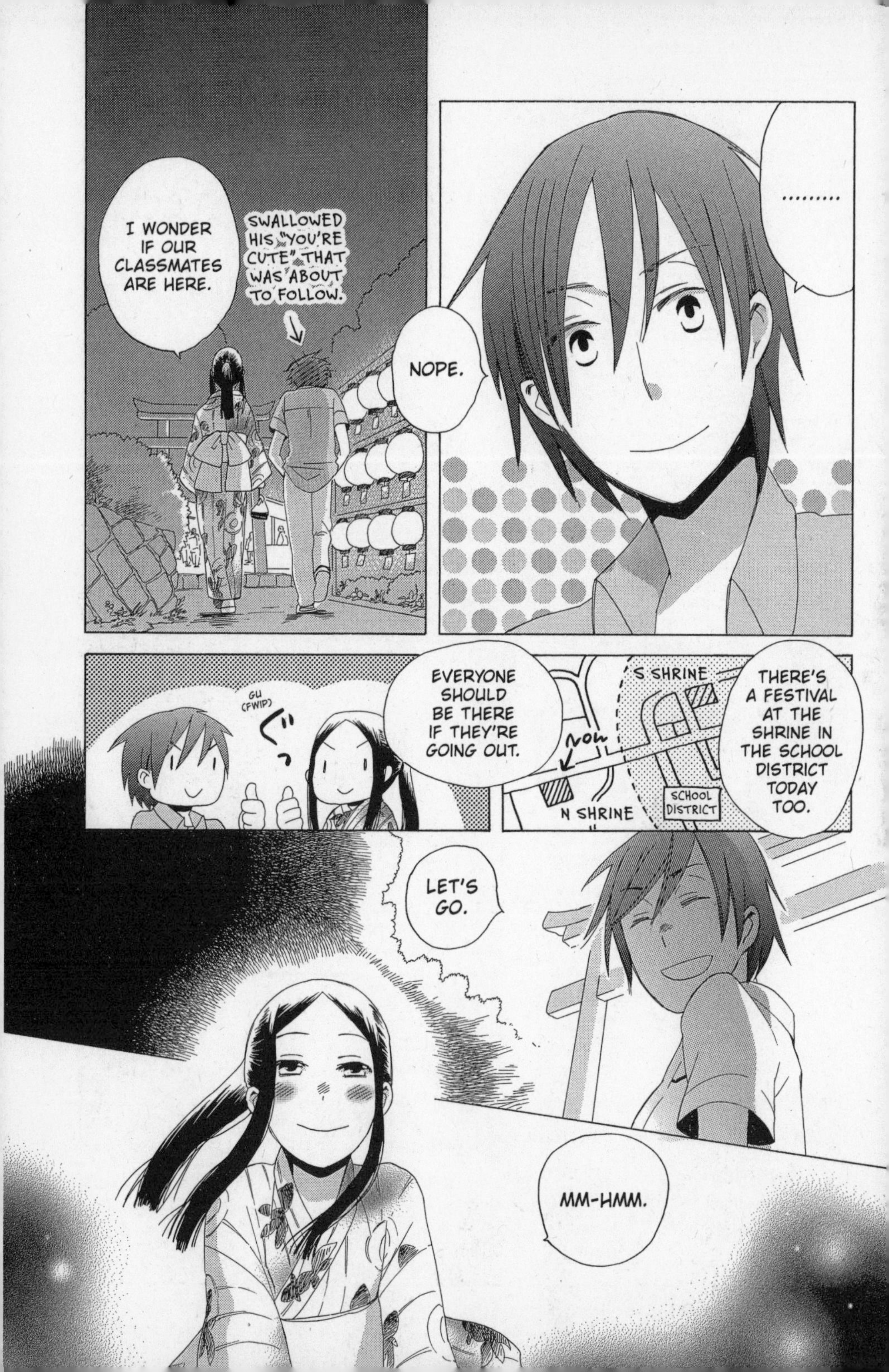
....
NOPE.
I WONDER IF OUR CLASSMATES ARE HERE.
SWALLOWED HIS "YOU'RE CUTE" THAT WAS ABOUT TO FOLLOW.
THERE'S A FESTIVAL AT THE SHRINE IN THE SCHOOL DISTRICT TODAY TOO.
S SHRINE
now
N SHRINE
SCHOOL DISTRICT
EVERYONE SHOULD BE THERE IF THEY'RE GOING OUT.
GU (FWIP)
LET'S GO.
MM-HMM.

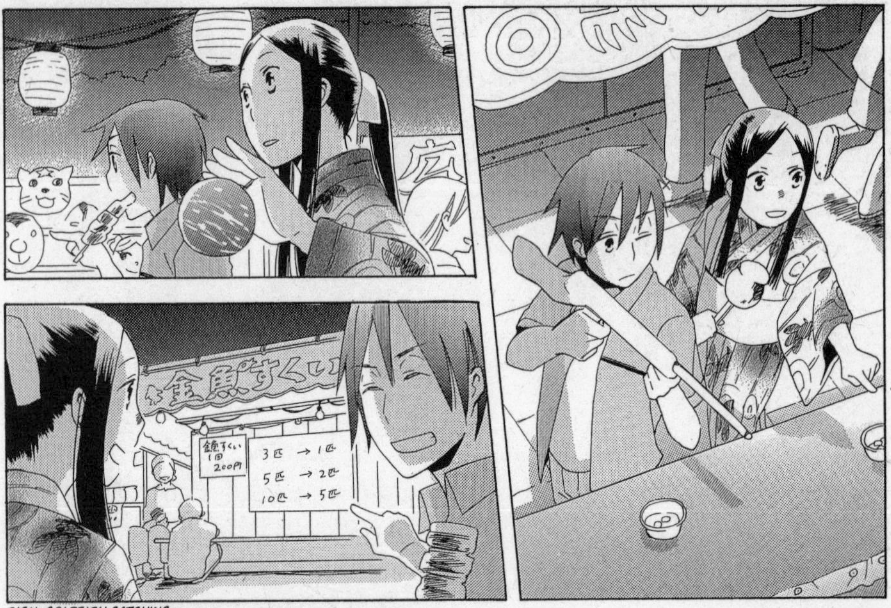
金魚すくい
3匹 → 1匹
5匹 → 2匹
10匹 → 5匹

SIGN: GOLDFISH CATCHING

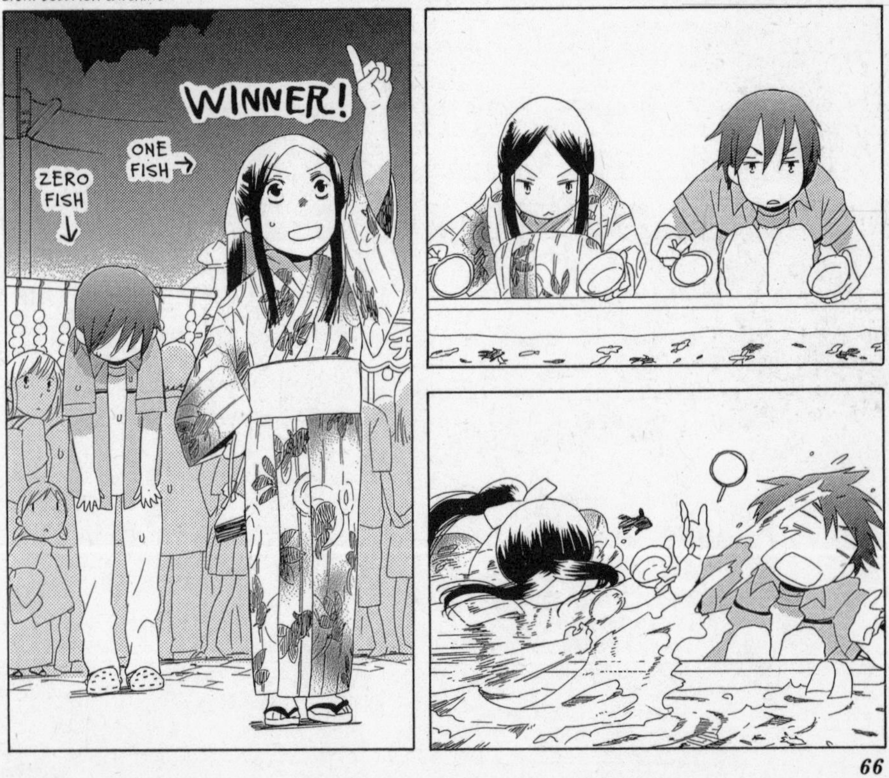
WINNER!
ONE FISH →
ZERO FISH ↓

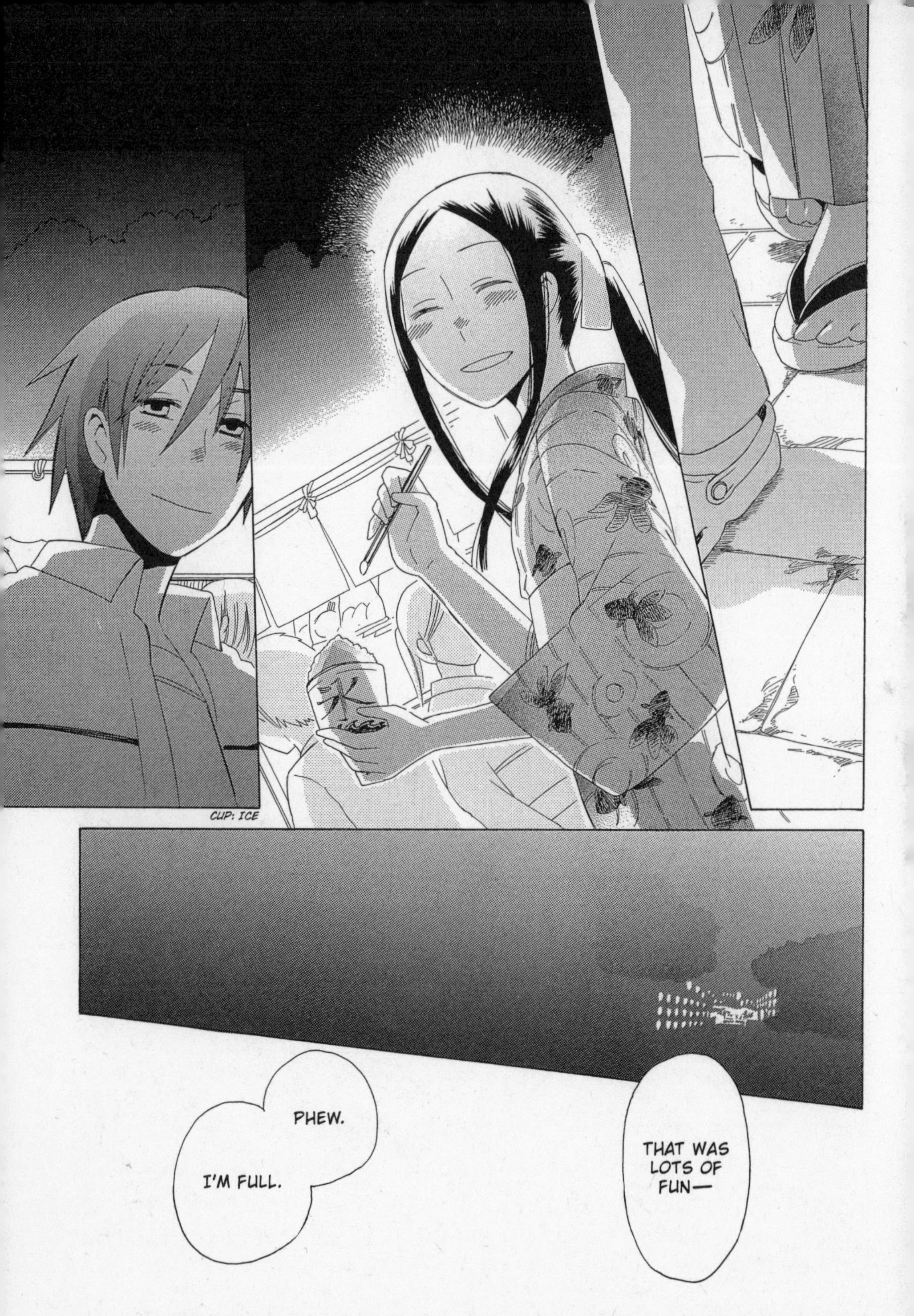
CUP: ICE
THAT WAS LOTS OF FUN—
PHEW.
I'M FULL.

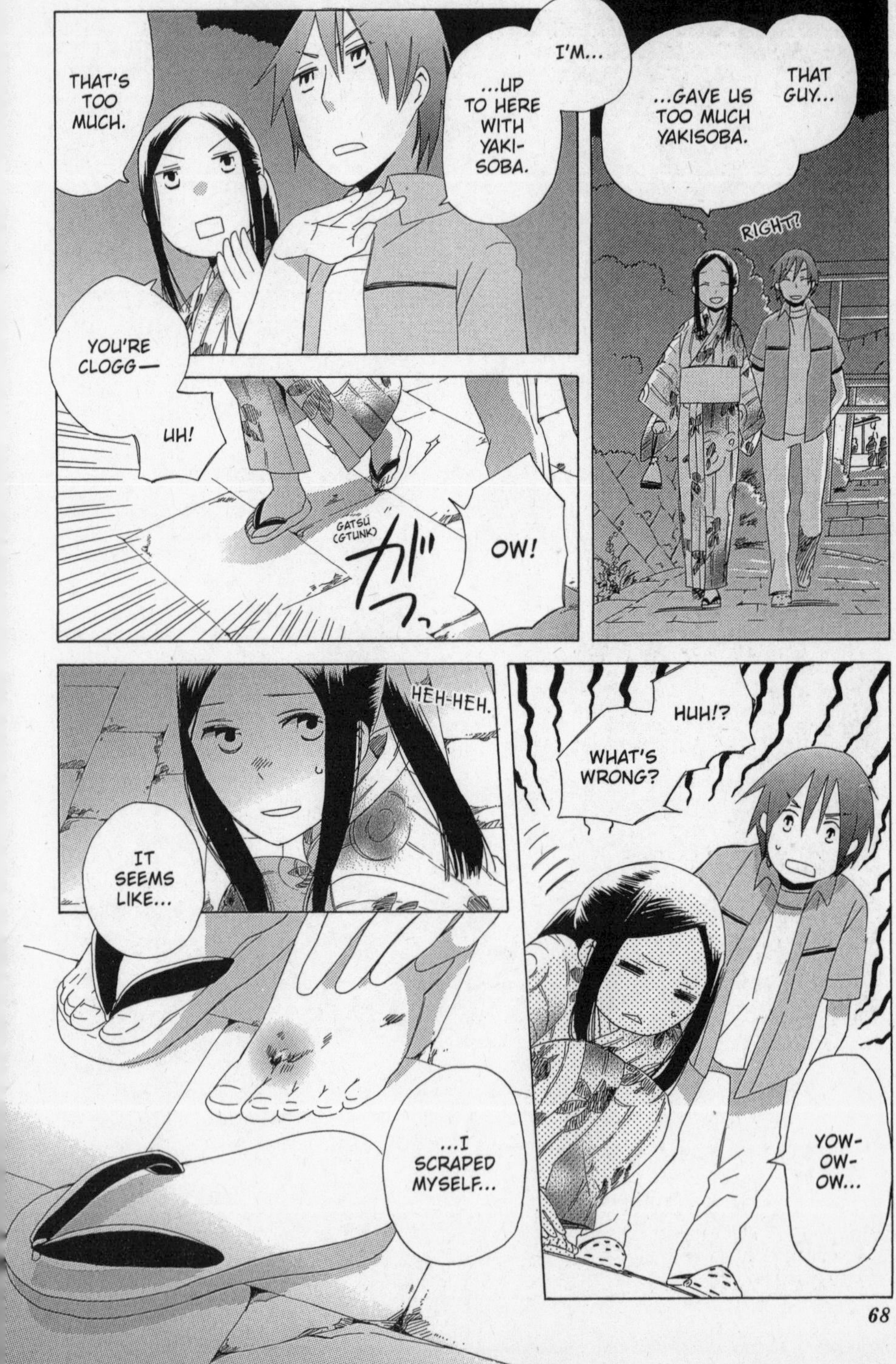
THAT GUY...
...GAVE US TOO MUCH YAKISOBA.
RIGHT?
I'M...
...UP TO HERE WITH YAKI-SOBA.
THAT'S TOO MUCH.
YOU'RE CLOGG—
UH!
GATSU (GTUNK)
OW!
HUH!?
WHAT'S WRONG?
YOW-OW-OW...
HEH-HEH.
IT SEEMS LIKE...
...I SCRAPED MYSELF...

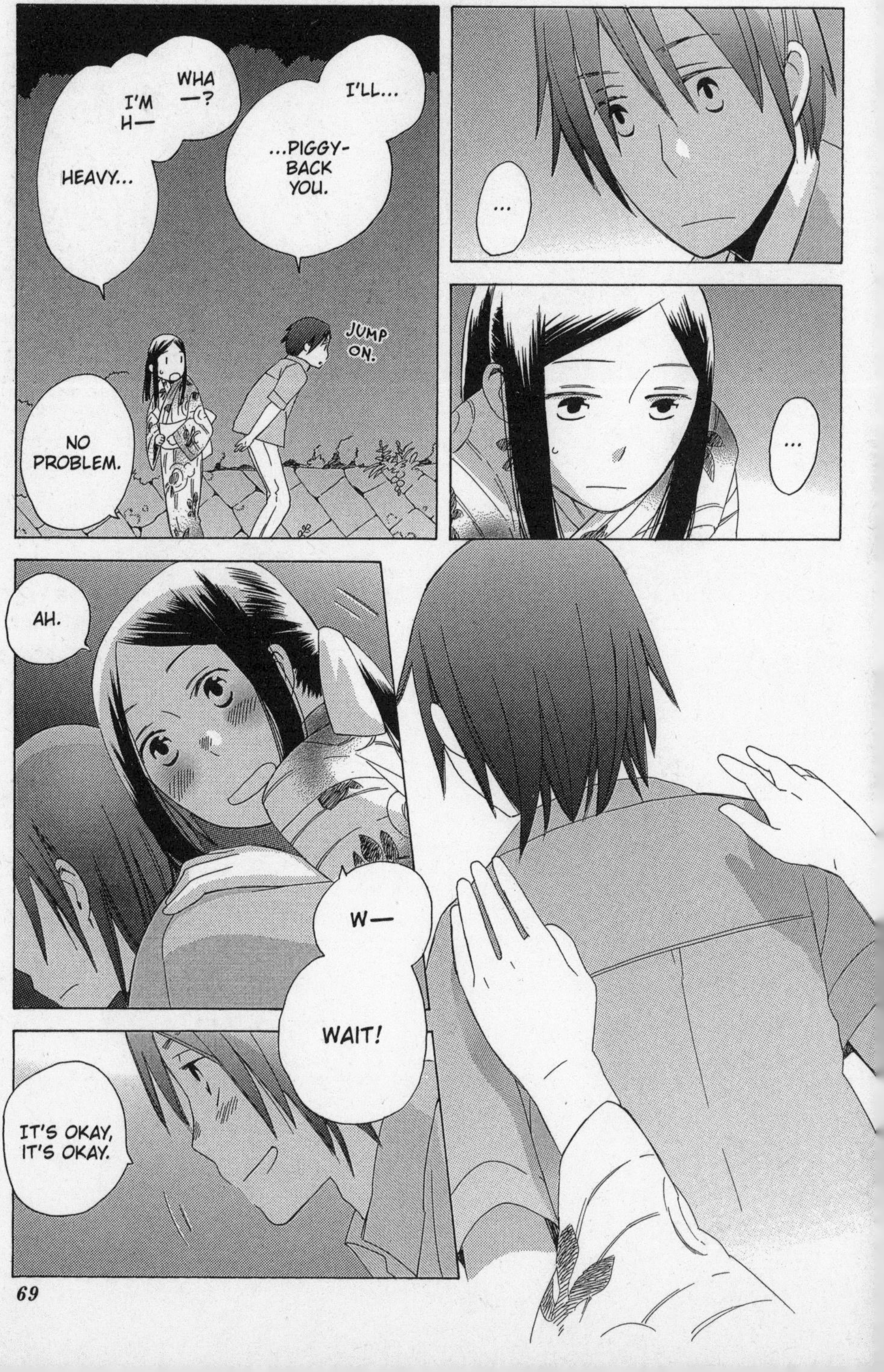
...
...
I'LL...
...PIGGY-BACK YOU.
WHA—?
I'M H—
HEAVY...
JUMP ON.
NO PROBLEM.
W—
WAIT!
AH.
IT'S OKAY, IT'S OKAY.

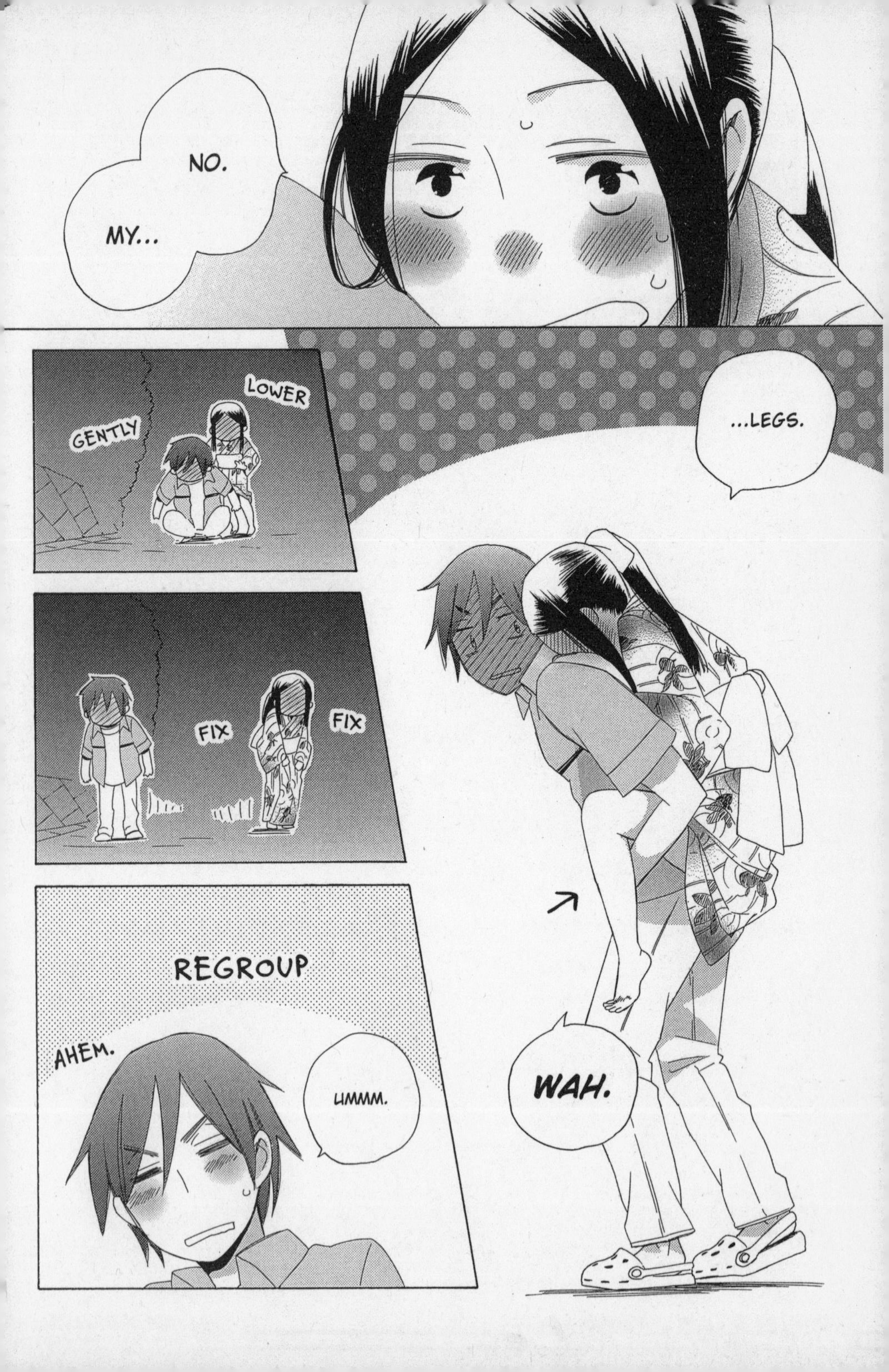
NO.
MY...
...LEGS.
WAH.
LOWER
GENTLY
FIX
FIX
REGROUP
UMMM.
AHEM.

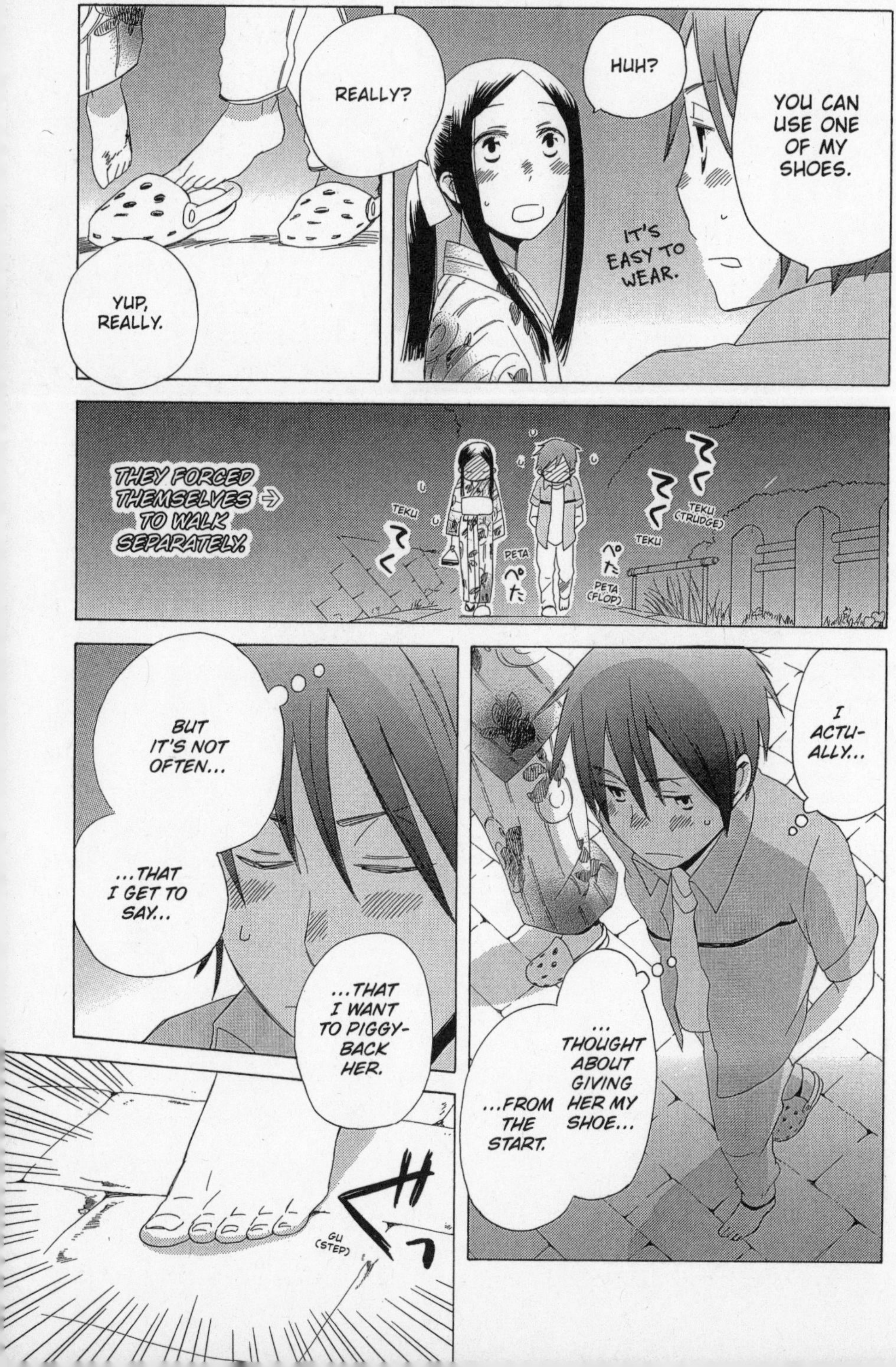
YOU CAN USE ONE OF MY SHOES.
HUH?
IT'S EASY TO WEAR.
REALLY?
YUP, REALLY.
てく
TEKU (TRUDGE)
てく
TEKU
ぺた
PETA (FLOP)
ぺた
PETA
てく
TEKU
THEY FORCED THEMSELVES → TO WALK SEPARATELY.
I ACTU-ALLY...
... THOUGHT ABOUT GIVING HER MY SHOE...
...FROM THE START.
BUT IT'S NOT OFTEN...
...THAT I GET TO SAY...
...THAT I WANT TO PIGGY-BACK HER.
ぐっ
GU (STEP)

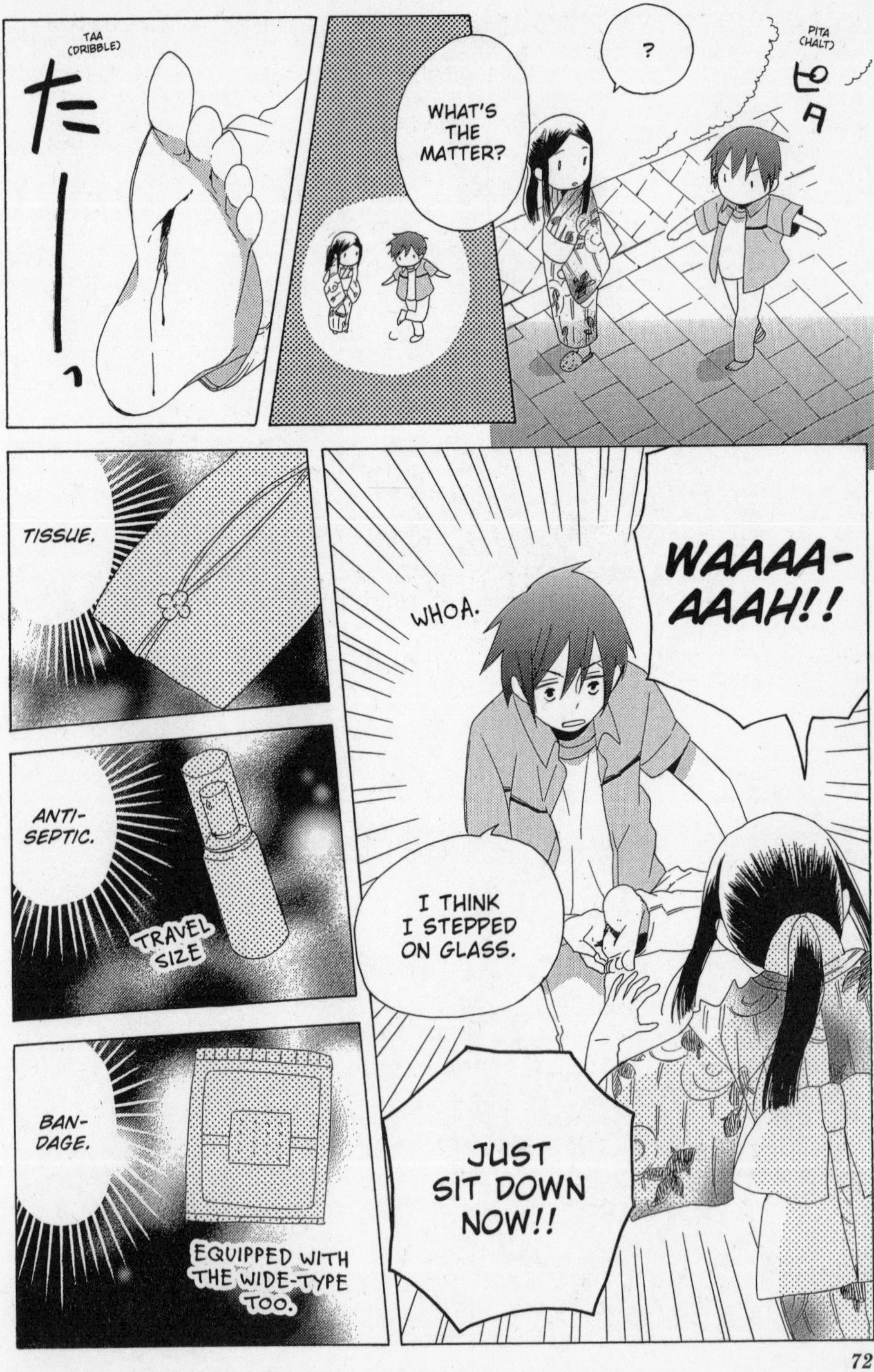
PITA (HALT)
ピタ
?
WHAT'S THE MATTER?
TAA (DRIBBLE)
たー
WAAAA-AAAH!!
WHOA.
I THINK I STEPPED ON GLASS.
JUST SIT DOWN NOW!!
TISSUE.
ANTI-SEPTIC.
TRAVEL SIZE
BAN-DAGE.
EQUIPPED WITH THE WIDE-TYPE TOO.

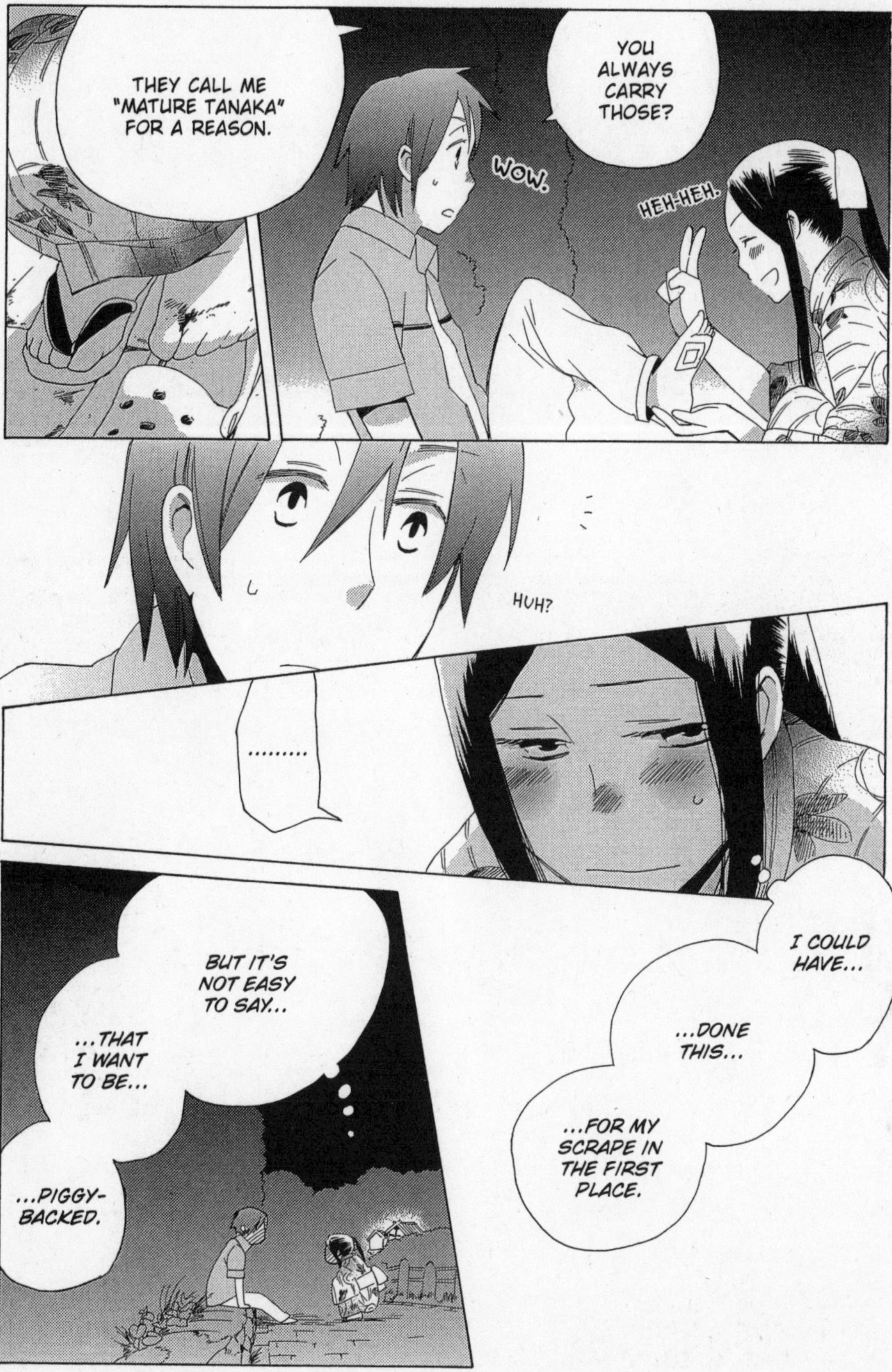
YOU ALWAYS CARRY THOSE?
HEH-HEH.
WOW.
THEY CALL ME "MATURE TANAKA" FOR A REASON.
HUH?
....
I COULD HAVE...
...DONE THIS...
...FOR MY SCRAPE IN THE FIRST PLACE.
BUT IT'S NOT EASY TO SAY...
...THAT I WANT TO BE...
...PIGGY-BACKED.

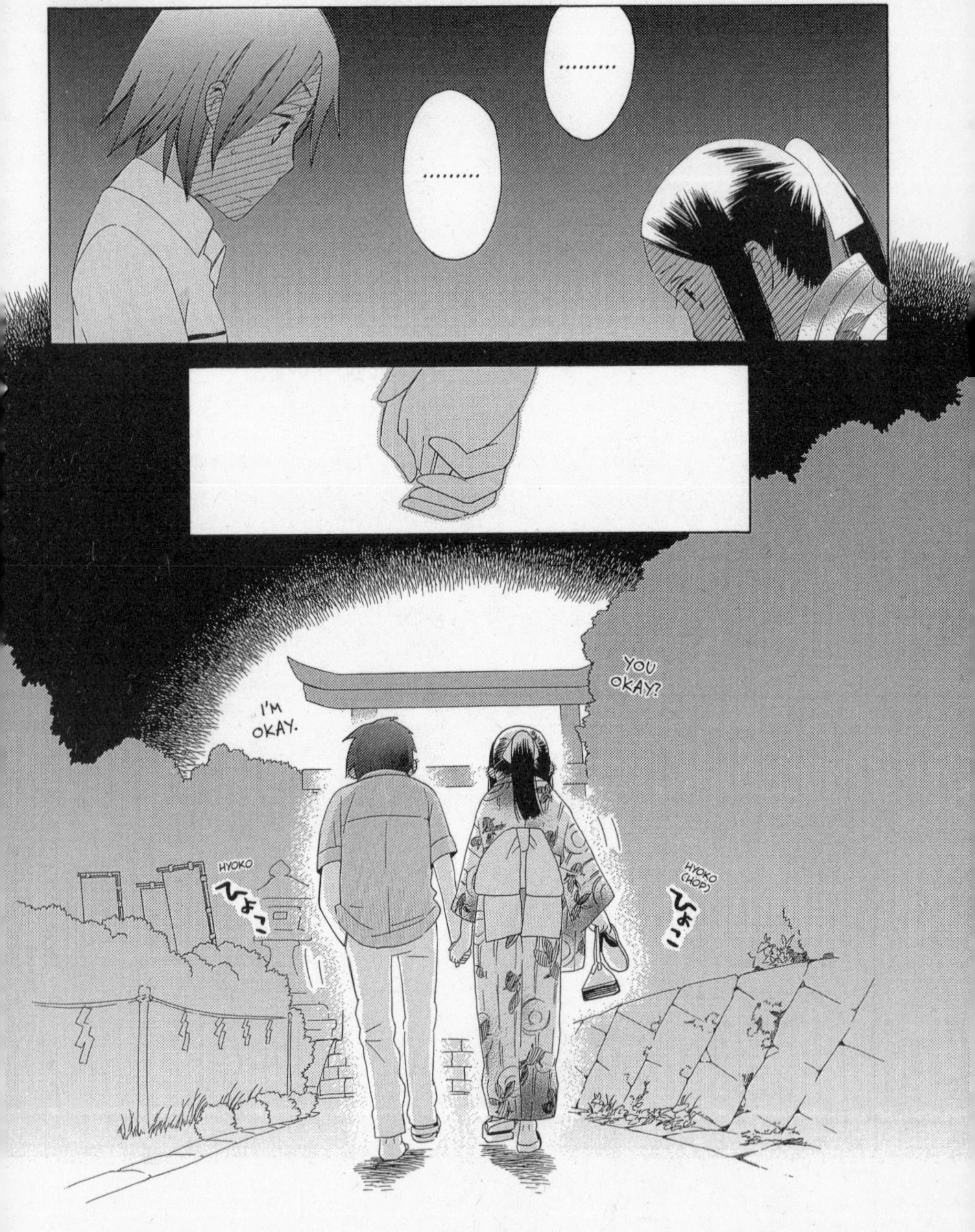

………
………
YOU OKAY?
I'M OKAY.
HYOKO (HOP)
ひょこ
HYOKO
ひょこ

Fin

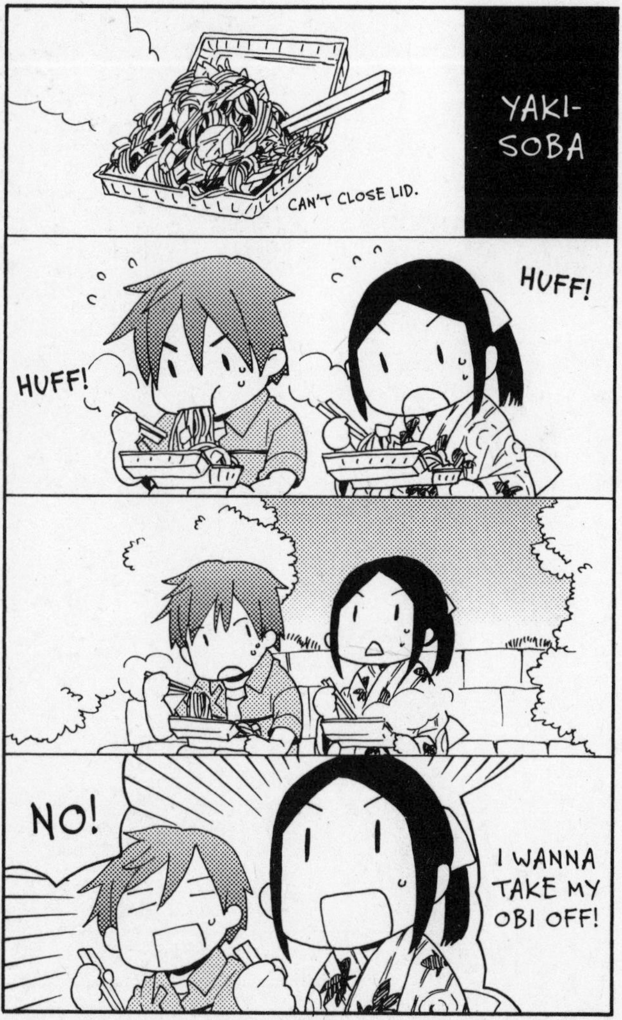
YAKI-
SOBA
CAN'T CLOSE LID.
HUFF!
HUFF!
I WANNA
TAKE MY
OBI OFF!
NO!

Love at Fourteen

Fuka Mizutani

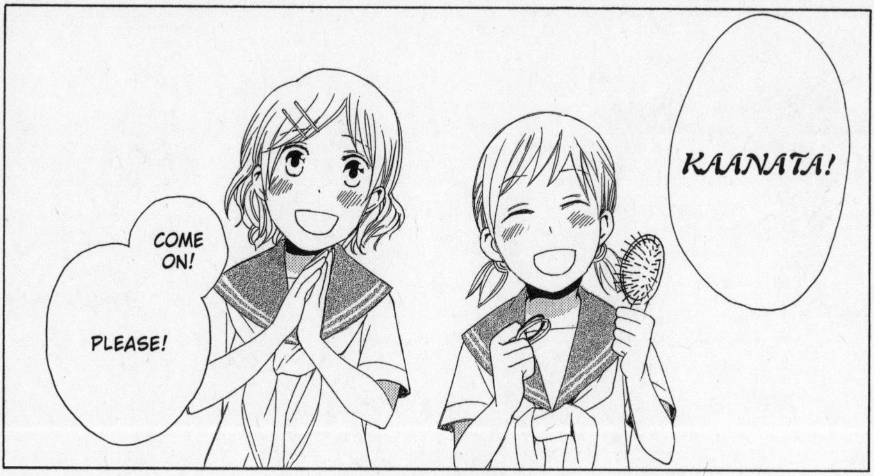
KAANATA!
COME ON!
PLEASE!

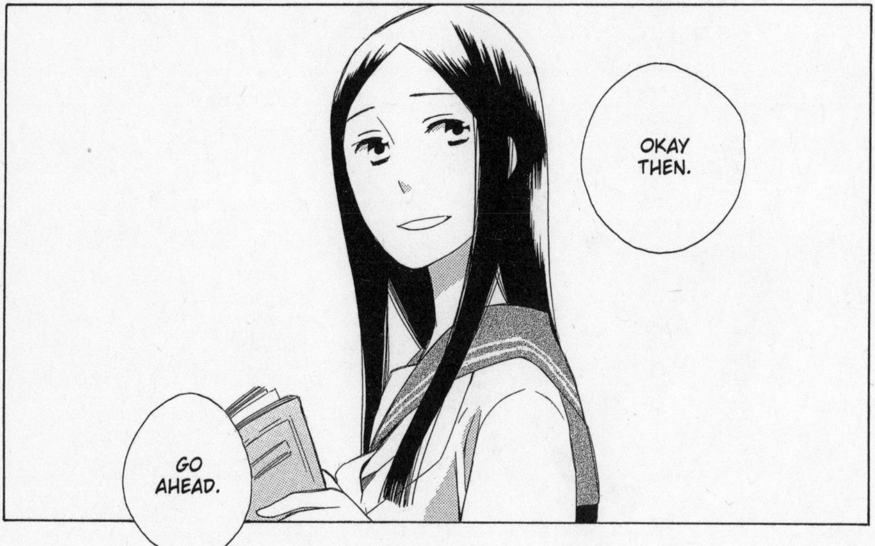
OKAY THEN.
GO AHEAD.

Love at Fourteen

[Intermission 3]

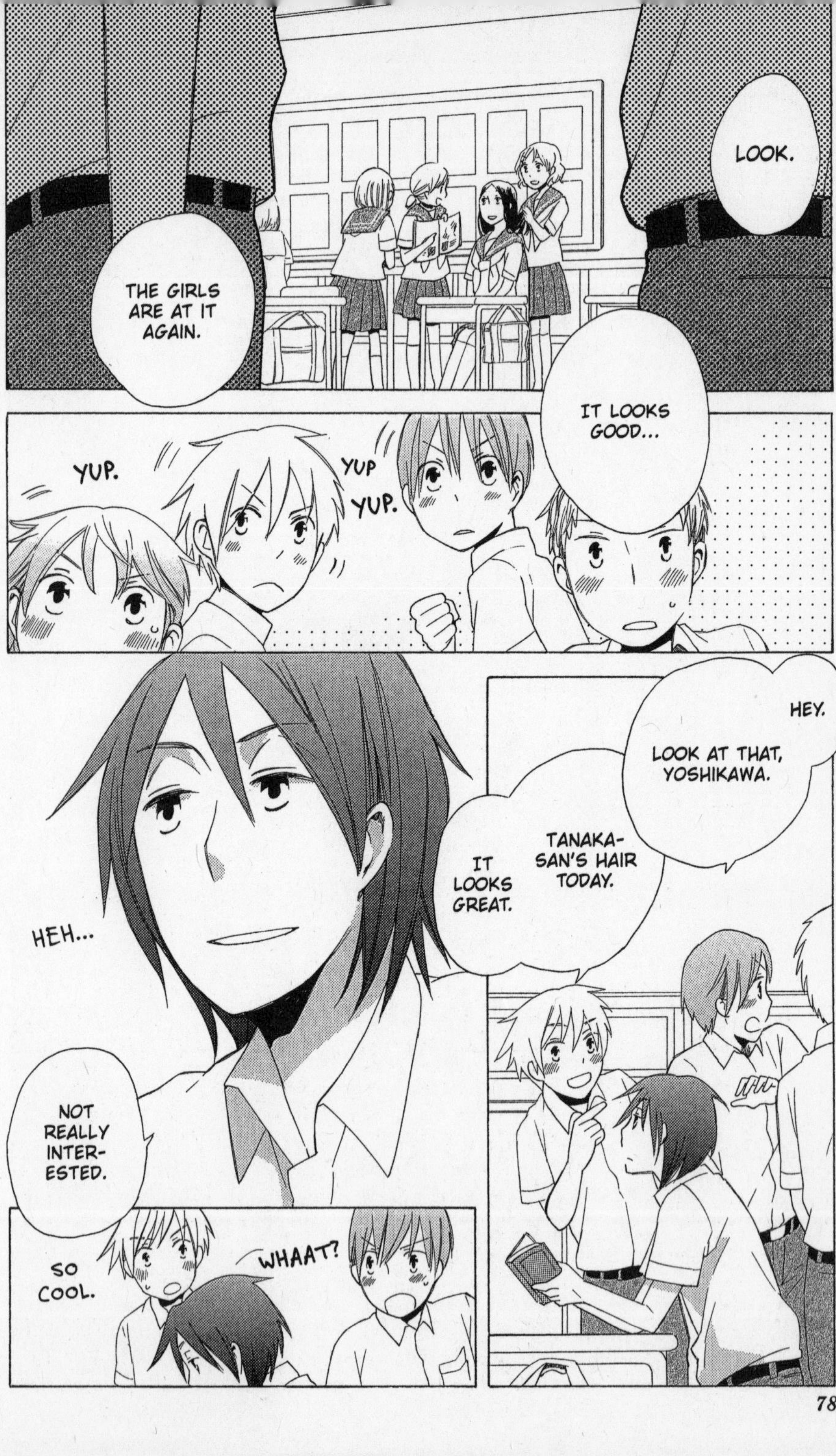
LOOK.
THE GIRLS ARE AT IT AGAIN.
IT LOOKS GOOD...
YUP YUP.
YUP.
HEY.
LOOK AT THAT, YOSHIKAWA.
TANAKA-SAN'S HAIR TODAY.
IT LOOKS GREAT.
HEH...
NOT REALLY INTER-ESTED.
WHAAT?
SO COOL.

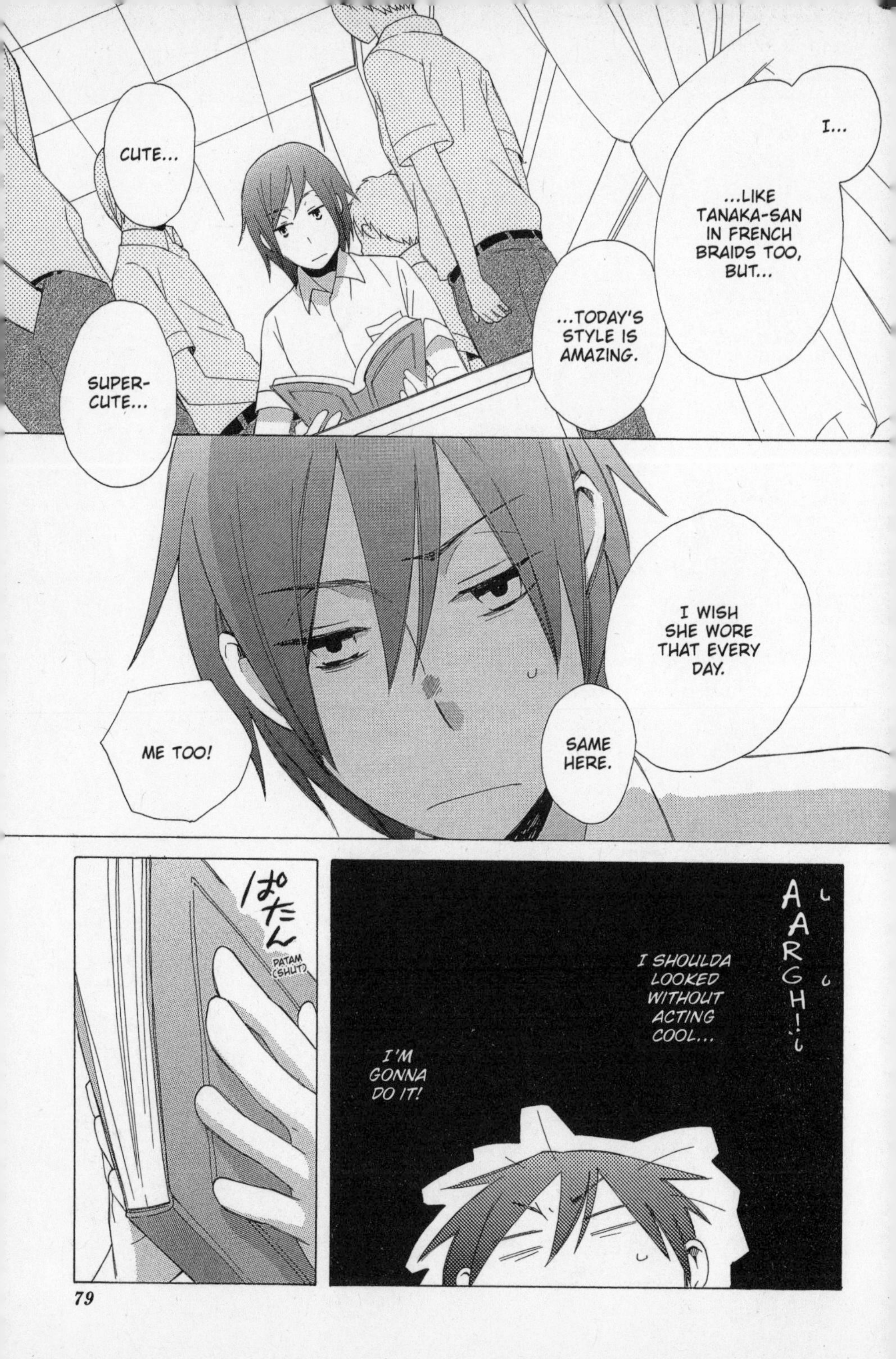
I...
...LIKE TANAKA-SAN IN FRENCH BRAIDS TOO, BUT...
...TODAY'S STYLE IS AMAZING.
CUTE...
SUPER-CUTE...
I WISH SHE WORE THAT EVERY DAY.
SAME HERE.
ME TOO!
AARGH!
I SHOULDA LOOKED WITHOUT ACTING COOL...
I'M GONNA DO IT!
ぱたん
PATAM (SHUT)

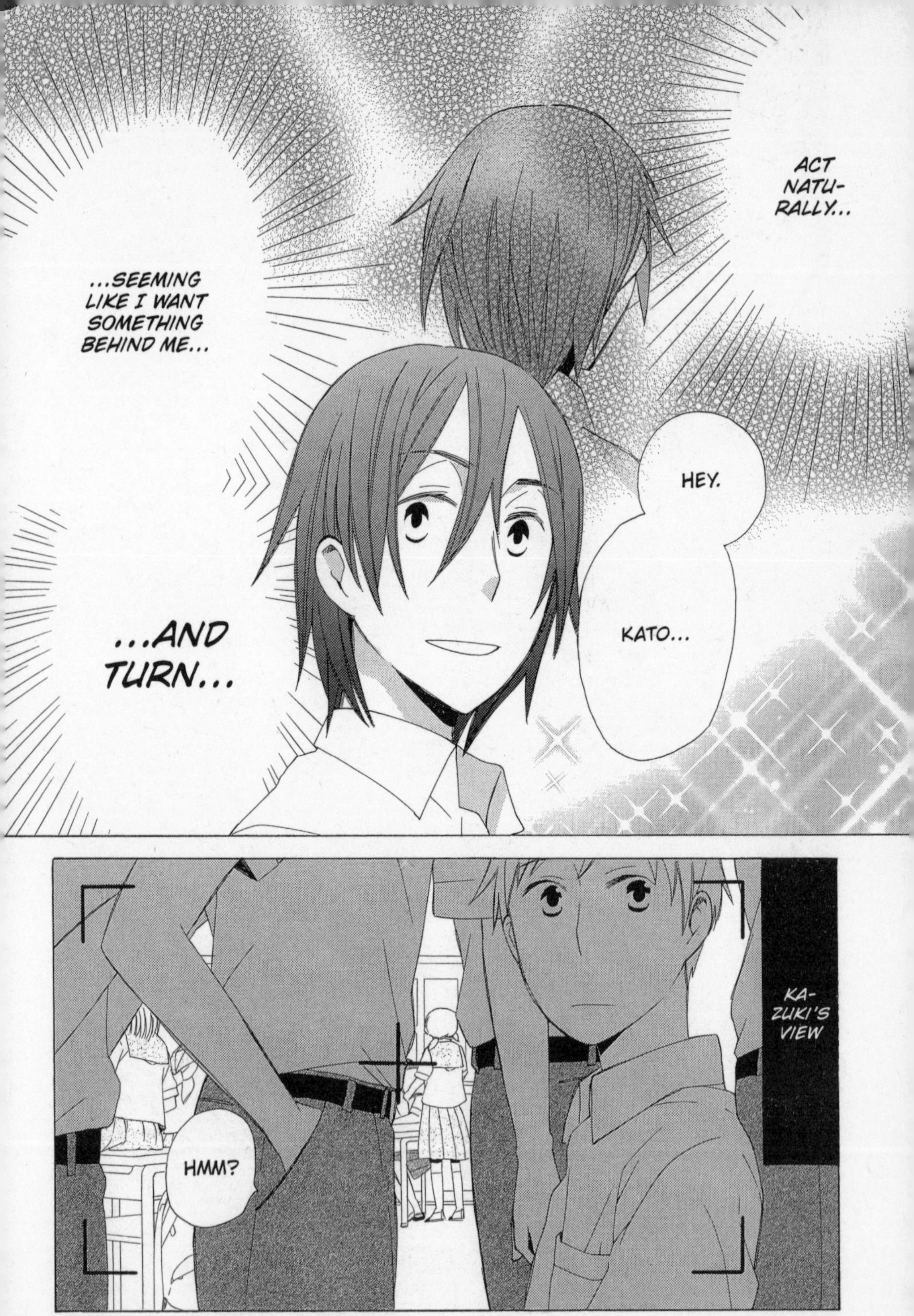
ACT NATU-RALLY...
...SEEMING LIKE I WANT SOMETHING BEHIND ME...
...AND TURN...
HEY.
KATO...
KA-ZUKI'S VIEW
HMM?

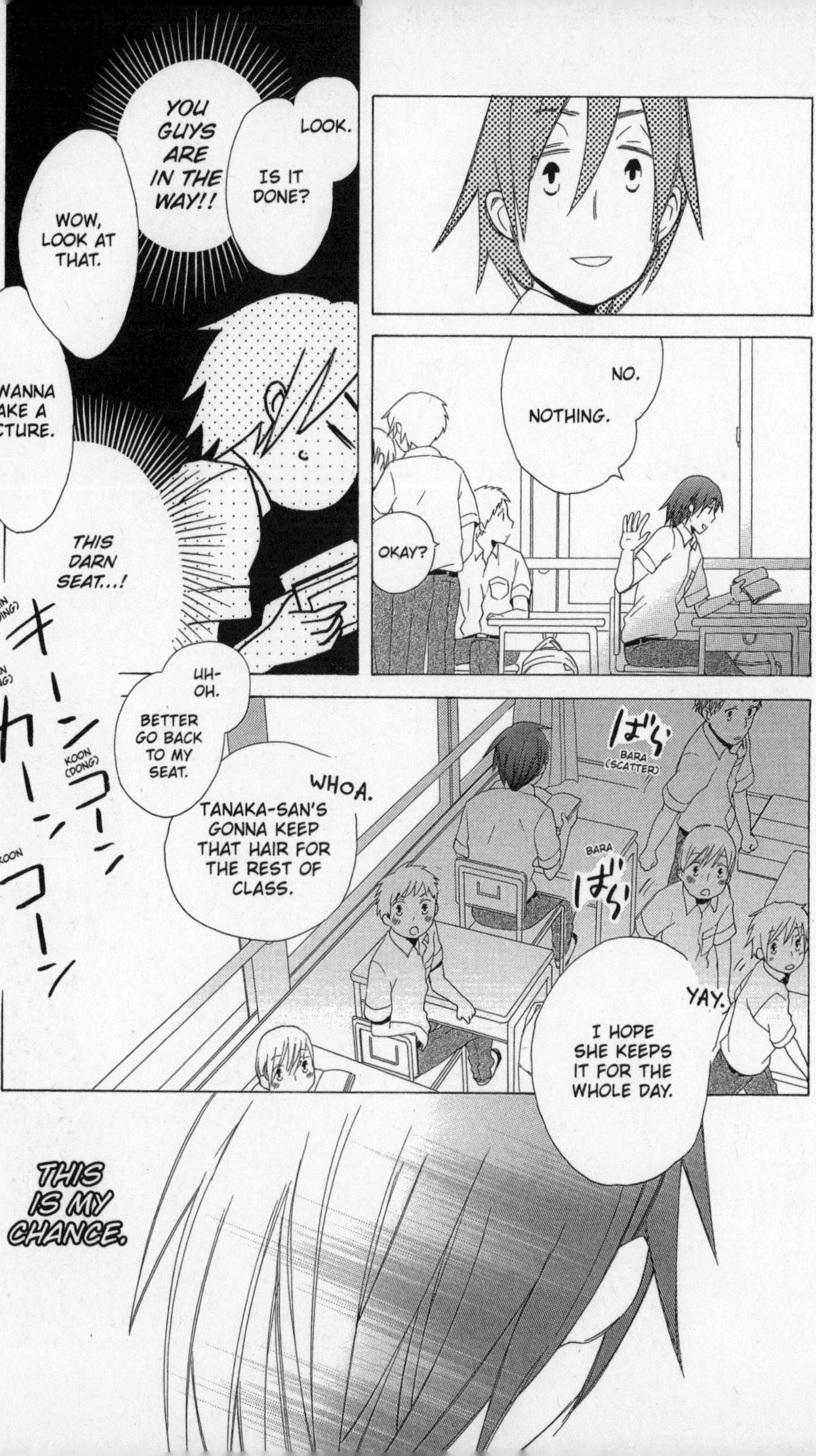
NO.
NOTHING.
OKAY?
LOOK.
IS IT DONE?
YOU GUYS ARE IN THE WAY!!
WOW, LOOK AT THAT.
I WANNA TAKE A PICTURE.
THIS DARN SEAT...!
ばら
BARA (SCATTER)
BARA
ばら
WHOA.
TANAKA-SAN'S GONNA KEEP THAT HAIR FOR THE REST OF CLASS.
UH-OH.
BETTER GO BACK TO MY SEAT.
キーンカーンコーンコーン
KIIN (DING)
KAAN (DING)
KOON (DONG)
KOON
YAY.
I HOPE SHE KEEPS IT FOR THE WHOLE DAY.
THIS IS MY CHANCE.

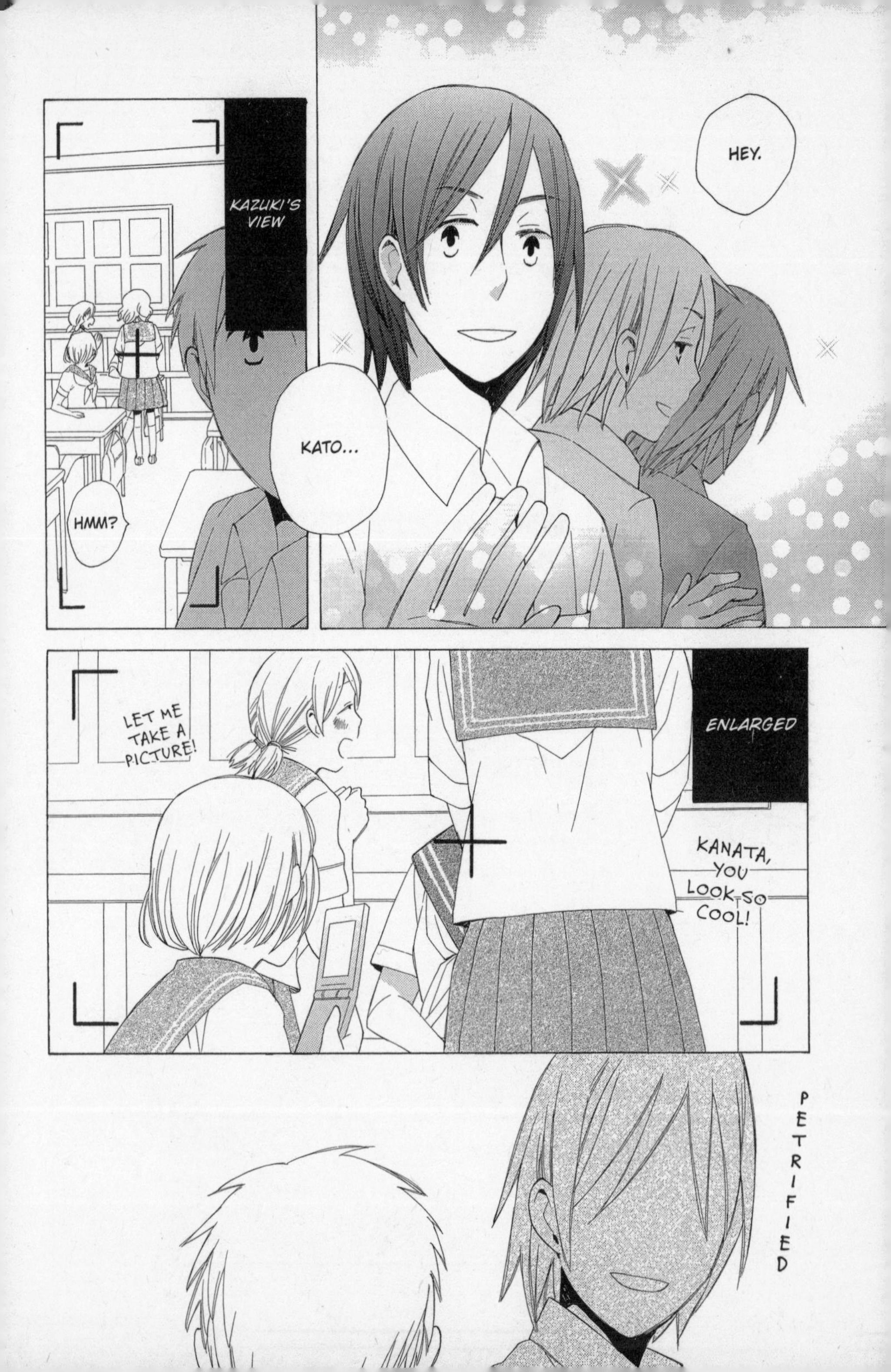
HEY.
KATO...
KAZUKI'S VIEW
HMM?
ENLARGED
KANATA, YOU LOOK SO COOL!
LET ME TAKE A PICTURE!
PETRIFIED

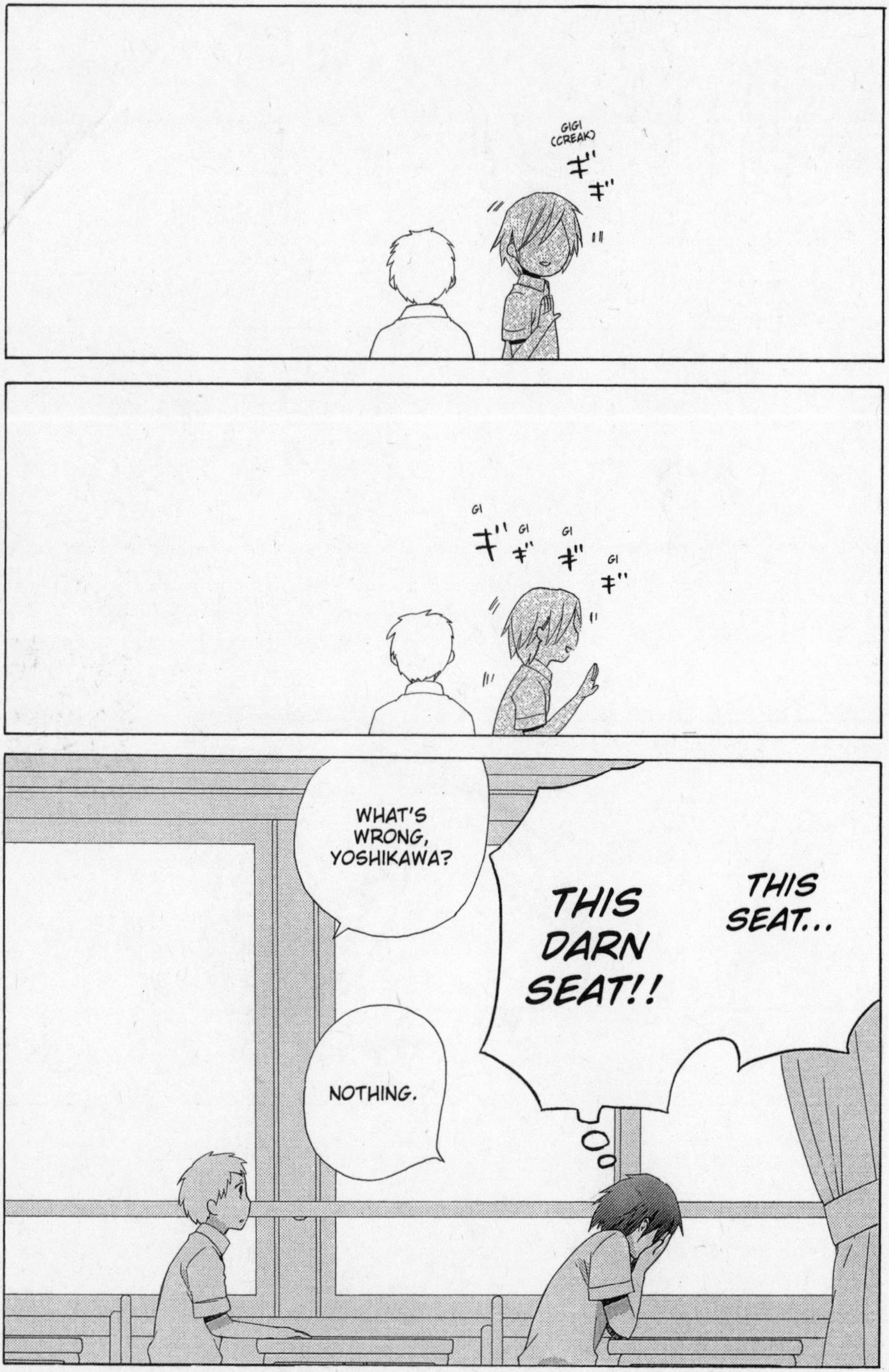
ギギ
GIGI
(CREAK)
ギギギギ
GI GI GI GI
THIS SEAT...
THIS DARN SEAT!!
WHAT'S WRONG, YOSHIKAWA?
NOTHING.

Fin

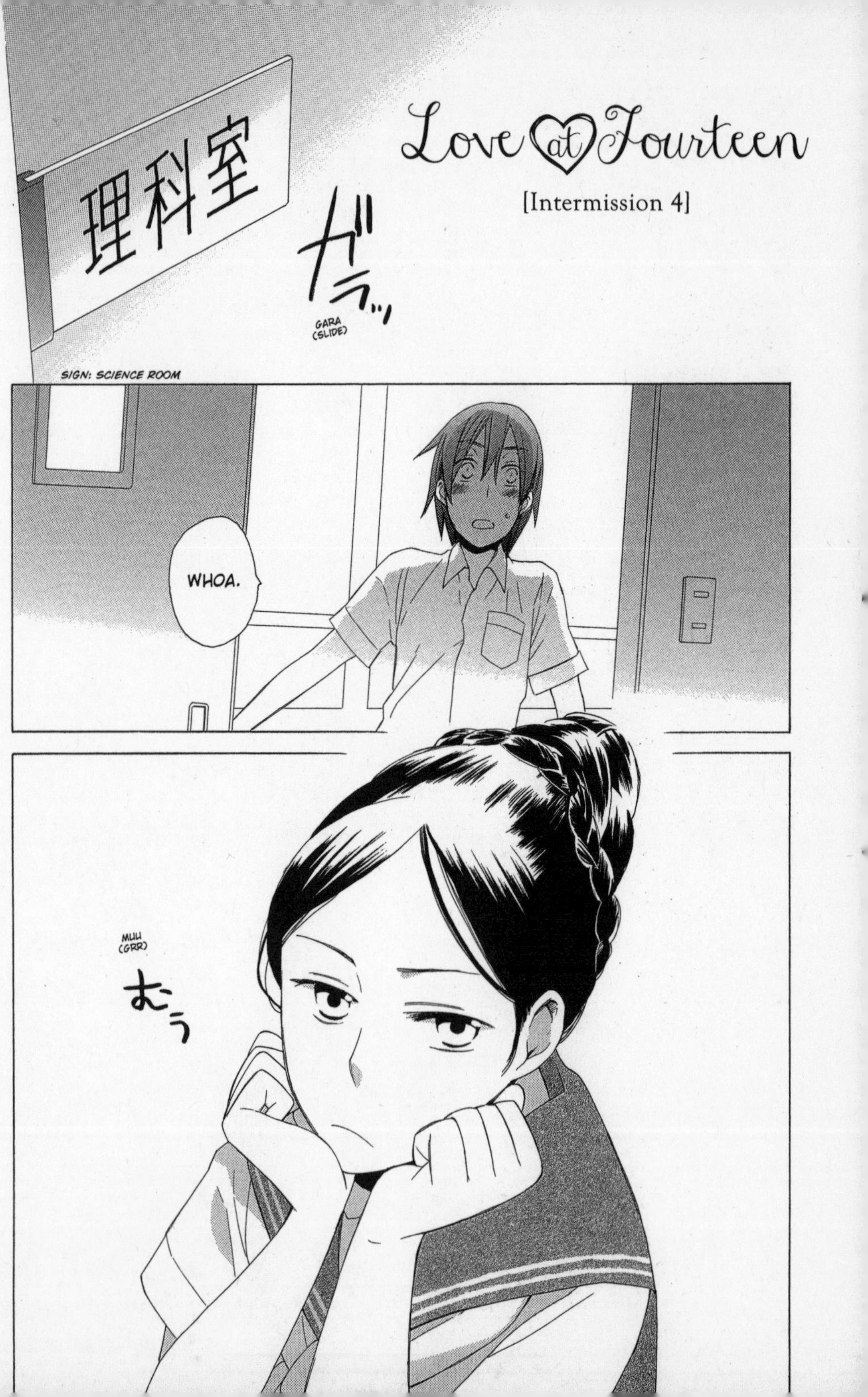
Love at Fourteen
[Intermission 4]
GARA (SLIDE)
理科室
SIGN: SCIENCE ROOM
WHOA.
MUU (GRR)

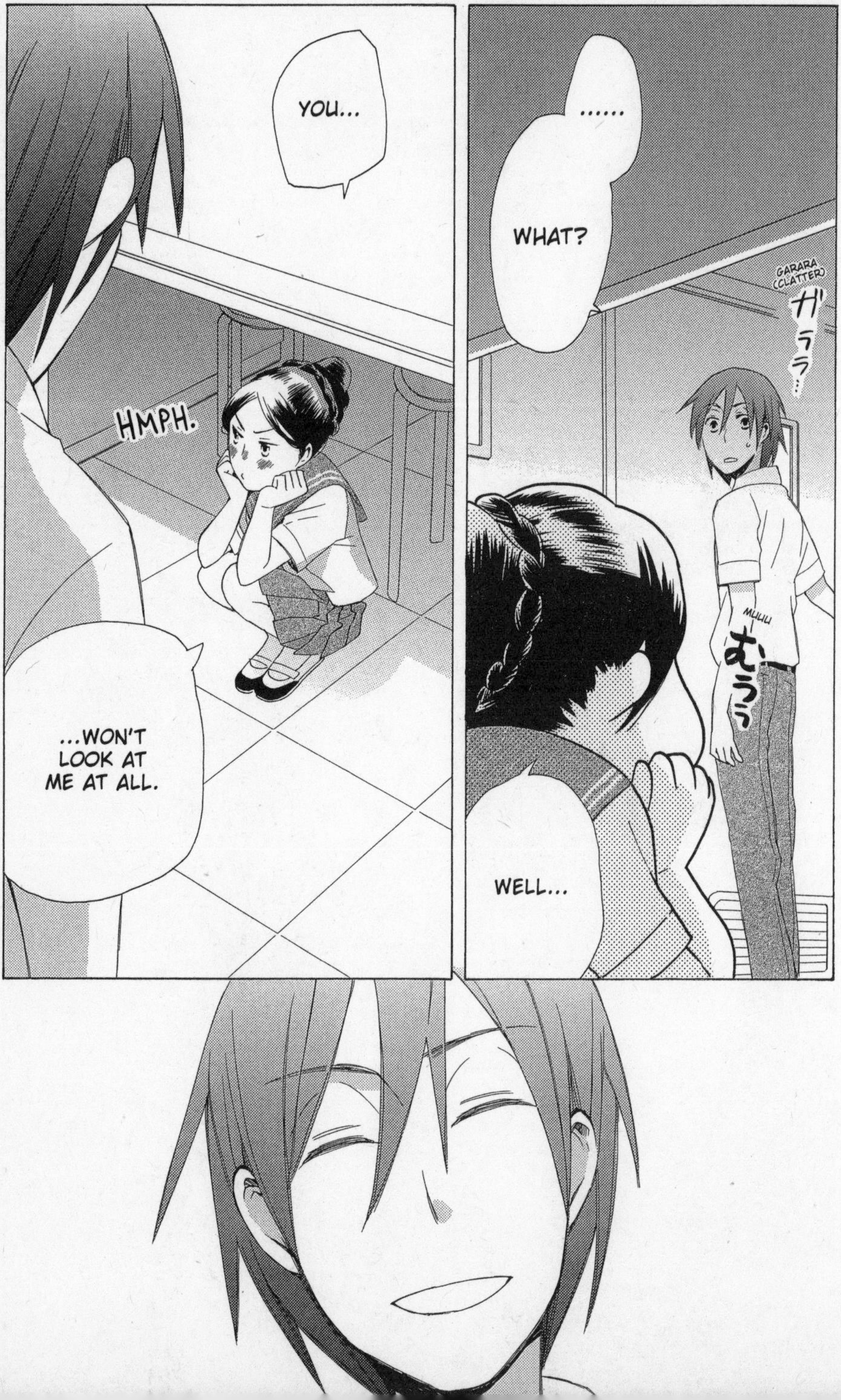
......
WHAT?
GARARA (CLATTER)
ガララ…
MUUU
むぅぅ
WELL...
YOU...
HMPH.
...WON'T LOOK AT ME AT ALL.

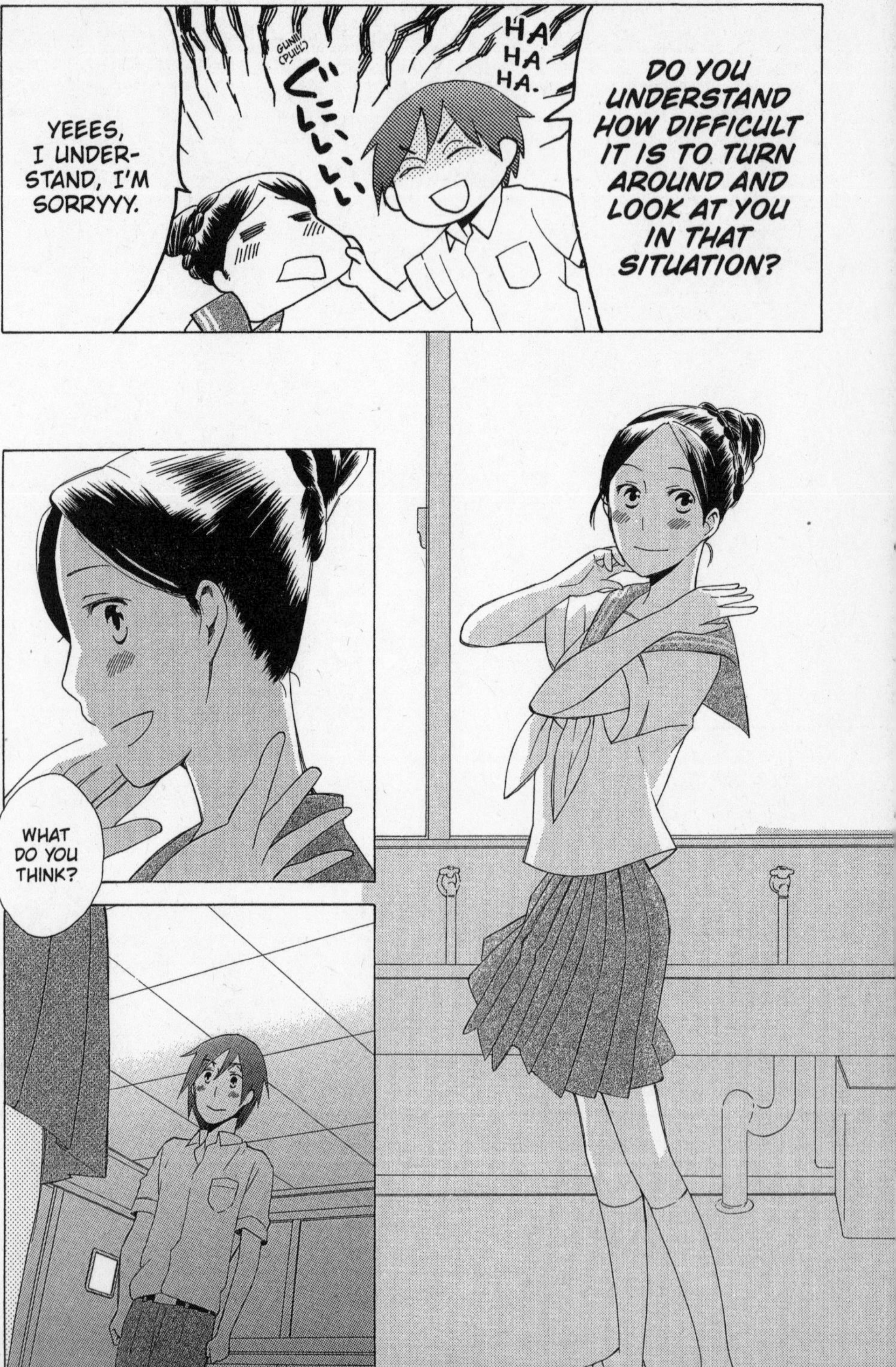
DO YOU UNDERSTAND HOW DIFFICULT IT IS TO TURN AROUND AND LOOK AT YOU IN THAT SITUATION?
HA HA HA.
GUNII (PULL)
YEEES, I UNDER-STAND, I'M SORRYYY.
WHAT DO YOU THINK?

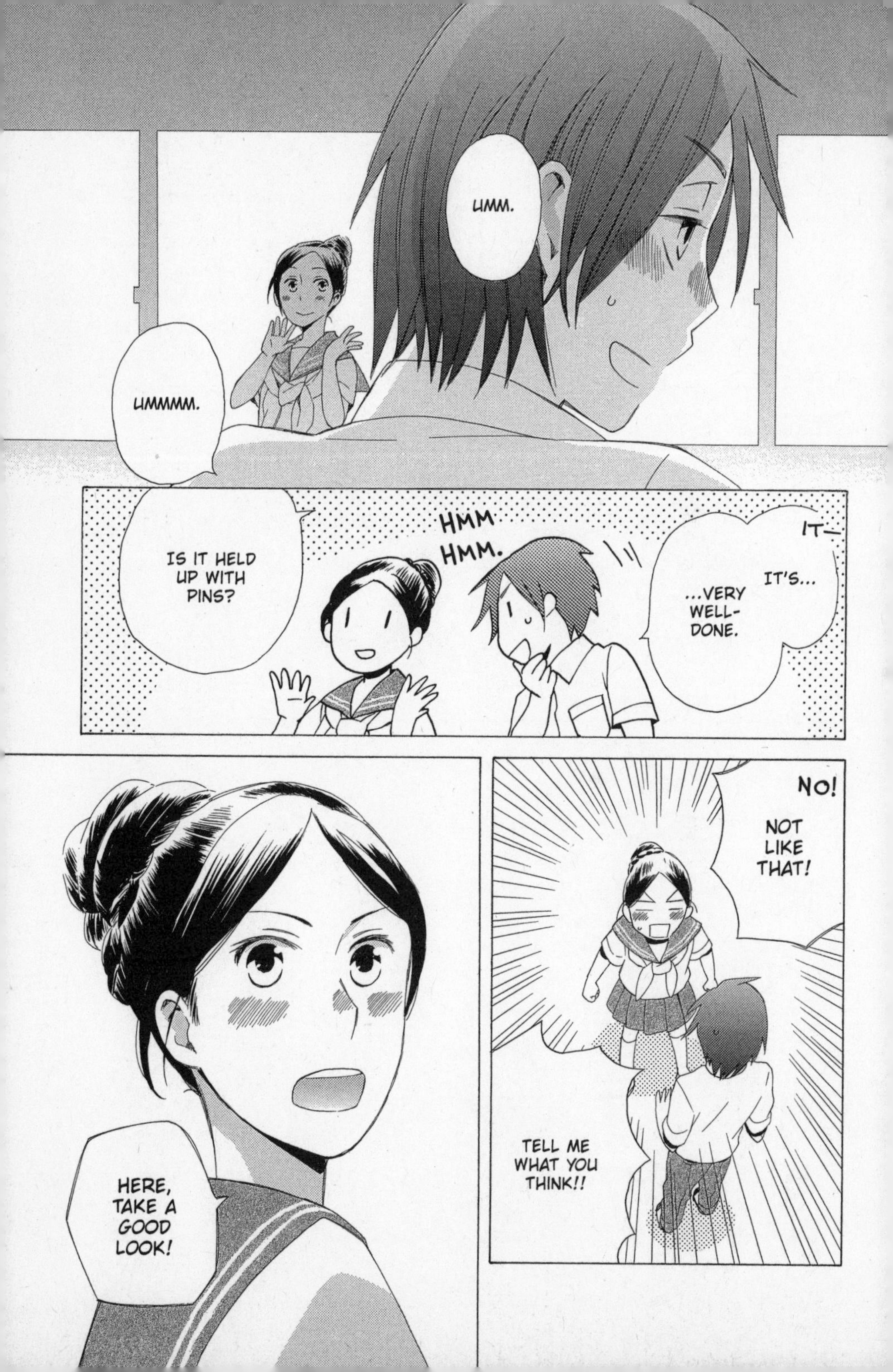
UMM.
UMMMM.
IT— IT'S... ...VERY WELL-DONE.
HMM HMM.
IS IT HELD UP WITH PINS?
NO! NOT LIKE THAT!
TELL ME WHAT YOU THINK!!
HERE, TAKE A GOOD LOOK!

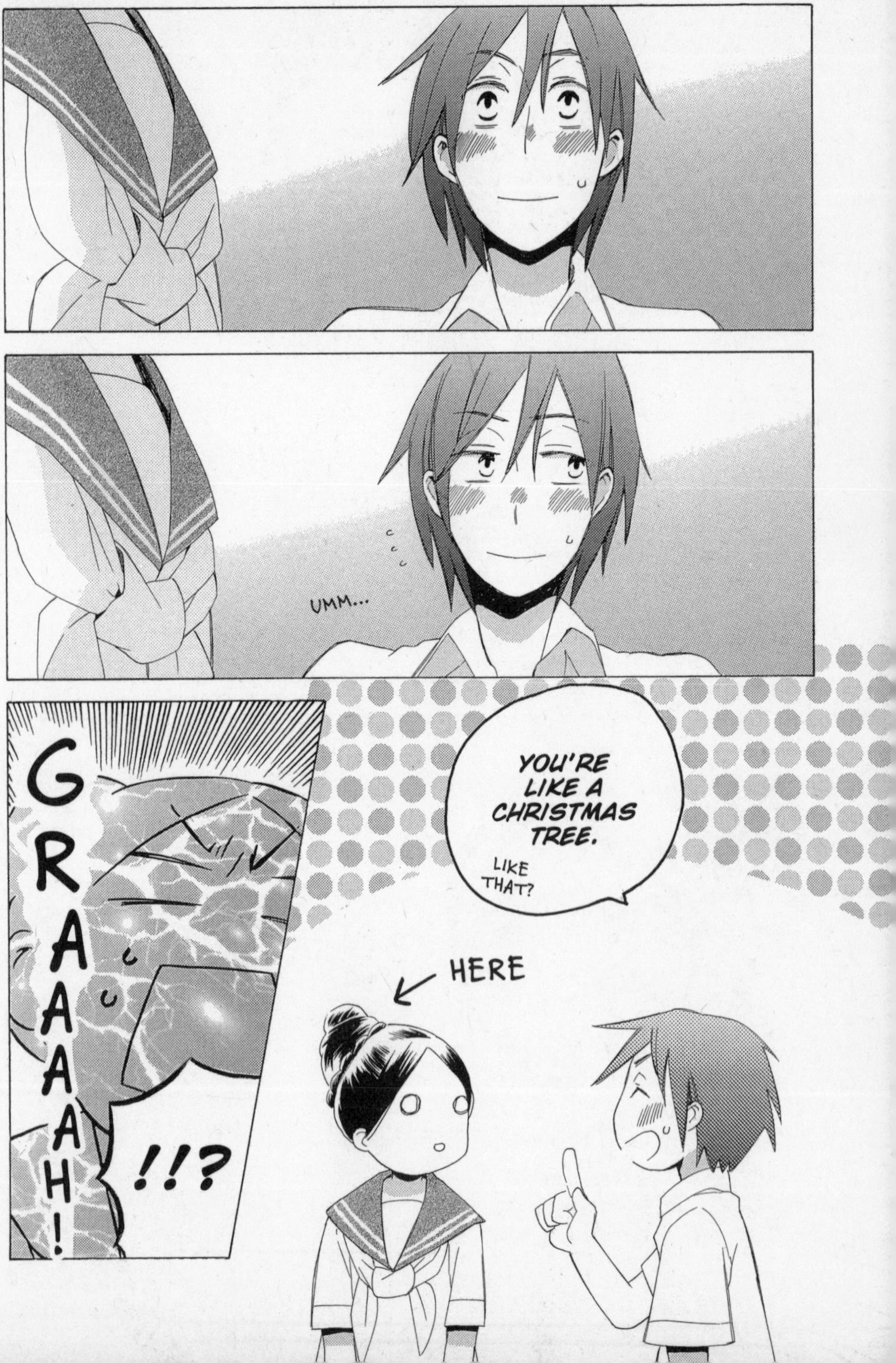
UMM...
YOU'RE LIKE A CHRISTMAS TREE.
LIKE THAT?
HERE
GRAAAAH!
!!?

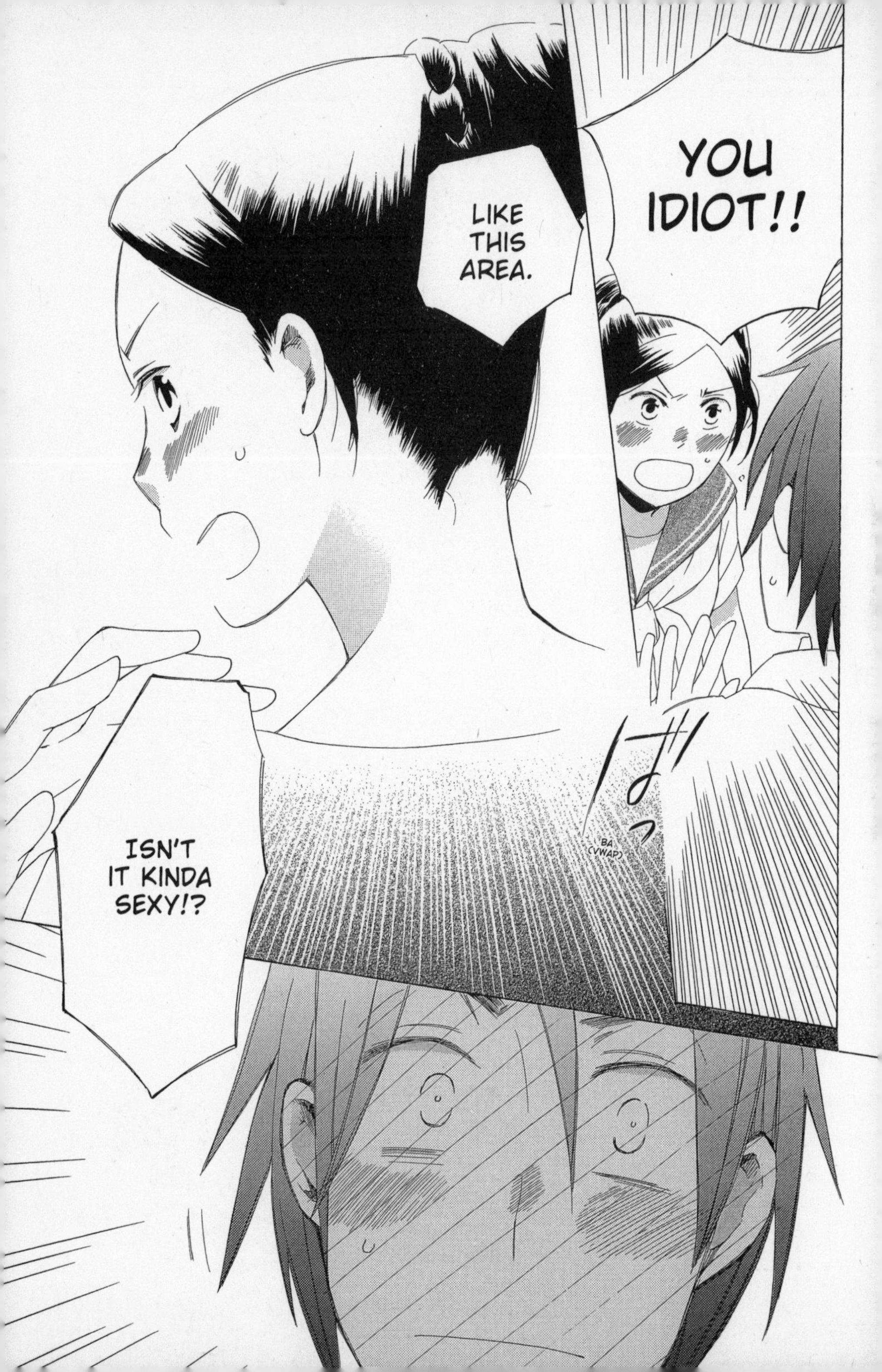
LIKE THIS AREA.
ISN'T IT KINDA SEXY!?
YOU IDIOT!!
BA (VWAP)

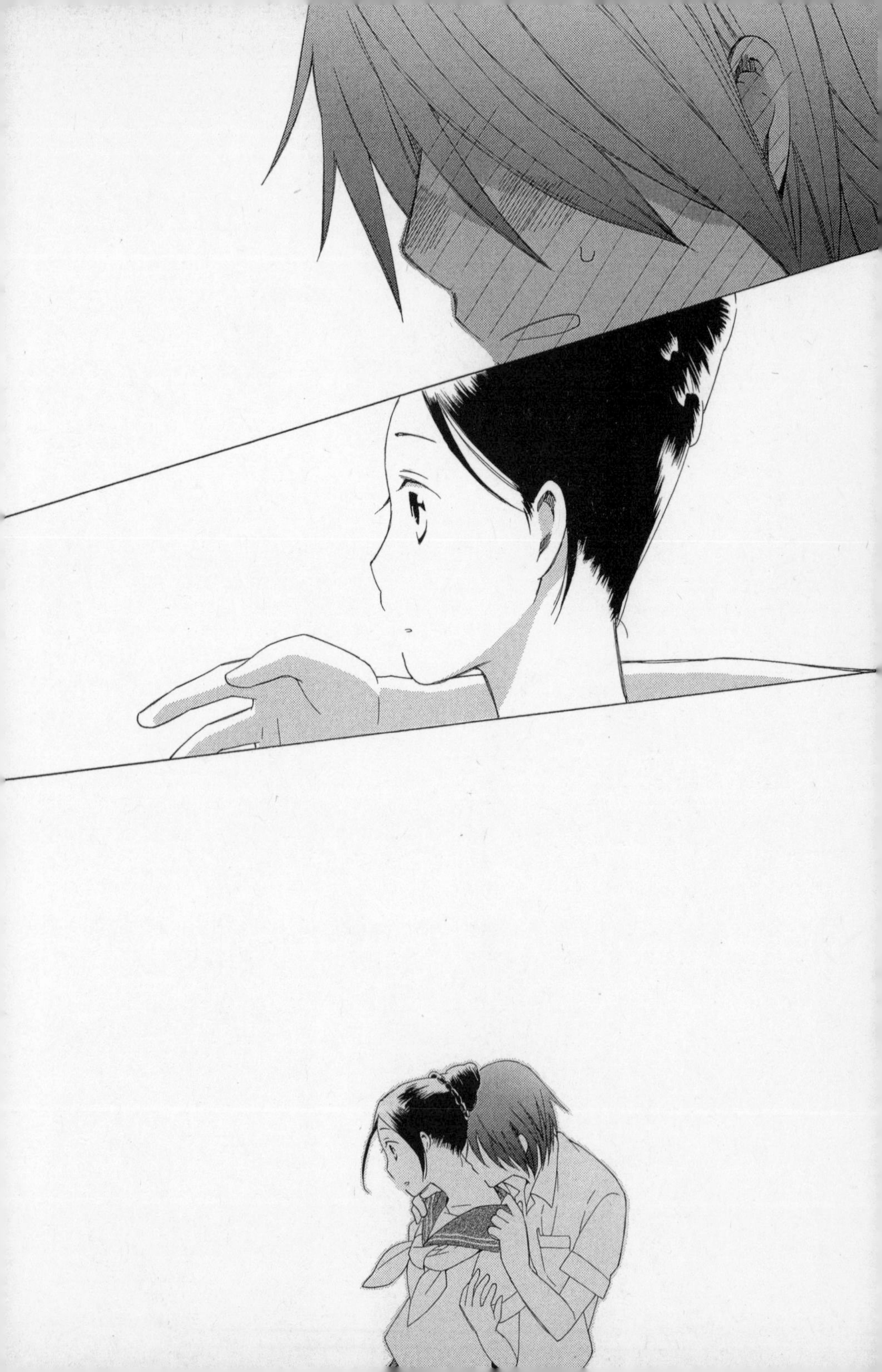

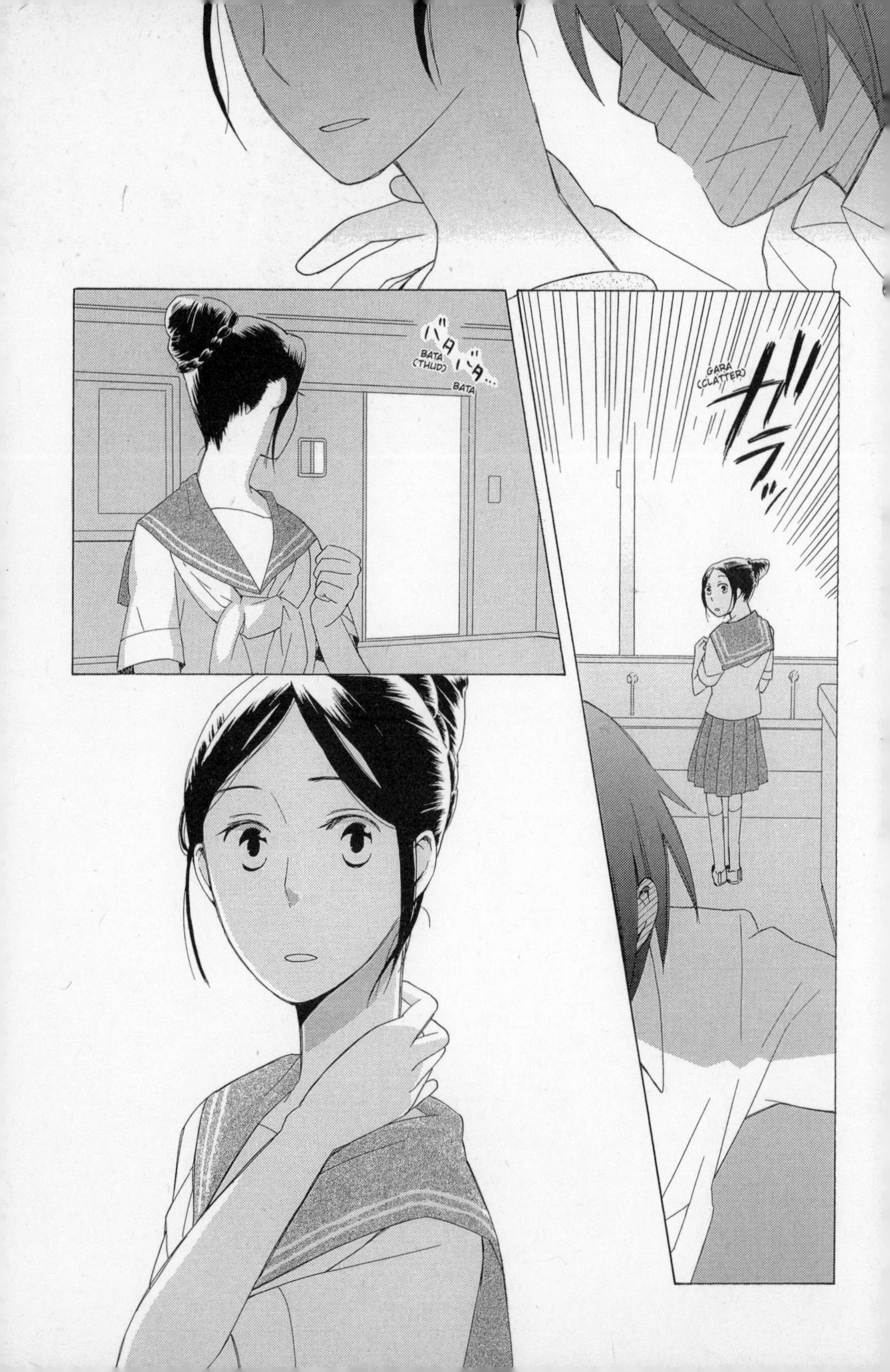
ガラッ
GARA (CLATTER)
バタバタ…
BATA (THUD) BATA

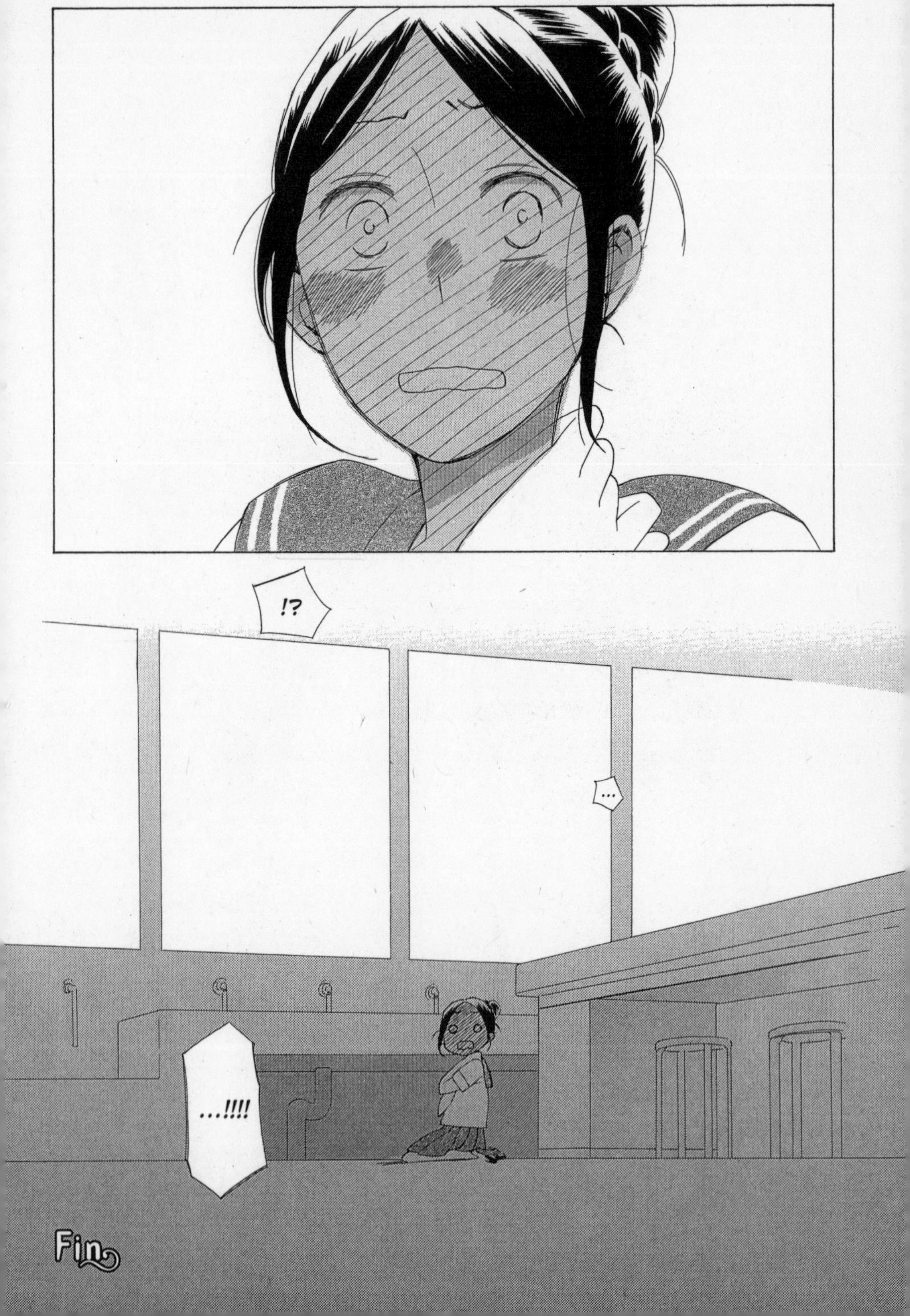
!?
...
...!!!!
Fin

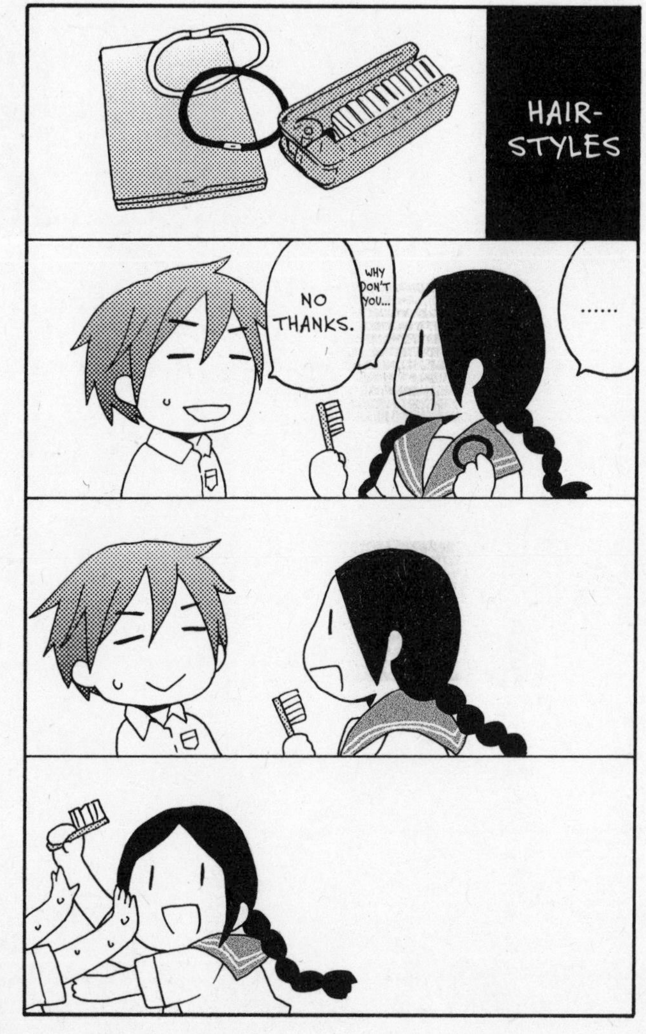
HAIR-STYLES
......
WHY DON'T YOU...
NO THANKS.

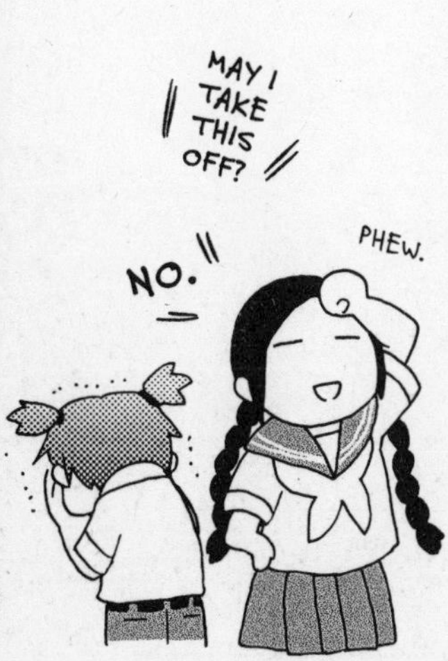
MAY I TAKE THIS OFF?
PHEW.
NO.

Love at Fourteen

Fuka Mizutani

Love at Fourteen

[Chapter 4]

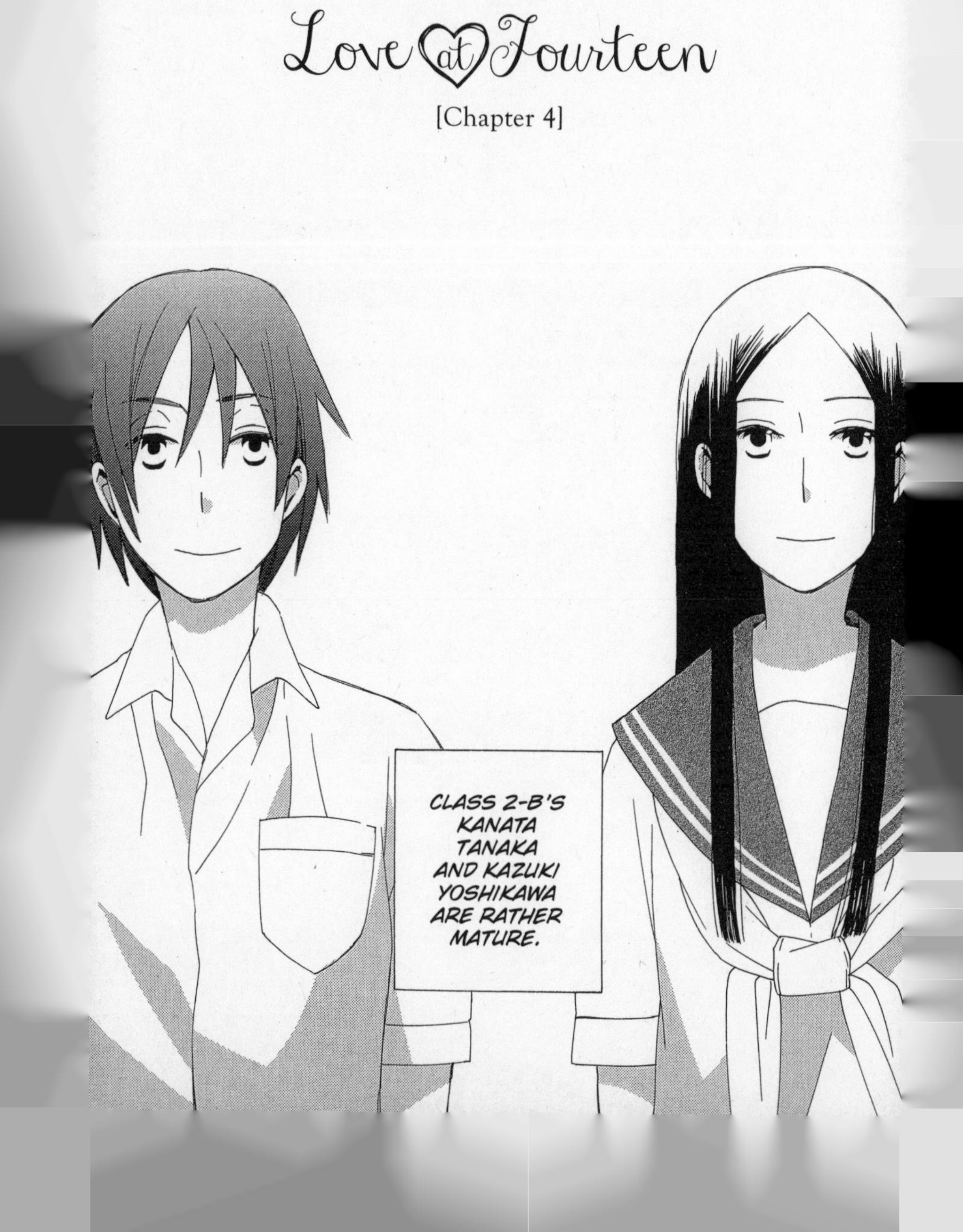
CLASS 2-B'S KANATA TANAKA AND KAZUKI YOSHIKAWA ARE RATHER MATURE.

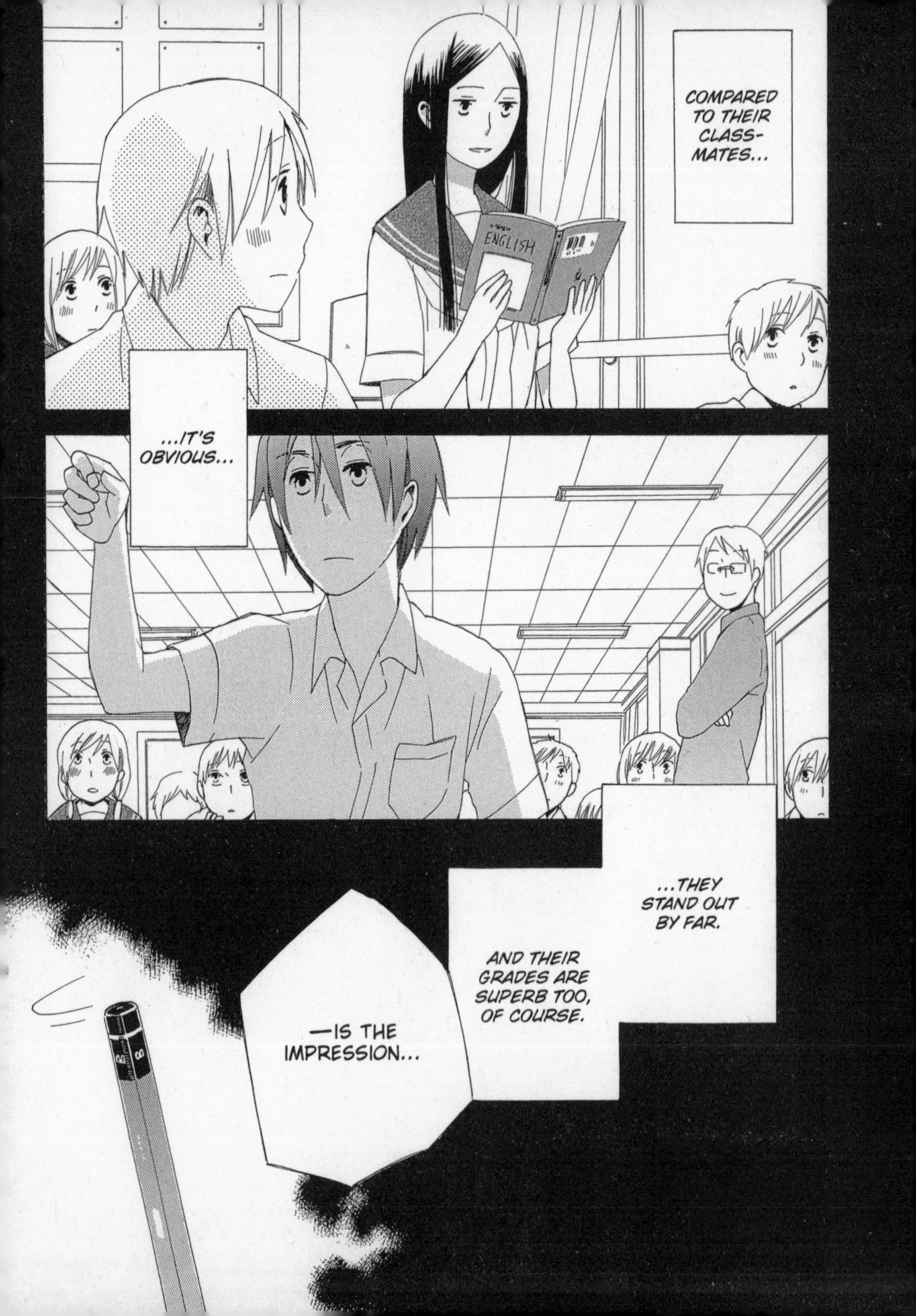
COMPARED TO THEIR CLASS-MATES...
ENGLISH
...IT'S OBVIOUS...
...THEY STAND OUT BY FAR.
AND THEIR GRADES ARE SUPERB TOO, OF COURSE.
—IS THE IMPRESSION...

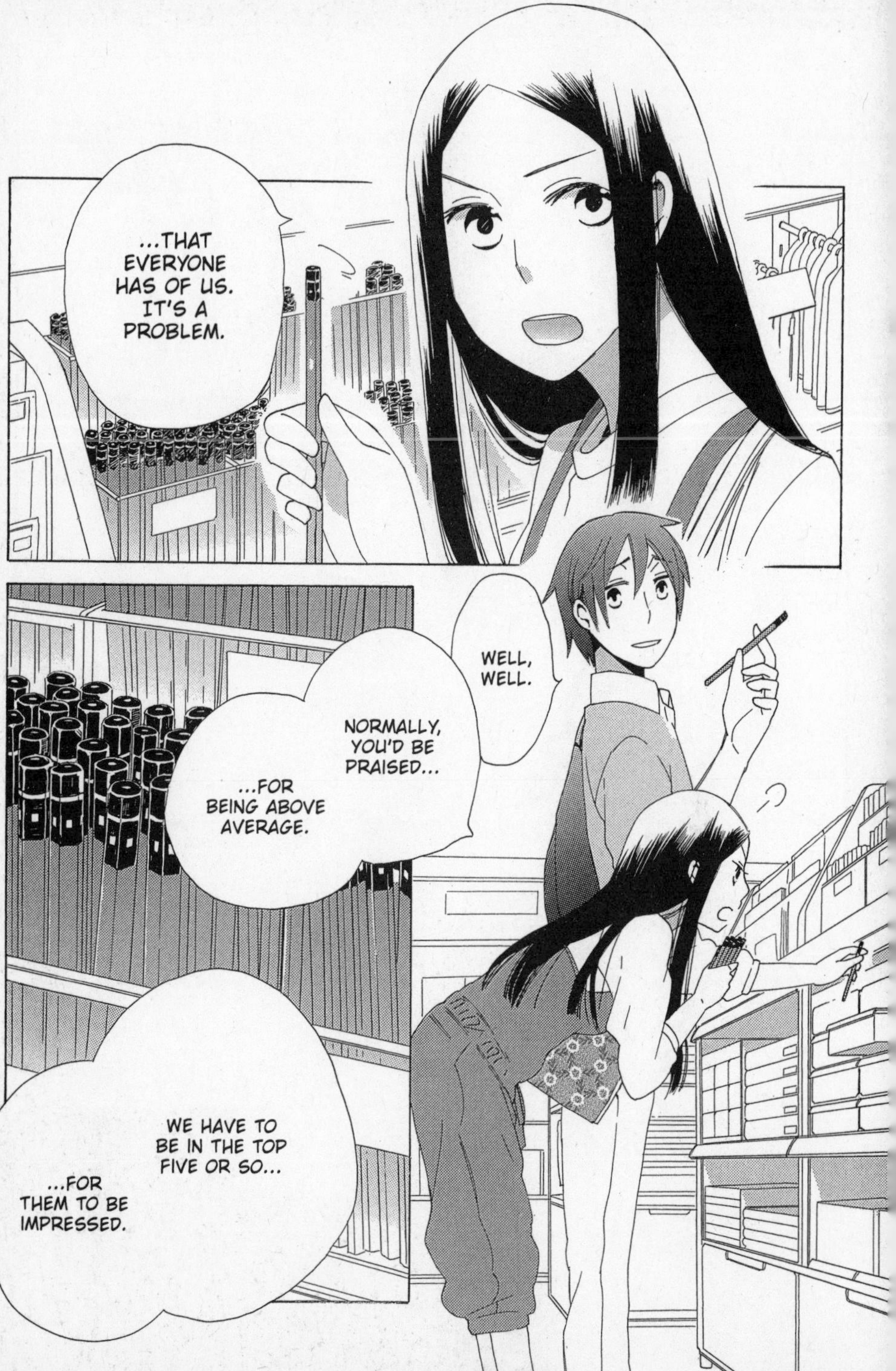
...THAT EVERYONE HAS OF US. IT'S A PROBLEM.
WELL, WELL.
NORMALLY, YOU'D BE PRAISED...
...FOR BEING ABOVE AVERAGE.
WE HAVE TO BE IN THE TOP FIVE OR SO...
...FOR THEM TO BE IMPRESSED.

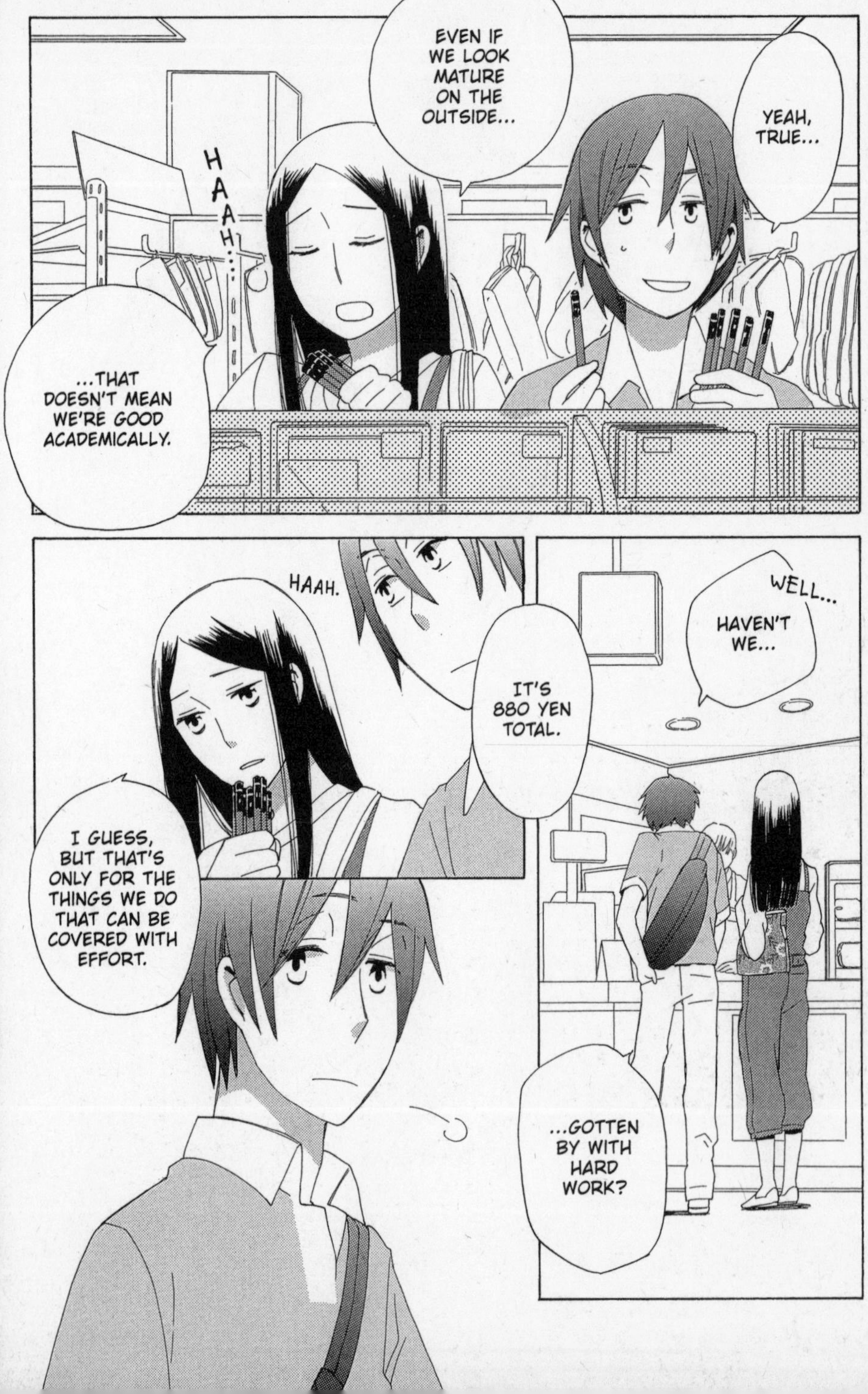
EVEN IF WE LOOK MATURE ON THE OUTSIDE...
YEAH, TRUE...
HAAH...
...THAT DOESN'T MEAN WE'RE GOOD ACADEMICALLY.
WELL...
HAVEN'T WE...
...GOTTEN BY WITH HARD WORK?
HAAH.
IT'S 880 YEN TOTAL.
I GUESS, BUT THAT'S ONLY FOR THE THINGS WE DO THAT CAN BE COVERED WITH EFFORT.

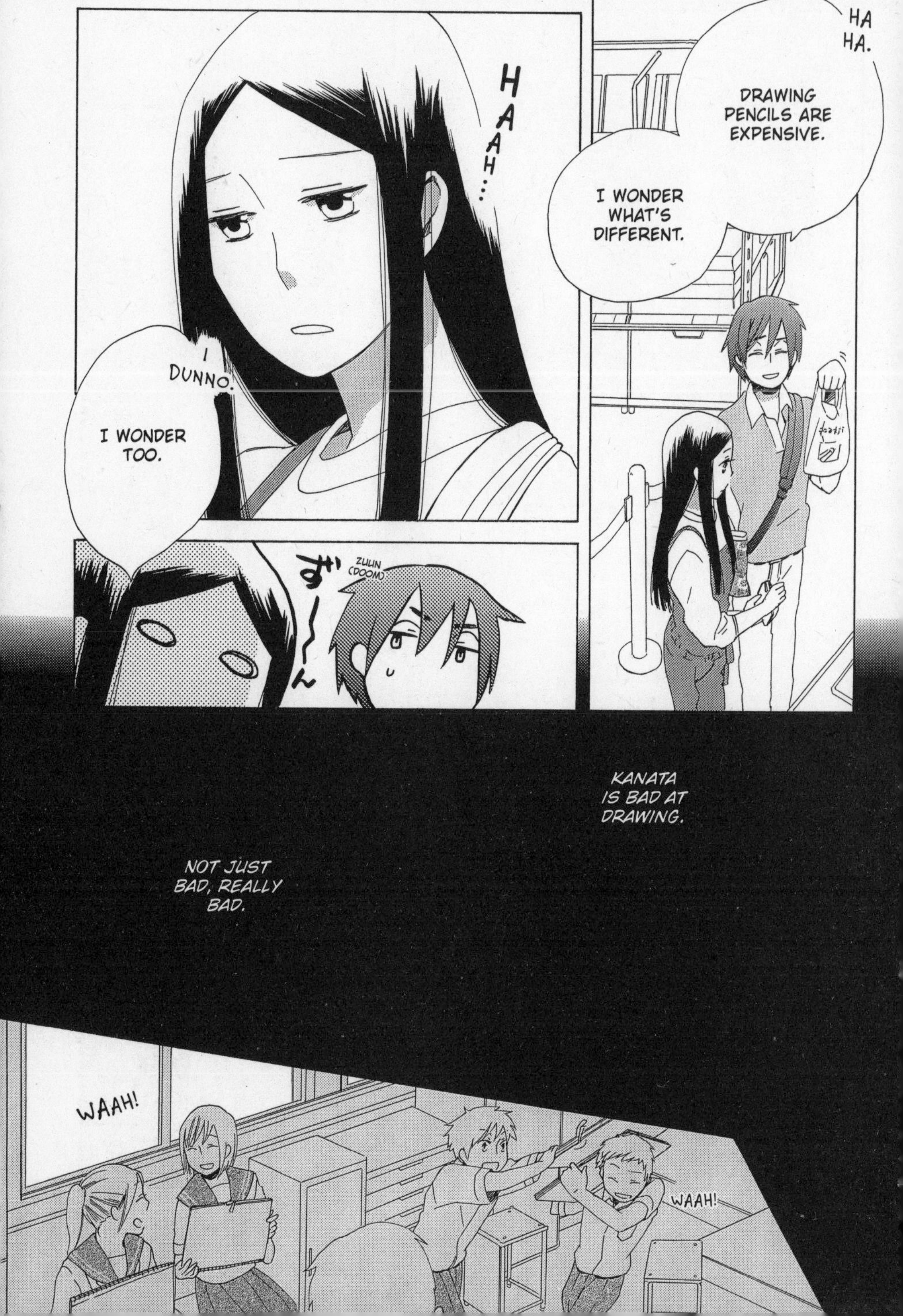
HA HA.
DRAWING PENCILS ARE EXPENSIVE.
I WONDER WHAT'S DIFFERENT.
HAAAH...
I DUNNO.
I WONDER TOO.
ず〜〜ん
ZUUN (DOOM)
KANATA IS BAD AT DRAWING.
NOT JUST BAD, REALLY BAD.
WAAH!
WAAH!

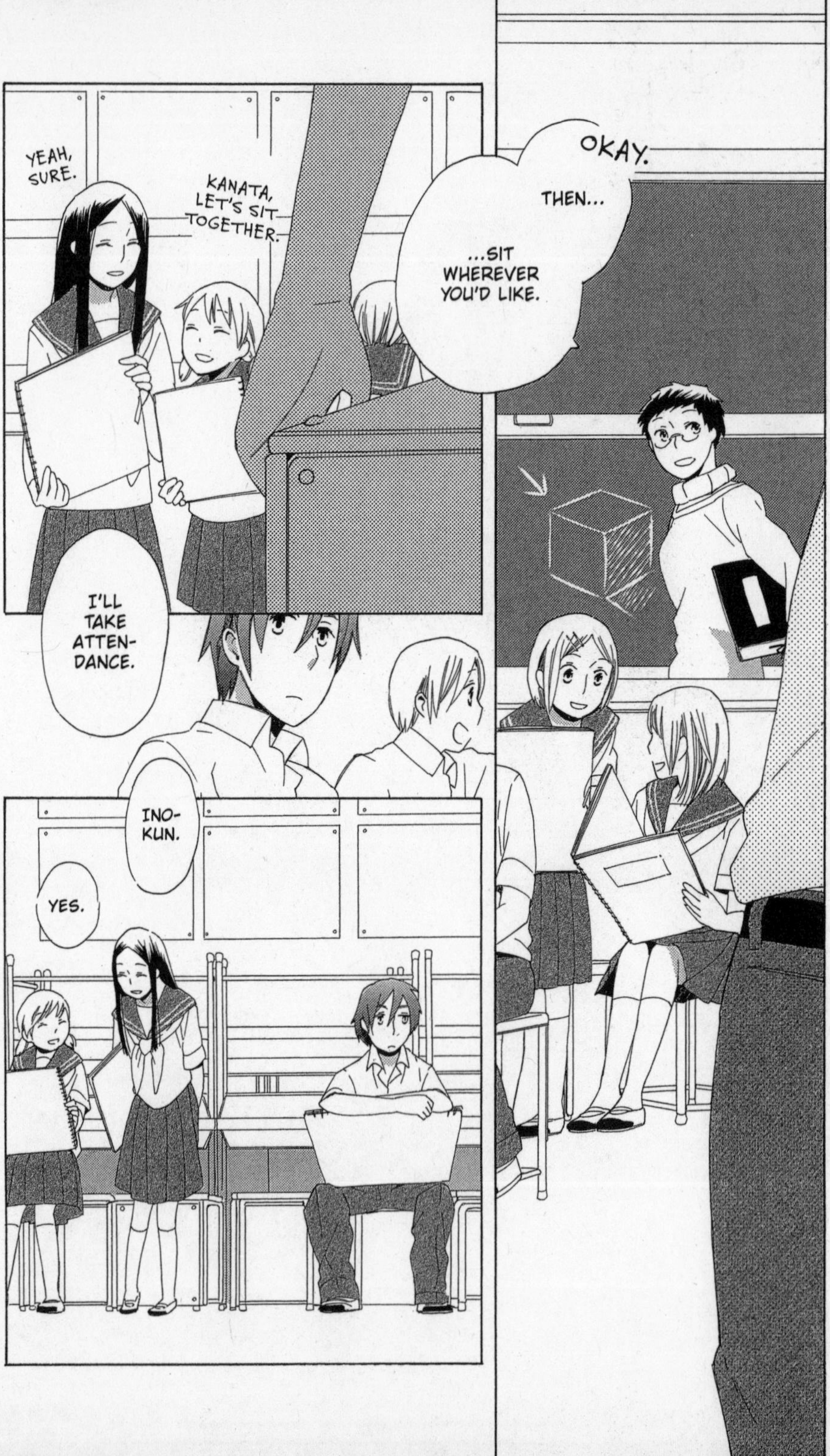
OKAY.
THEN...
...SIT WHEREVER YOU'D LIKE.
KANATA, LET'S SIT TOGETHER.
YEAH, SURE.
I'LL TAKE ATTEN-DANCE.
INO-KUN.
YES.

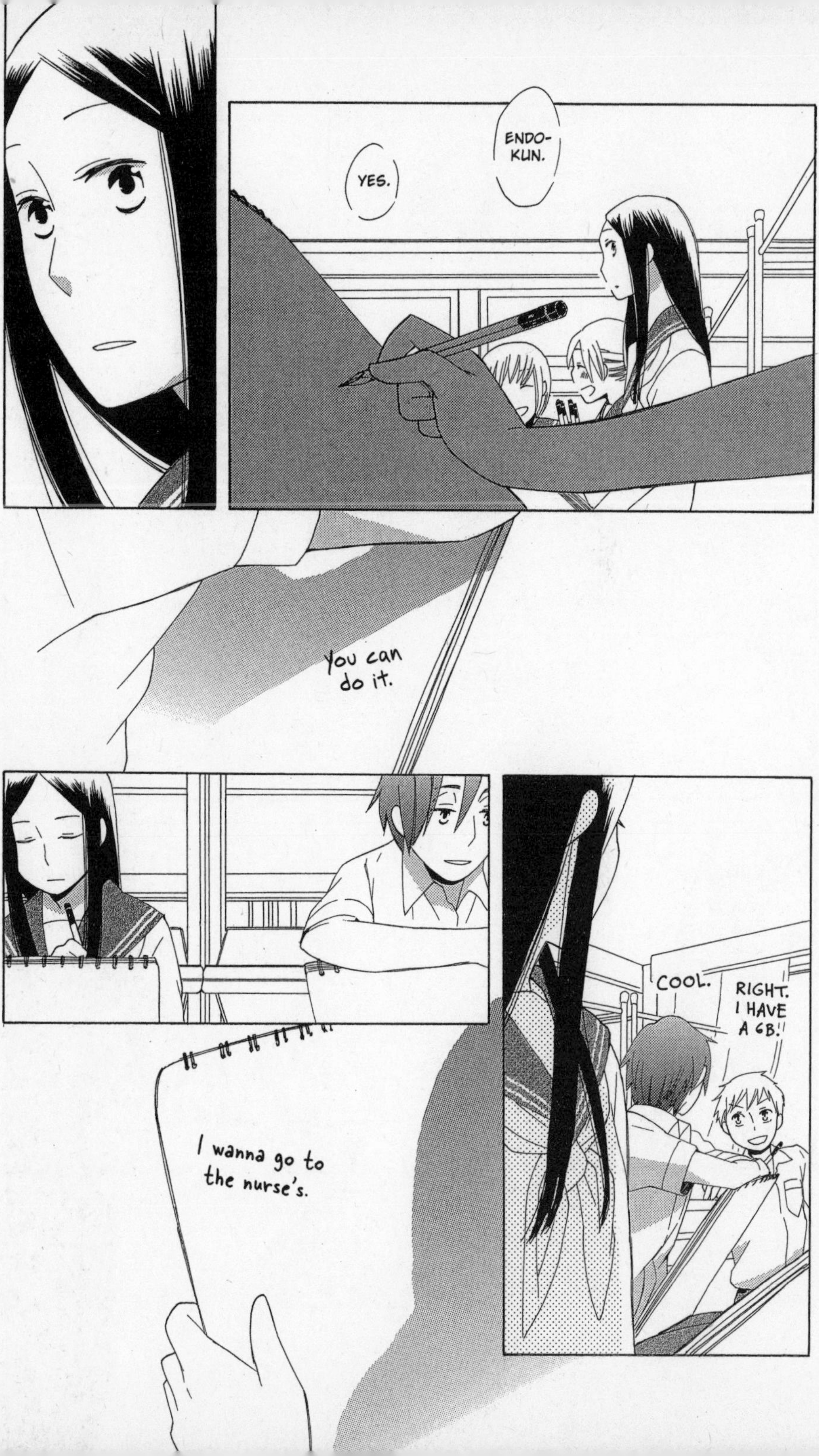
ENDO-KUN.
YES.
You can do it.
RIGHT. I HAVE A 6B!
COOL.
I wanna go to the nurse's.

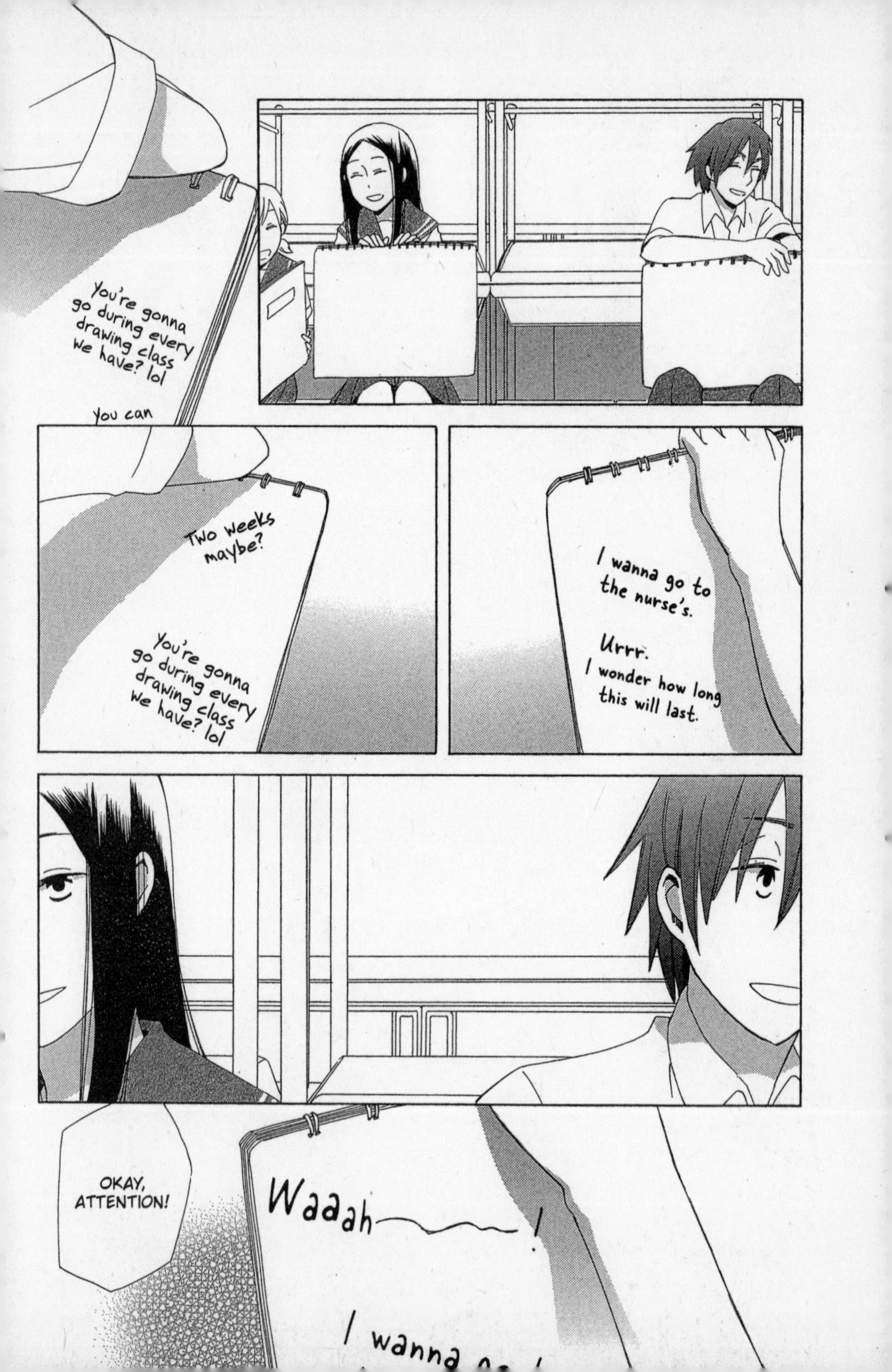

You're gonna go during every drawing class we have? lol
You can
I wanna go to the nurse's.
Urrr.
I wonder how long this will last.
Two weeks maybe?
You're gonna go during every drawing class we have? lol
Waaah—!
I wanna
OKAY, ATTENTION!

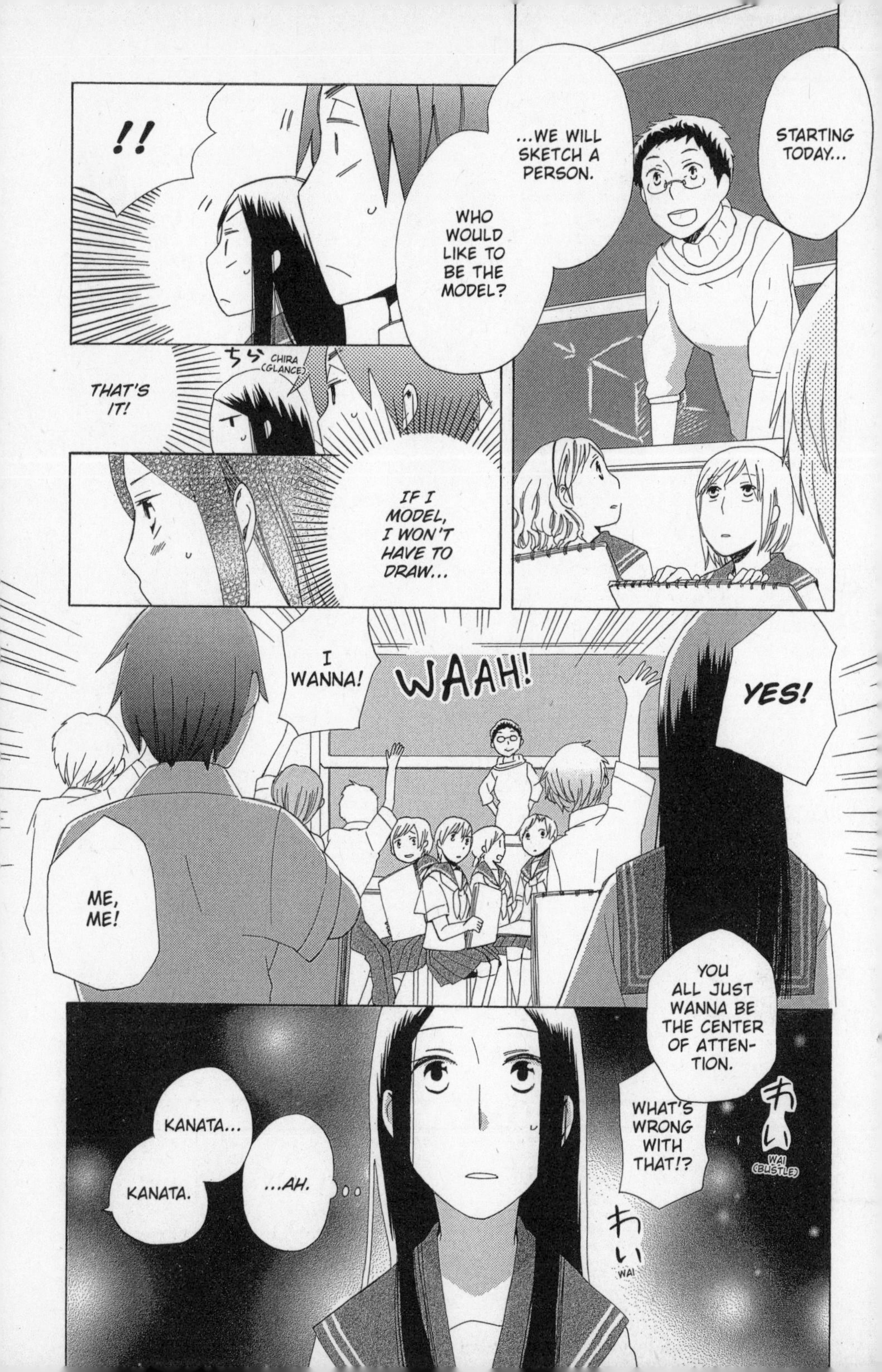
STARTING TODAY...
...WE WILL SKETCH A PERSON.
WHO WOULD LIKE TO BE THE MODEL?
!!
ちら CHIRA (GLANCE)
THAT'S IT!
IF I MODEL, I WON'T HAVE TO DRAW...
YES!
WAAH!
I WANNA!
ME, ME!
YOU ALL JUST WANNA BE THE CENTER OF ATTEN-TION.
WHAT'S WRONG WITH THAT!?
わい WAI (BUSTLE)
わい WAI
KANATA...
KANATA.
...AH.

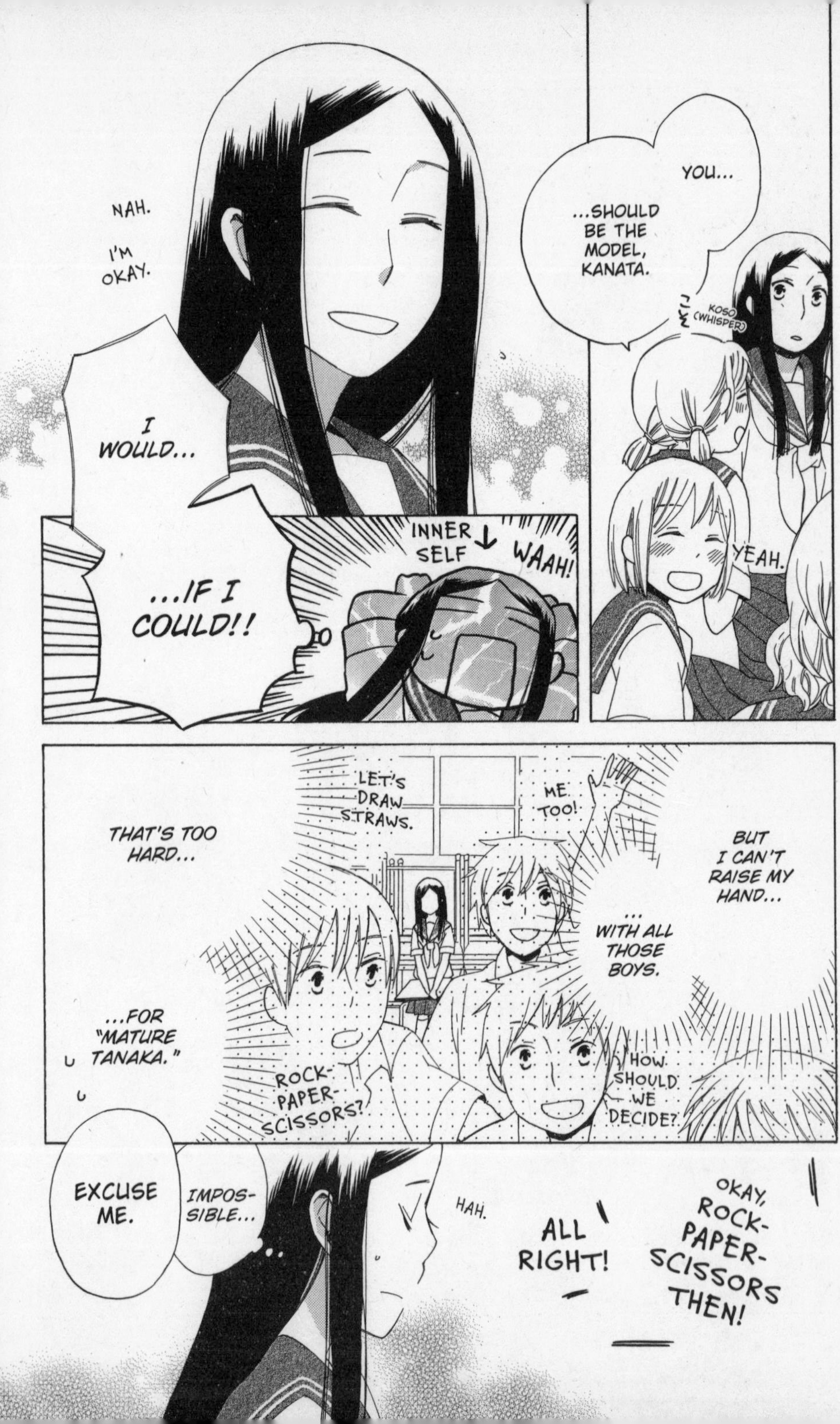
YOU...
...SHOULD BE THE MODEL, KANATA.
KOSO (WHISPER)
YEAH.
NAH.
I'M OKAY.
I WOULD...
...IF I COULD!!
INNER SELF
WAAH!
BUT I CAN'T RAISE MY HAND...
... WITH ALL THOSE BOYS.
ME TOO!
LET'S DRAW STRAWS.
HOW SHOULD WE DECIDE?
ROCK-PAPER-SCISSORS?
THAT'S TOO HARD...
...FOR "MATURE TANAKA."
OKAY, ROCK-PAPER-SCISSORS THEN!
ALL RIGHT!
HAH.
IMPOSSIBLE...
EXCUSE ME.

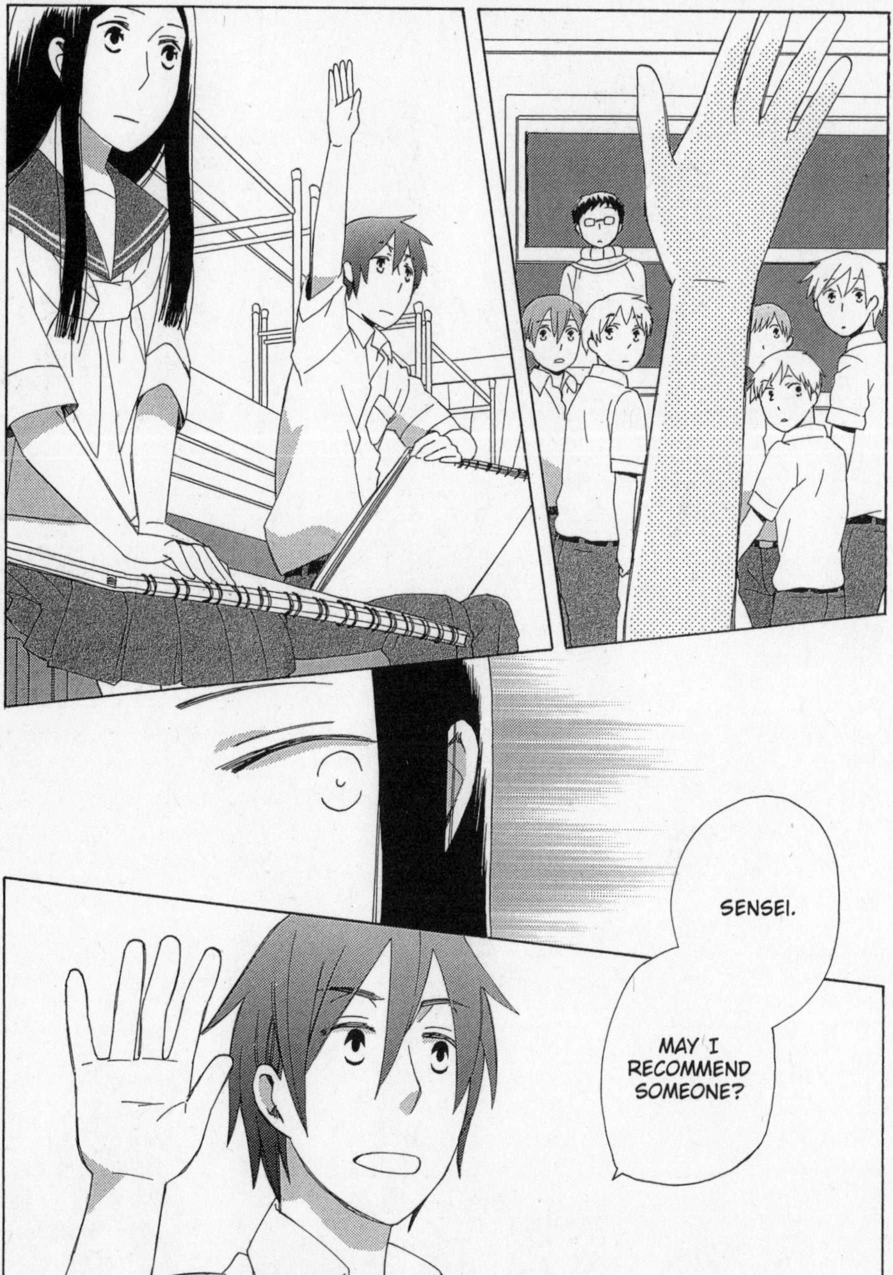
SENSEI.
MAY I RECOMMEND SOMEONE?

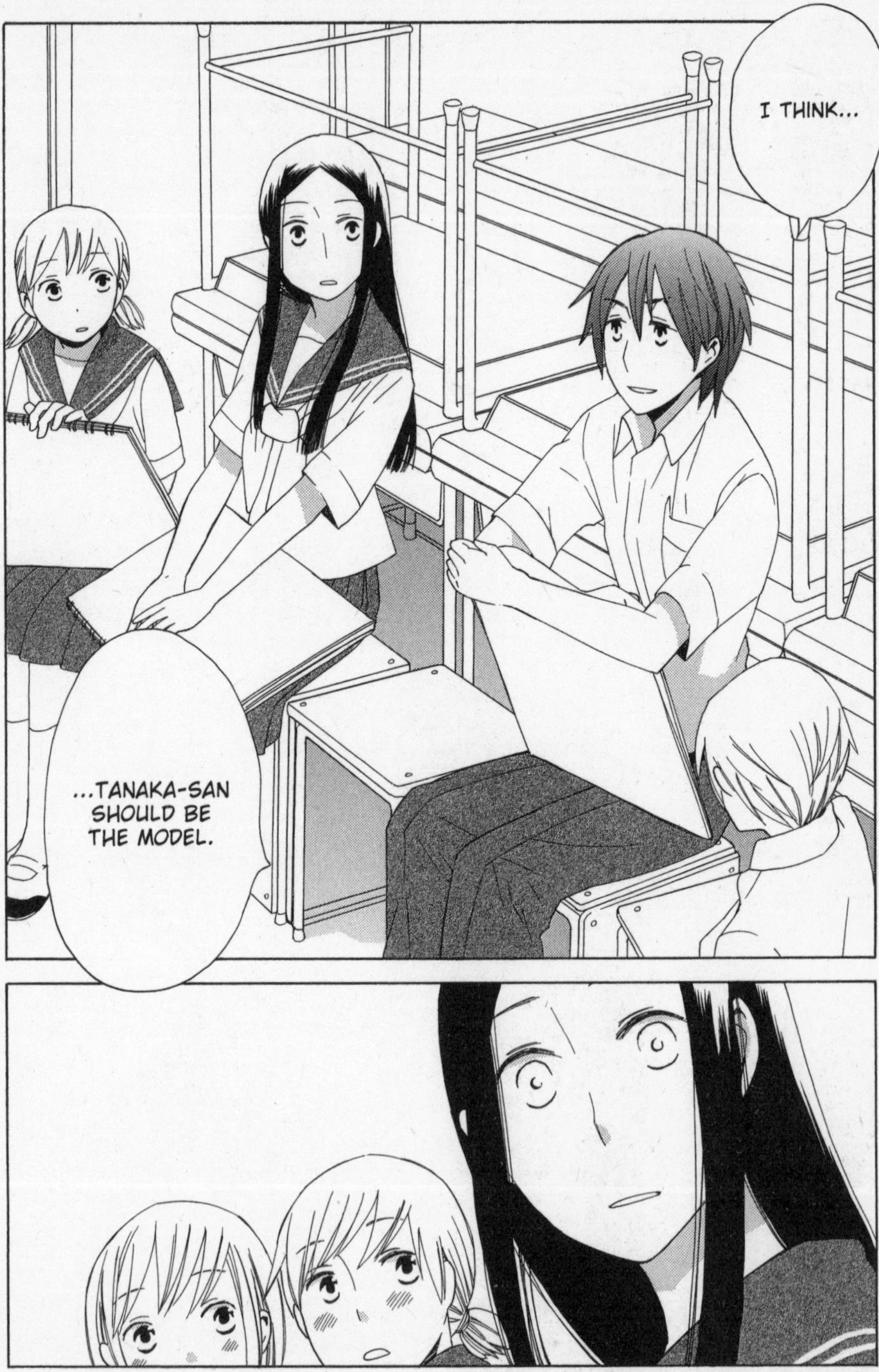
I THINK...
...TANAKA-SAN SHOULD BE THE MODEL.

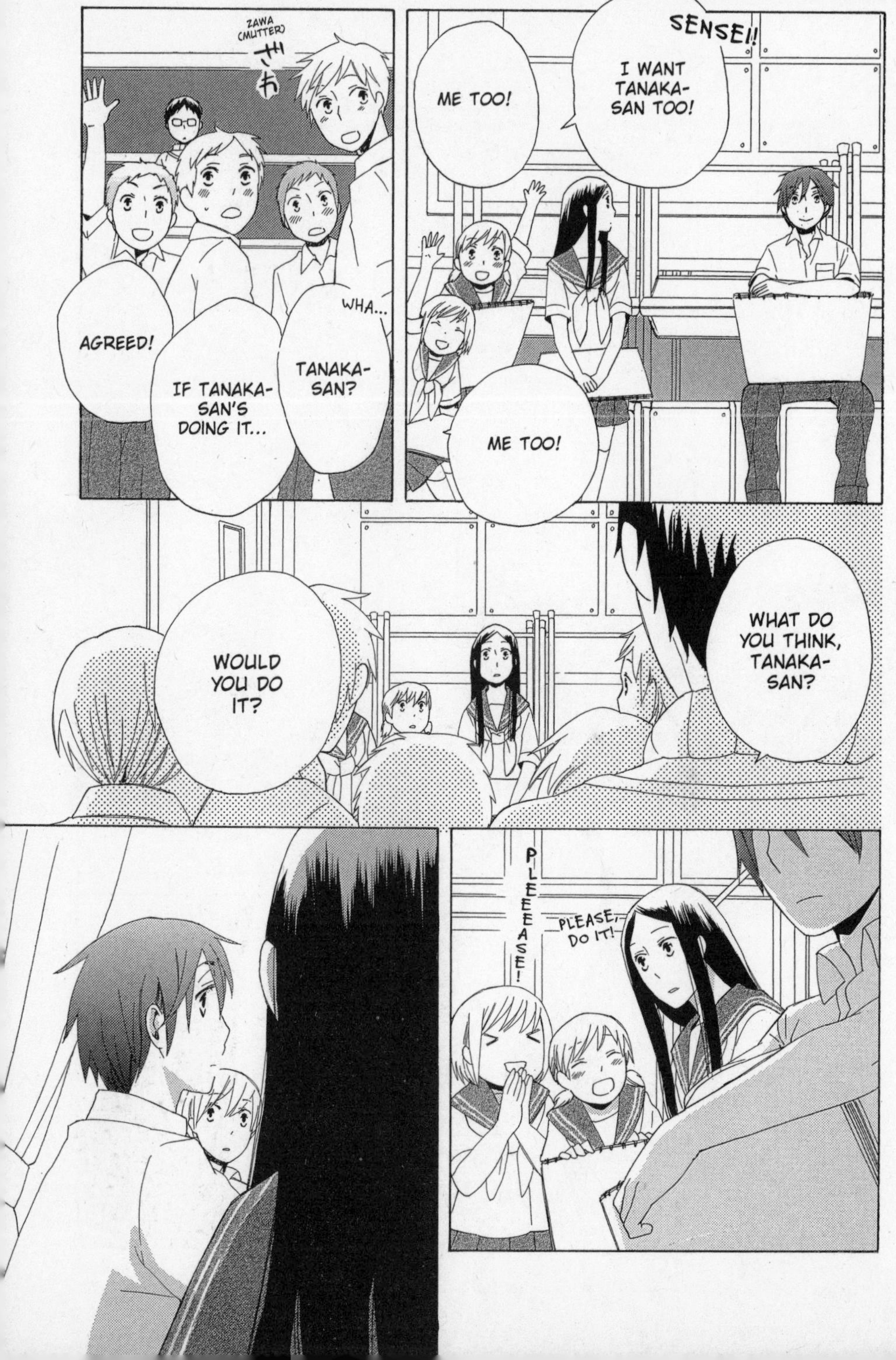
SENSEI!!
I WANT TANAKA-SAN TOO!
ME TOO!
ME TOO!
ZAWA (MUTTER)
ざわ
WHA...
TANAKA-SAN?
IF TANAKA-SAN'S DOING IT...
AGREED!
WHAT DO YOU THINK, TANAKA-SAN?
WOULD YOU DO IT?
PLEEEASE!
PLEASE, DO IT!

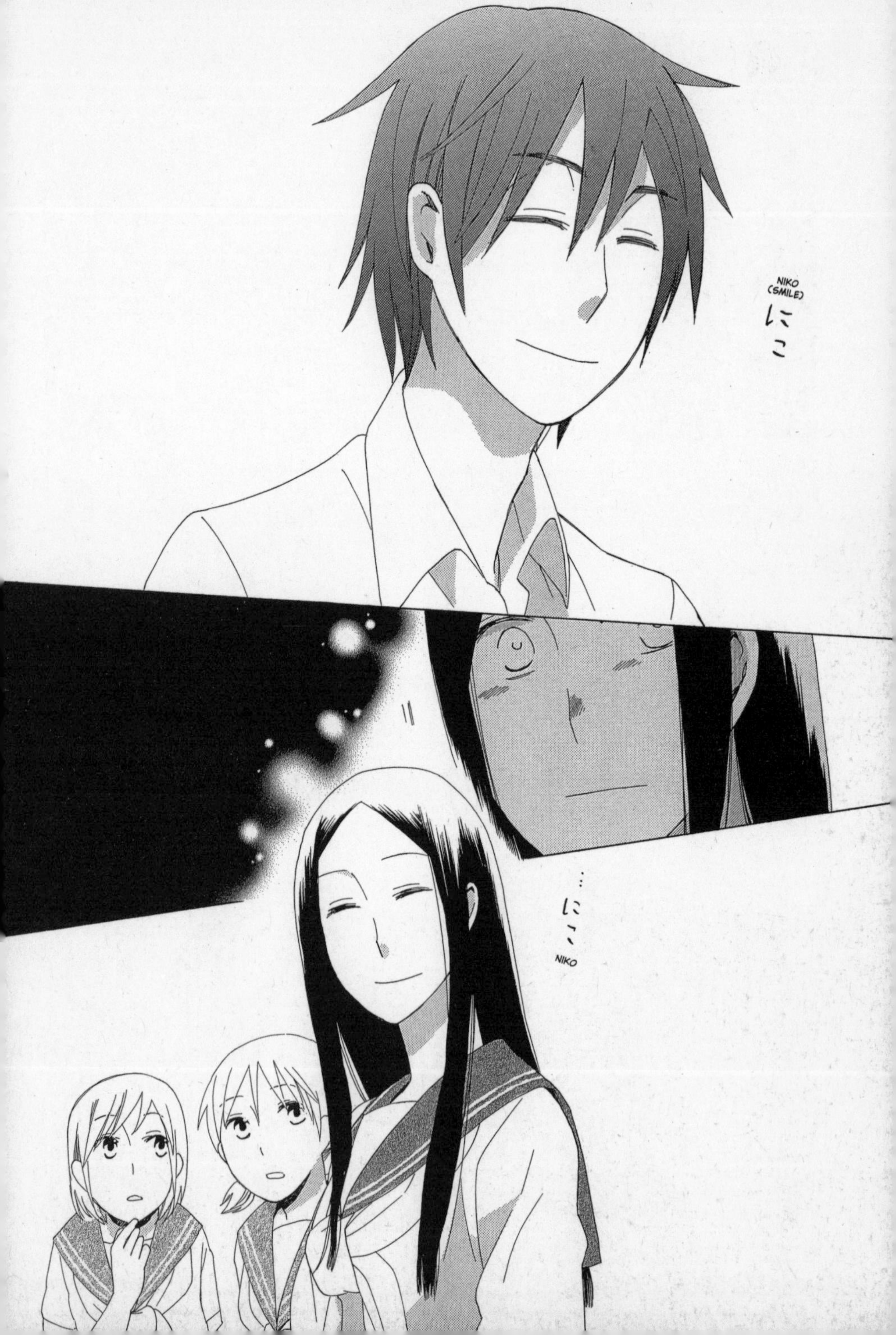
NIKO (SMILE)
にこ
…にこ
NIKO

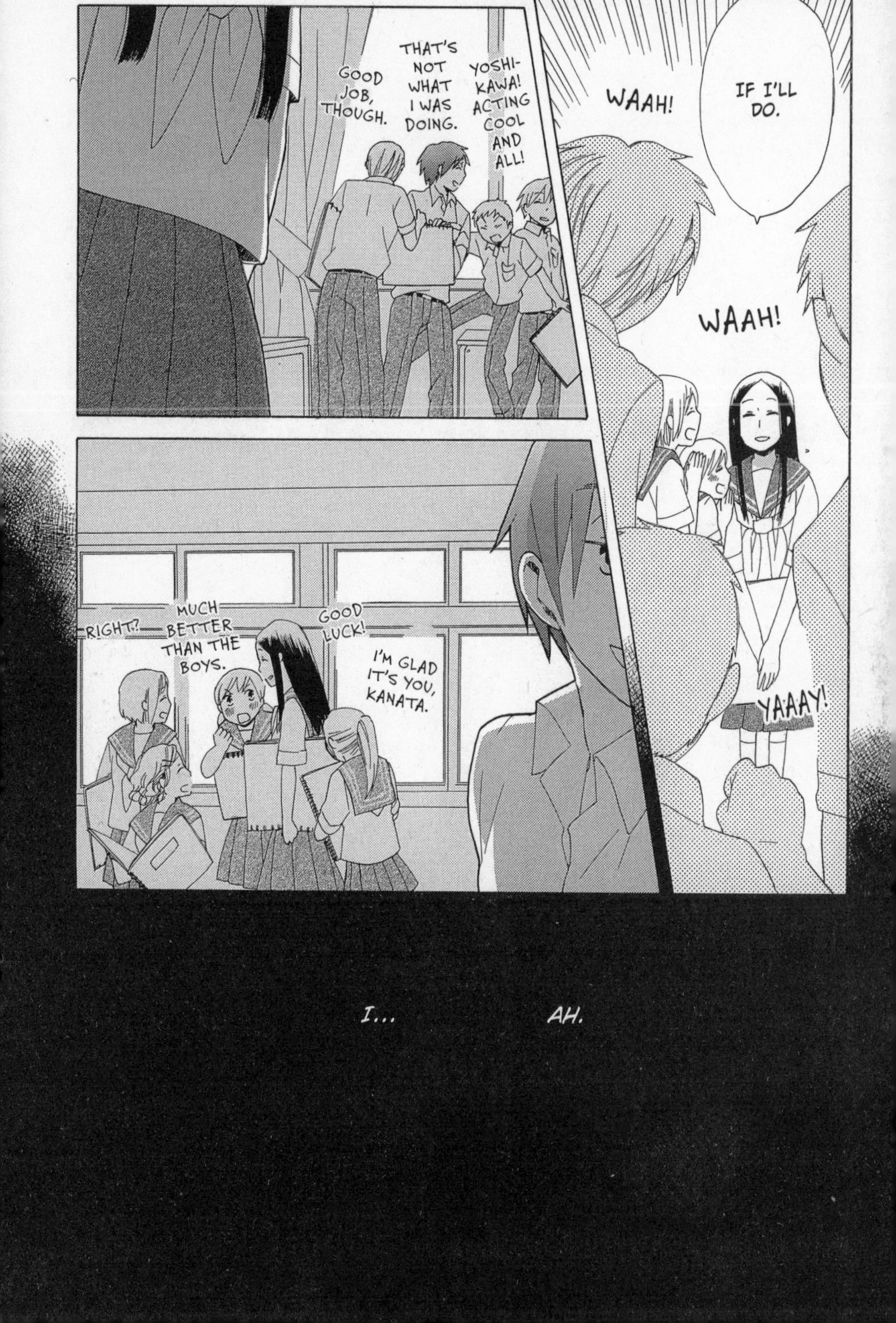
IF I'LL DO.
WAAH!
WAAH!
YAAAY!
YOSHI-KAWA! ACTING COOL AND ALL!
THAT'S NOT WHAT I WAS DOING.
GOOD JOB, THOUGH.
I'M GLAD IT'S YOU, KANATA.
GOOD LUCK!
MUCH BETTER THAN THE BOYS.
RIGHT?
AH.
I...

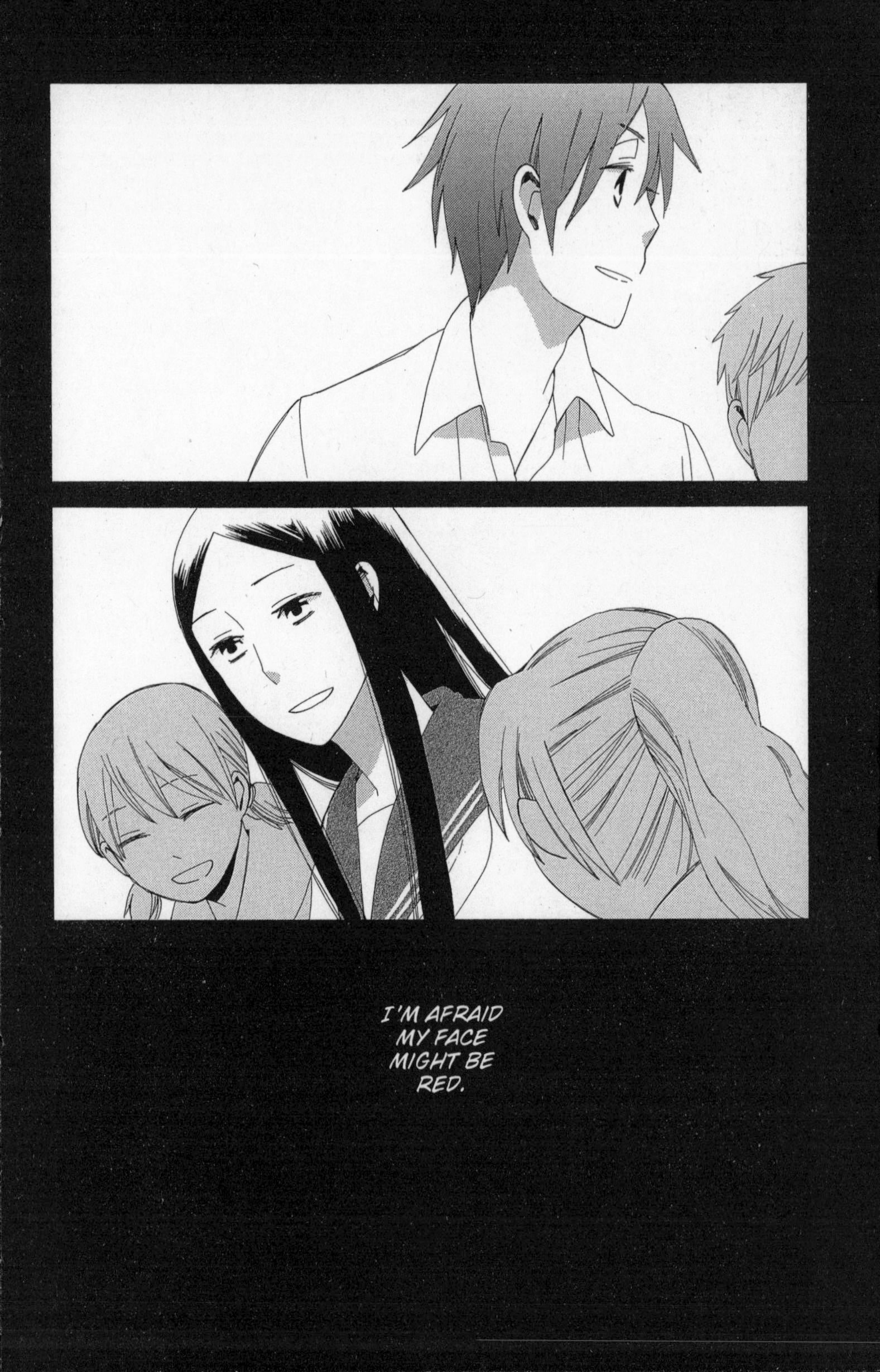
I'M AFRAID MY FACE MIGHT BE RED.

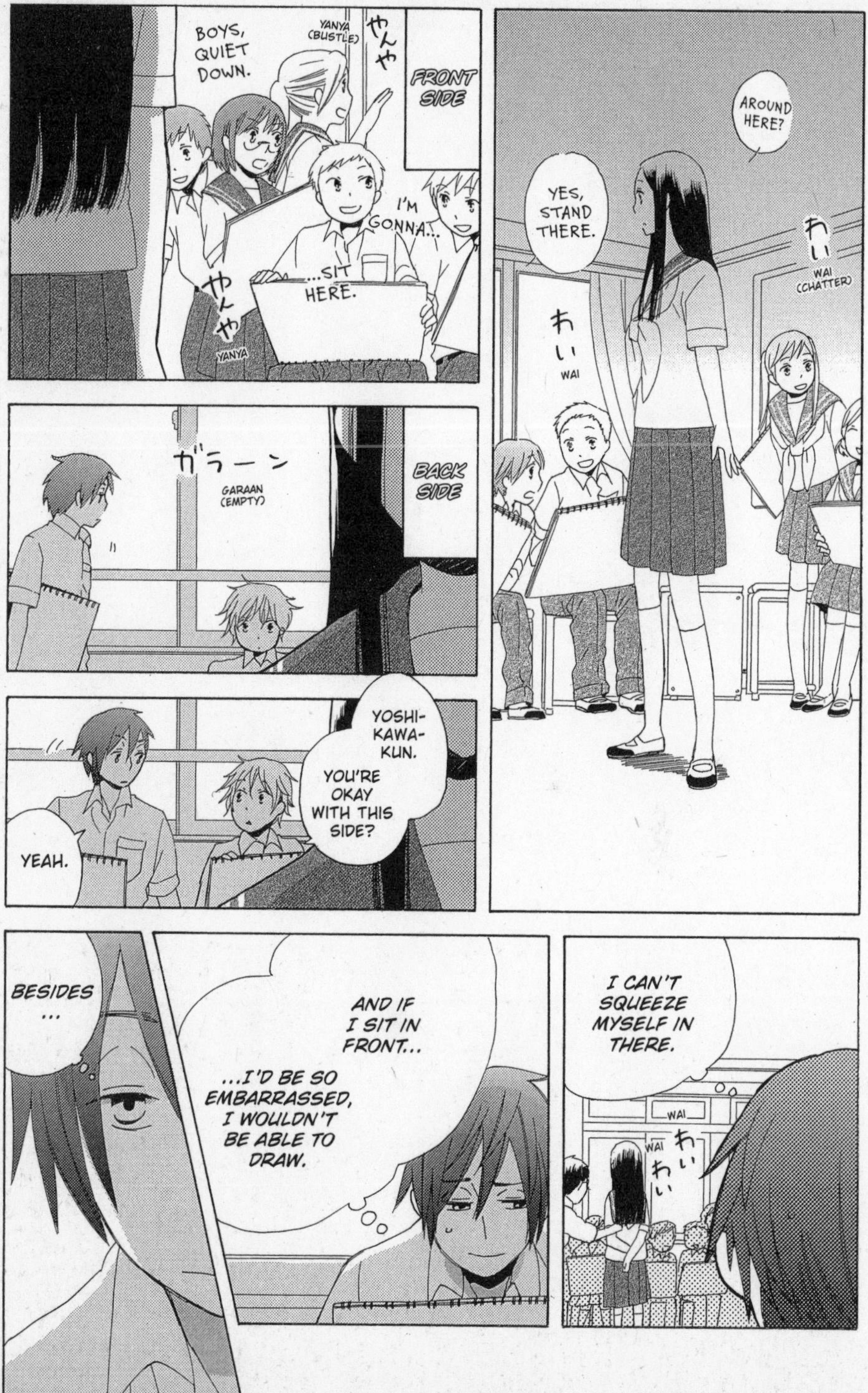
AROUND HERE?
わい
WAI (CHATTER)
YES, STAND THERE.
わい
WAI
やんや
YANYA (BUSTLE)
FRONT SIDE
BOYS, QUIET DOWN.
I'M GONNA...
...SIT HERE.
やんや
YANYA
BACK SIDE
ガラーン
GARAAN (EMPTY)
YOSHI-KAWA-KUN.
YOU'RE OKAY WITH THIS SIDE?
YEAH.
I CAN'T SQUEEZE MYSELF IN THERE.
WAI
わい わい
WAI
AND IF I SIT IN FRONT...
...I'D BE SO EMBARRASSED, I WOULDN'T BE ABLE TO DRAW.
BESIDES...

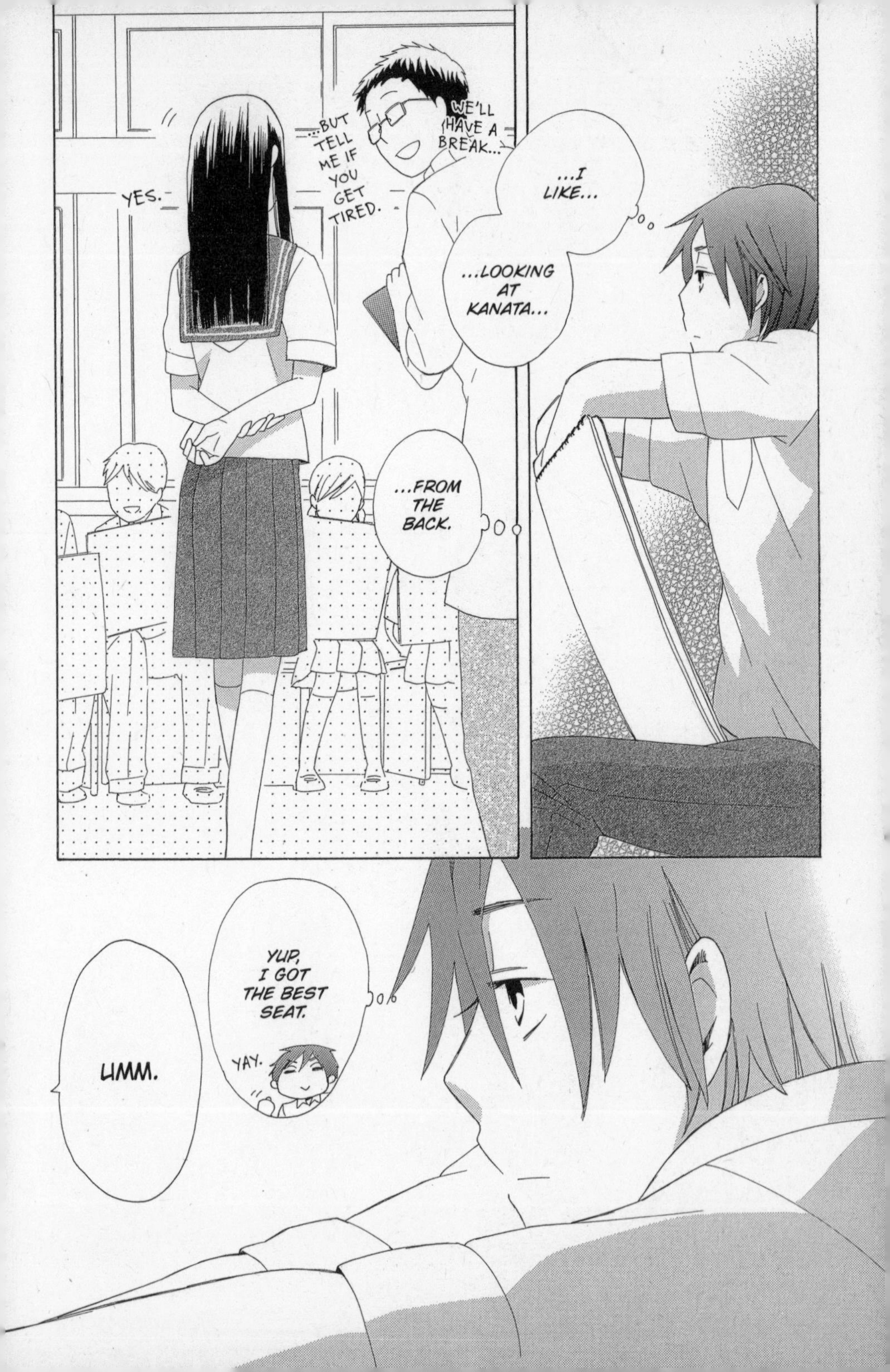
...I LIKE...
...LOOKING AT KANATA...
WE'LL HAVE A BREAK...
...BUT TELL ME IF YOU GET TIRED.
YES.
...FROM THE BACK.
YUP, I GOT THE BEST SEAT.
YAY.
UMM.

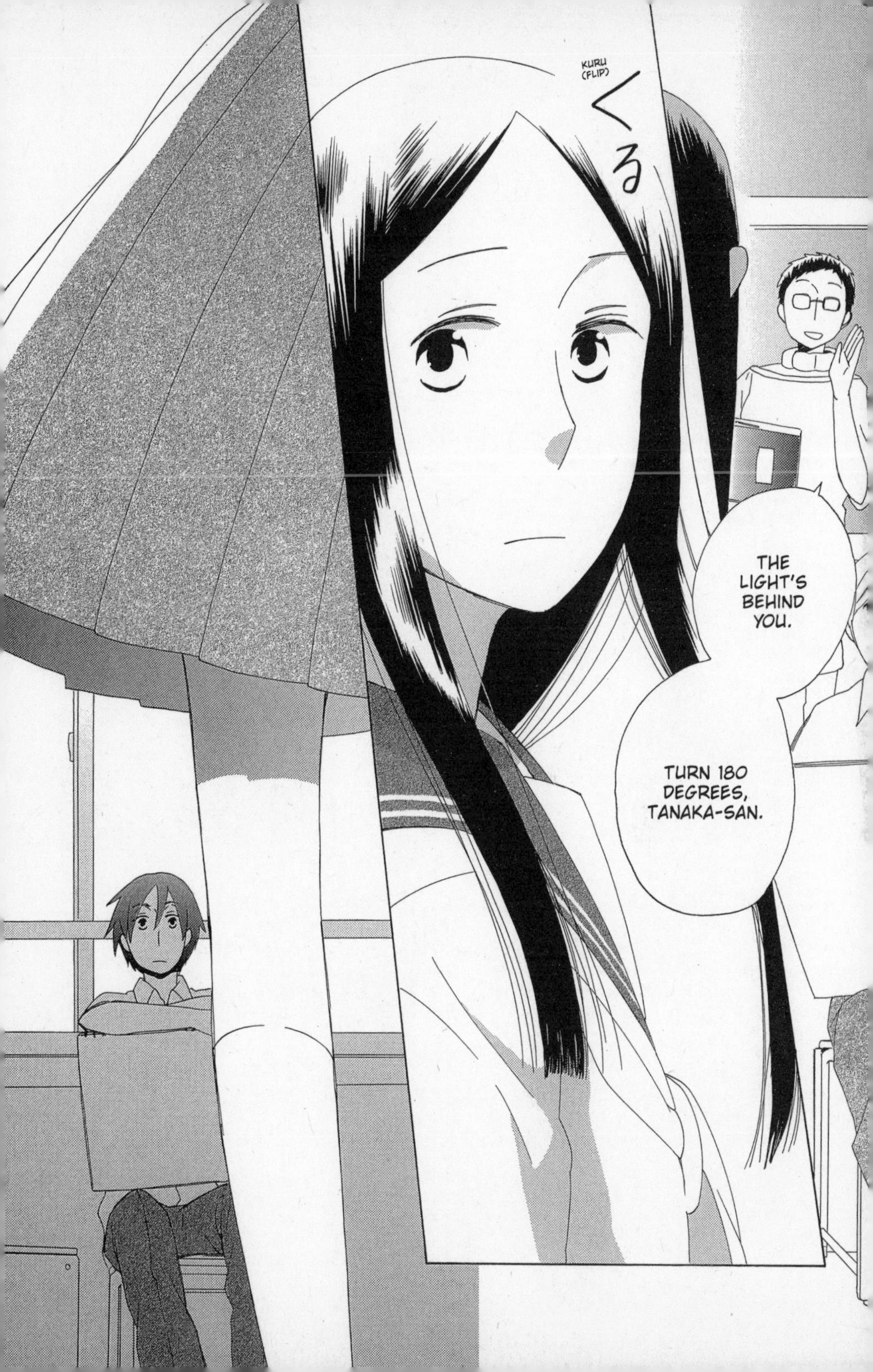
KURU (FLIP)
くる
THE LIGHT'S BEHIND YOU.
TURN 180 DEGREES, TANAKA-SAN.

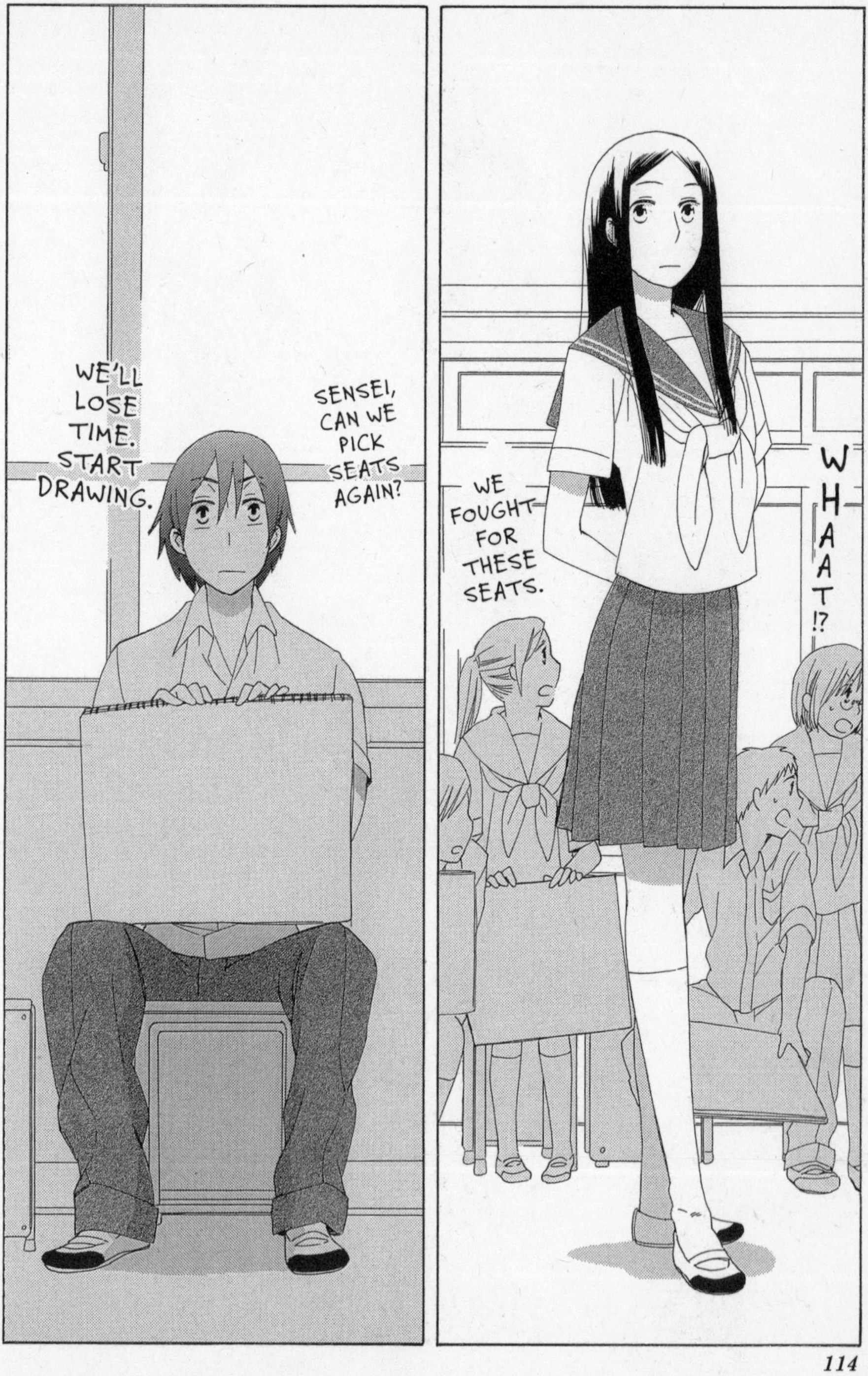
WHAAT!?
WE FOUGHT FOR THESE SEATS.
SENSEI, CAN WE PICK SEATS AGAIN?
WE'LL LOSE TIME. START DRAWING.

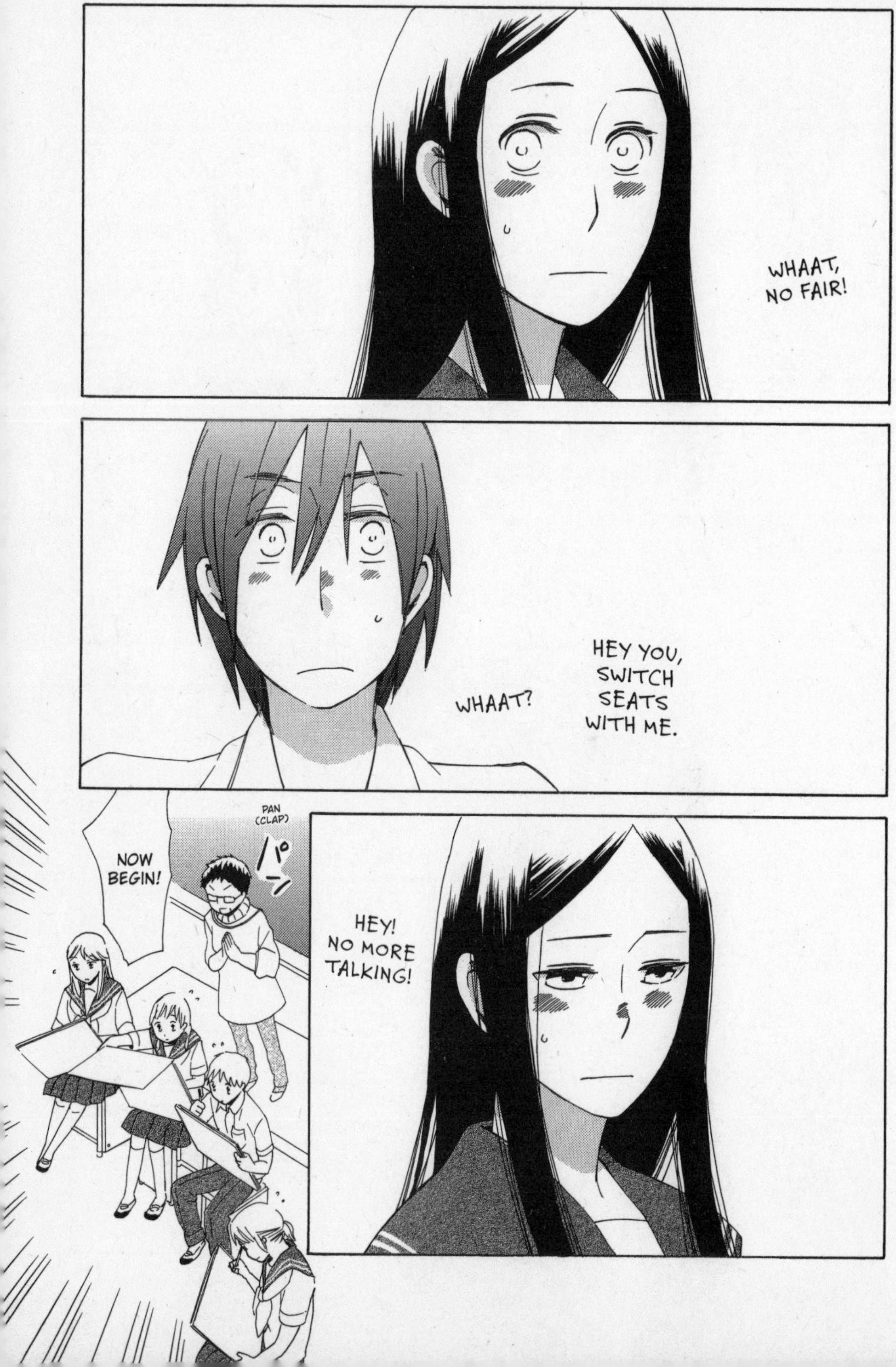
WHAAT, NO FAIR!
HEY YOU, SWITCH SEATS WITH ME.
WHAAT?
HEY! NO MORE TALKING!
PAN (CLAP)
NOW BEGIN!

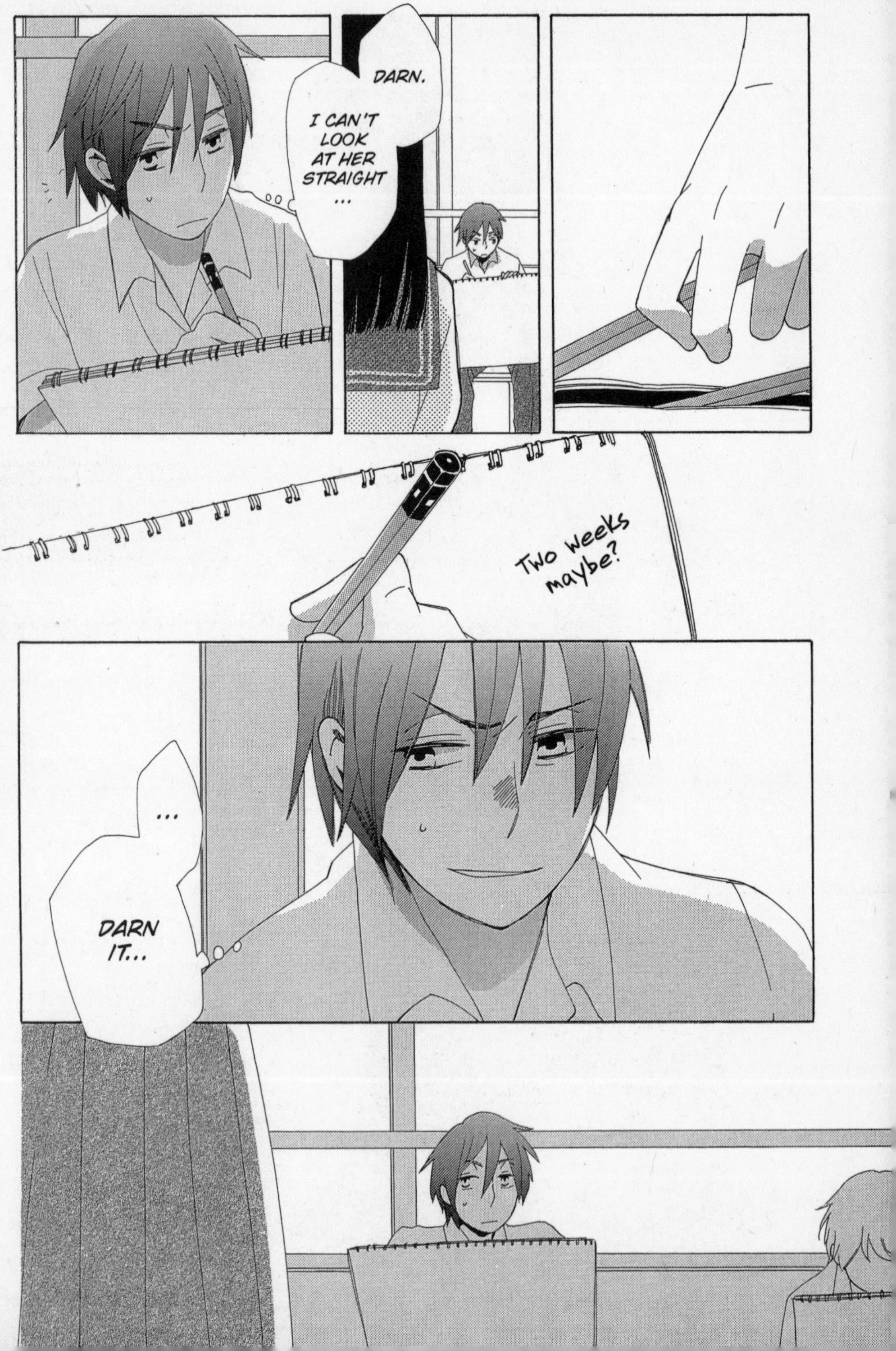
DARN.
I CAN'T LOOK AT HER STRAIGHT ...
Two weeks maybe?
...
DARN IT...

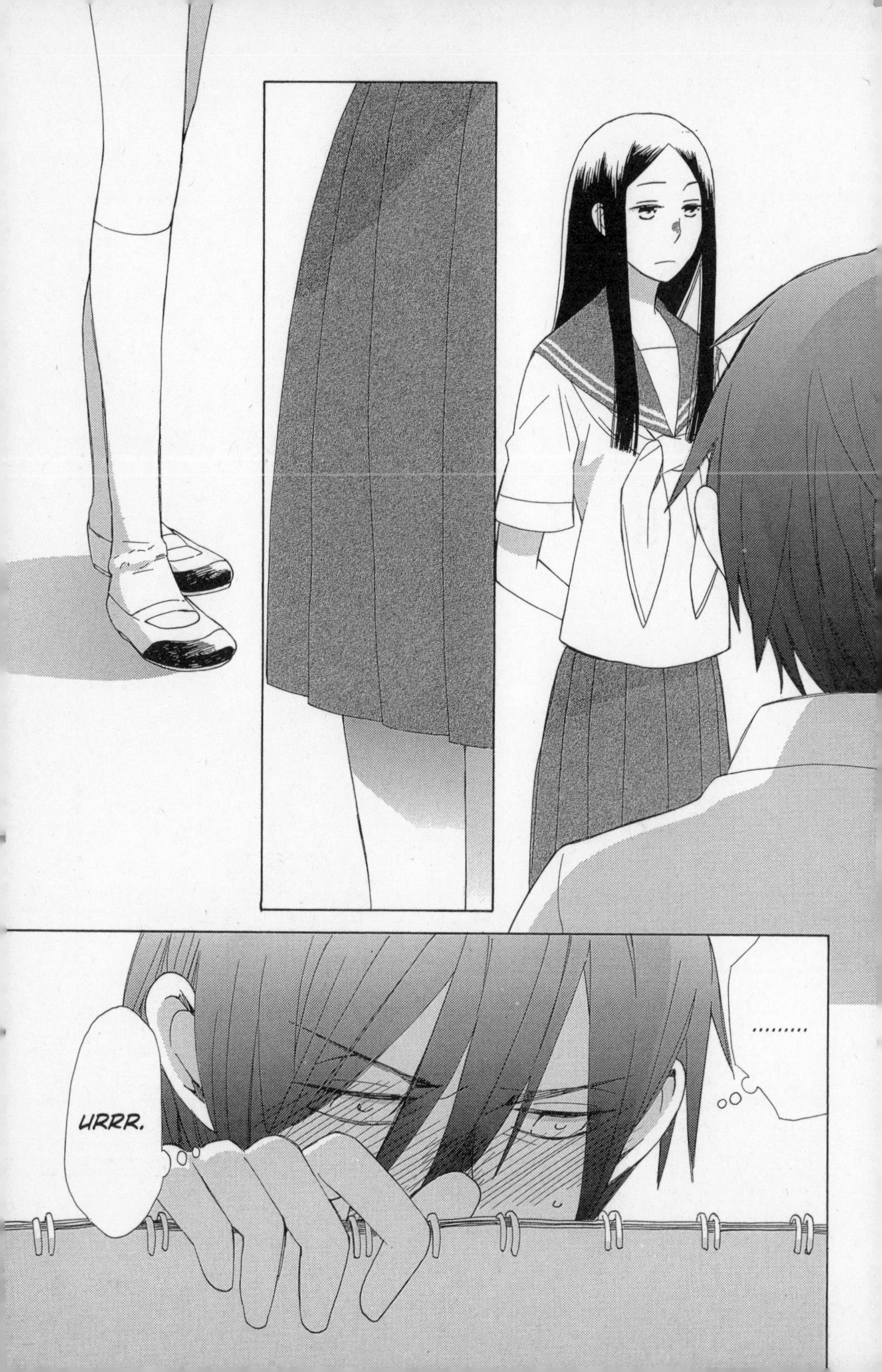
....
URRR.

I WANNA GO...
...TO THE NURSE'S.

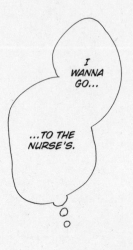

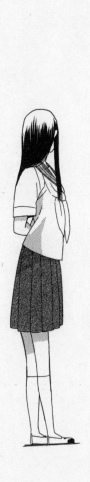

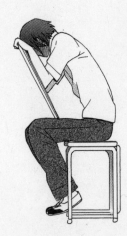

Fin

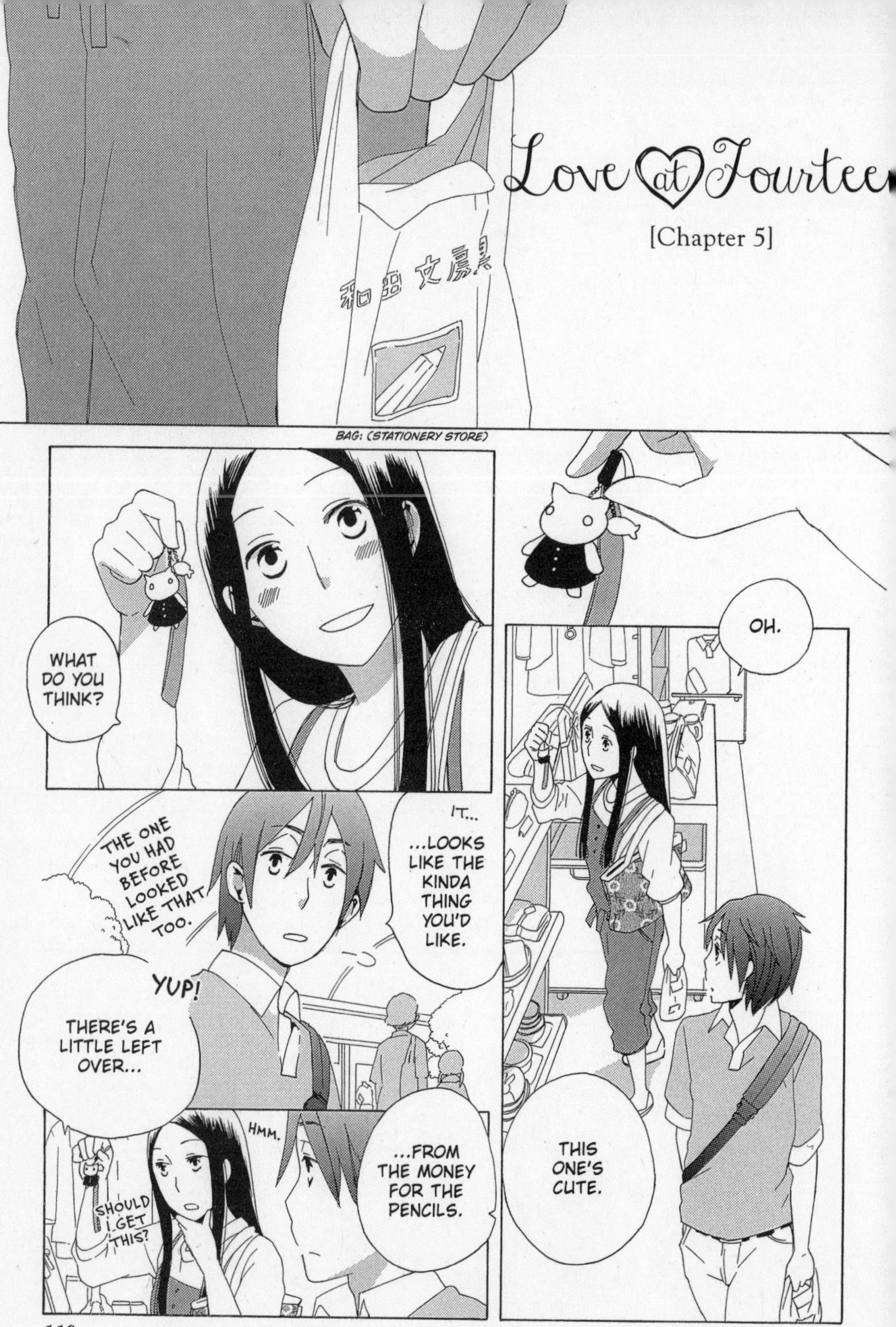
Love at Fourtee
[Chapter 5]
BAG: (STATIONERY STORE)
OH.
THIS ONE'S CUTE.
WHAT DO YOU THINK?
IT...
...LOOKS LIKE THE KINDA THING YOU'D LIKE.
THE ONE YOU HAD BEFORE LOOKED LIKE THAT TOO.
YUP!
THERE'S A LITTLE LEFT OVER...
...FROM THE MONEY FOR THE PENCILS.
HMM.
SHOULD I GET THIS?

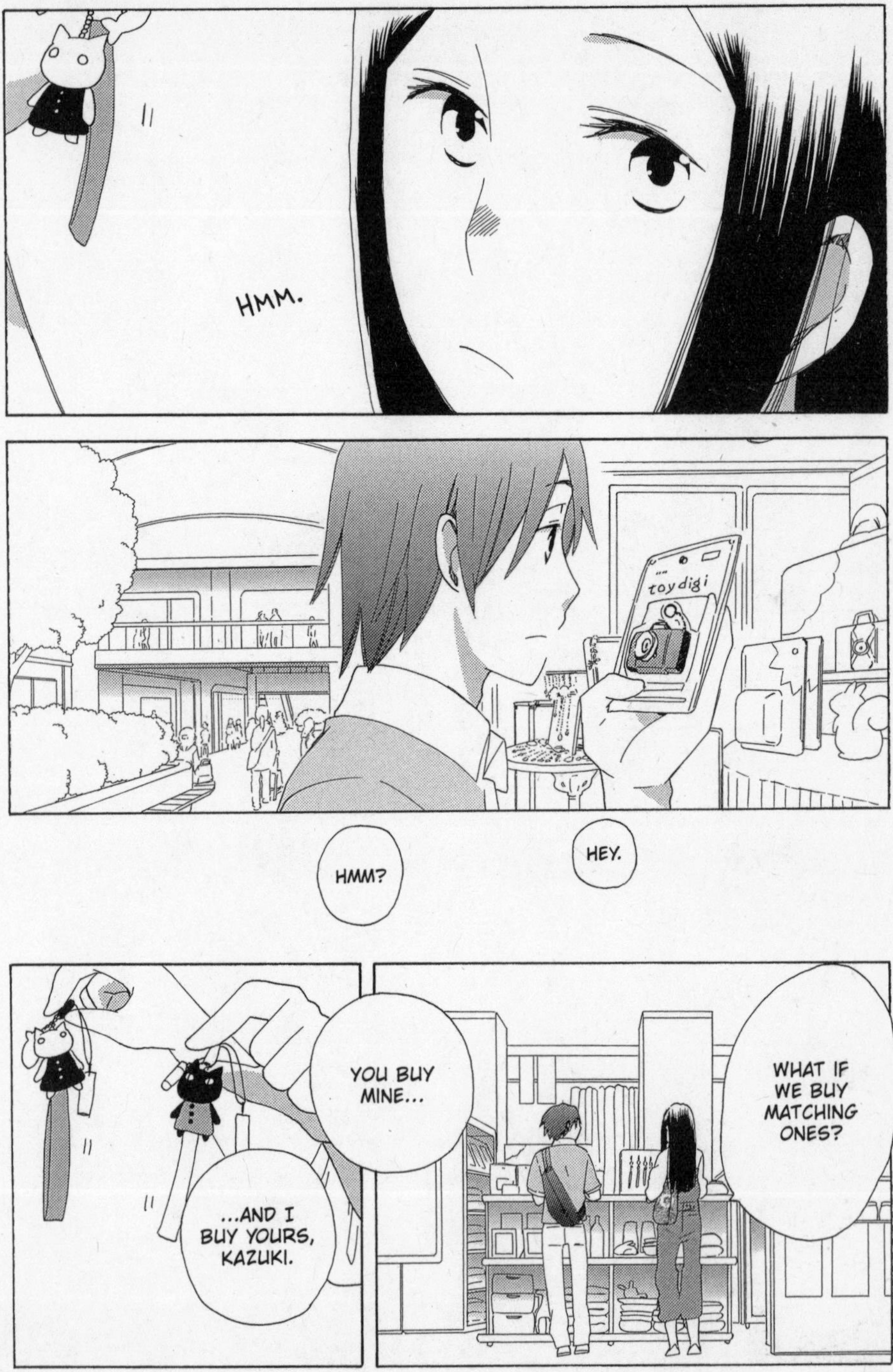
HMM.
toydigi
HEY.
HMM?
WHAT IF WE BUY MATCHING ONES?
YOU BUY MINE...
...AND I BUY YOURS, KAZUKI.

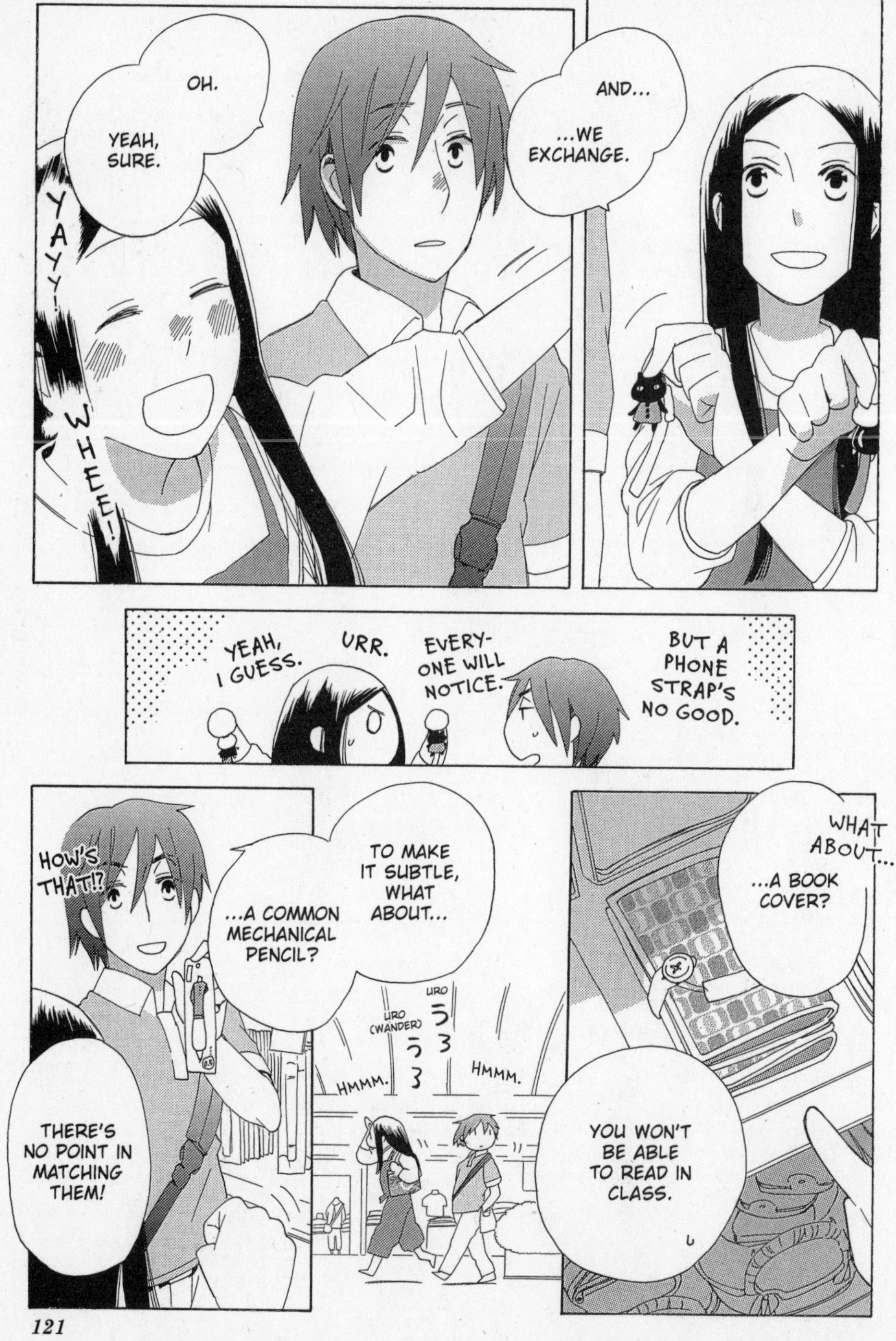
AND...
...WE EXCHANGE.
OH.
YEAH, SURE.
YAYY!
WHEE!
BUT A PHONE STRAP'S NO GOOD.
EVERY-ONE WILL NOTICE.
URR.
YEAH, I GUESS.
WHAT ABOUT...
...A BOOK COVER?
YOU WON'T BE ABLE TO READ IN CLASS.
TO MAKE IT SUBTLE, WHAT ABOUT...
...A COMMON MECHANICAL PENCIL?
HOW'S THAT!?
URO
うろ
URO (WANDER)
うろ
HMMM.
HMMM.
THERE'S NO POINT IN MATCHING THEM!

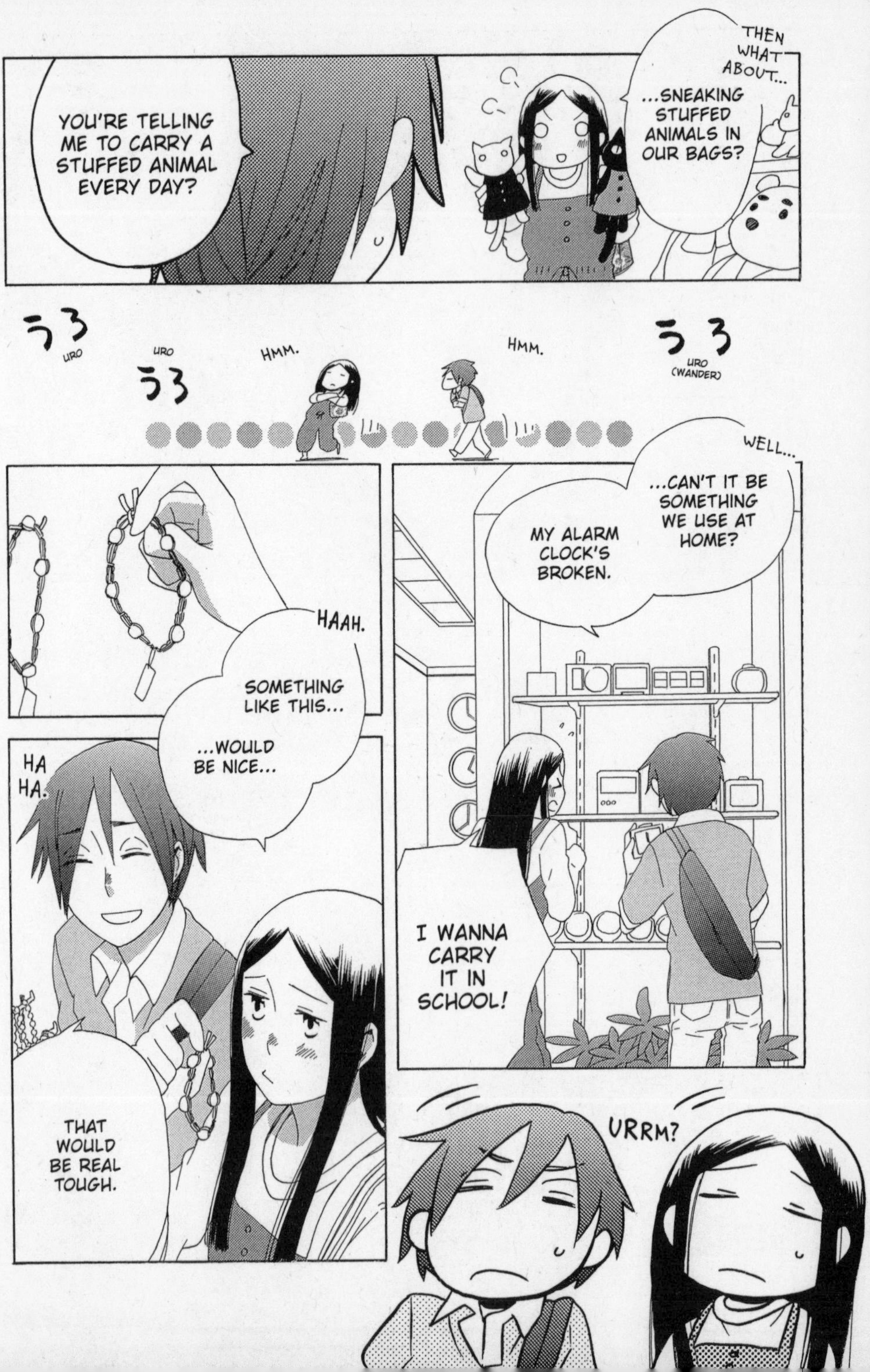
THEN WHAT ABOUT...
...SNEAKING STUFFED ANIMALS IN OUR BAGS?
YOU'RE TELLING ME TO CARRY A STUFFED ANIMAL EVERY DAY?
うろ URO (WANDER)
HMM.
HMM.
うろ URO
うろ URO
WELL...
...CAN'T IT BE SOMETHING WE USE AT HOME?
MY ALARM CLOCK'S BROKEN.
I WANNA CARRY IT IN SCHOOL!
HAAH.
SOMETHING LIKE THIS...
...WOULD BE NICE...
HA HA.
THAT WOULD BE REAL TOUGH.
URRM?

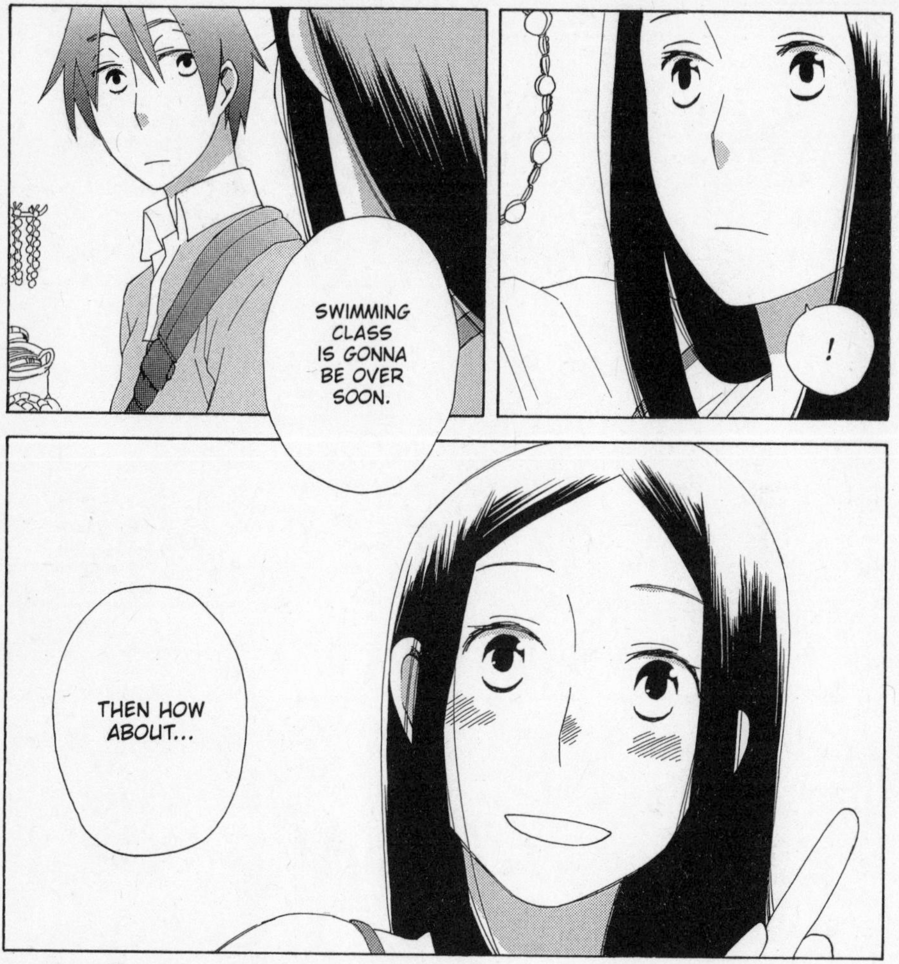
!
SWIMMING CLASS IS GONNA BE OVER SOON.
THEN HOW ABOUT...

SHOES: TANAKA, YOSHIKAWA

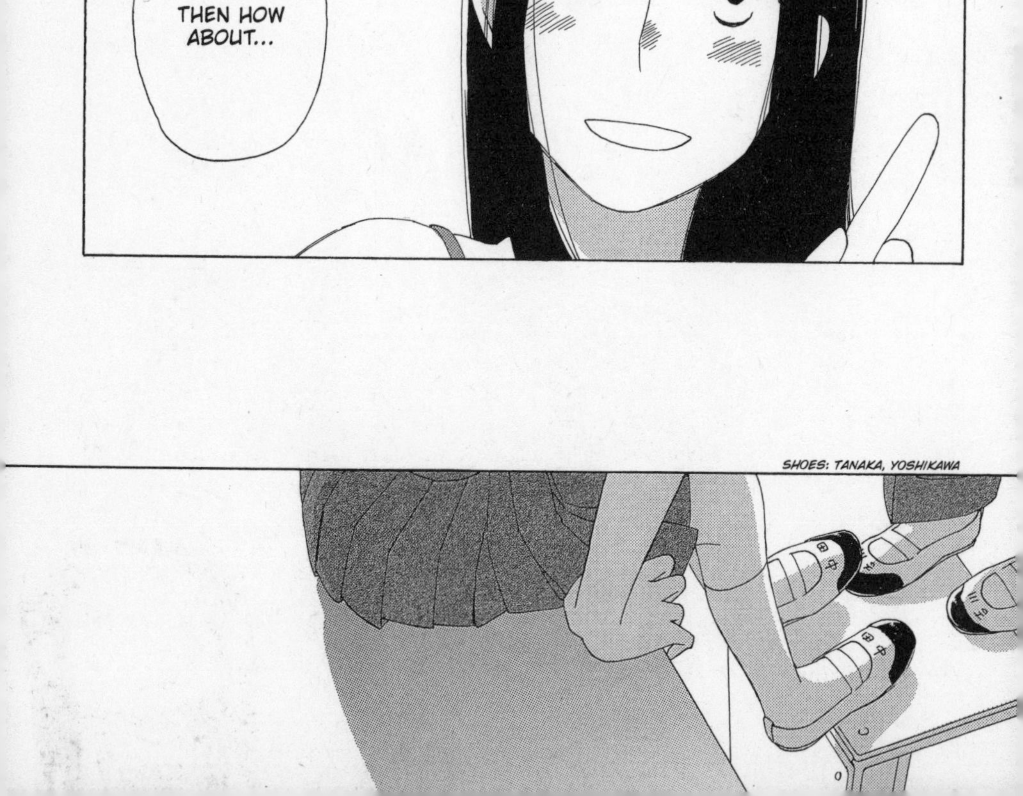

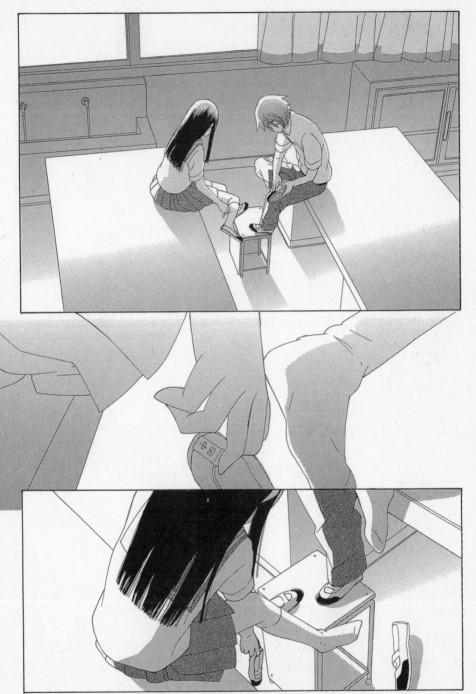

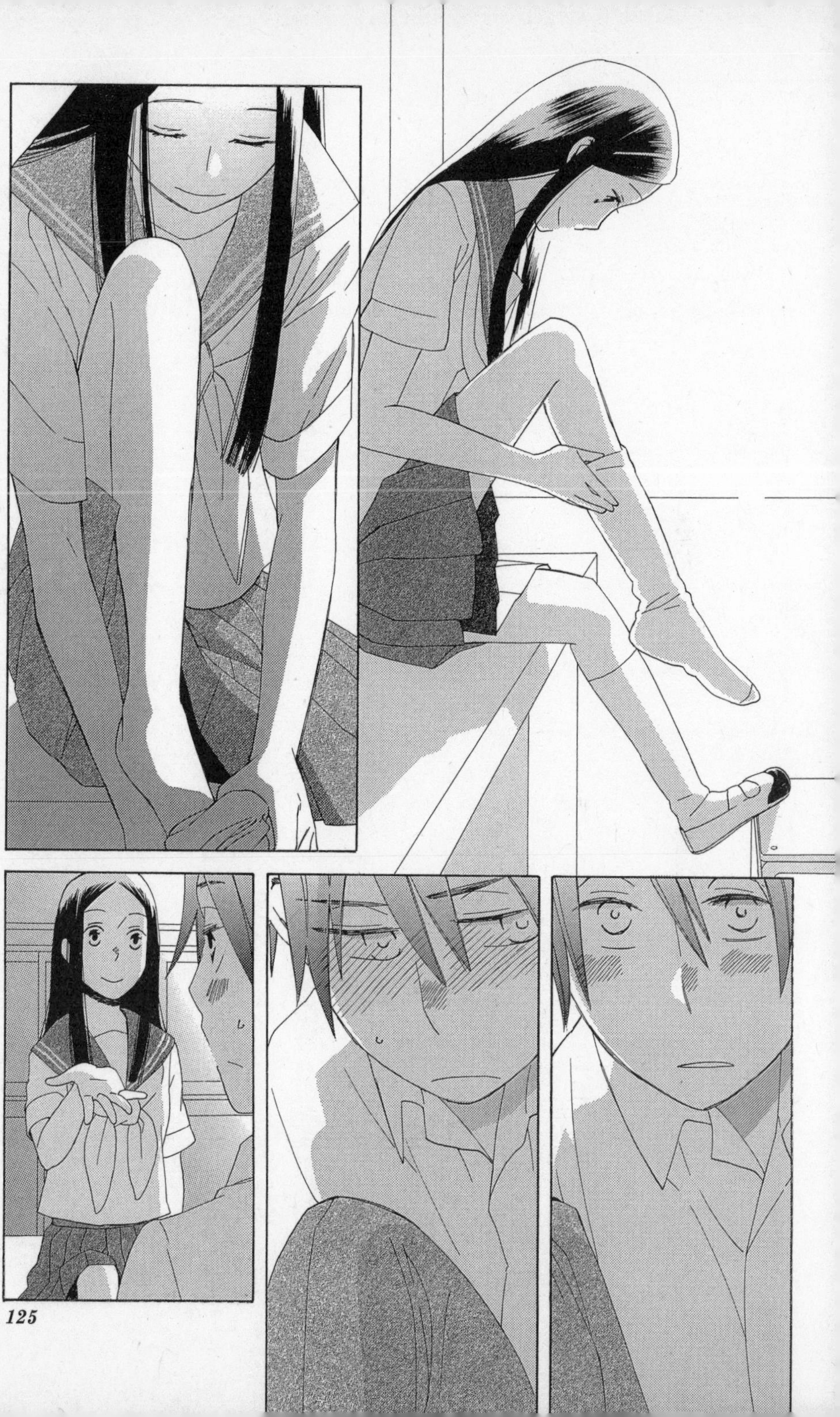

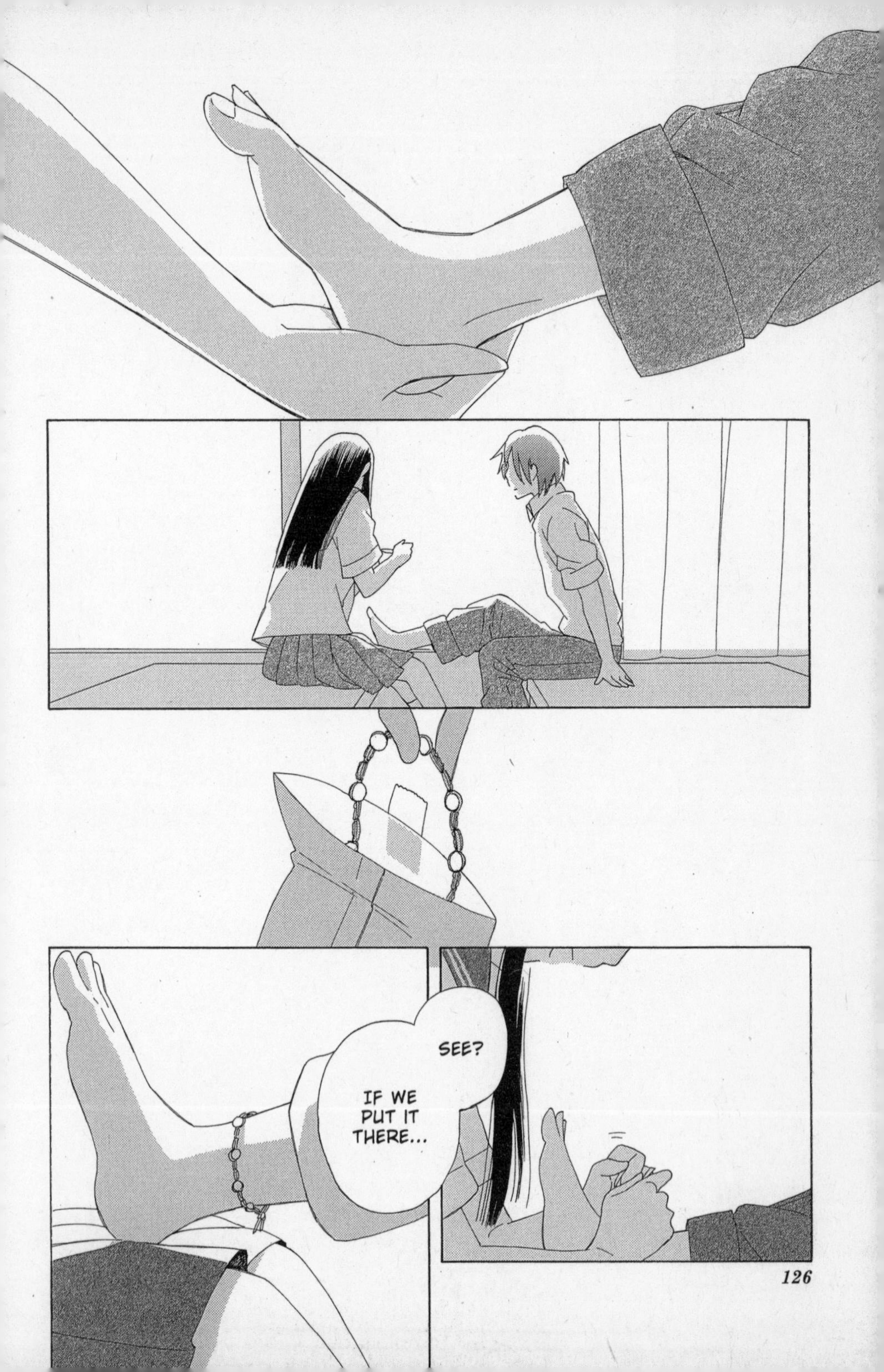
SEE?
IF WE PUT IT THERE...

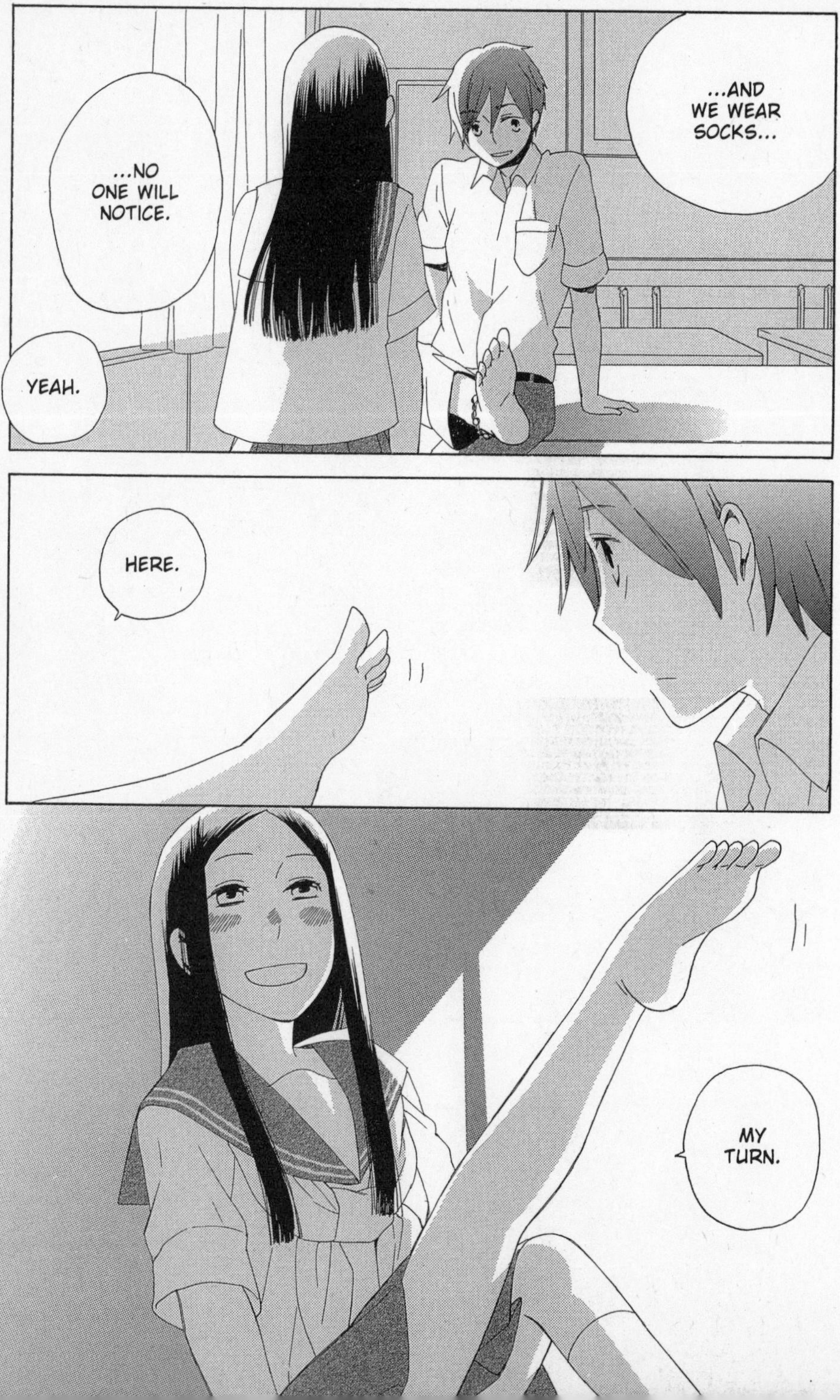
...AND WE WEAR SOCKS...
...NO ONE WILL NOTICE.
YEAH.
HERE.
MY TURN.

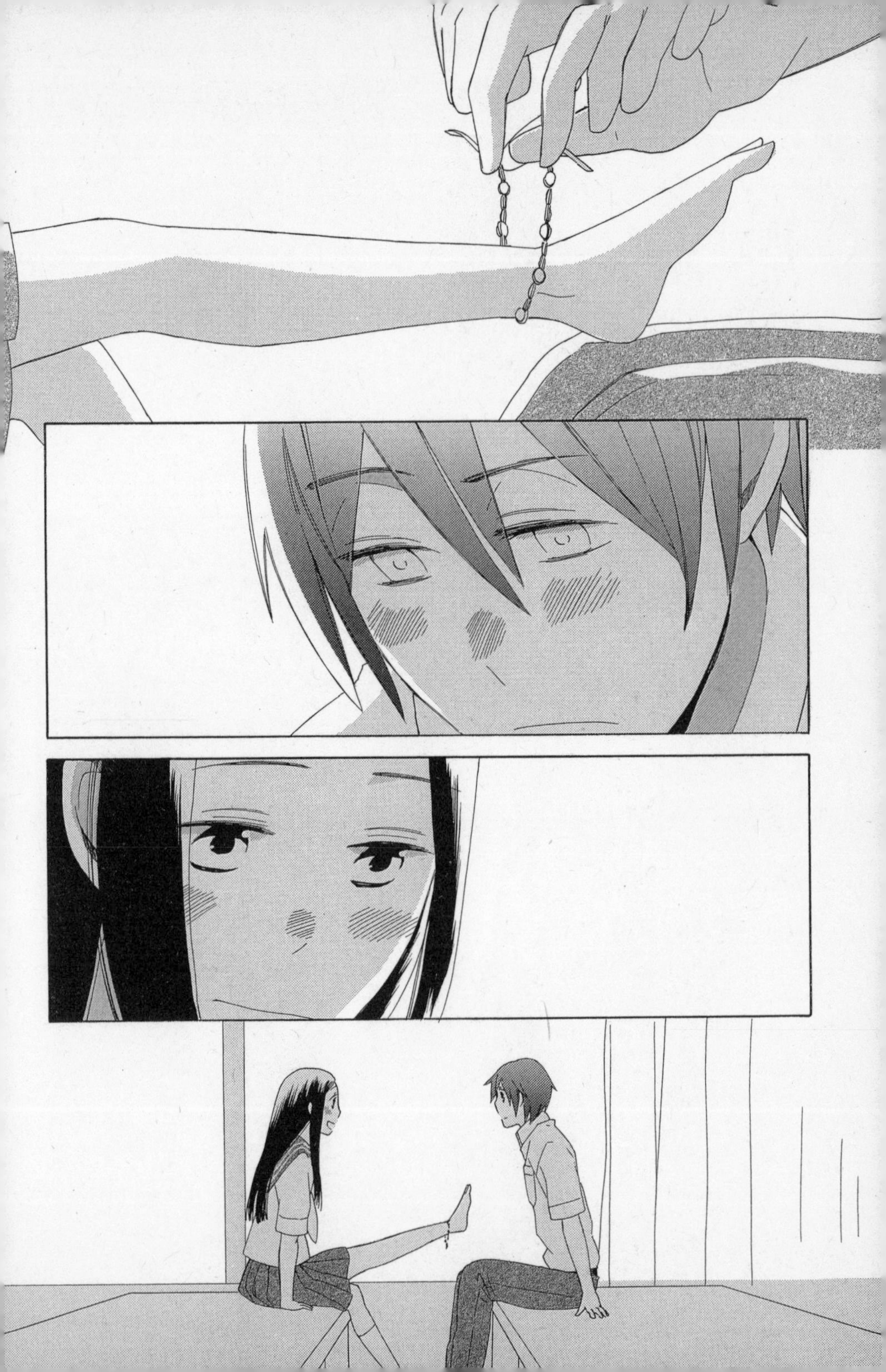

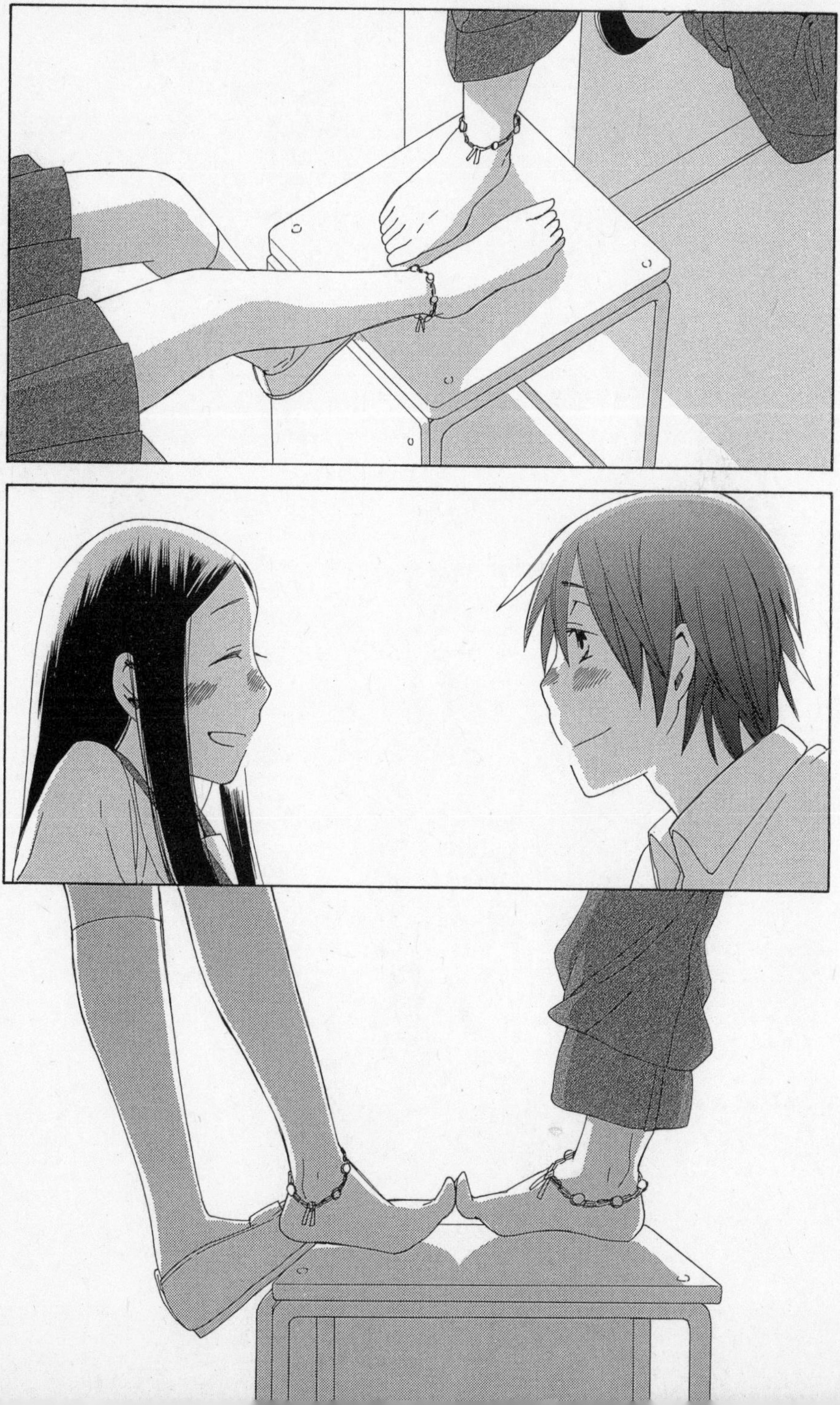

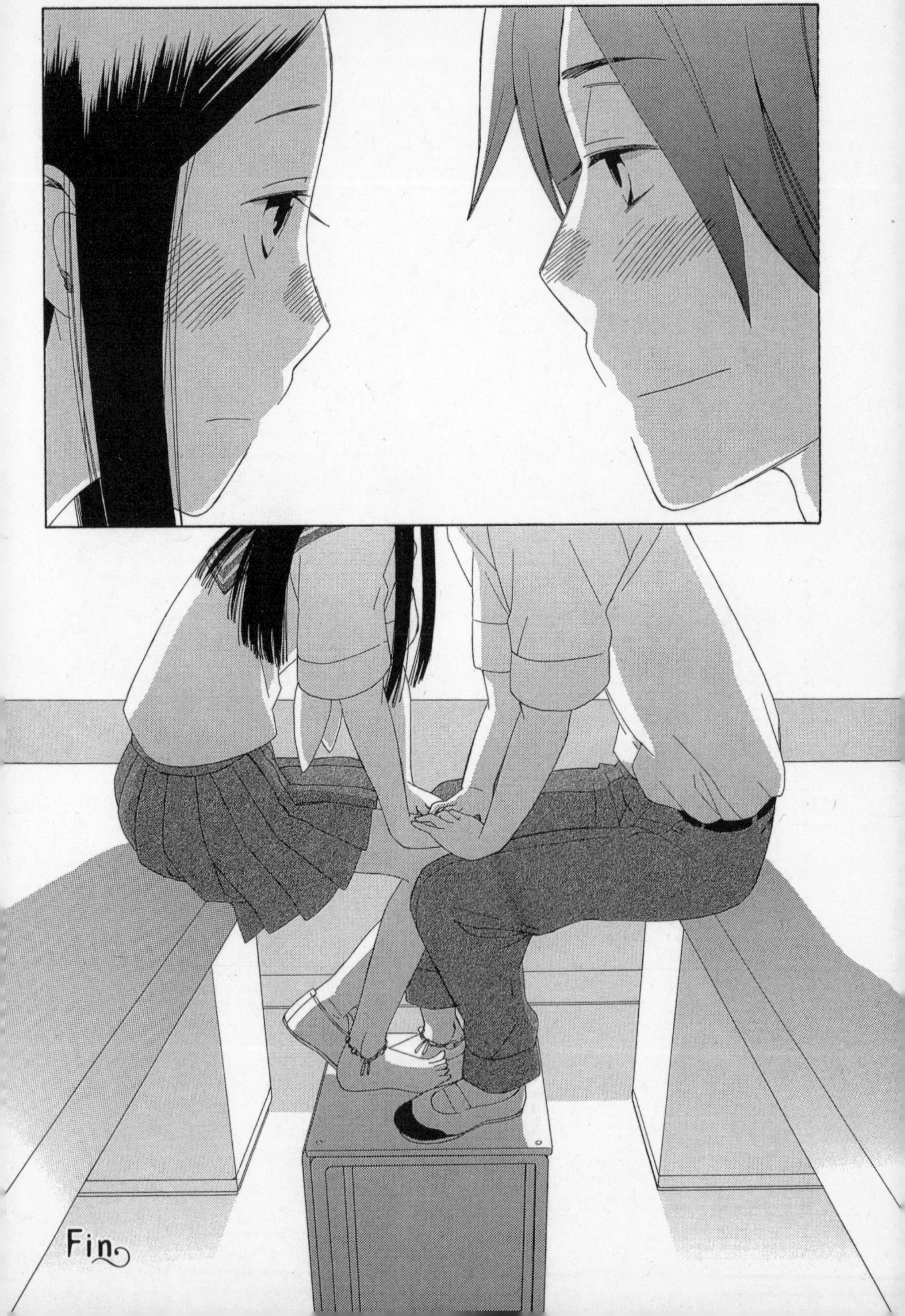
Fin.

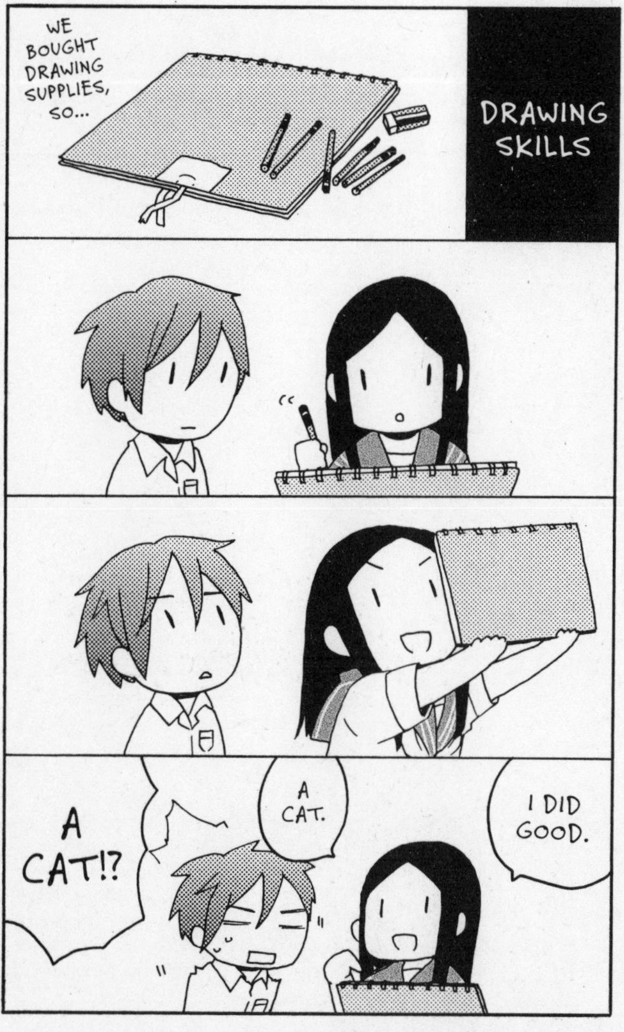
DRAWING SKILLS
WE BOUGHT DRAWING SUPPLIES, SO...
I DID GOOD.
A CAT.
A CAT!?

Love at Fourteen

Fuka Mizutani

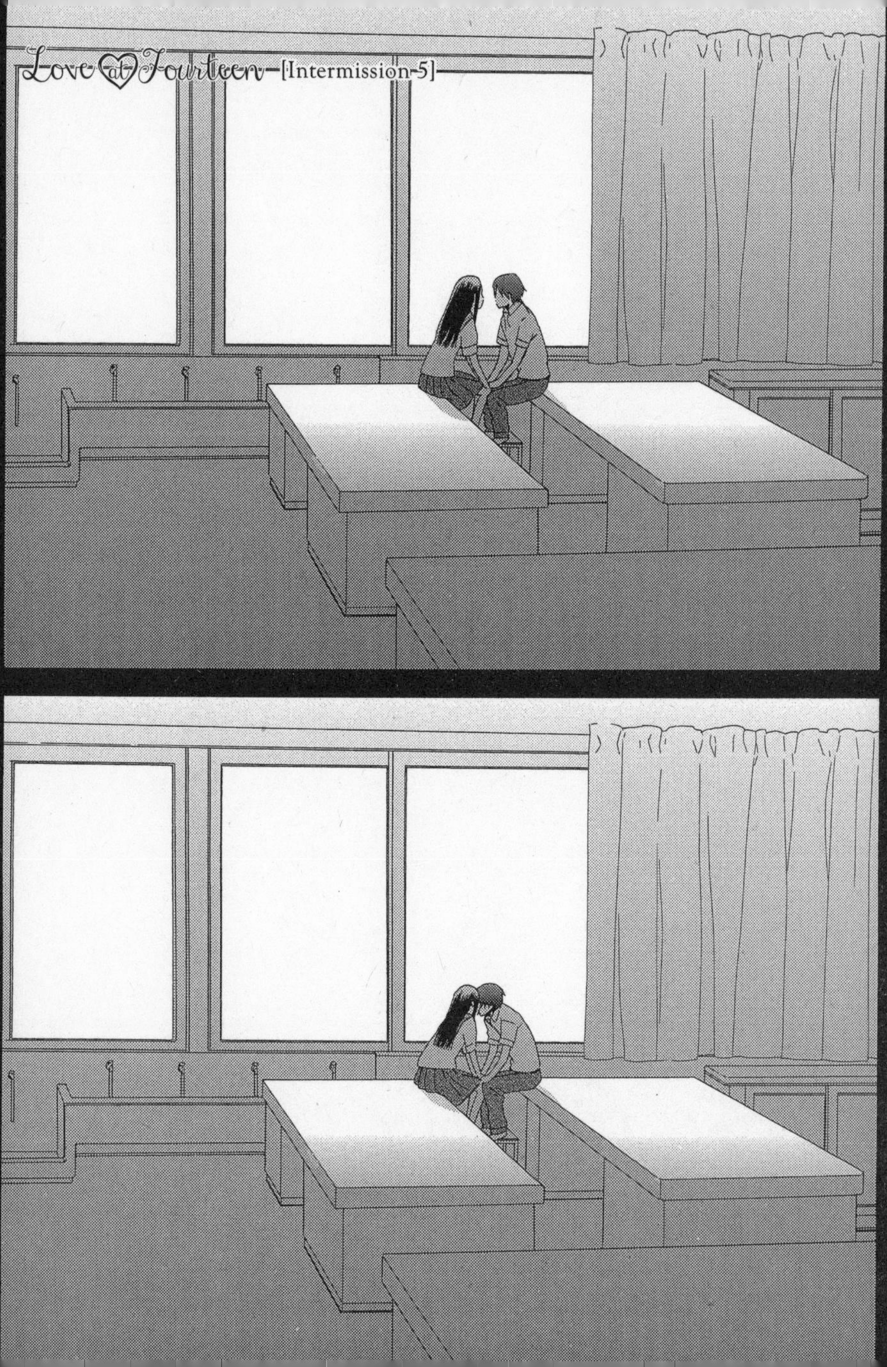
Love at Fourteen [Intermission-5]

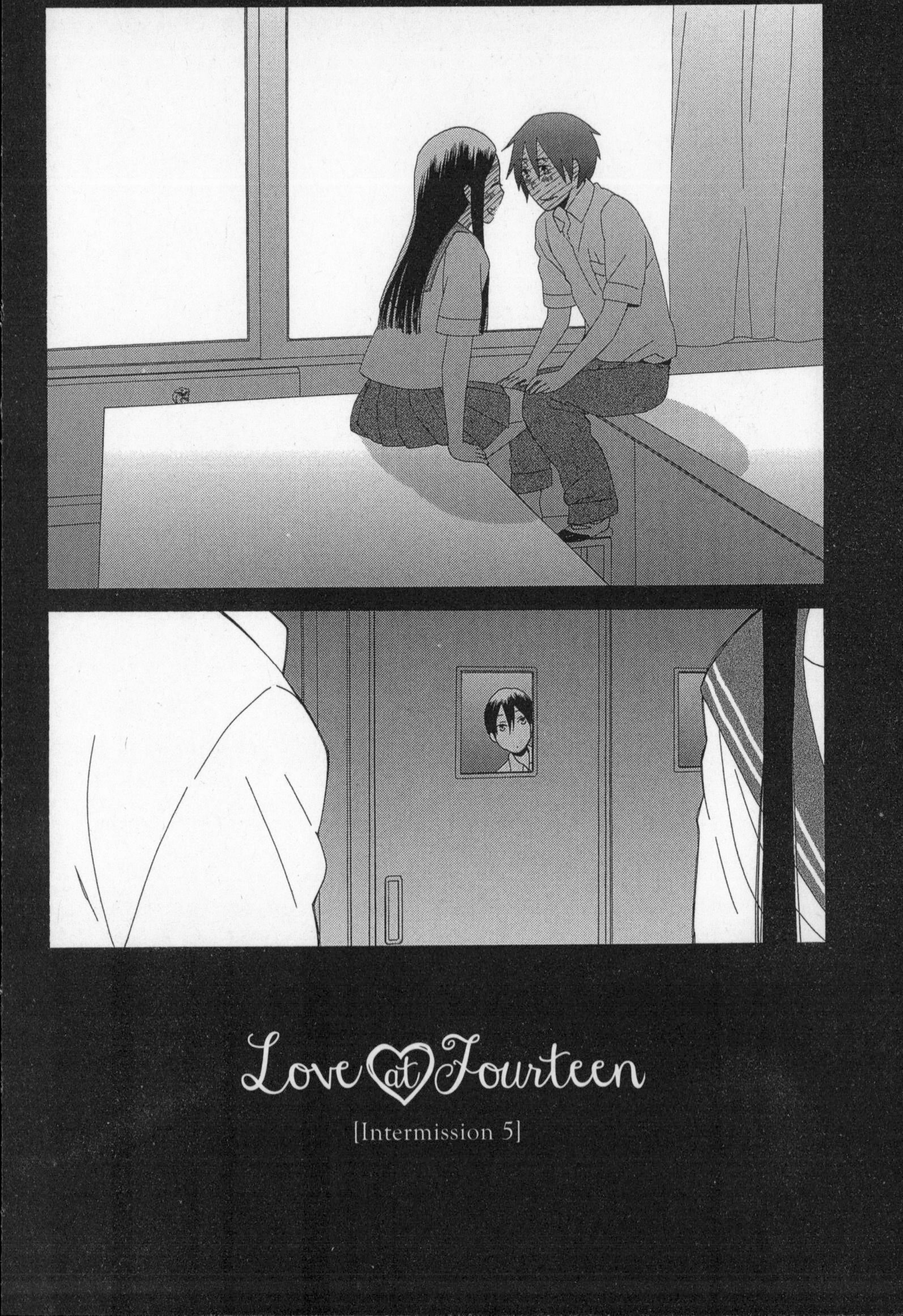

Love at Fourteen

[Intermission 5]

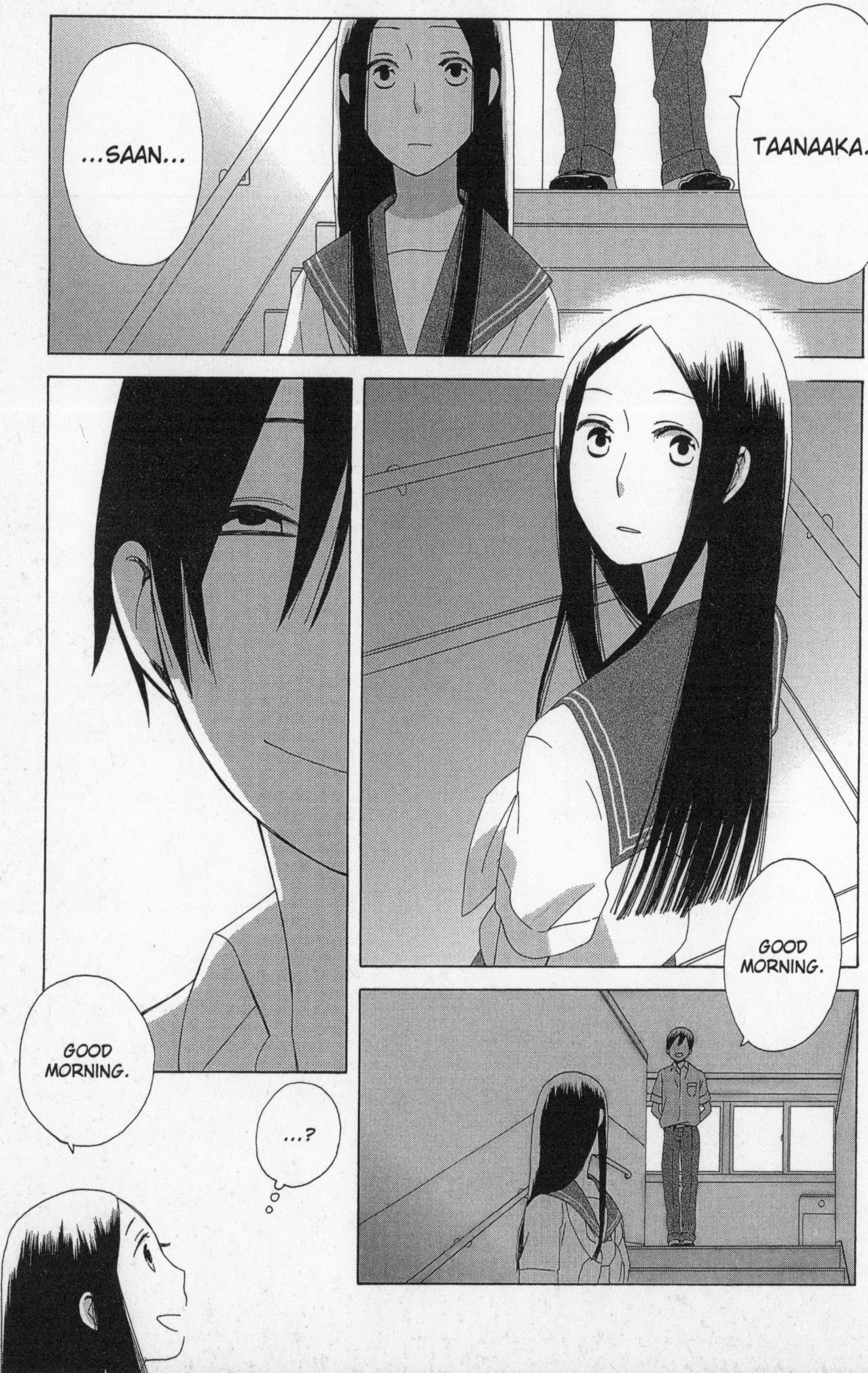
TAANAAKA...
...SAAN...
GOOD MORNING.
GOOD MORNING.
...?

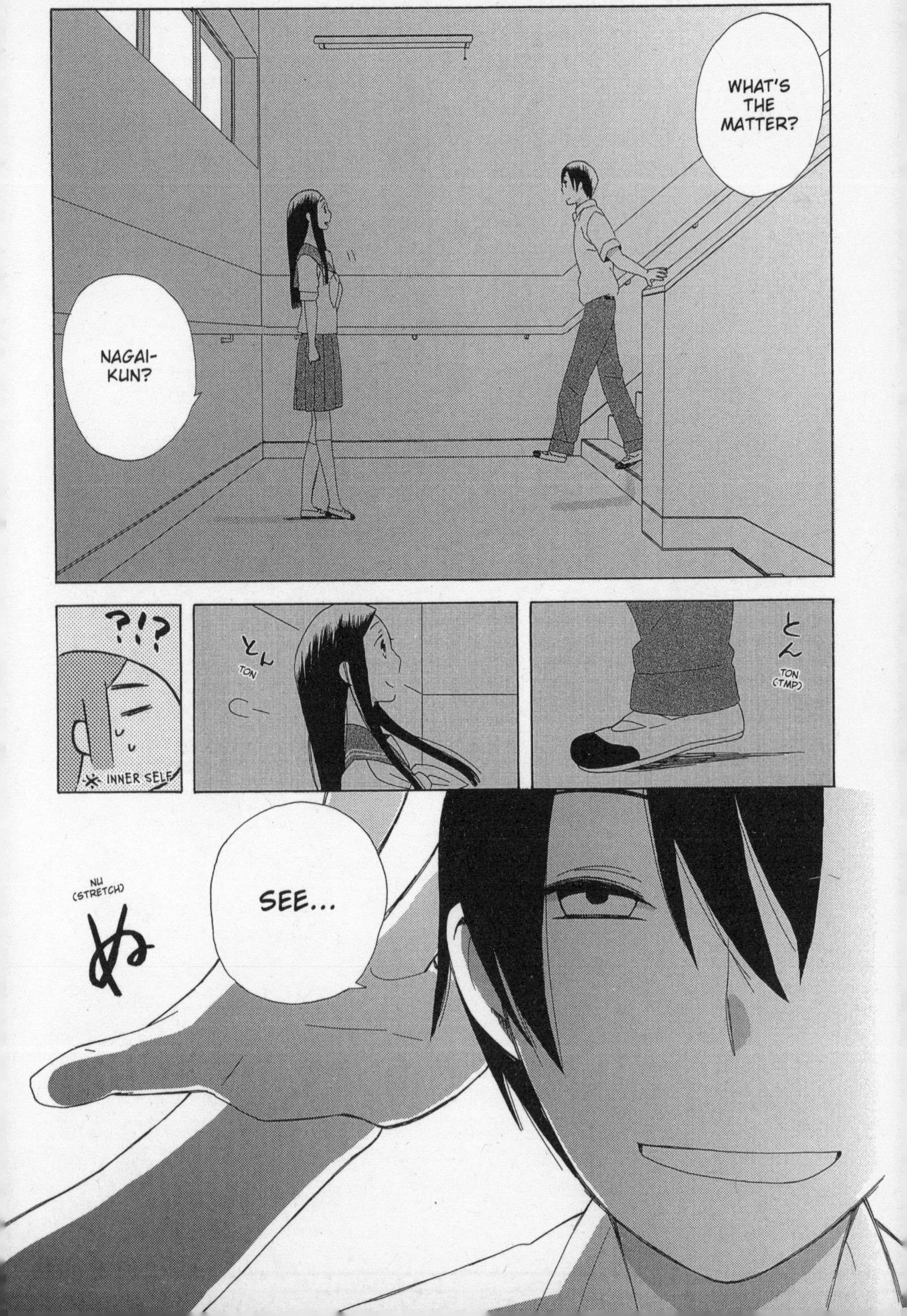
WHAT'S THE MATTER?
NAGAI-KUN?
とん
TON (TMP)
とん
TON
?!?
※ INNER SELF
SEE...
NU (STRETCH)
ぬ

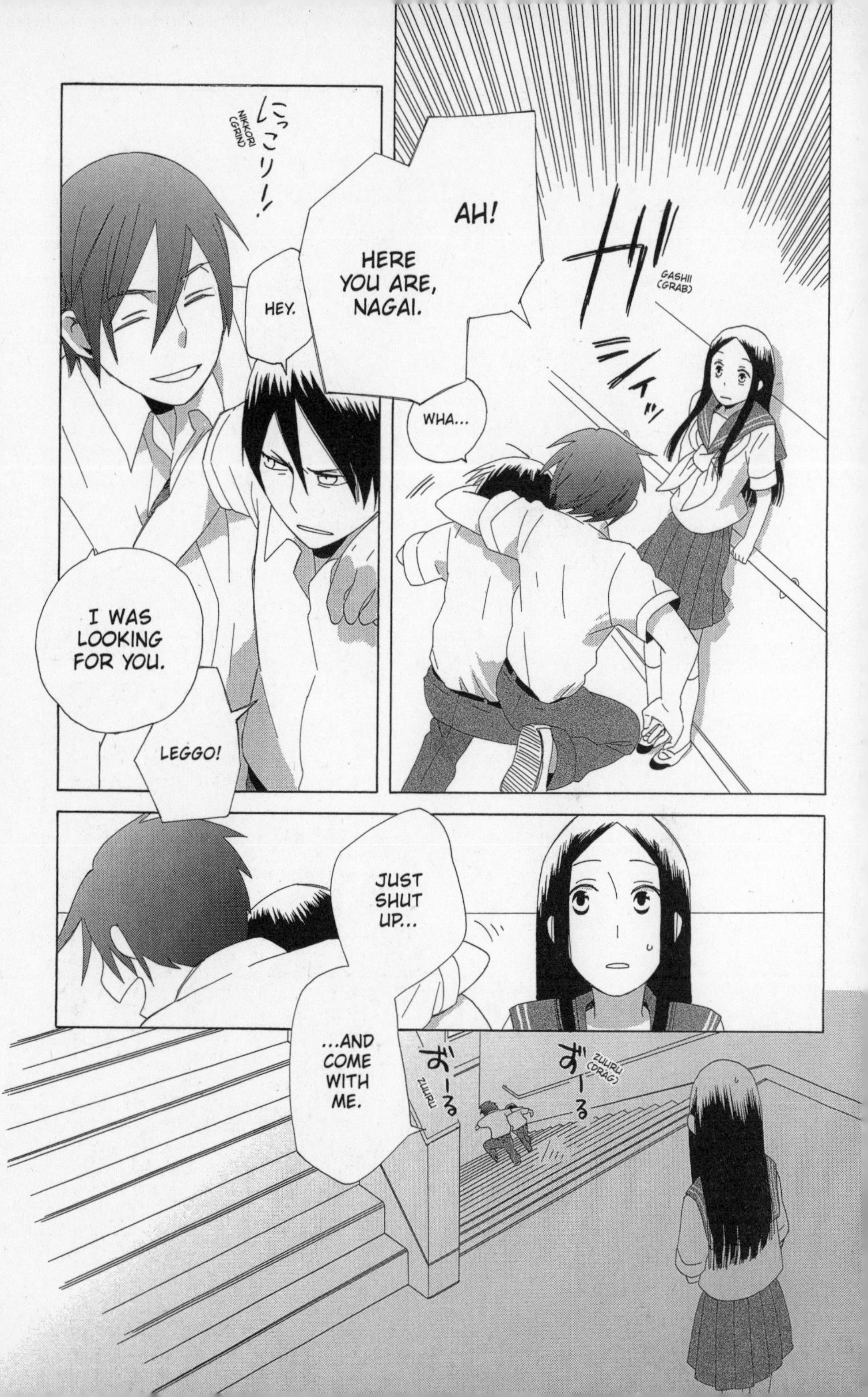
AH!
HERE YOU ARE, NAGAI.
GASHII (GRAB)
WHA...
にっこり!!
NIKKORI (GRIN)
HEY.
I WAS LOOKING FOR YOU.
LEGGO!
JUST SHUT UP...
...AND COME WITH ME.
ずーる
ZUURU (DRAG)
ずーる
ZUURU

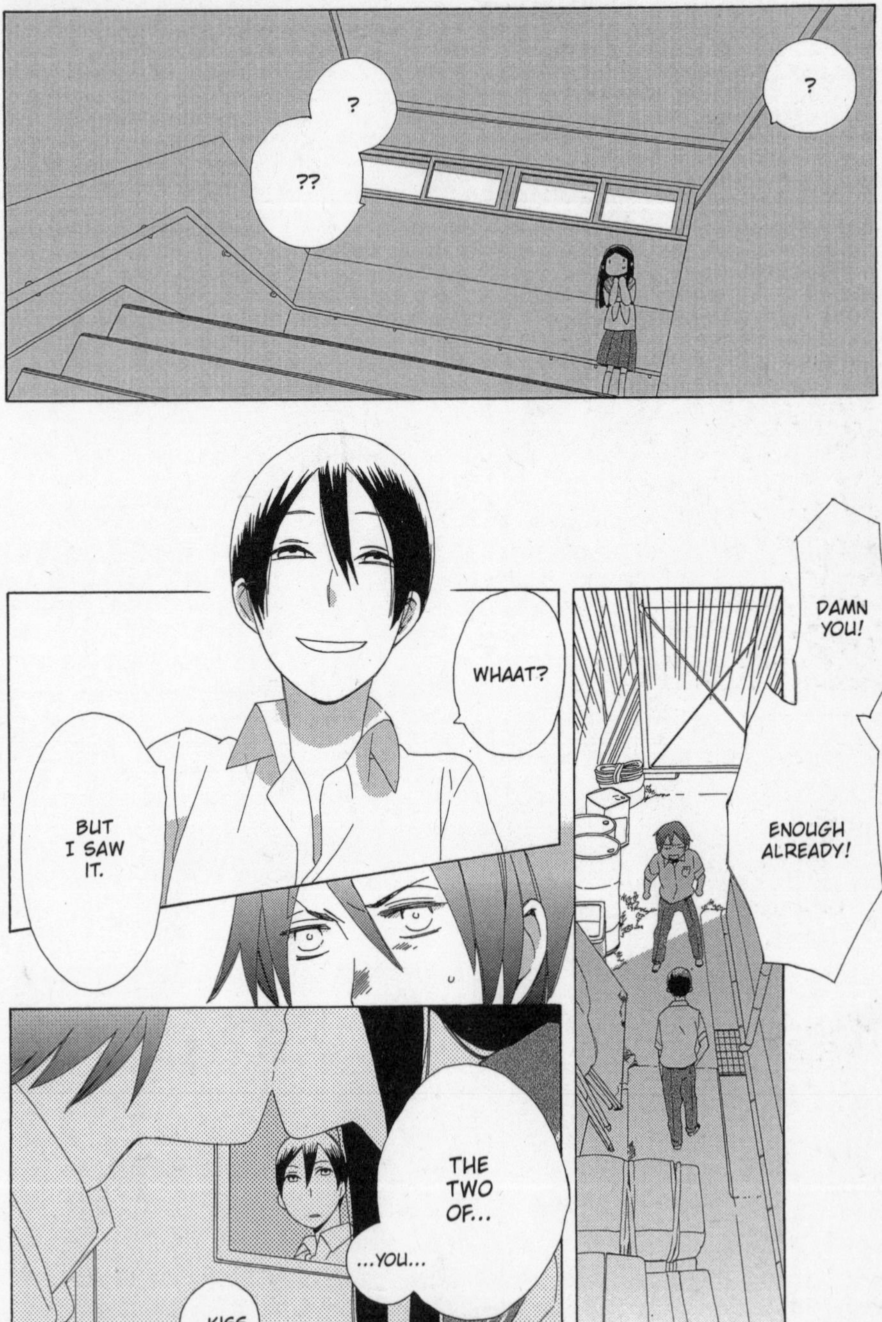
?
?
??
DAMN YOU!
ENOUGH ALREADY!
WHAAT?
BUT I SAW IT.
THE TWO OF...
...YOU...
...KISS.

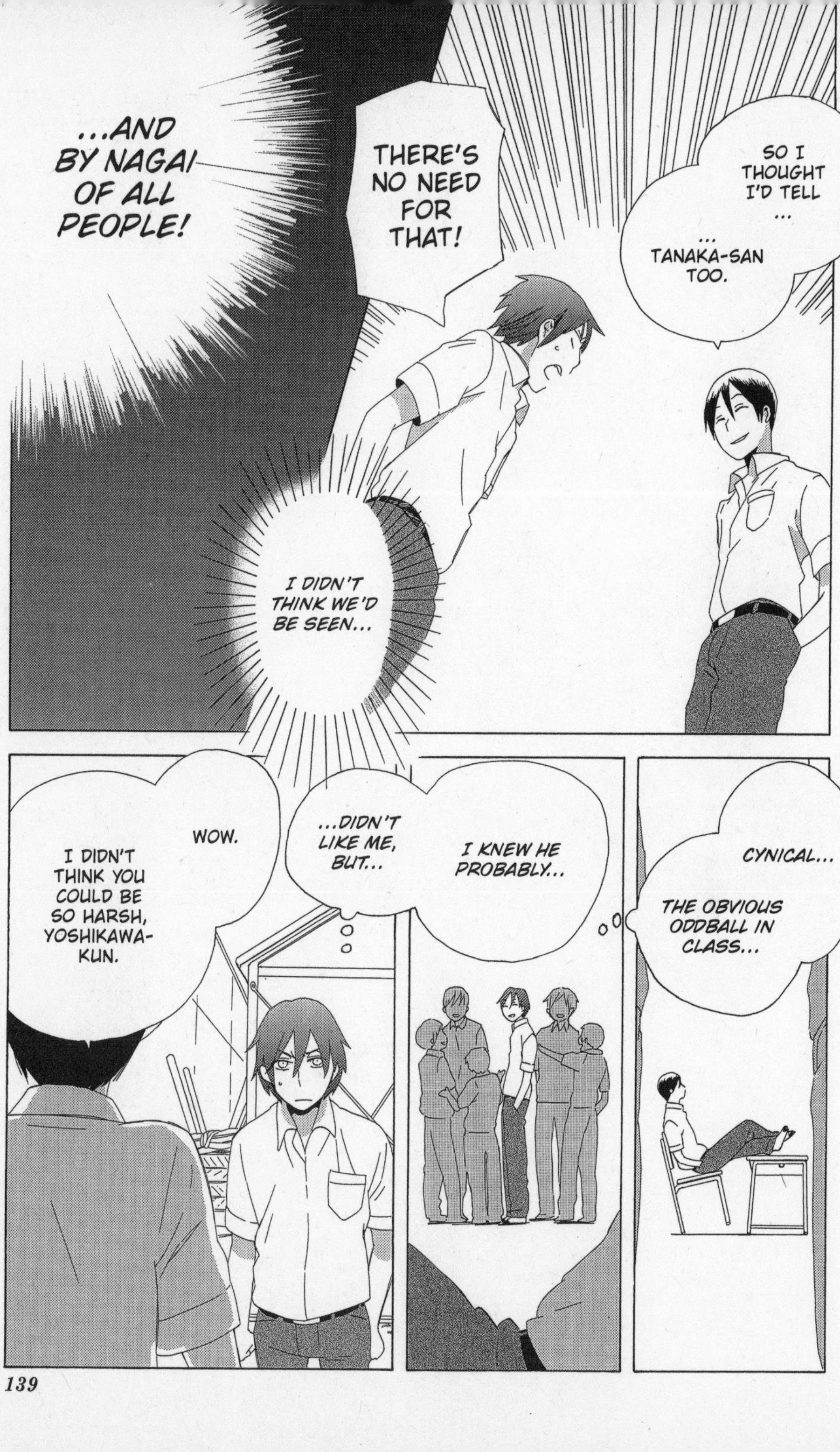
SO I THOUGHT I'D TELL ... ... TANAKA-SAN TOO.
THERE'S NO NEED FOR THAT!
...AND BY NAGAI OF ALL PEOPLE!
I DIDN'T THINK WE'D BE SEEN...
CYNICAL...
THE OBVIOUS ODDBALL IN CLASS...
I KNEW HE PROBABLY...
...DIDN'T LIKE ME, BUT...
WOW.
I DIDN'T THINK YOU COULD BE SO HARSH, YOSHIKAWA-KUN.

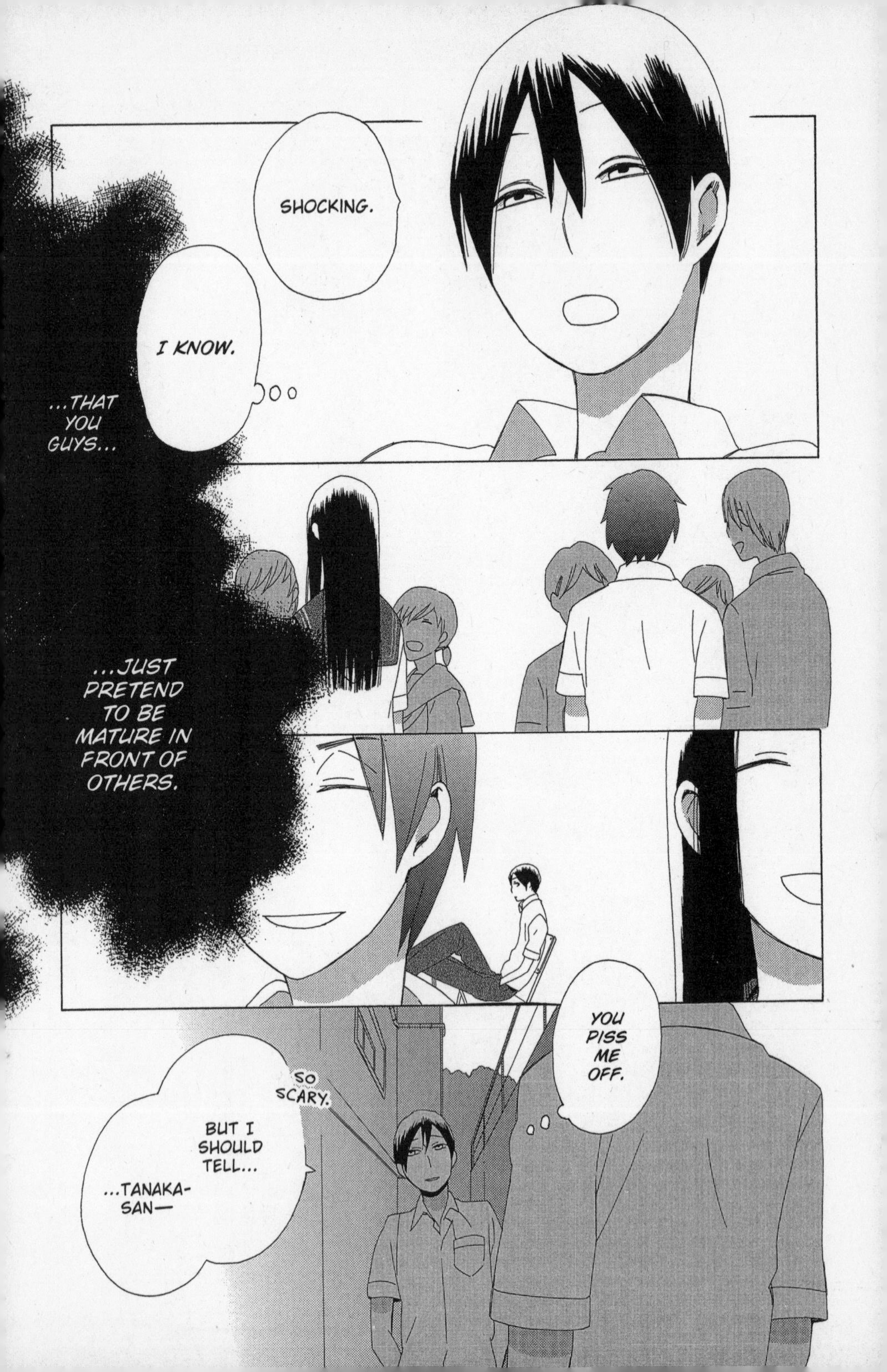
SHOCKING.
I KNOW.
...THAT YOU GUYS...
...JUST PRETEND TO BE MATURE IN FRONT OF OTHERS.
YOU PISS ME OFF.
SO SCARY.
BUT I SHOULD TELL... ...TANAKA-SAN—

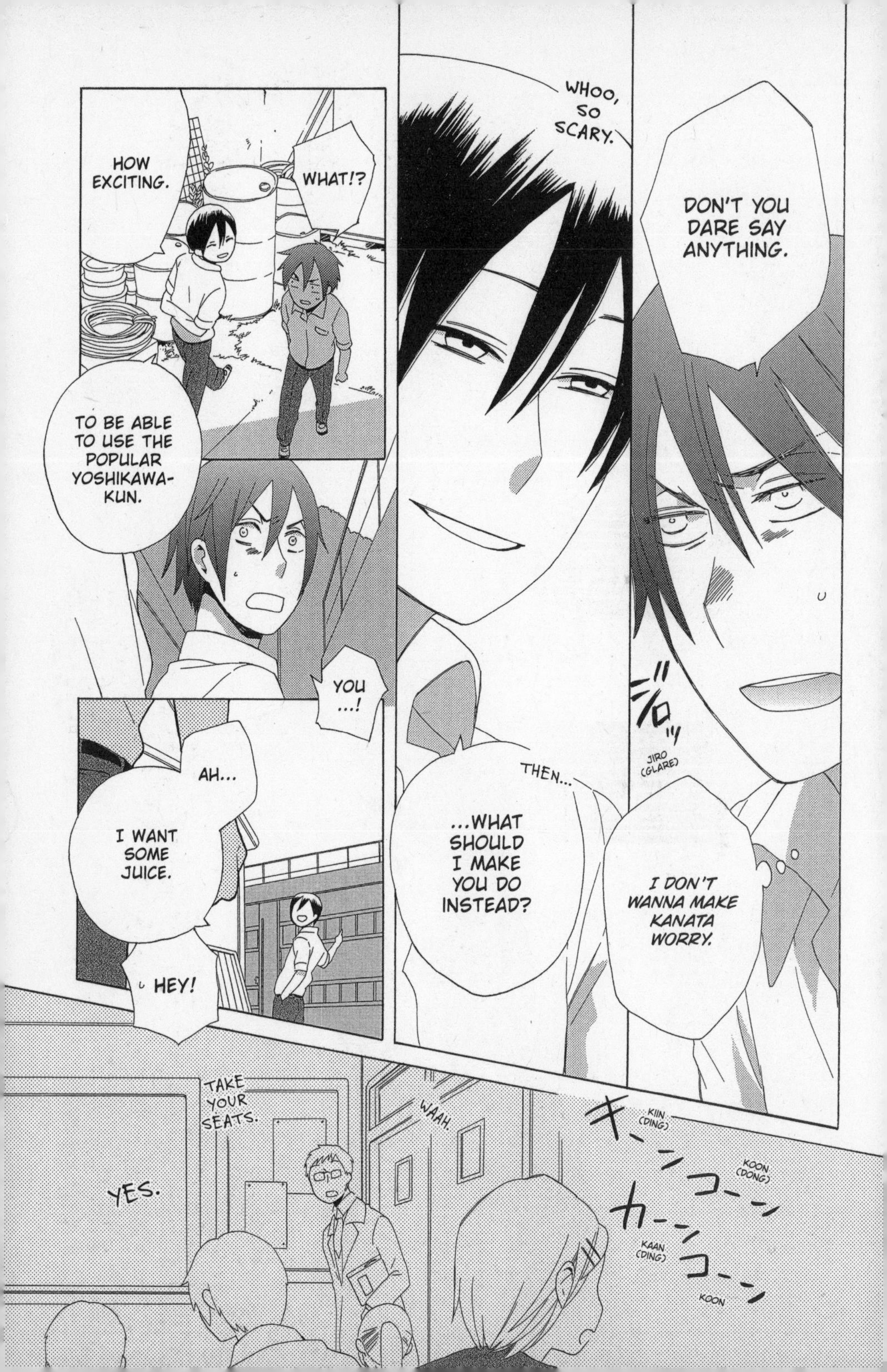
DON'T YOU DARE SAY ANYTHING.
JIRO (GLARE)
I DON'T WANNA MAKE KANATA WORRY.
WHOO, SO SCARY.
THEN...
...WHAT SHOULD I MAKE YOU DO INSTEAD?
HOW EXCITING.
WHAT!?
TO BE ABLE TO USE THE POPULAR YOSHIKAWA-KUN.
YOU ...!
AH...
I WANT SOME JUICE.
HEY!
KIIN (DING)
KOON (DONG)
KAAN (DING)
KOON
WAAH.
TAKE YOUR SEATS.
YES.

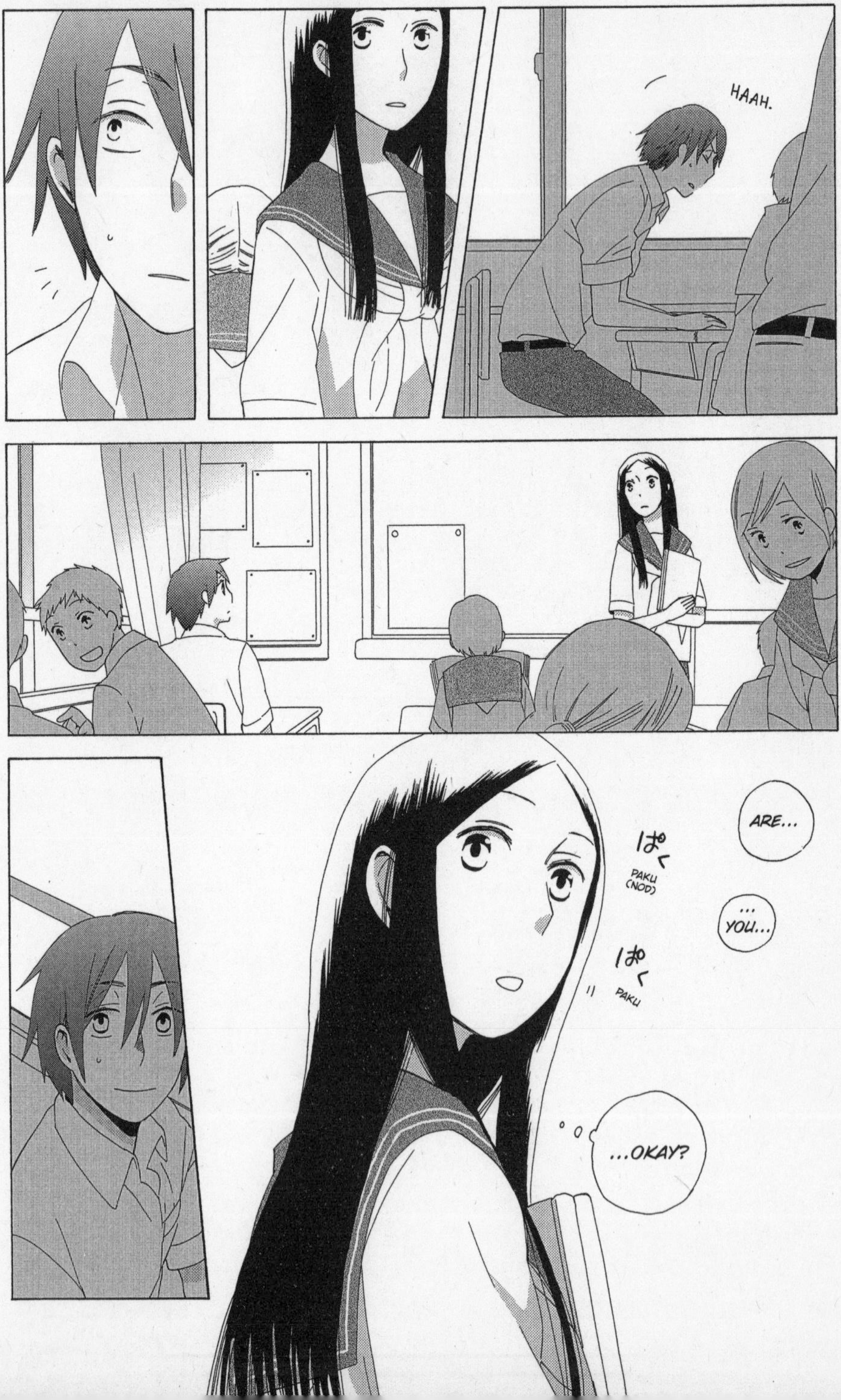
HAAH.
ARE...
ぱく
PAKU (NOD)
...YOU...
ぱく
PAKU
...OKAY?

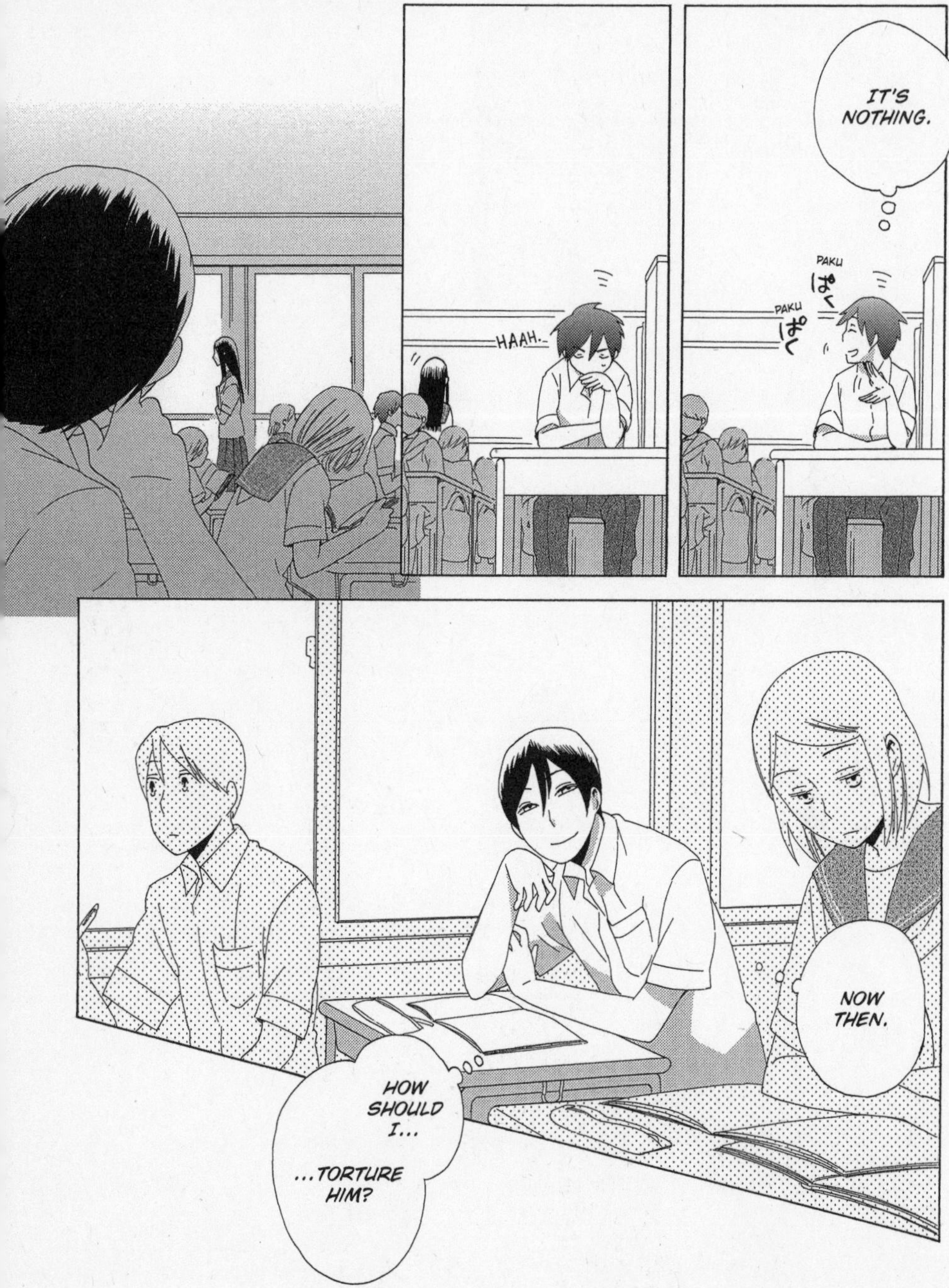
IT'S NOTHING.
PAKU
ぱく
PAKU
ぱく
HAAH.
NOW THEN.
HOW SHOULD I...
...TORTURE HIM?

Fin

Love at Fourteen

Fuka Mizutani

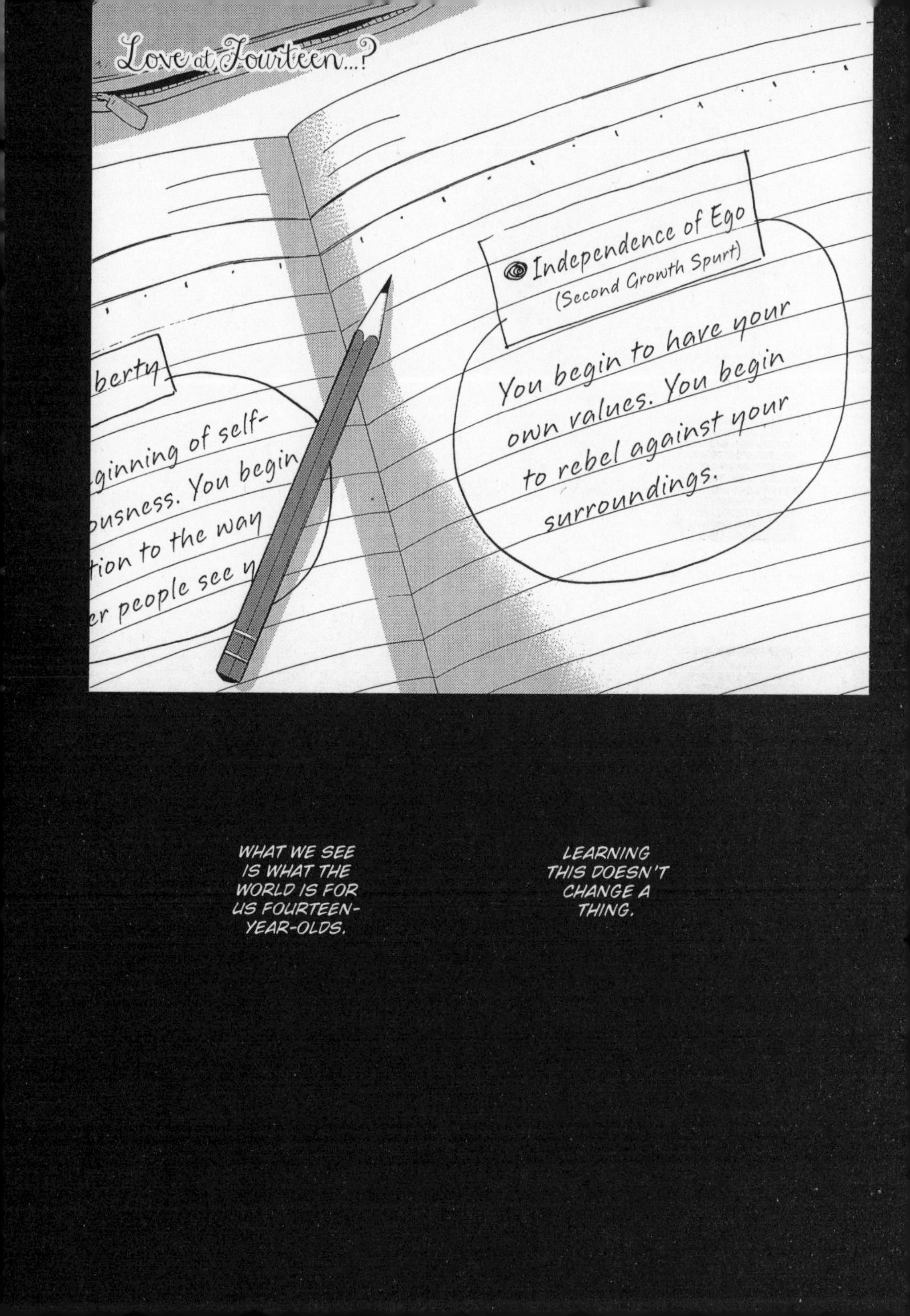
Love at Fourteen...?
Independence of Ego
(Second Growth Spurt)
You begin to have your own values. You begin to rebel against your surroundings.
berty
ginning of self-
usness. You begin
tion to the way
er people see y
WHAT WE SEE IS WHAT THE WORLD IS FOR US FOURTEEN-YEAR-OLDS.
LEARNING THIS DOESN'T CHANGE A THING.

Love at Fourteen...?

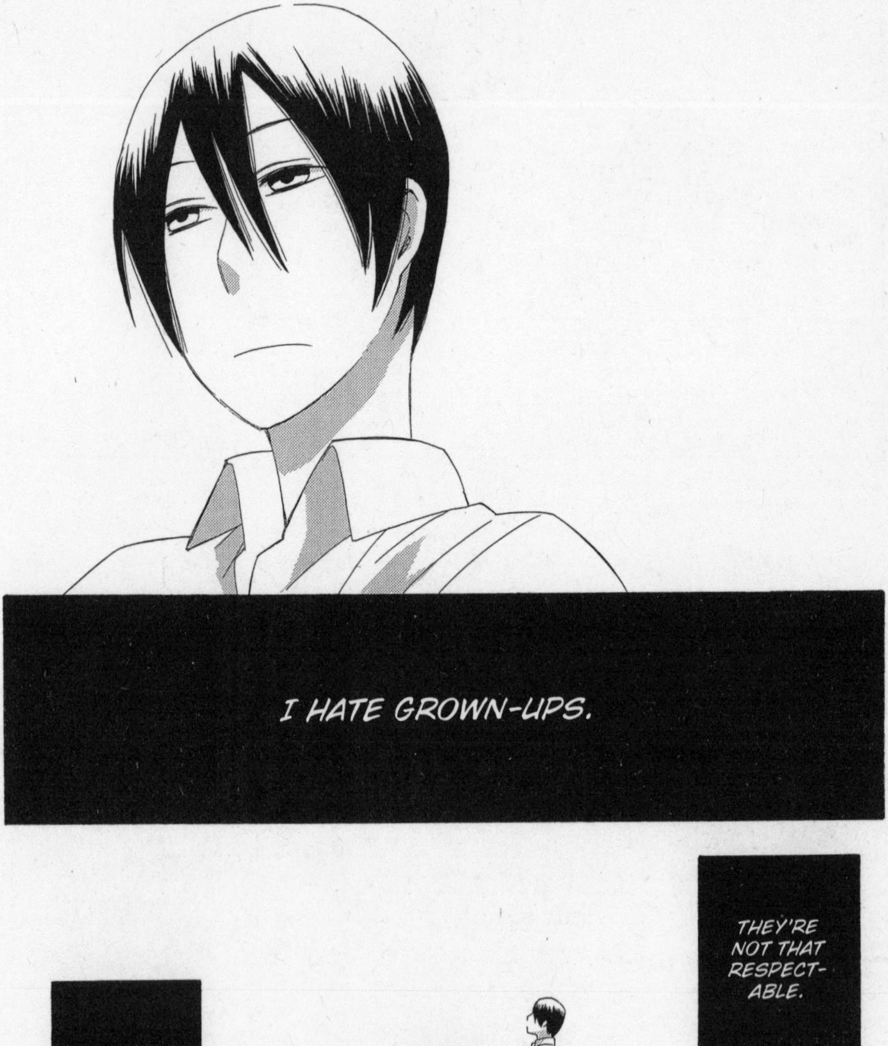
I HATE GROWN-UPS.
THEY'RE NOT THAT RESPECT-ABLE.
BUT THEY TALK SO BIG.

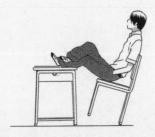

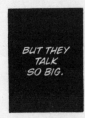

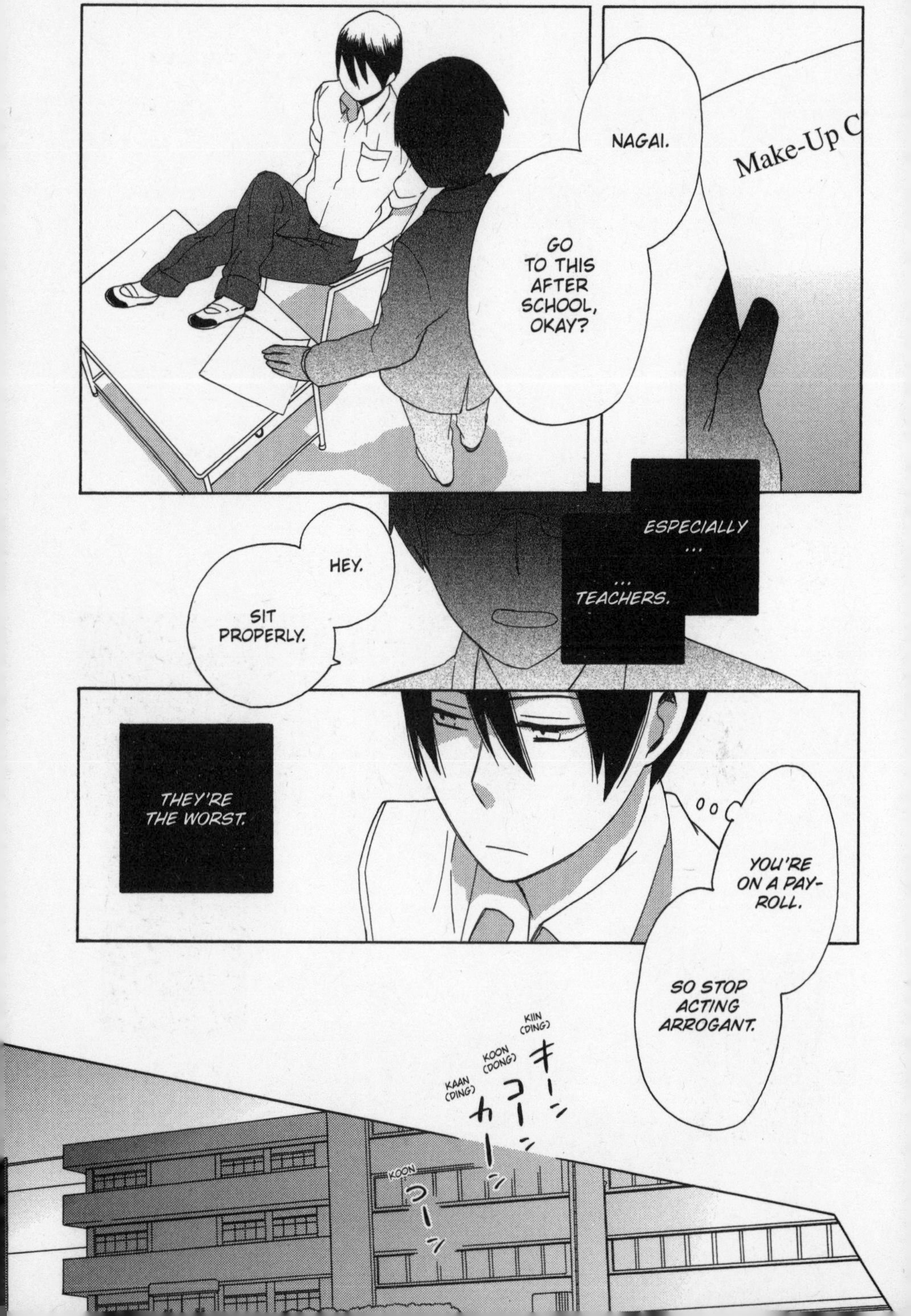
Make-Up C
NAGAI.
GO TO THIS AFTER SCHOOL, OKAY?
ESPECIALLY...
...TEACHERS.
HEY.
SIT PROPERLY.
...
YOU'RE ON A PAYROLL.
SO STOP ACTING ARROGANT.
THEY'RE THE WORST.
KIIN (DING)
キーン
KOON (DONG)
コーン
KAAN (DING)
カーン
KOON
コーン

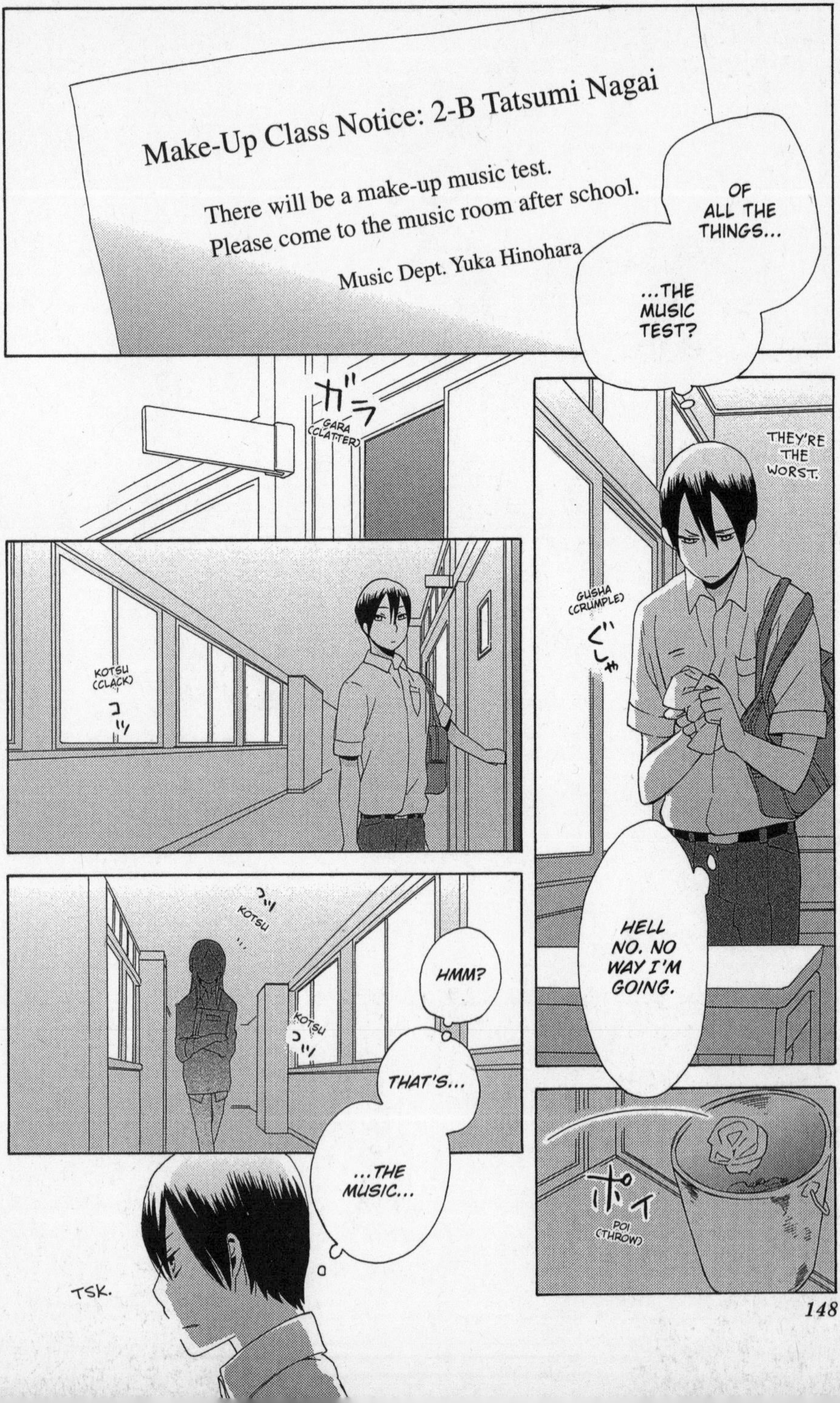
Make-Up Class Notice: 2-B Tatsumi Nagai
There will be a make-up music test.
Please come to the music room after school.
Music Dept. Yuka Hinohara
OF ALL THE THINGS...
...THE MUSIC TEST?
THEY'RE THE WORST.
ぐしゃ
GUSHA (CRUMPLE)
HELL NO. NO WAY I'M GOING.
ポイ
POI (THROW)
ガラ
GARA (CLATTER)
コツ
KOTSU (CLACK)
コツ
KOTSU
コツ
KOTSU
HMM?
THAT'S...
...THE MUSIC...
TSK.

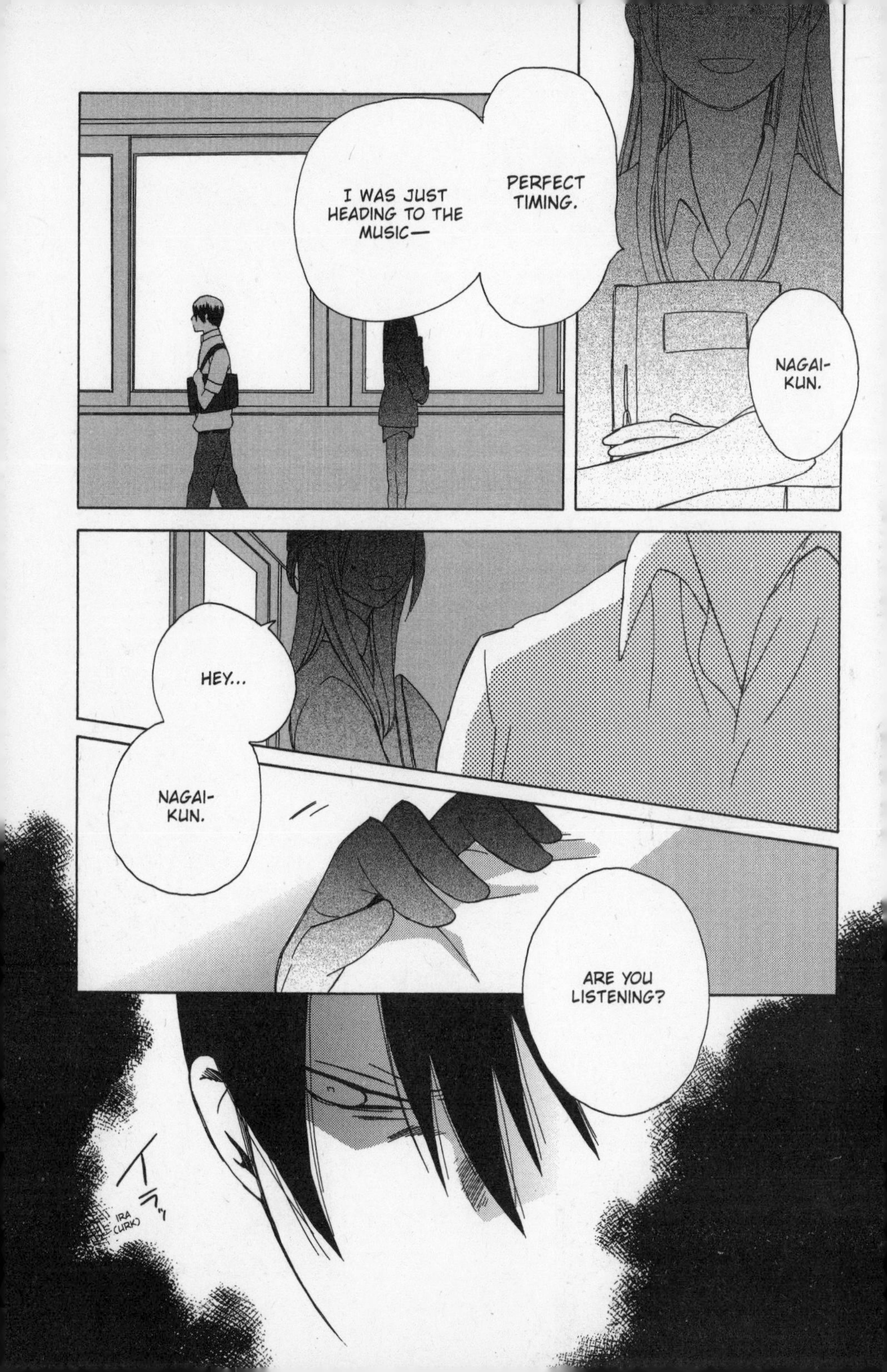
NAGAI-KUN.
PERFECT TIMING.
I WAS JUST HEADING TO THE MUSIC—
HEY...
NAGAI-KUN.
ARE YOU LISTENING?
IRA (URK)

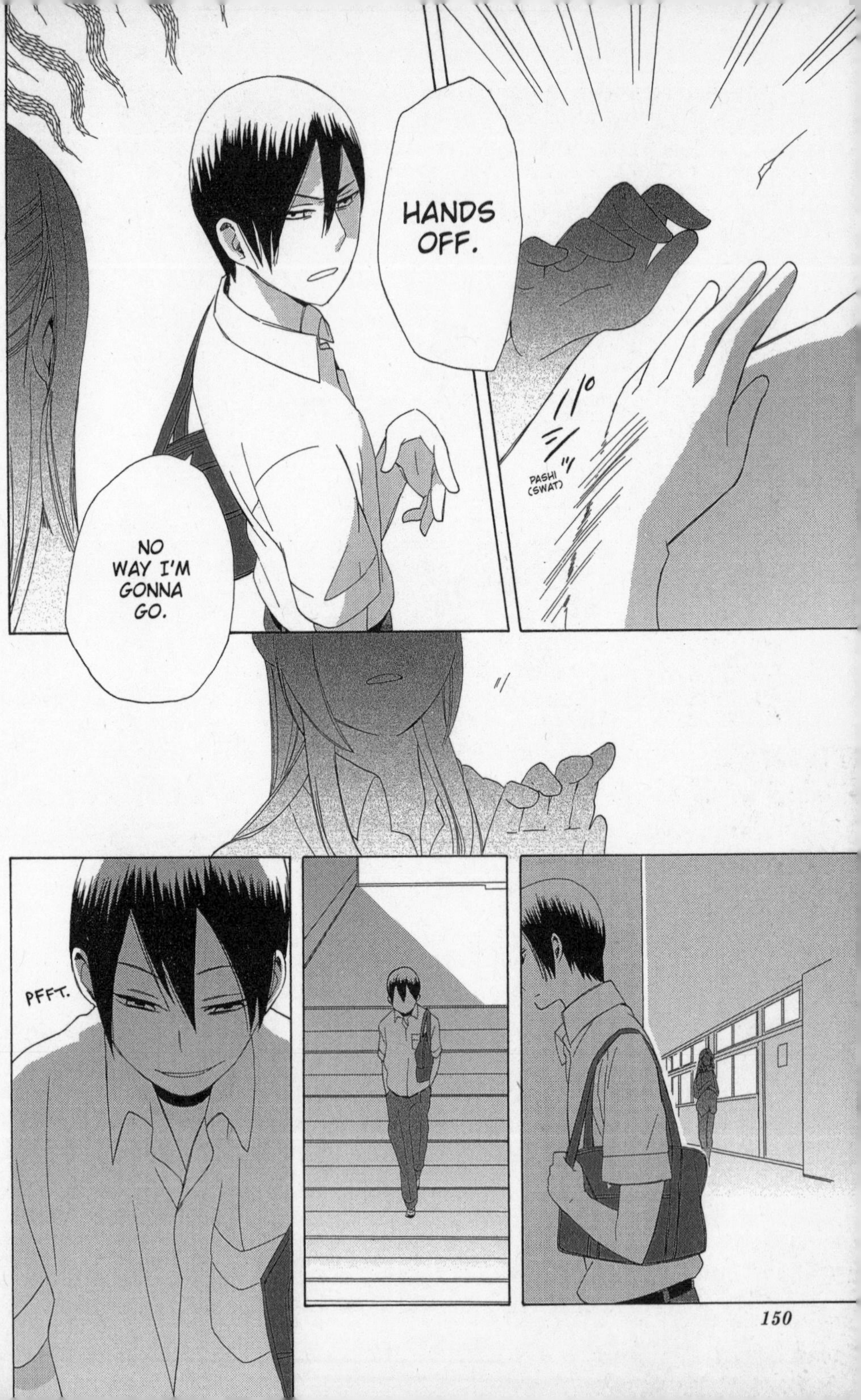
PASHI (SWAT)
HANDS OFF.
NO WAY I'M GONNA GO.
PFFT.

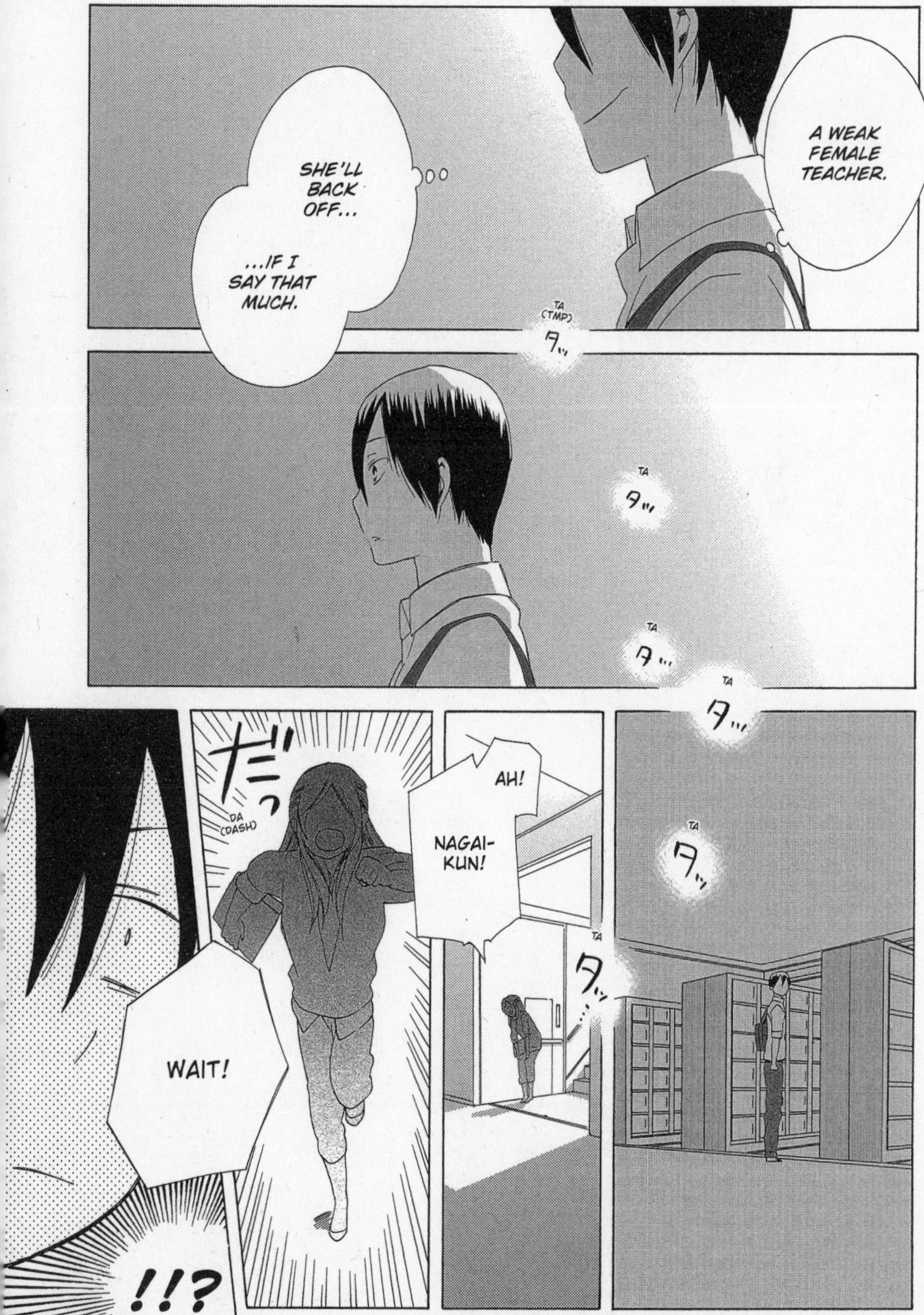
A WEAK FEMALE TEACHER.
SHE'LL BACK OFF...
...IF I SAY THAT MUCH.
TA (TMP)
タッ
TA
タッ
TA
タッ
TA
タッ
TA
タッ
TA
タッ
AH!
NAGAI-KUN!
だっ
DA (DASH)
WAIT!
!!?

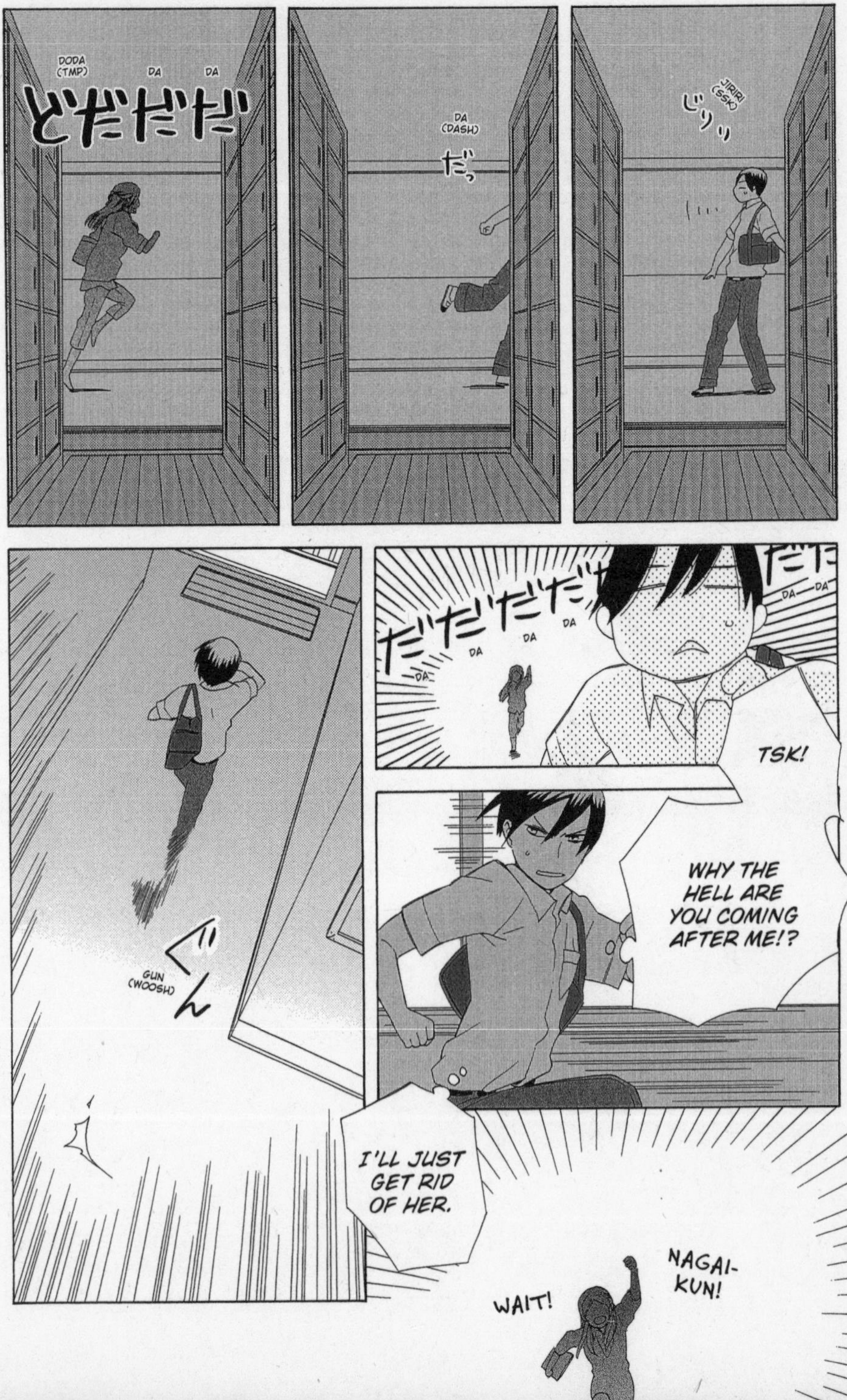
JIRIRI (SSK)
じりり
DA (DASH)
だっ
DODA (TMP) DA DA
どだだだ
だだ
DA DA
だだだだだ
DA DA DA DA
TSK!
WHY THE HELL ARE YOU COMING AFTER ME!?
GUN (WOOSH)
ぐん
I'LL JUST GET RID OF HER.
NAGAI-KUN!
WAIT!

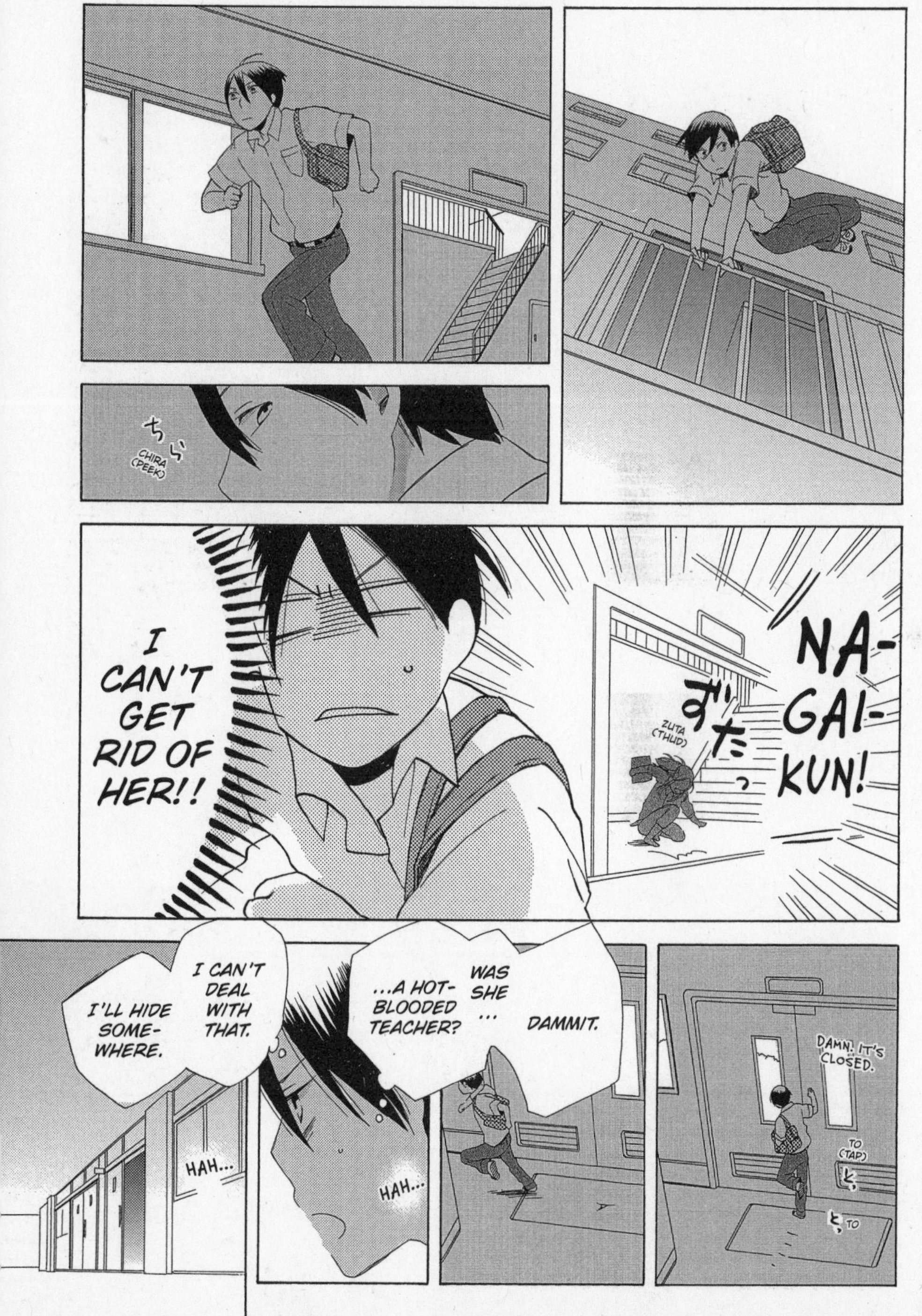
ちら
CHIRA (PEEK)
NA-GAI-KUN!
ずたっ
ZUTA (THUD)
I CAN'T GET RID OF HER!!
DAMN. IT'S CLOSED.
と、と
TO (TAP)
TO
DAMMIT.
WAS SHE ...
...A HOT-BLOODED TEACHER?
HAH...
HAH...
I CAN'T DEAL WITH THAT.
I'LL HIDE SOMEWHERE.

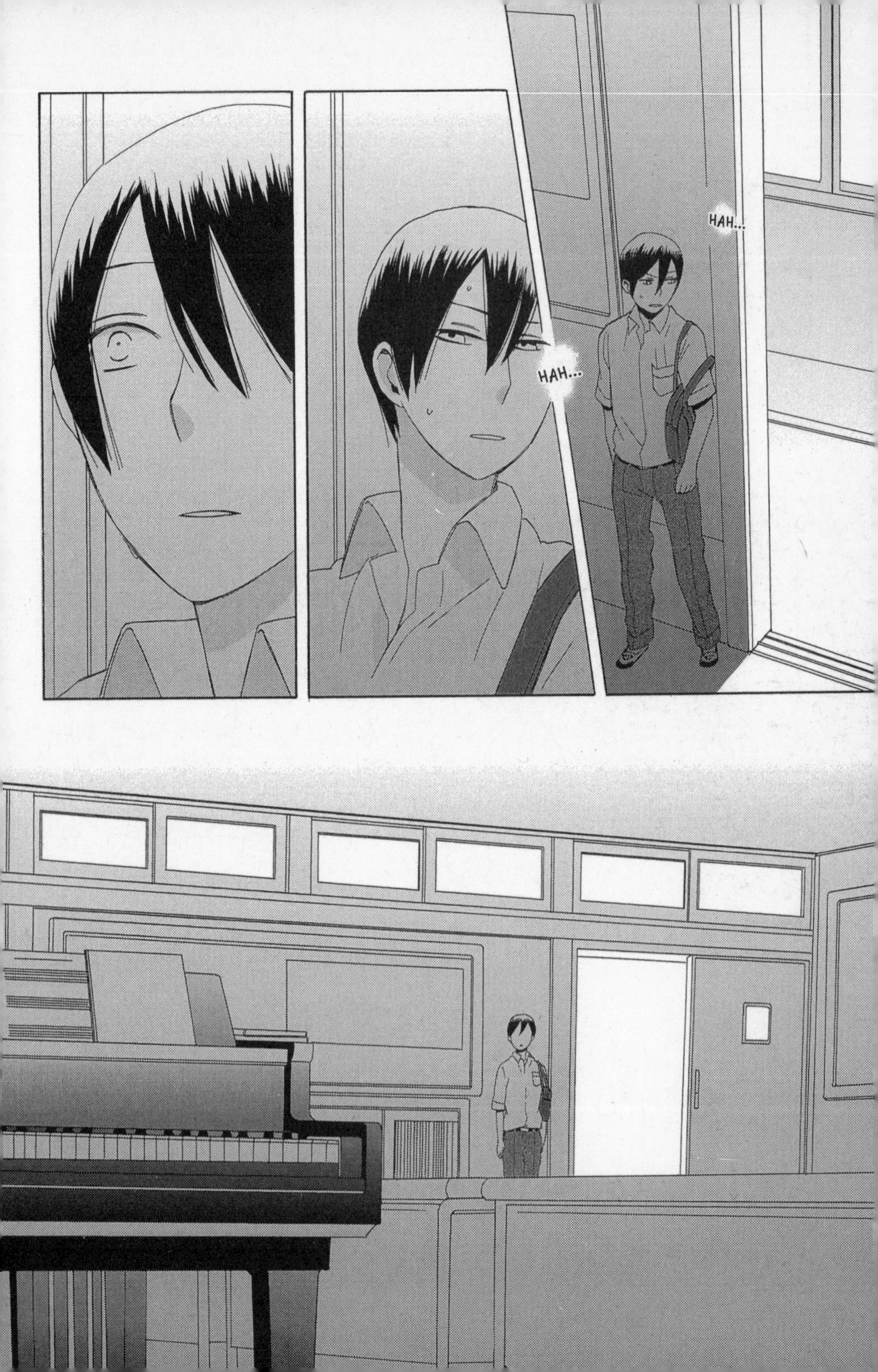
HAH...
HAH...

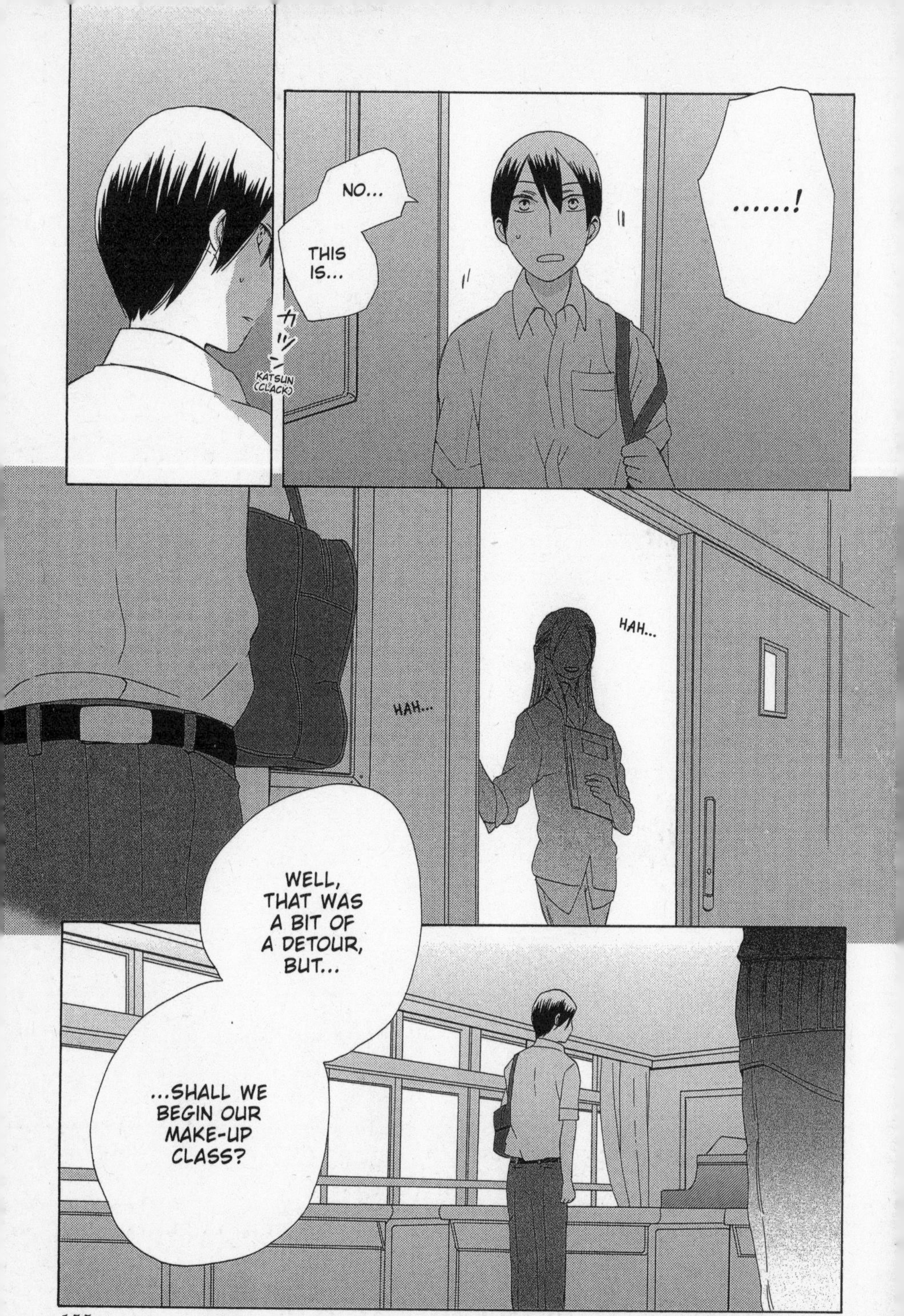

......!
NO...
THIS IS...
KATSUN (CLACK)
HAH...
HAH...
WELL, THAT WAS A BIT OF A DETOUR, BUT...
...SHALL WE BEGIN OUR MAKE-UP CLASS?

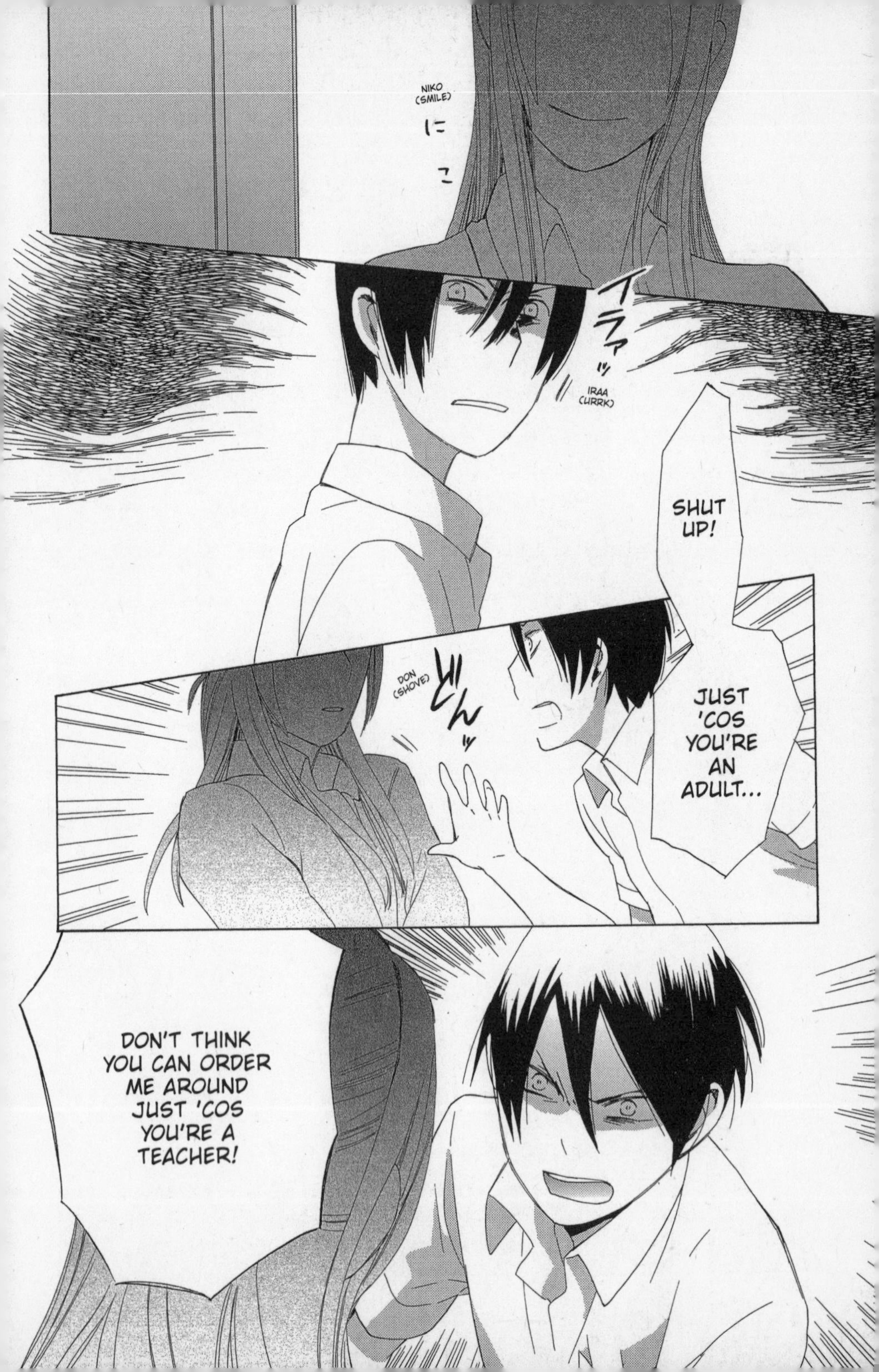
にこ
NIKO (SMILE)
イラァッ
IRAA (URRK)
SHUT UP!
JUST 'COS YOU'RE AN ADULT...
どんッ
DON (SHOVE)
DON'T THINK YOU CAN ORDER ME AROUND JUST 'COS YOU'RE A TEACHER!

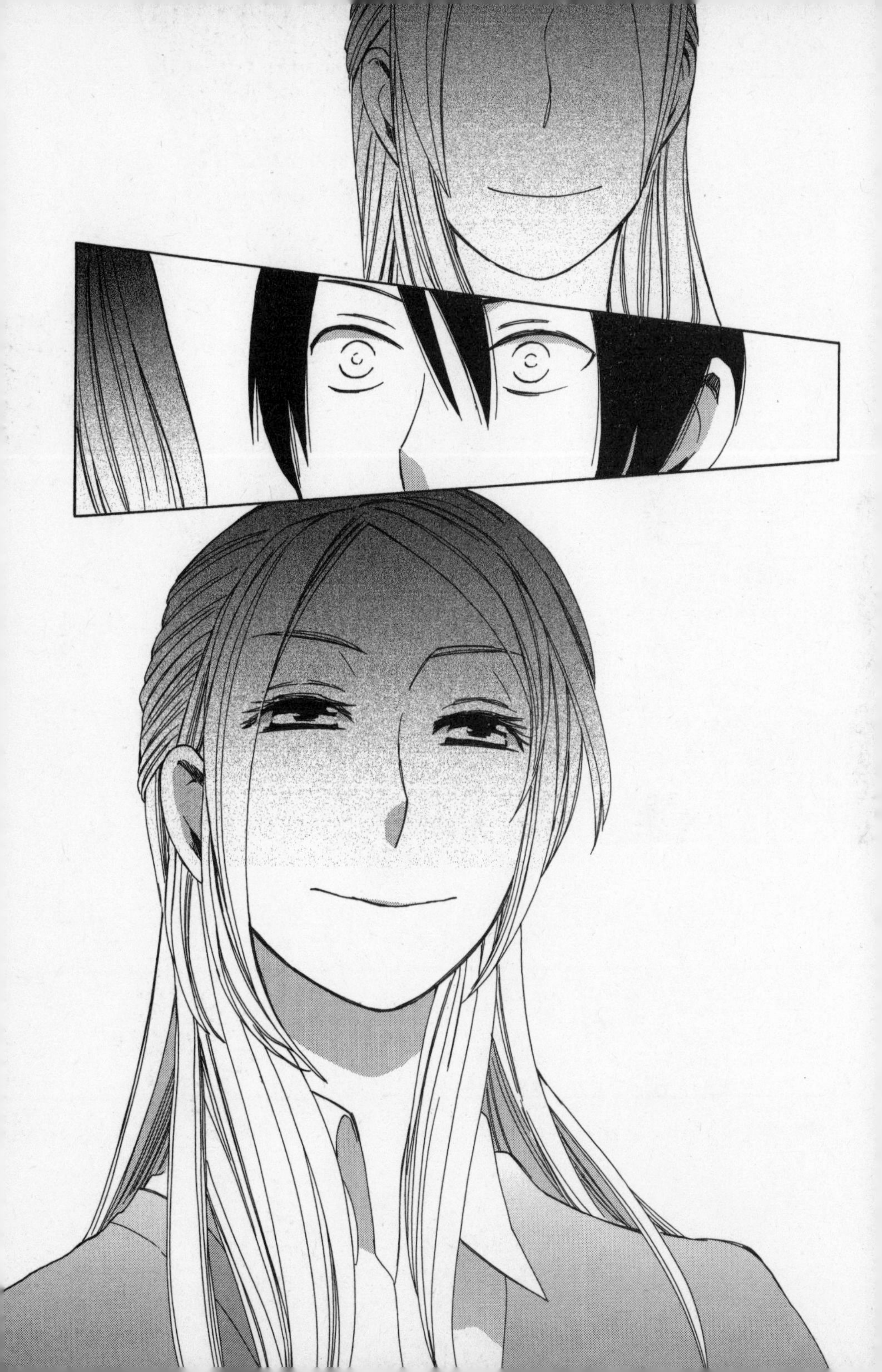

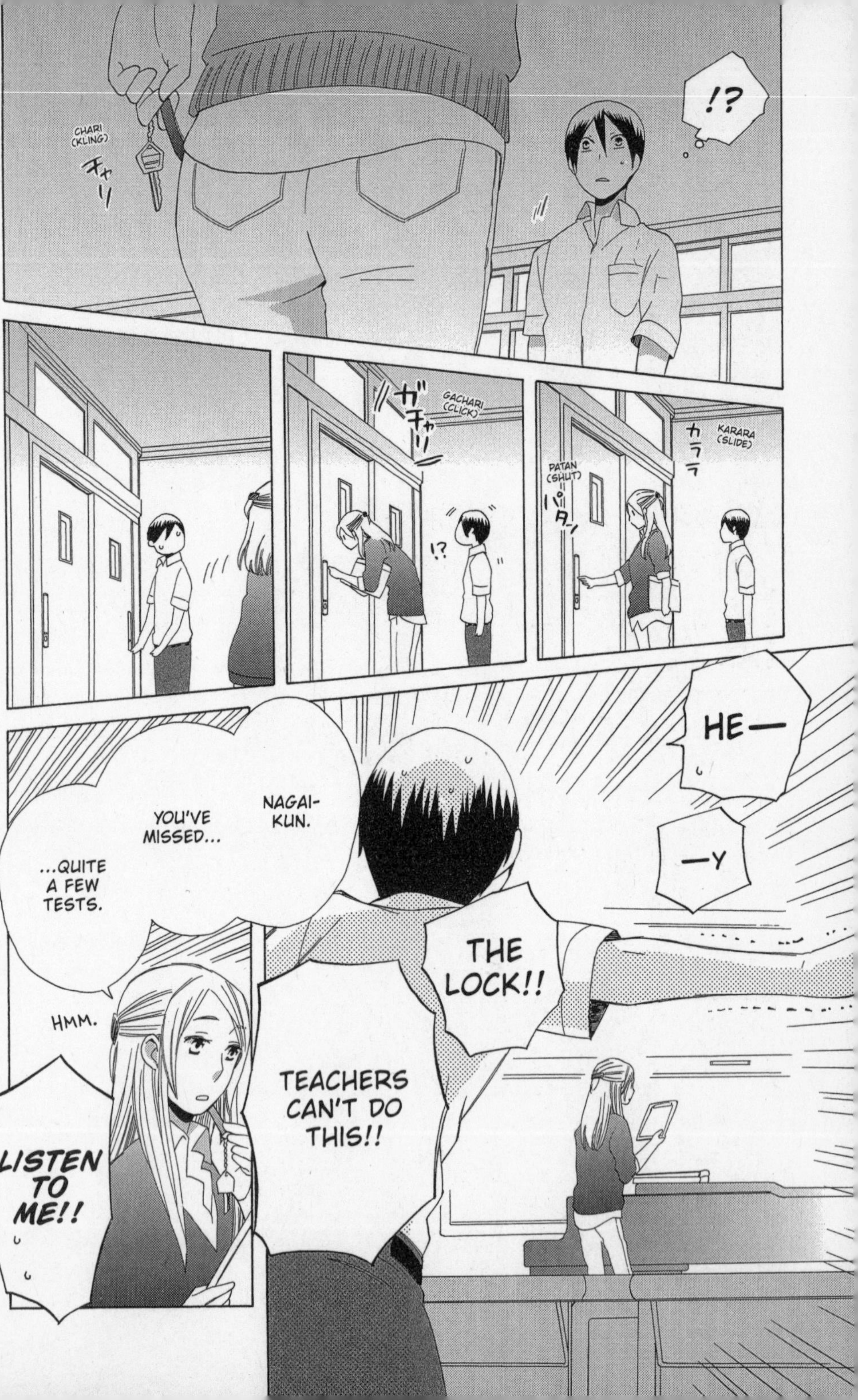
!?
CHARI (KLING)
チャリ
KARARA (SLIDE)
カララ
PATAN (SHUT)
パタン
GACHARI (CLICK)
ガチャリ
!?
HE—
—Y
THE LOCK!!
TEACHERS CAN'T DO THIS!!
NAGAI-KUN.
YOU'VE MISSED...
...QUITE A FEW TESTS.
HMM.
LISTEN TO ME!!

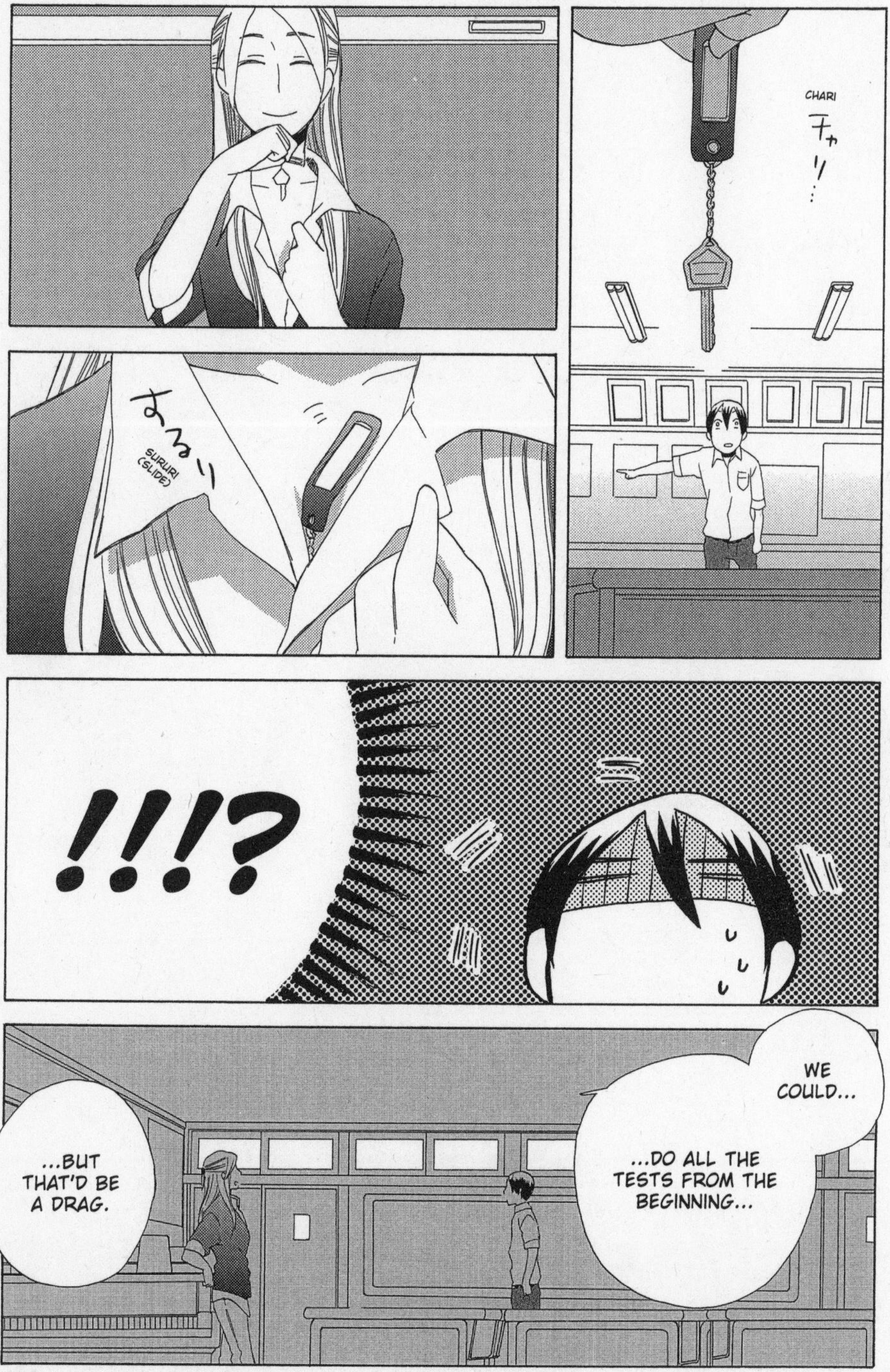
CHARI
チャリ…
するり
SURURI (SLIDE)
!!!?
WE COULD...
...DO ALL THE TESTS FROM THE BEGINNING...
...BUT THAT'D BE A DRAG.

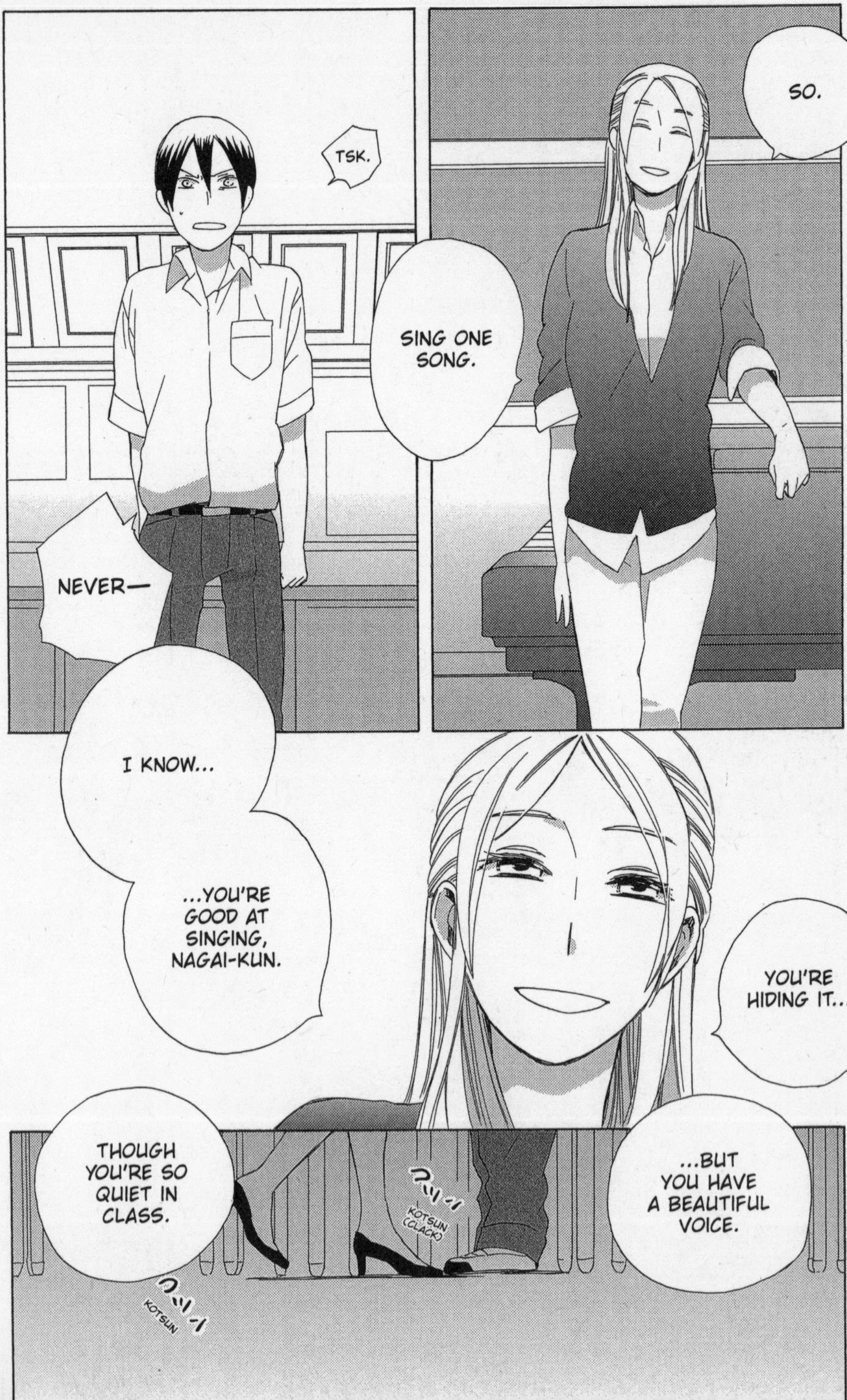
SO.
SING ONE SONG.
TSK.
NEVER—
I KNOW...
...YOU'RE GOOD AT SINGING, NAGAI-KUN.
YOU'RE HIDING IT...
...BUT YOU HAVE A BEAUTIFUL VOICE.
THOUGH YOU'RE SO QUIET IN CLASS.
KOTSUN (CLACK)
KOTSUN

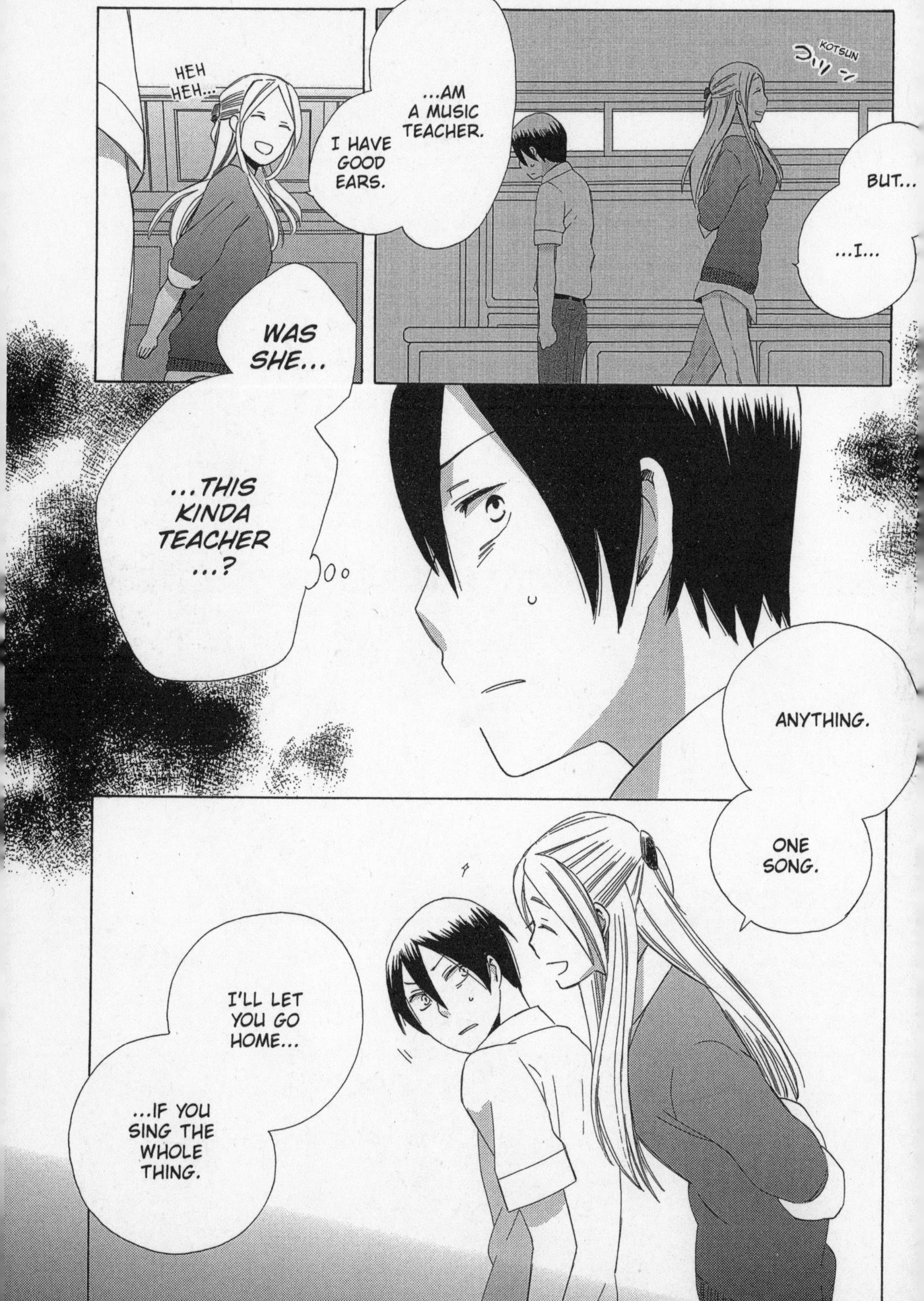
KOTSUN
BUT...
...I...
...AM A MUSIC TEACHER.
I HAVE GOOD EARS.
HEH HEH...
WAS SHE...
...THIS KINDA TEACHER ...?
ANYTHING.
ONE SONG.
I'LL LET YOU GO HOME...
...IF YOU SING THE WHOLE THING.

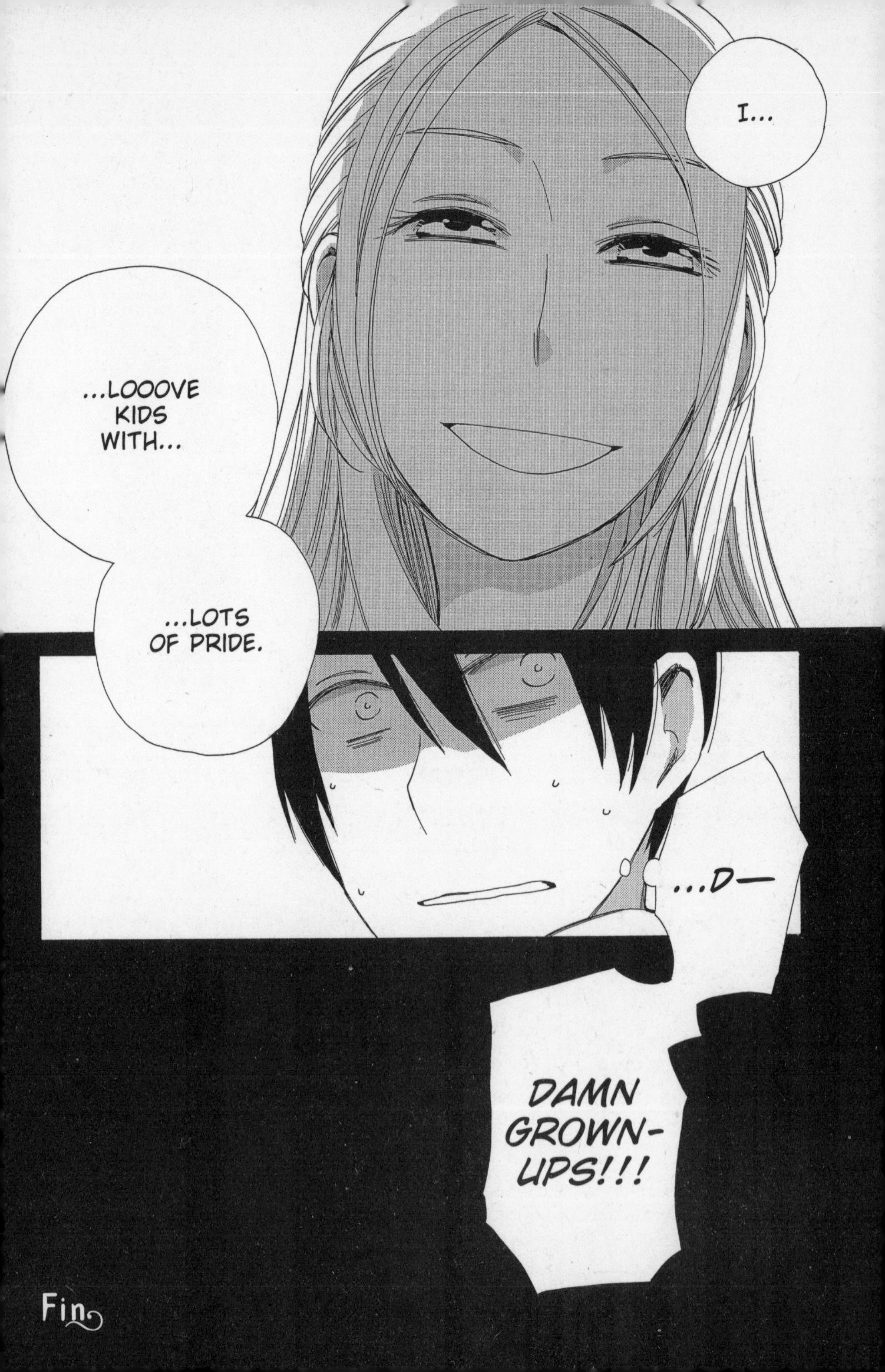
I...
...LOOOVE KIDS WITH...
...LOTS OF PRIDE.
...D—
DAMN GROWN-UPS!!!
Fin

Love at Fourteen

[Intermission 6]

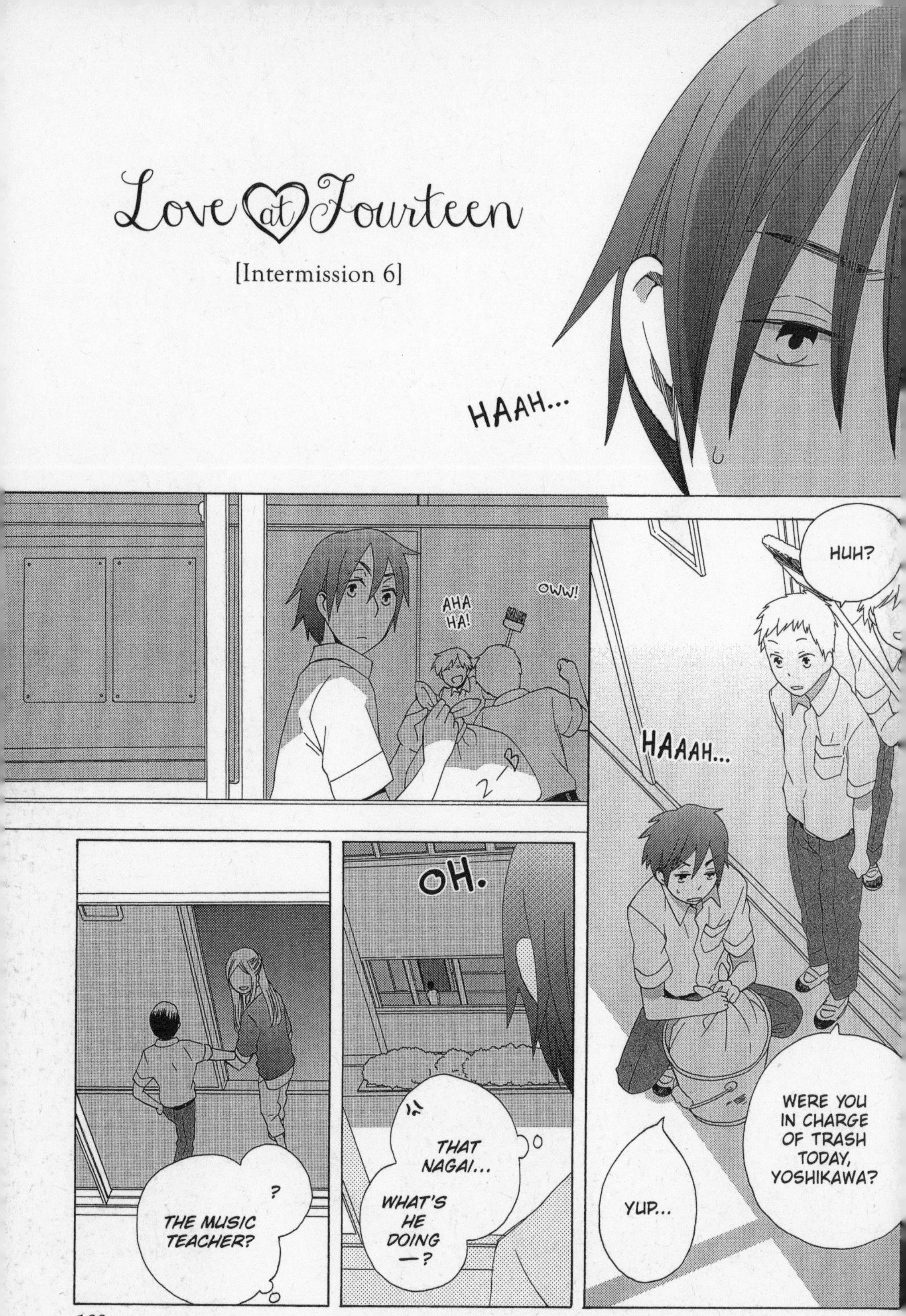
HAAH...
HUH?
HAAAH...
WERE YOU IN CHARGE OF TRASH TODAY, YOSHIKAWA?
YUP...
OWW!
AHA HA!
OH.
THAT NAGAI...
WHAT'S HE DOING—?
?
THE MUSIC TEACHER?

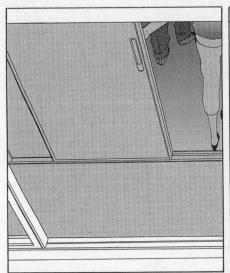

?

LEAVE ME ALONE!

DAMMIT!

HAH...

DOSA (THUD)

2 - B

164

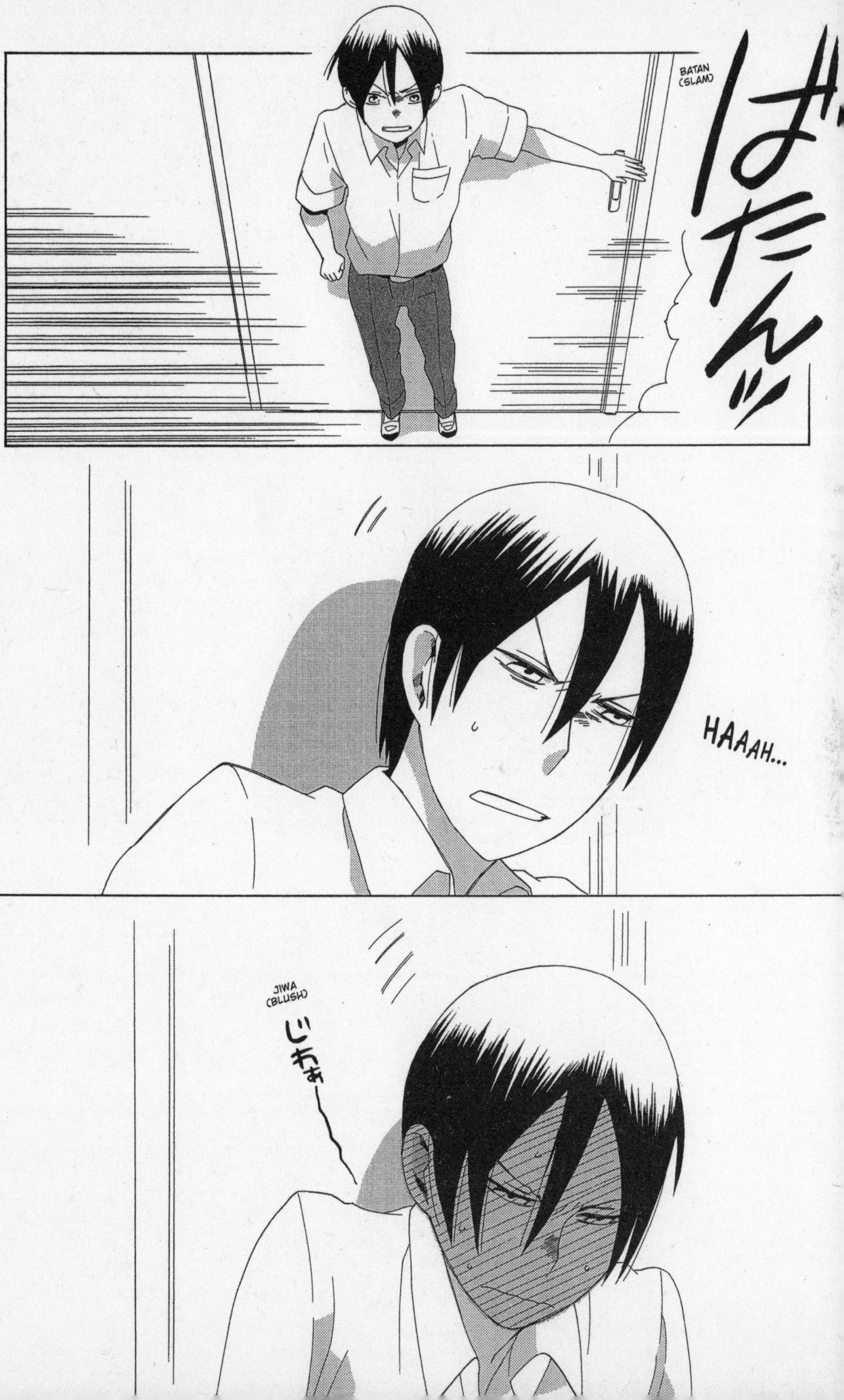
ばたんッ
BATAN (SLAM)
HAAAH...
じわぁ～
JIWA (BLUSH)

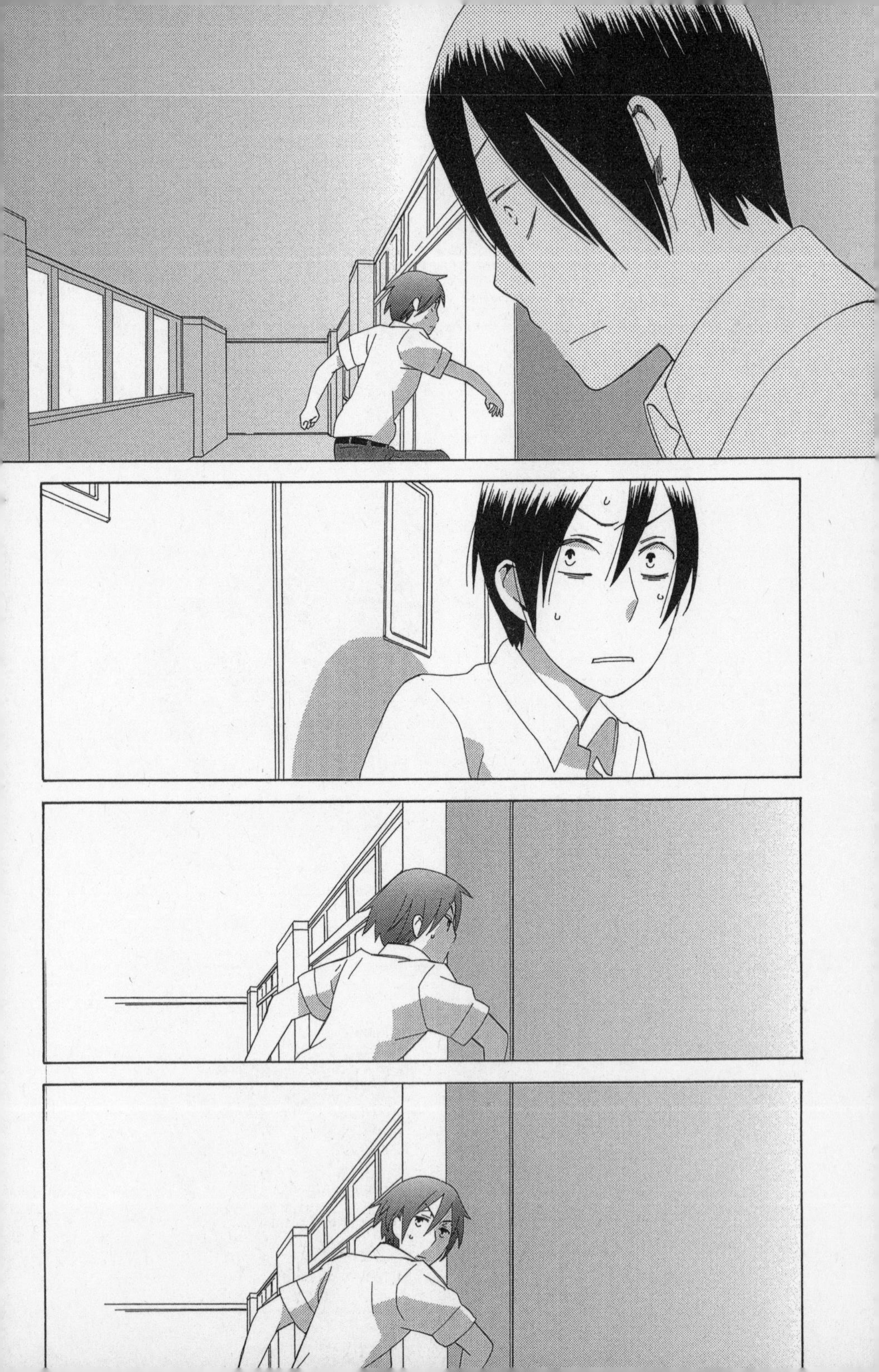

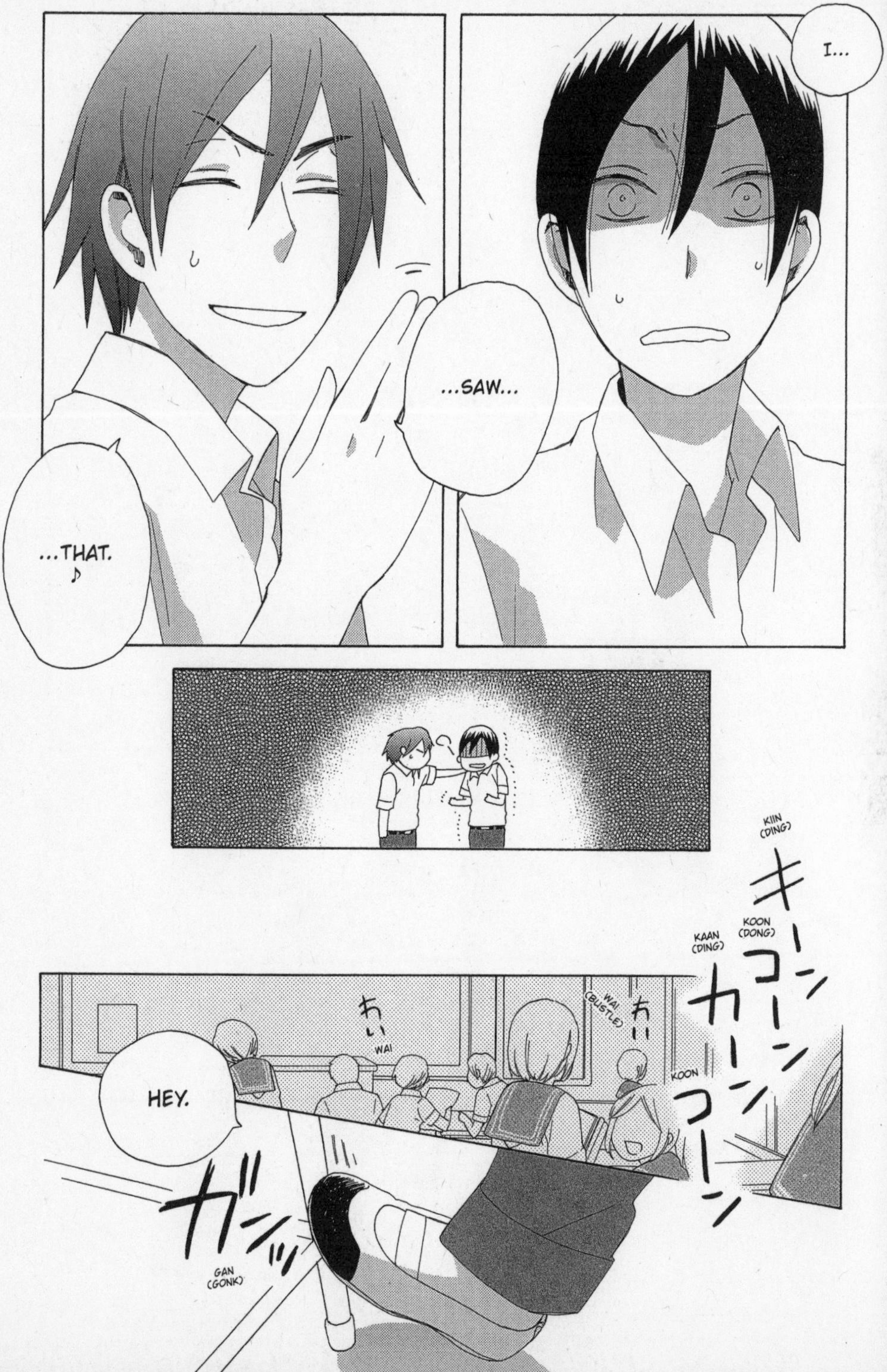
I...
...SAW...
...THAT. ♪
KIIN (DING)
KOON (DONG)
KAAN (DING)
KOON
キーンコーンカーンコーン
WAI (BUSTLE)
わい
WAI
わい
HEY.
GAN (GONK)
ガンッ

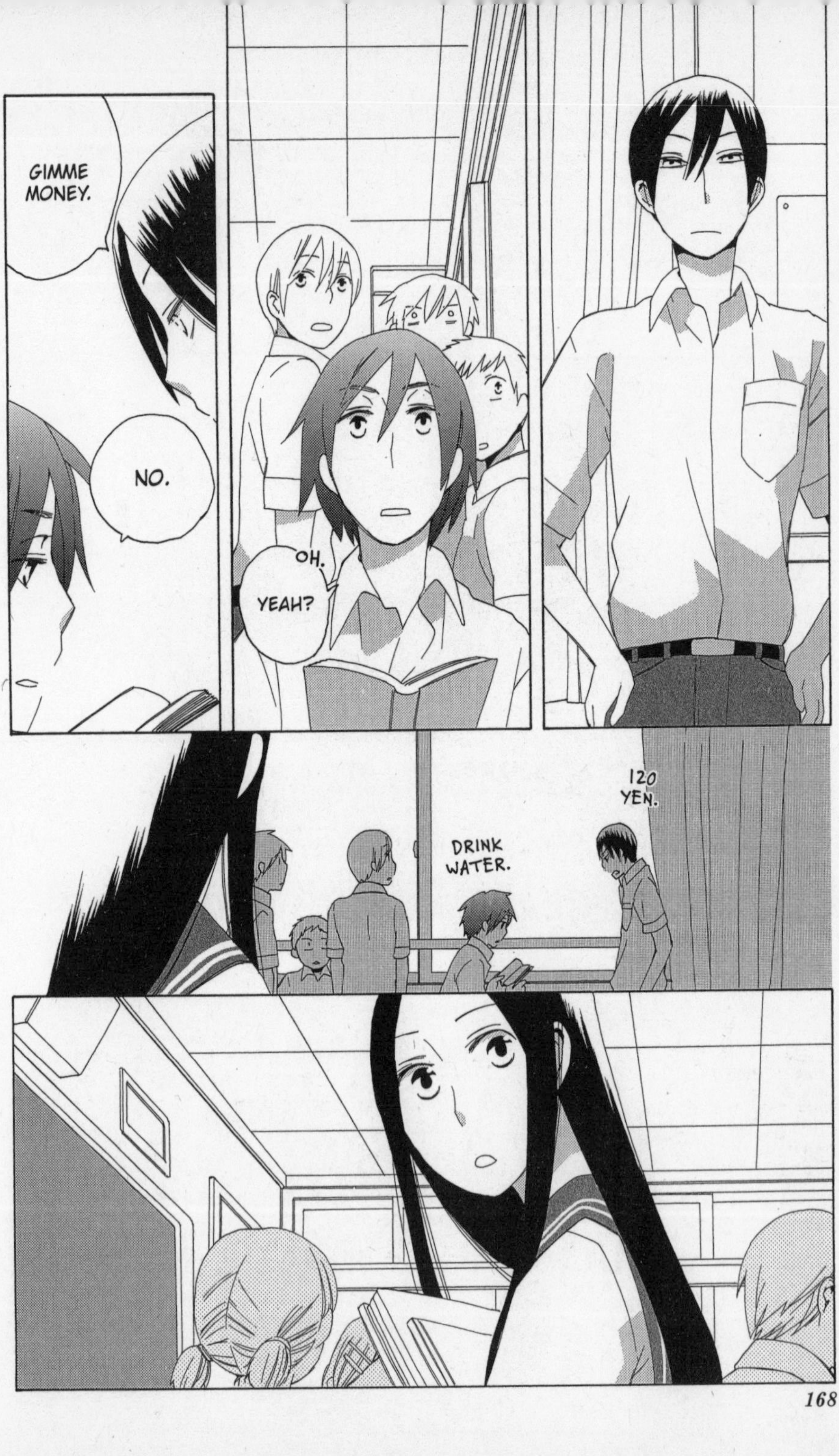
OH.
YEAH?
GIMME MONEY.
NO.
120 YEN.
DRINK WATER.

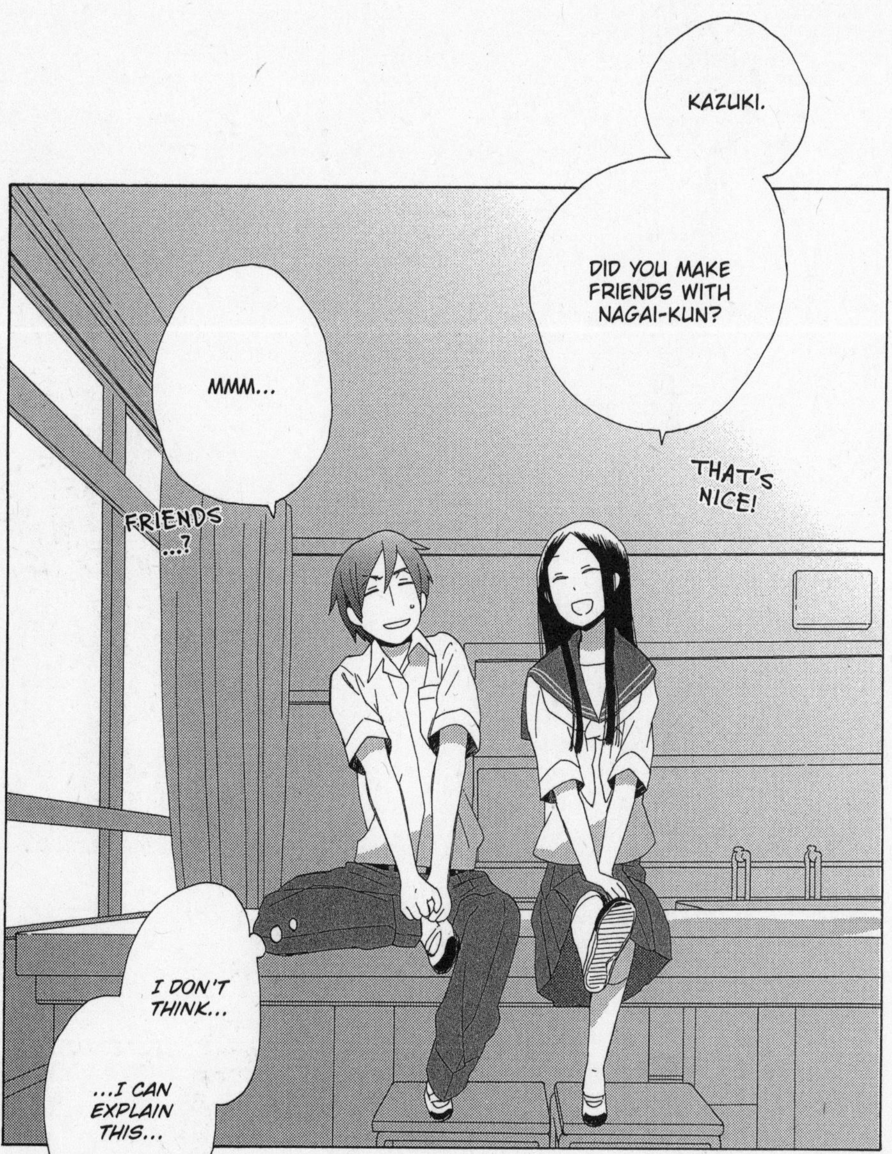
KAZUKI.
DID YOU MAKE FRIENDS WITH NAGAI-KUN?
THAT'S NICE!
MMM...
FRIENDS ...?
I DON'T THINK...
...I CAN EXPLAIN THIS...

Fin

Love at Fourteen

Fuka Mizutani

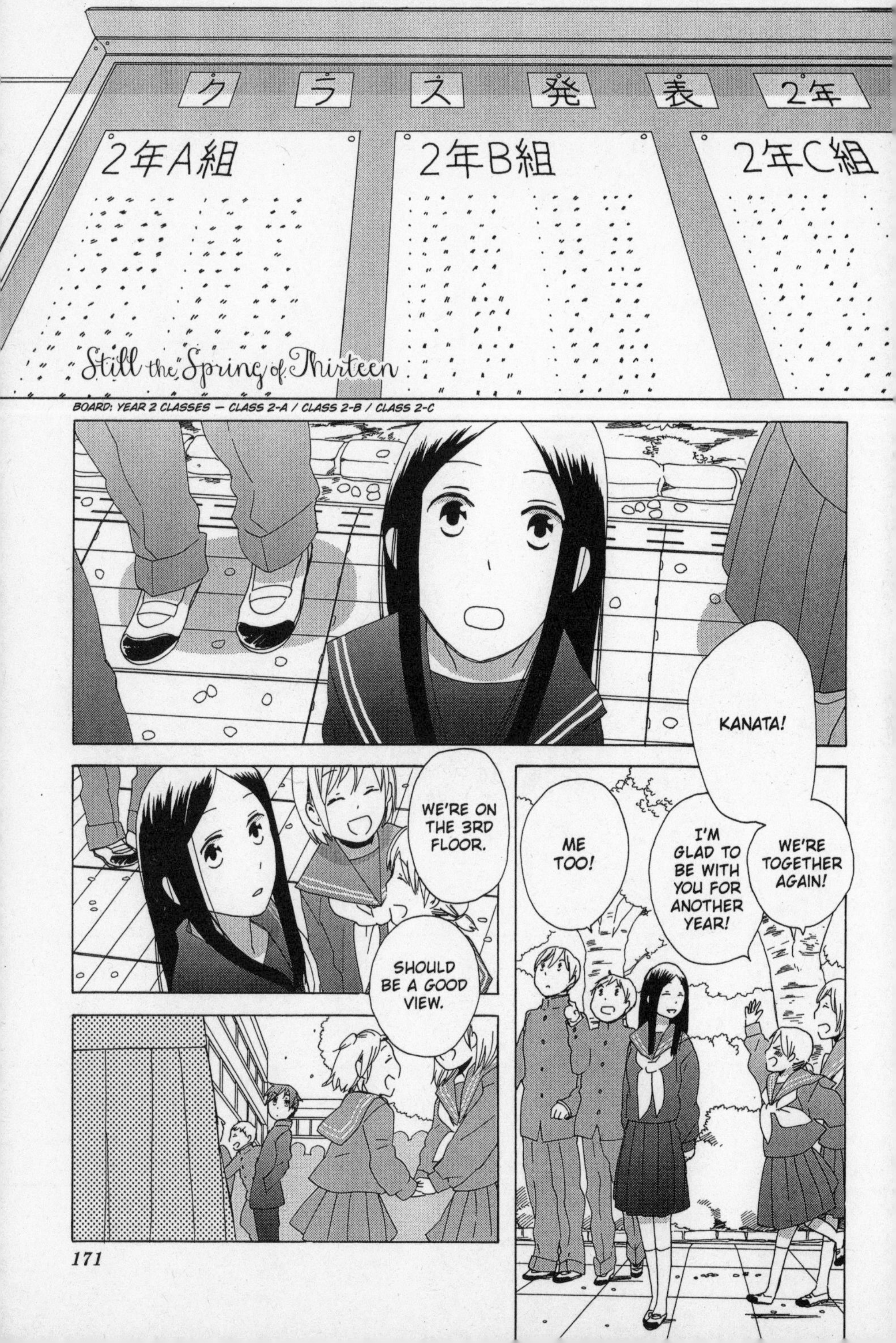
クラス発表2年
2年A組
2年B組
2年C組
Still the Spring of Thirteen
KANATA!
WE'RE TOGETHER AGAIN!
I'M GLAD TO BE WITH YOU FOR ANOTHER YEAR!
ME TOO!
WE'RE ON THE 3RD FLOOR.
SHOULD BE A GOOD VIEW.
BOARD: YEAR 2 CLASSES — CLASS 2-A / CLASS 2-B / CLASS 2-C

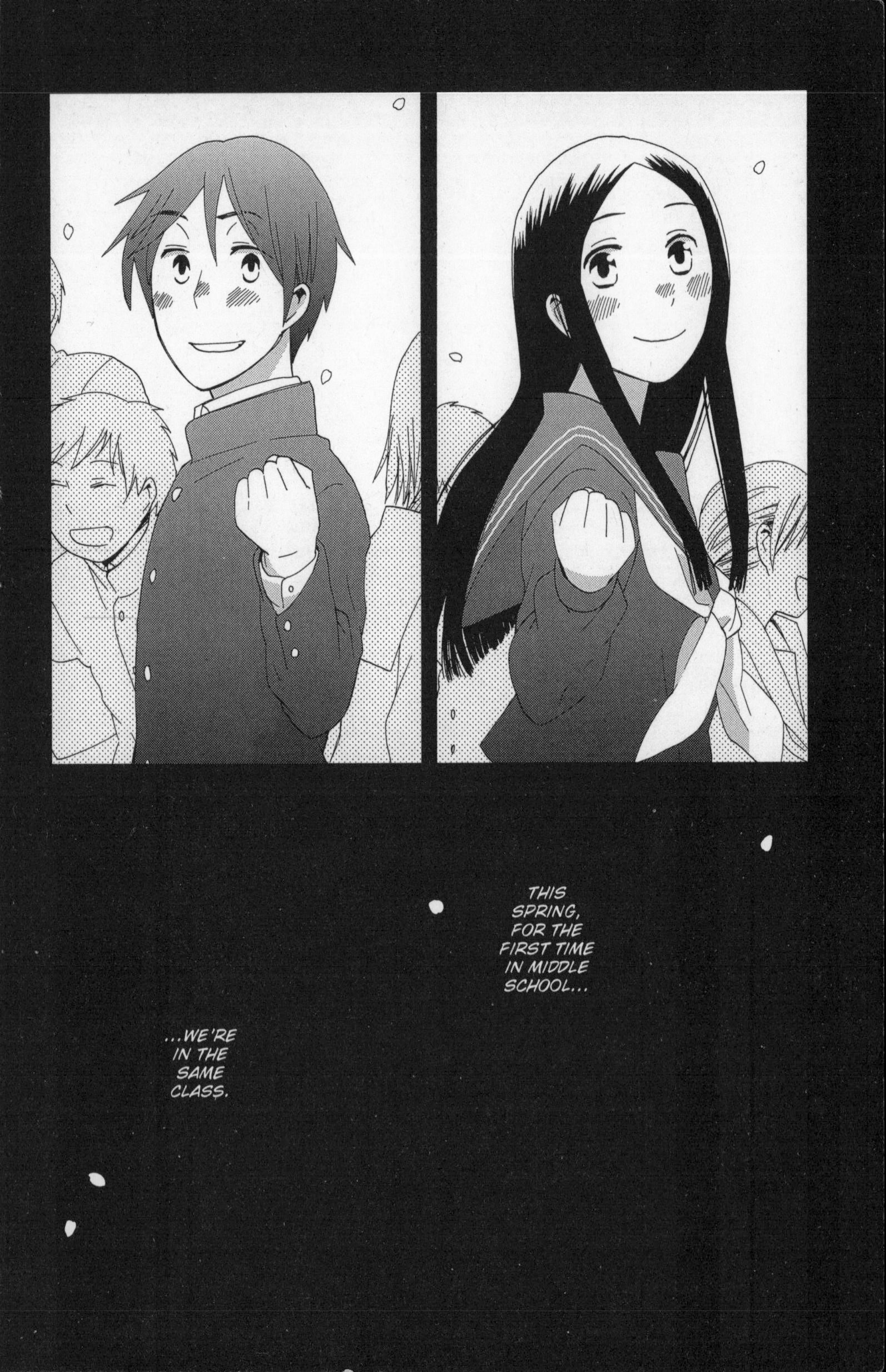
THIS SPRING, FOR THE FIRST TIME IN MIDDLE SCHOOL...
...WE'RE IN THE SAME CLASS.

Still the Spring of Thirteen

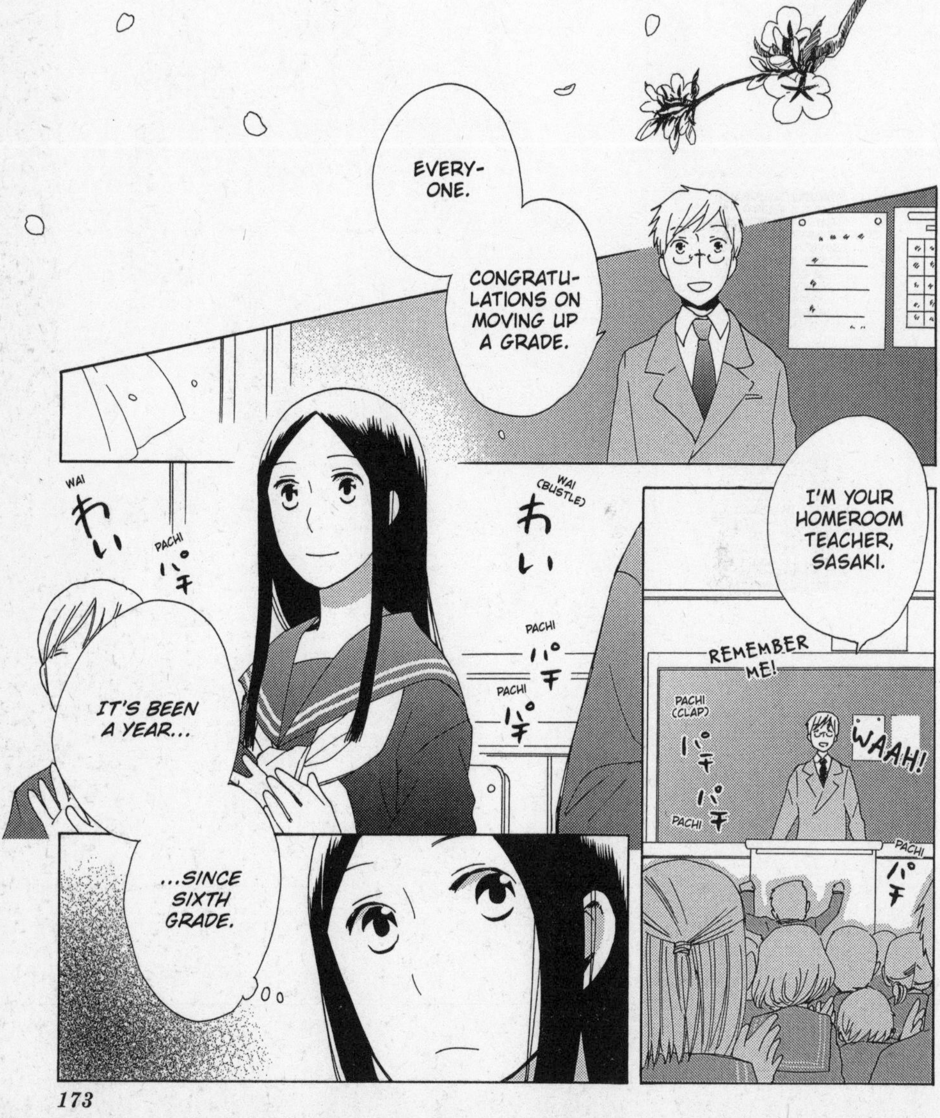
EVERY-ONE.
CONGRATULATIONS ON MOVING UP A GRADE.
I'M YOUR HOMEROOM TEACHER, SASAKI.
REMEMBER ME!
WAAH!
PACHI (CLAP) パチ
PACHI パチ
PACHI パチ
WAI (BUSTLE) わい
PACHI パチ
PACHI パチ
PACHI パチ
WAI わい
IT'S BEEN A YEAR...
...SINCE SIXTH GRADE.

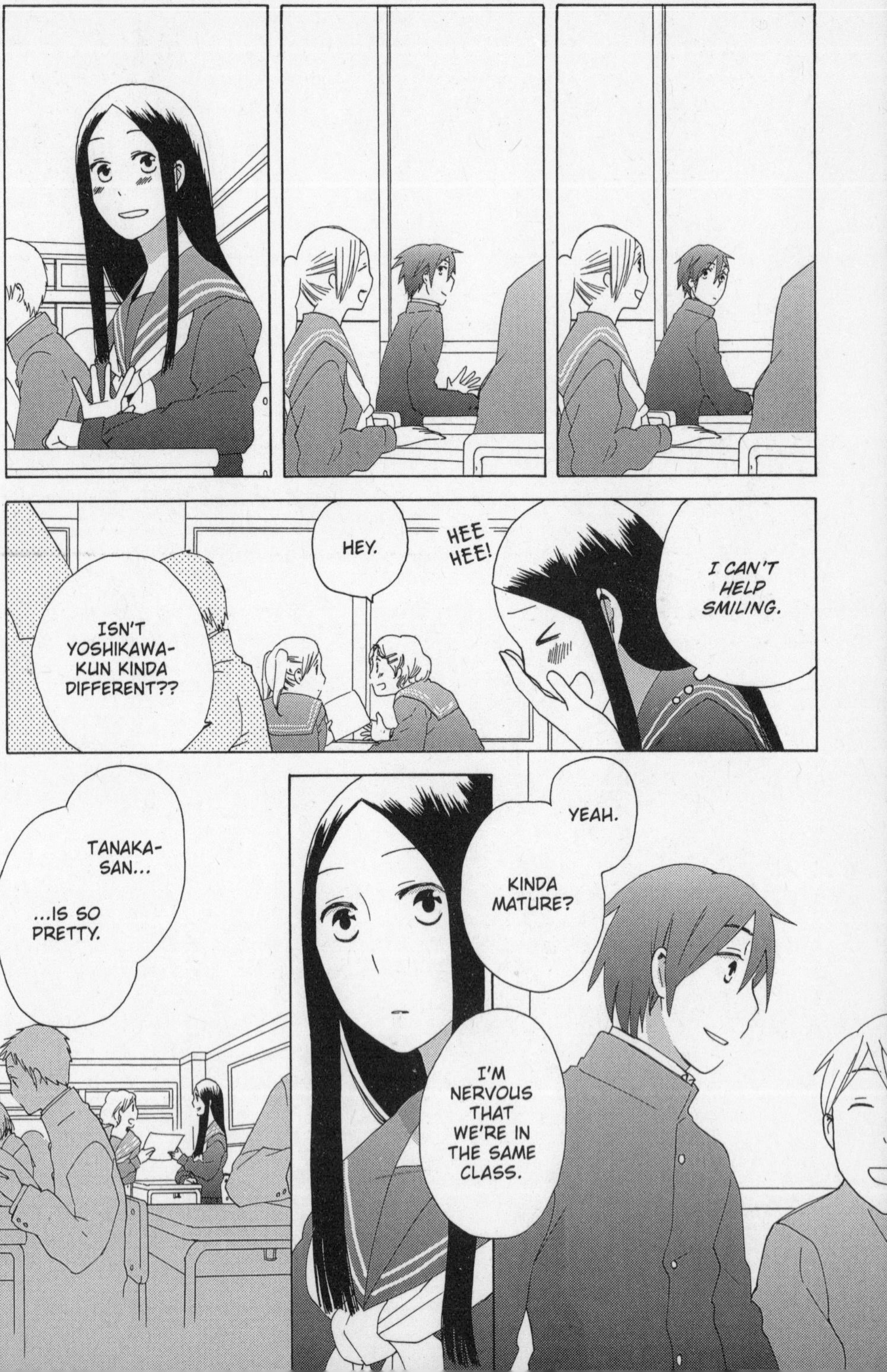
I CAN'T HELP SMILING.
HEE HEE!
HEY.
ISN'T YOSHIKAWA-KUN KINDA DIFFERENT??
YEAH.
KINDA MATURE?
I'M NERVOUS THAT WE'RE IN THE SAME CLASS.
TANAKA-SAN...
...IS SO PRETTY.

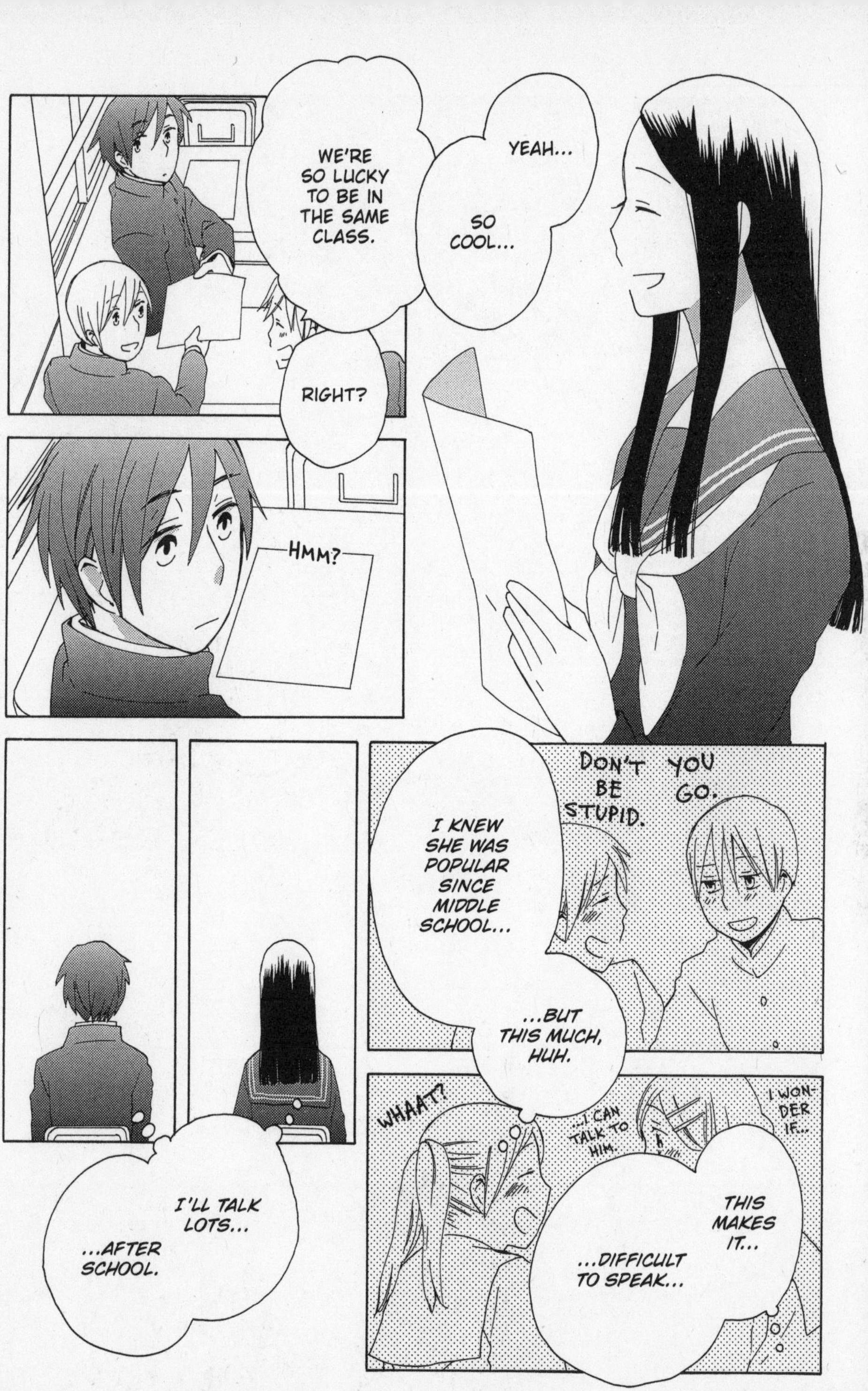
YEAH...
SO COOL...
WE'RE SO LUCKY TO BE IN THE SAME CLASS.
RIGHT?
HMM?
YOU GO.
DON'T BE STUPID.
I KNEW SHE WAS POPULAR SINCE MIDDLE SCHOOL...
...BUT THIS MUCH, HUH.
I WONDER IF...
...I CAN TALK TO HIM.
WHAAT?
THIS MAKES IT...
...DIFFICULT TO SPEAK...
I'LL TALK LOTS...
...AFTER SCHOOL.

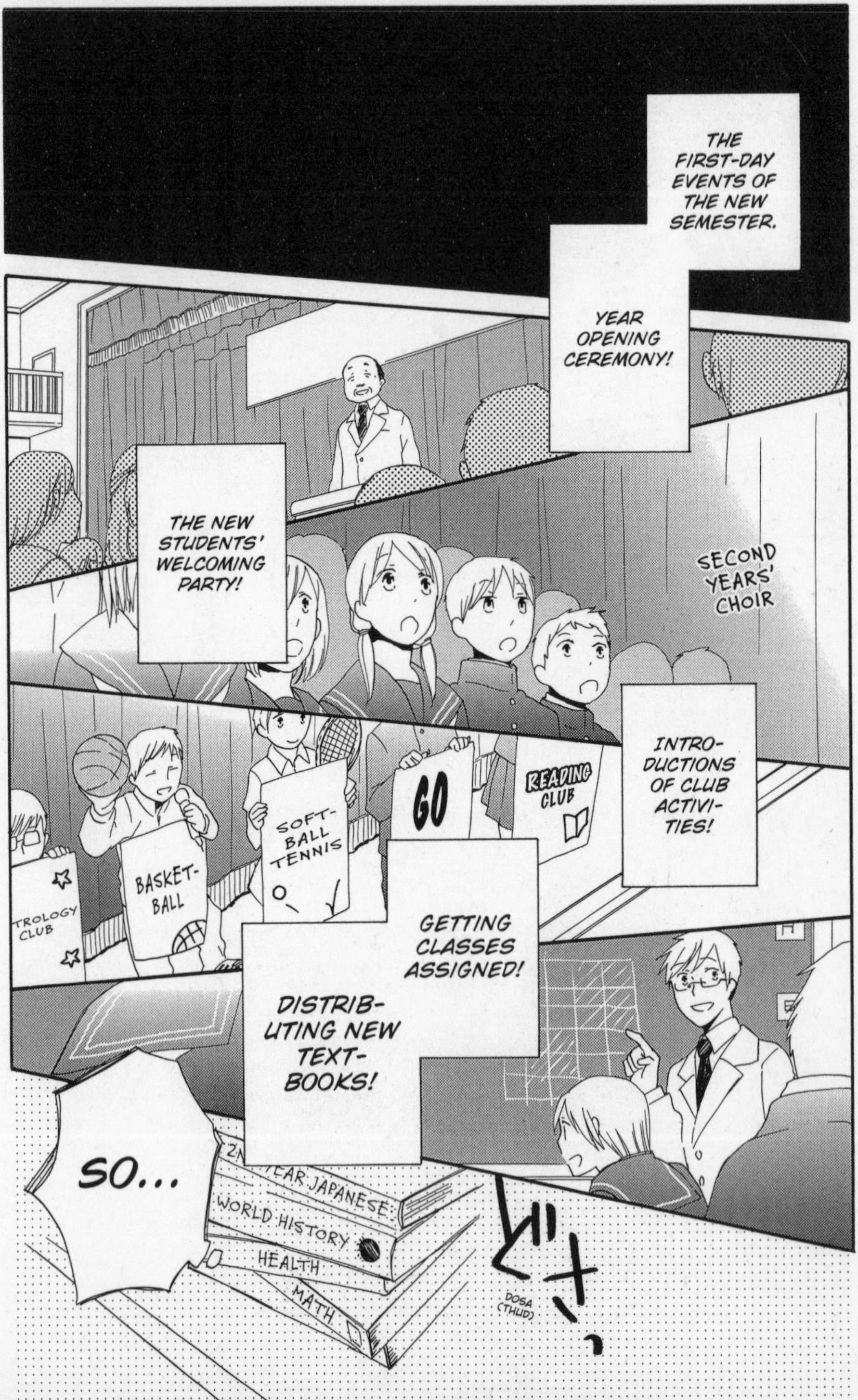
THE FIRST-DAY EVENTS OF THE NEW SEMESTER.
YEAR OPENING CEREMONY!
SECOND YEARS' CHOIR
THE NEW STUDENTS' WELCOMING PARTY!
INTRO-DUCTIONS OF CLUB ACTIVI-TIES!
READING CLUB
GO
SOFT-BALL TENNIS
BASKET-BALL
TROLOGY CLUB
GETTING CLASSES ASSIGNED!
DISTRIB-UTING NEW TEXT-BOOKS!
DOSA (THUD)
2N YEAR JAPANESE
WORLD HISTORY
HEALTH
MATH
SO...

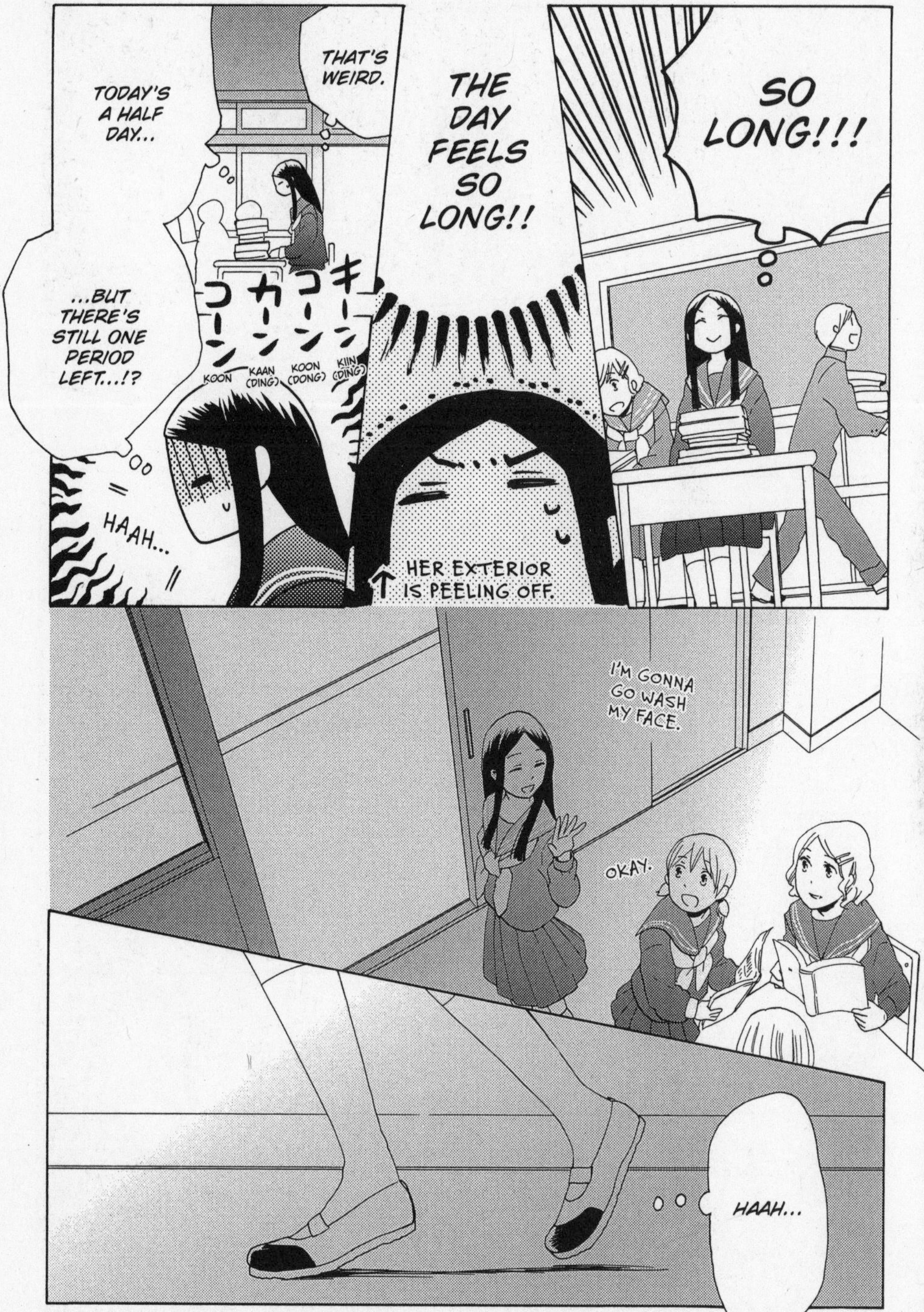
SO LONG!!!
THE DAY FEELS SO LONG!!
↑ HER EXTERIOR IS PEELING OFF.
キーン
KIIN (DING)
コーン
KOON (DONG)
カーン
KAAN (DING)
コーン
KOON
THAT'S WEIRD.
TODAY'S A HALF DAY...
...BUT THERE'S STILL ONE PERIOD LEFT...!?
HAAH...
I'M GONNA GO WASH MY FACE.
OKAY.
HAAH...

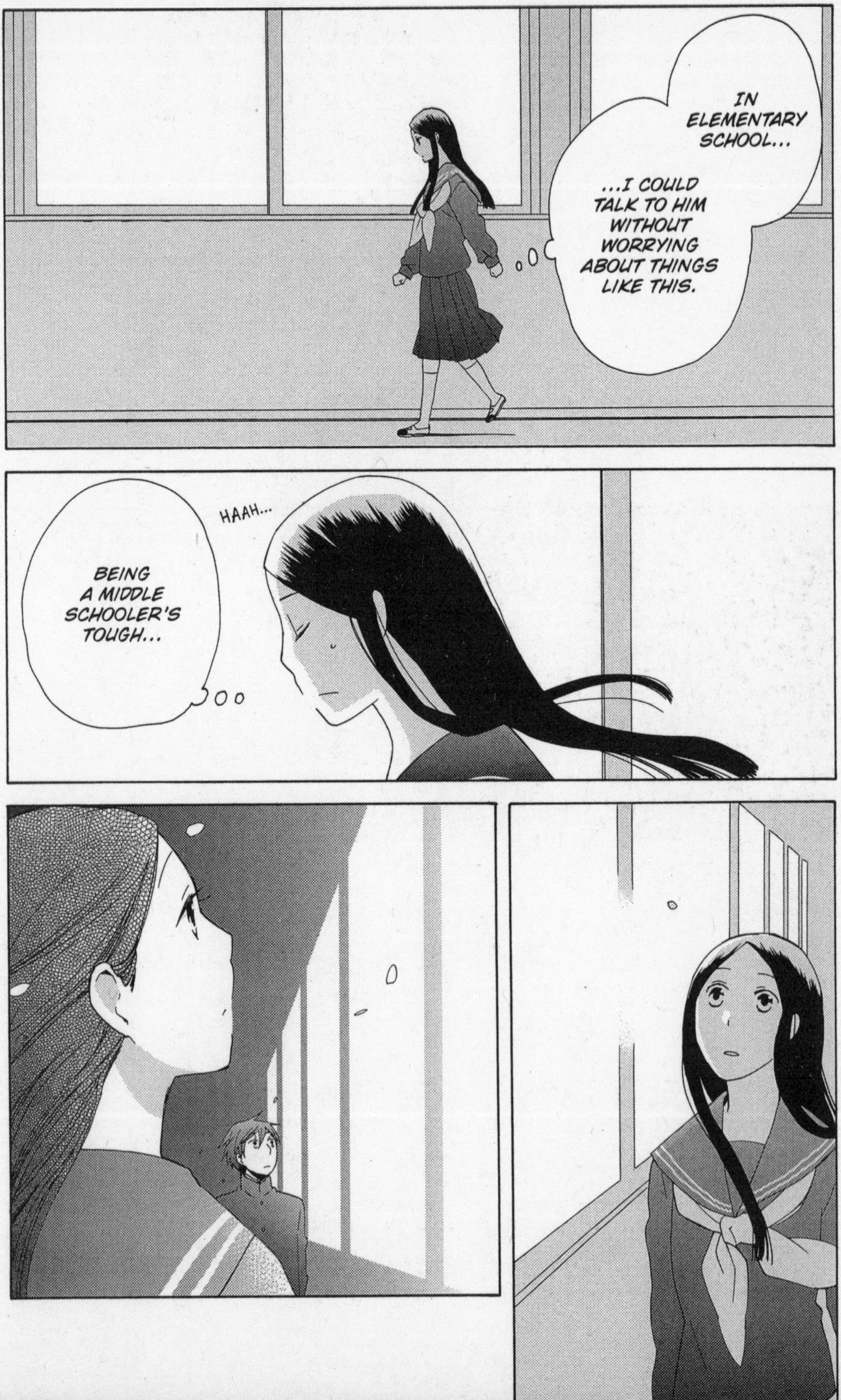
IN ELEMENTARY SCHOOL...
...I COULD TALK TO HIM WITHOUT WORRYING ABOUT THINGS LIKE THIS.
HAAH...
BEING A MIDDLE SCHOOLER'S TOUGH...

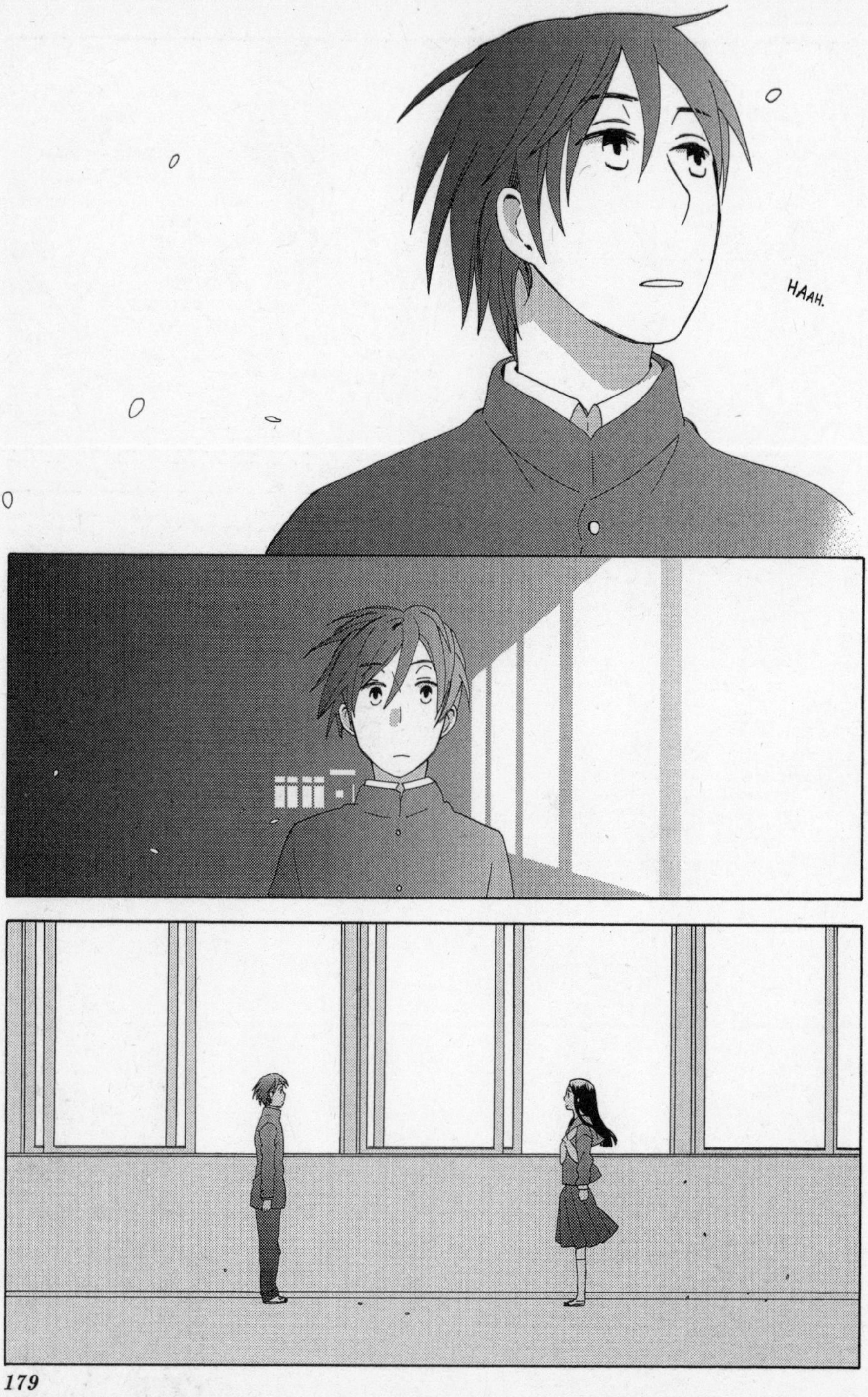
HAAH.

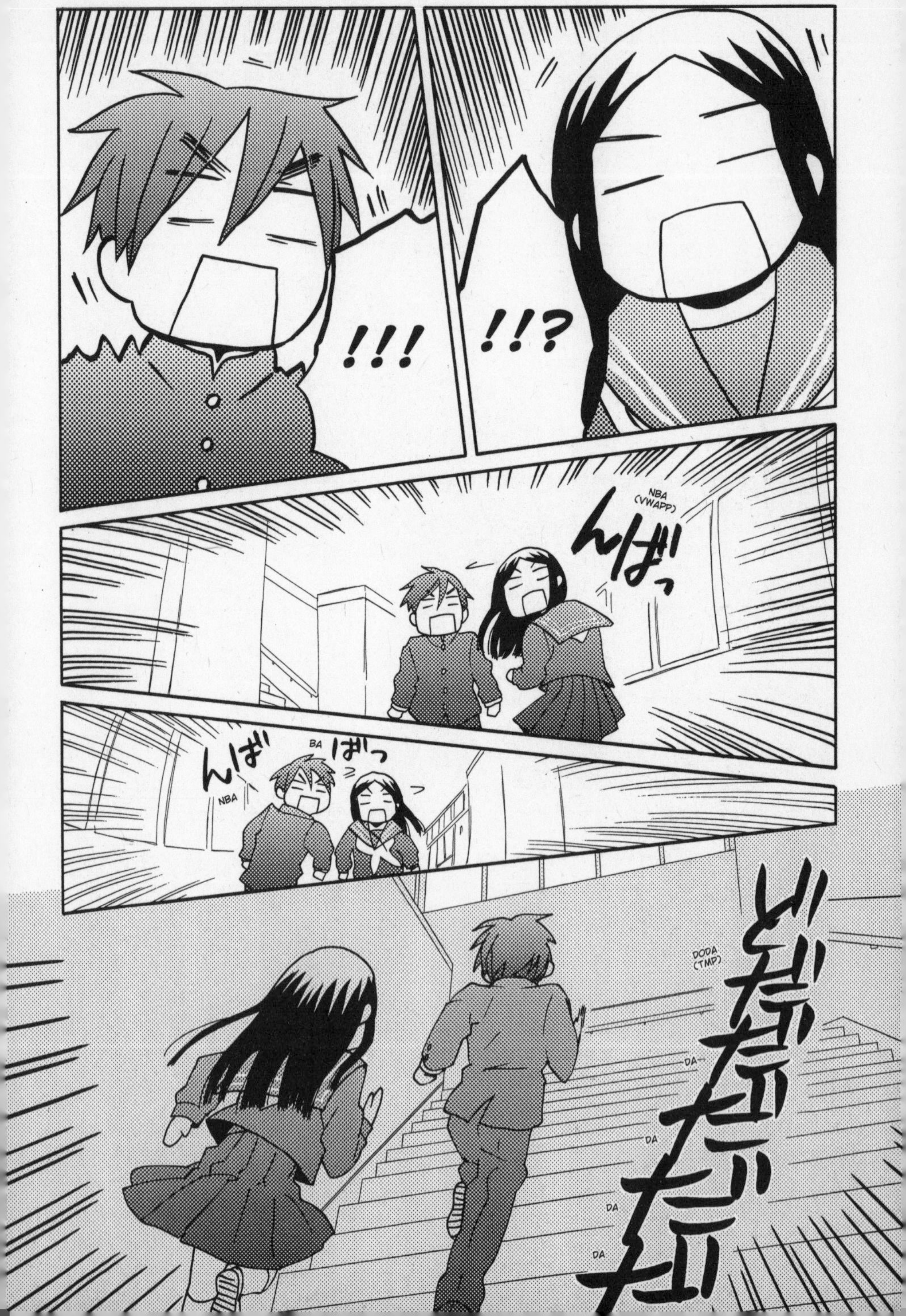
!!?
!!!
NBA (VWAPP)
んばっ
ばっ
BA
んば
NBA
DODA (TMP)
DA
DA
DA
DA

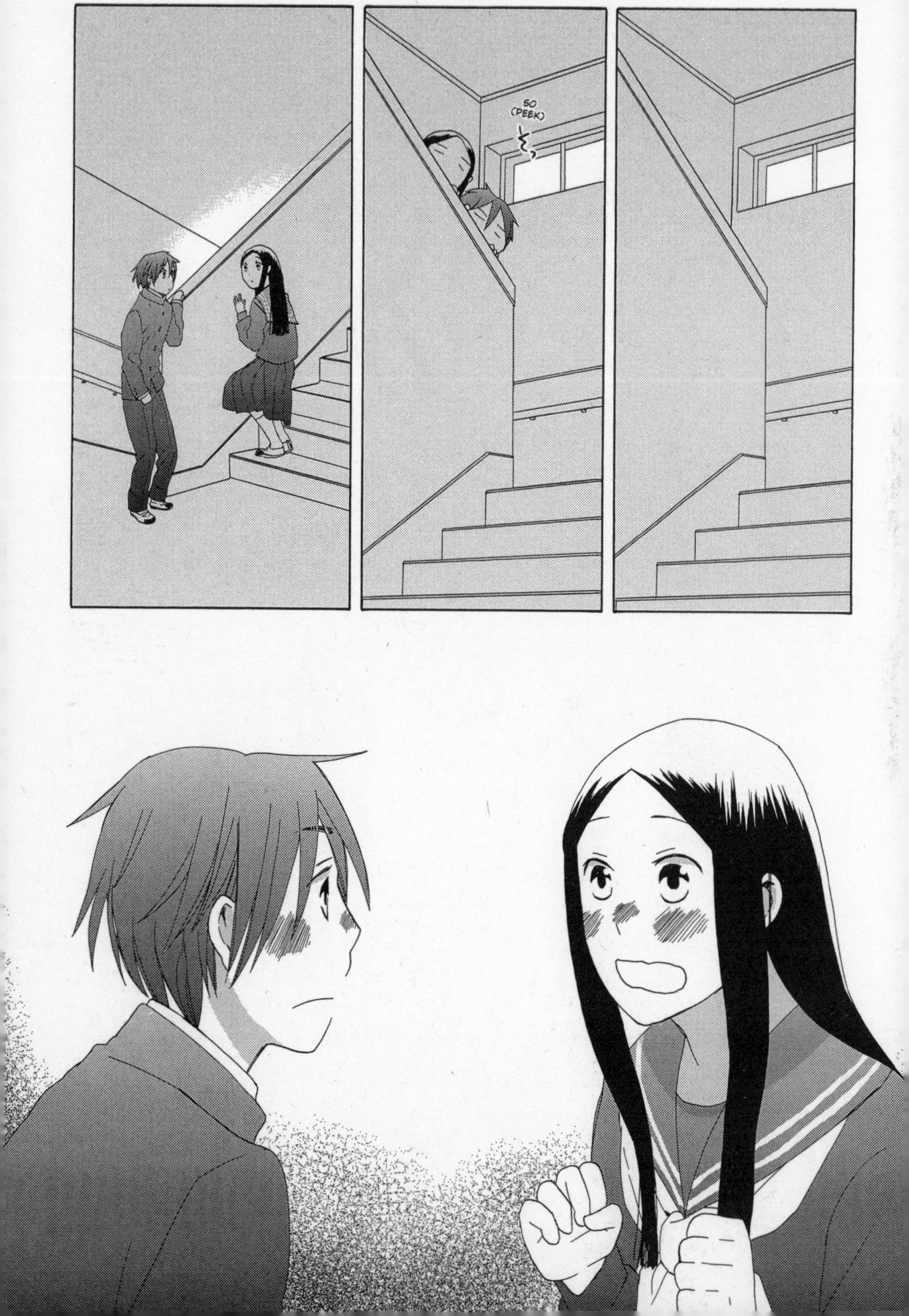
SO
(PEEK)

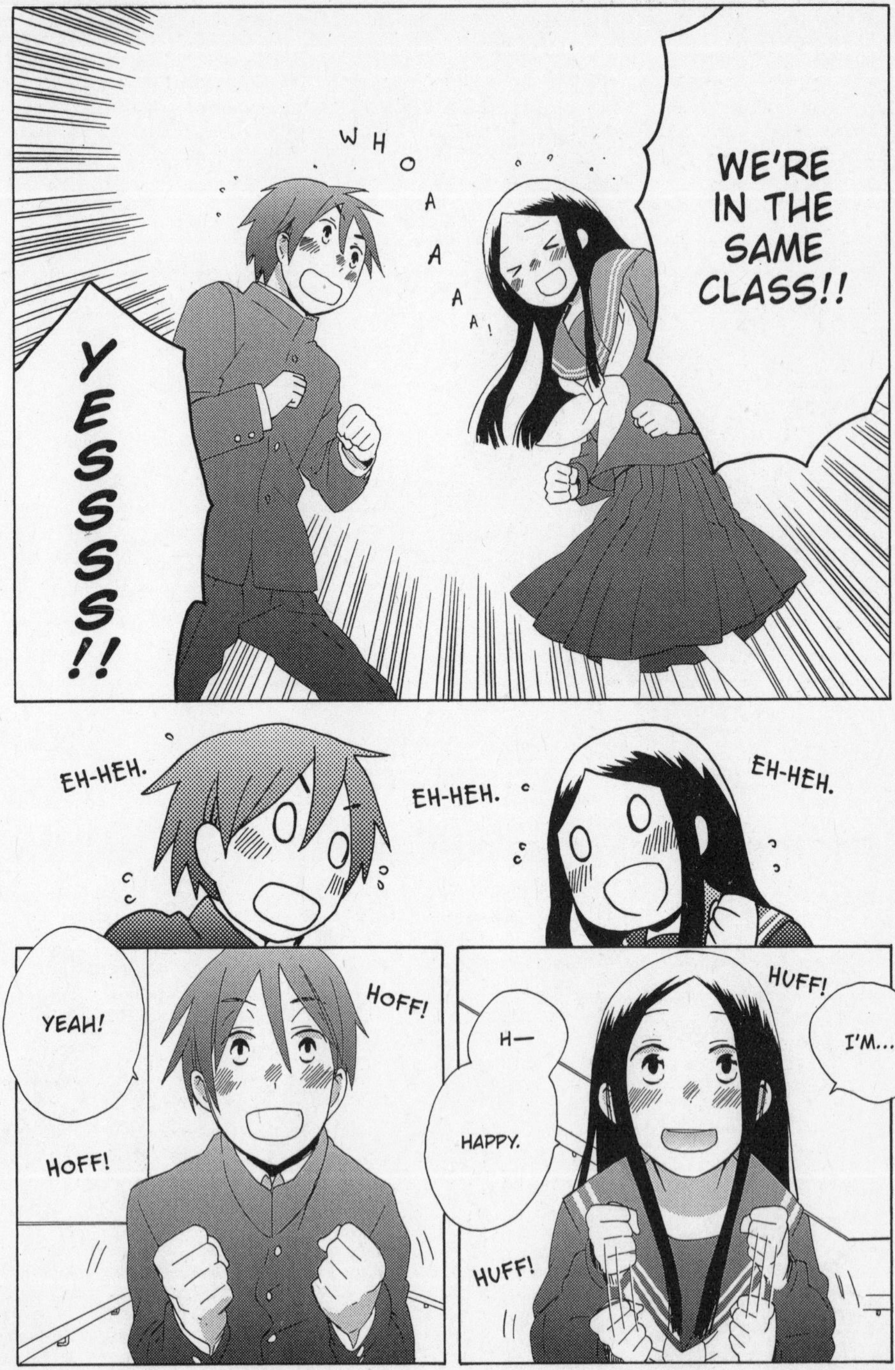
WE'RE IN THE SAME CLASS!!
WHOAAAAA!
YESSSSS!!
EH-HEH.
EH-HEH.
EH-HEH.
HUFF!
I'M...
H—
HAPPY.
HUFF!
HOFF!
YEAH!
HOFF!

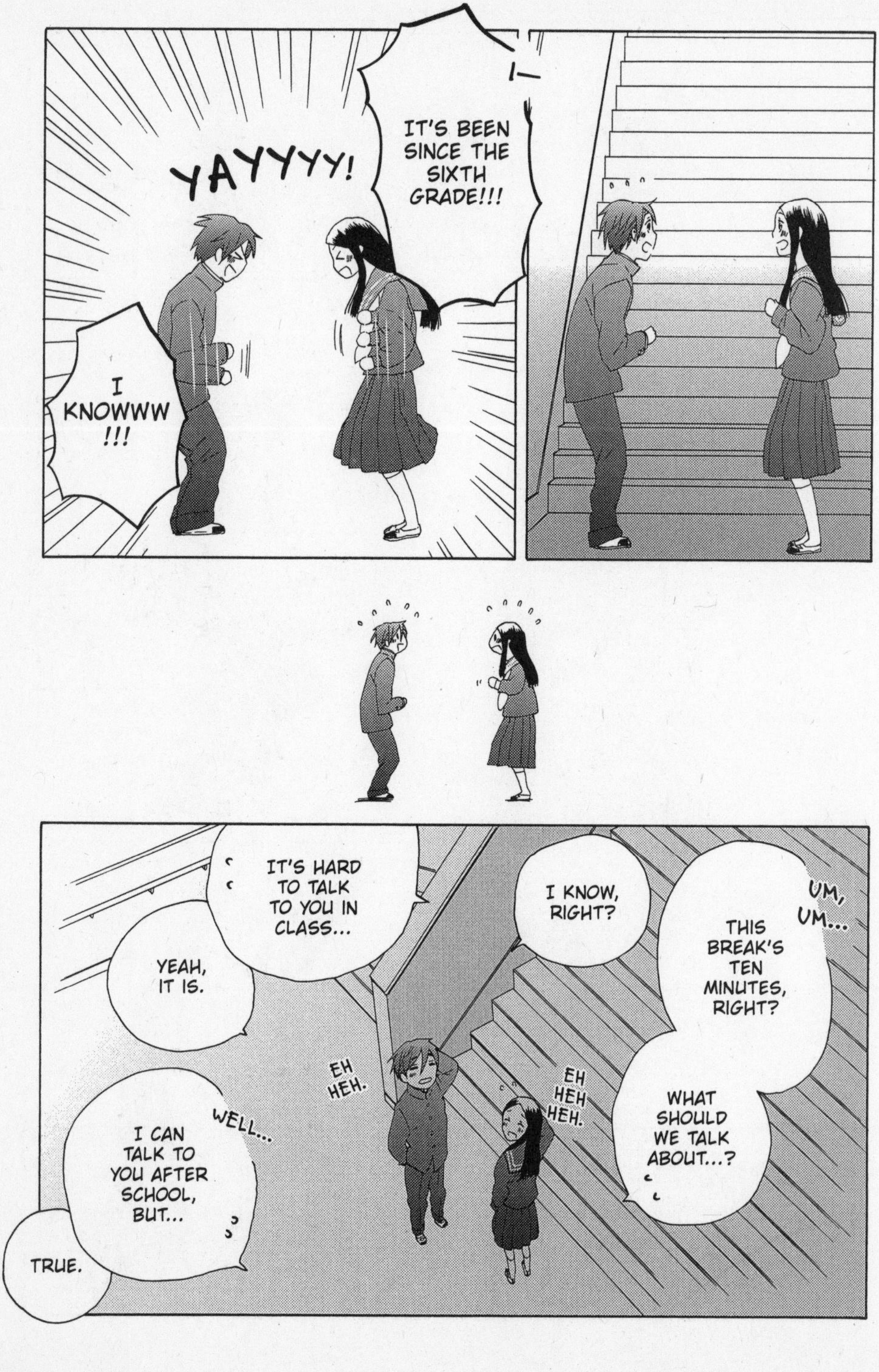
IT'S BEEN SINCE THE SIXTH GRADE!!!
YAYYYY!
I KNOWWW!!!
UM, UM...
THIS BREAK'S TEN MINUTES, RIGHT?
I KNOW, RIGHT?
IT'S HARD TO TALK TO YOU IN CLASS...
YEAH, IT IS.
WHAT SHOULD WE TALK ABOUT...?
EH HEH HEH.
EH HEH.
WELL...
I CAN TALK TO YOU AFTER SCHOOL, BUT...
TRUE.

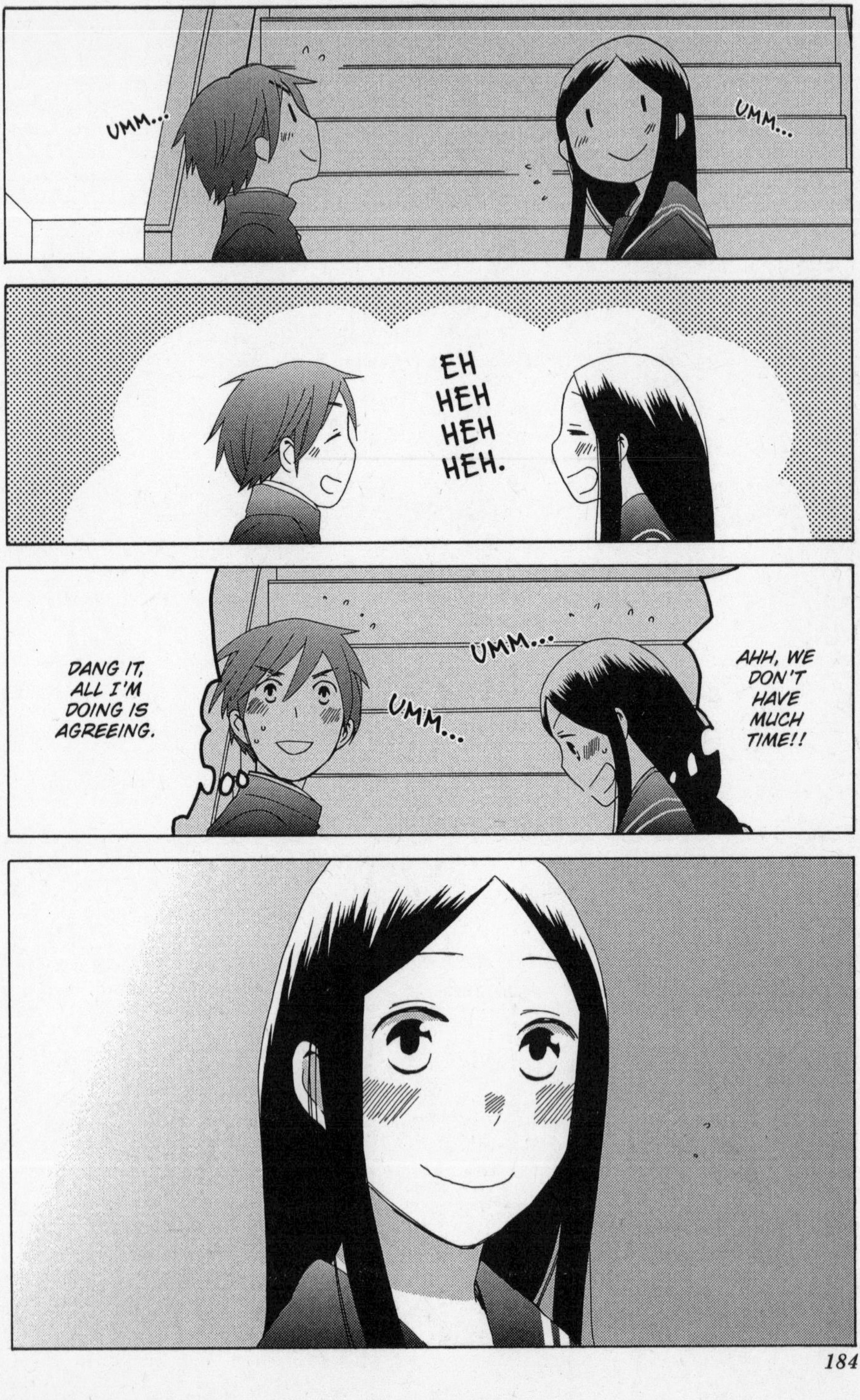
UMM...
UMM...
EH HEH HEH HEH.
AHH, WE DON'T HAVE MUCH TIME!!
UMM...
UMM...
DANG IT, ALL I'M DOING IS AGREEING.

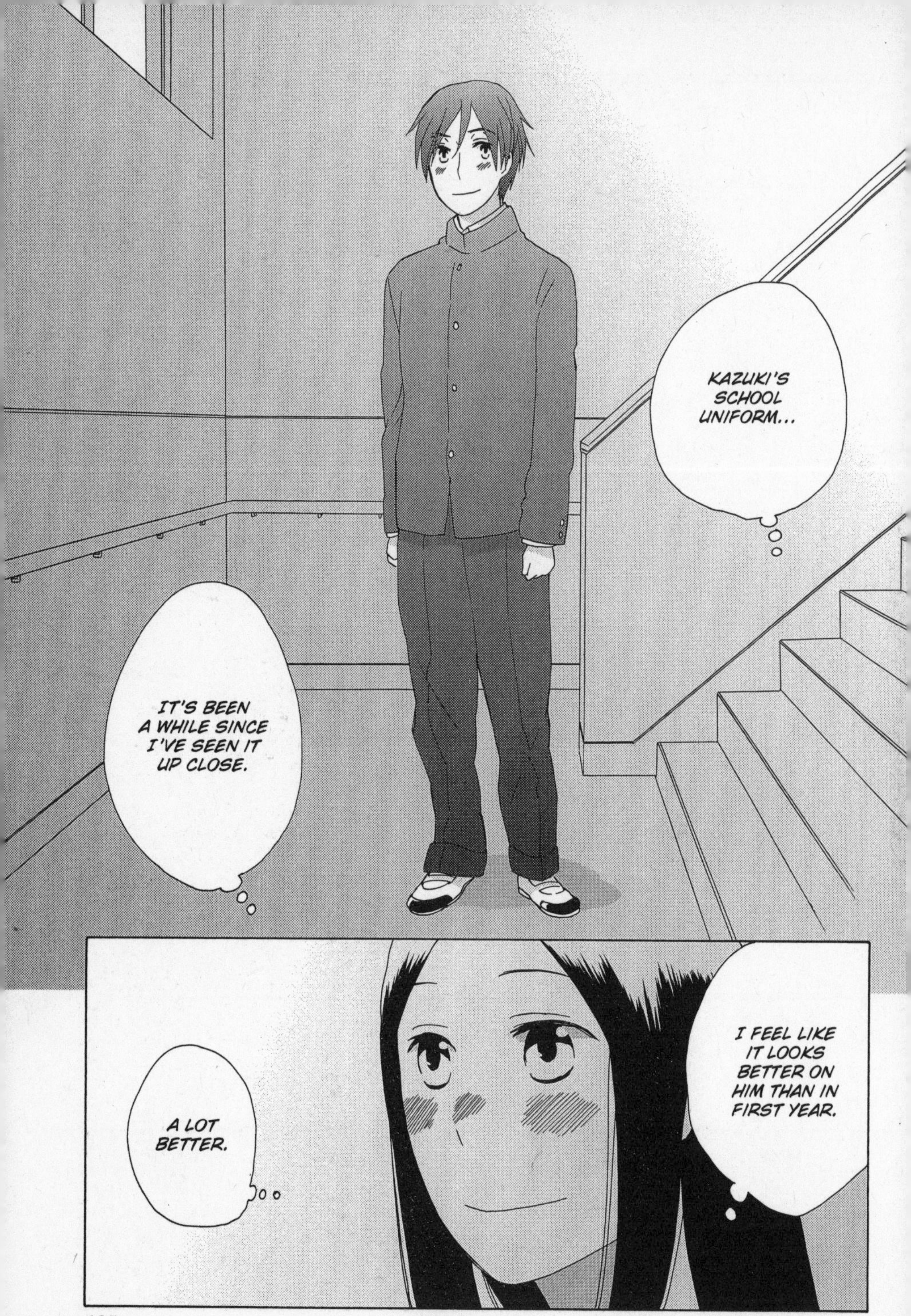
KAZUKI'S SCHOOL UNIFORM...
IT'S BEEN A WHILE SINCE I'VE SEEN IT UP CLOSE.
I FEEL LIKE IT LOOKS BETTER ON HIM THAN IN FIRST YEAR.
A LOT BETTER.

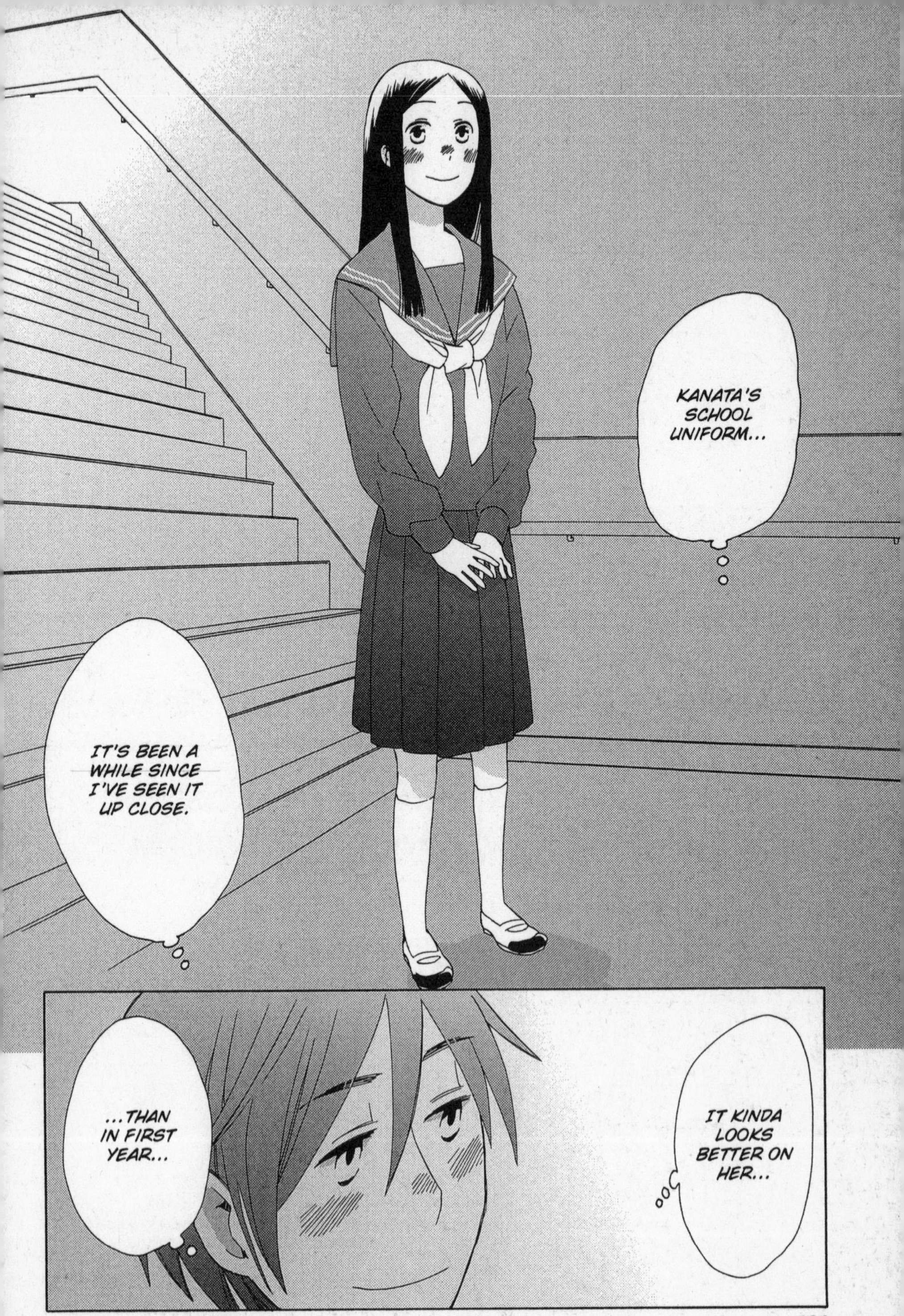
KANATA'S SCHOOL UNIFORM...
IT'S BEEN A WHILE SINCE I'VE SEEN IT UP CLOSE.
IT KINDA LOOKS BETTER ON HER...
...THAN IN FIRST YEAR...

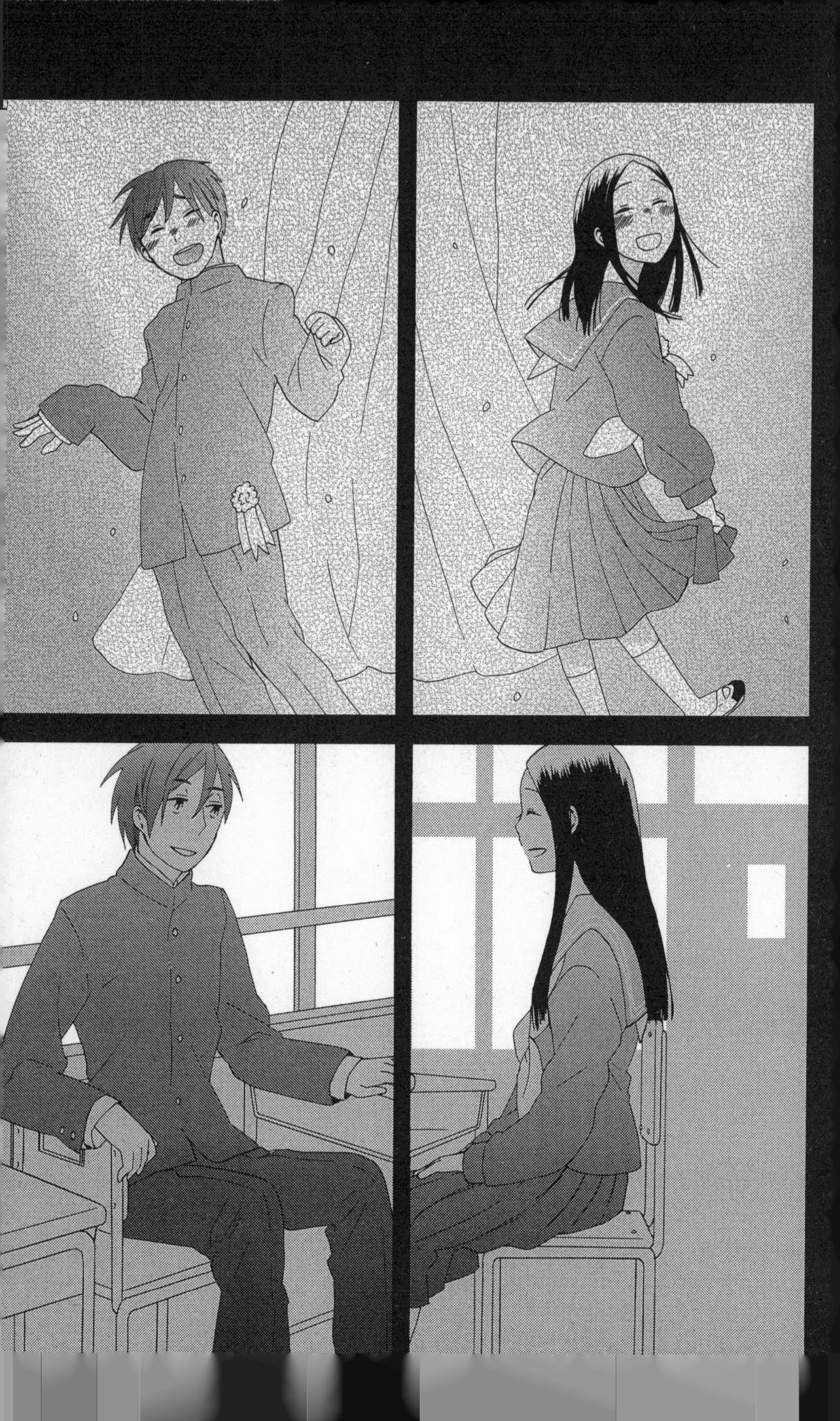

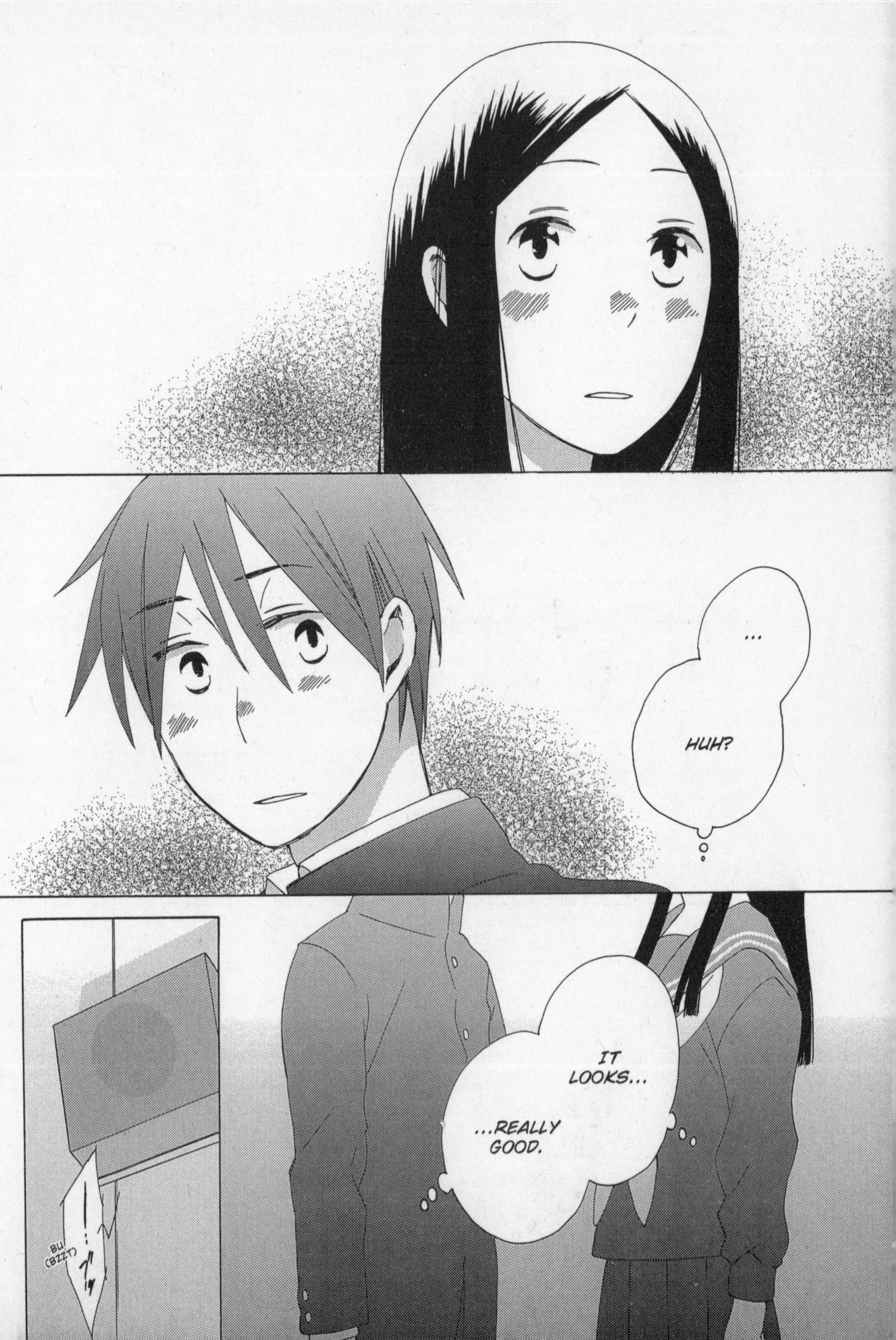
...
HUH?
IT LOOKS...
...REALLY GOOD.
BU (BZZT)

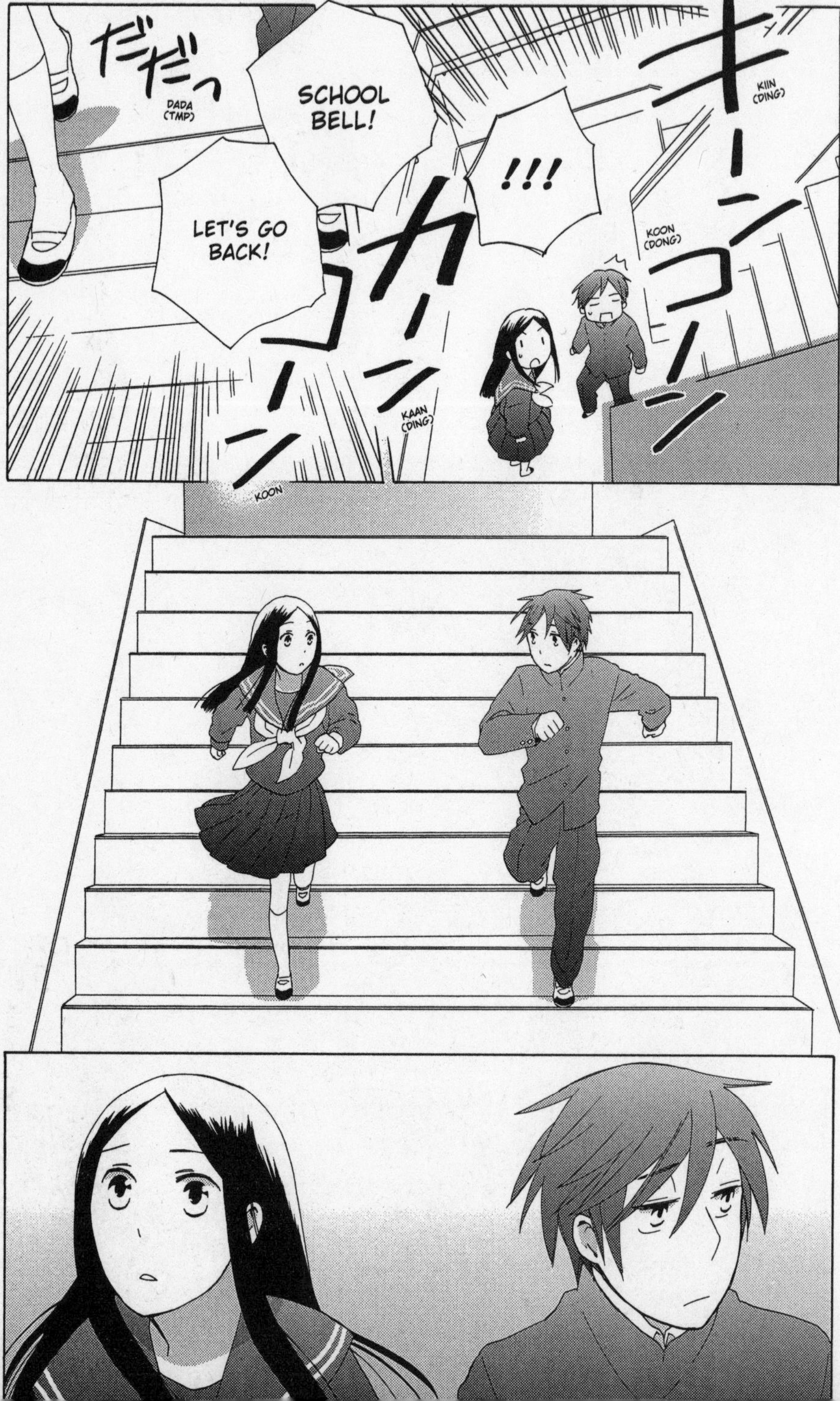
キーンコーン
KIIN (DING)
KOON (DONG)
!!!
SCHOOL BELL!
LET'S GO BACK!
カーンコーン
KAAN (DING)
KOON
だだっ
DADA (TMP)

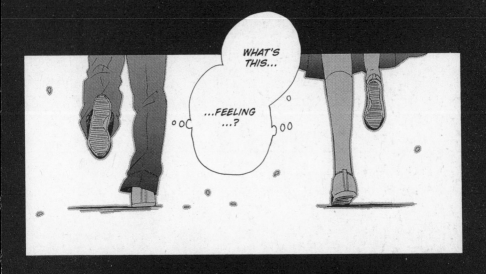

THE SPRING
OF THIRTEEN.

WE DON'T
YET KNOW...

...THE NAME
OF THAT
FEELING.

Fin

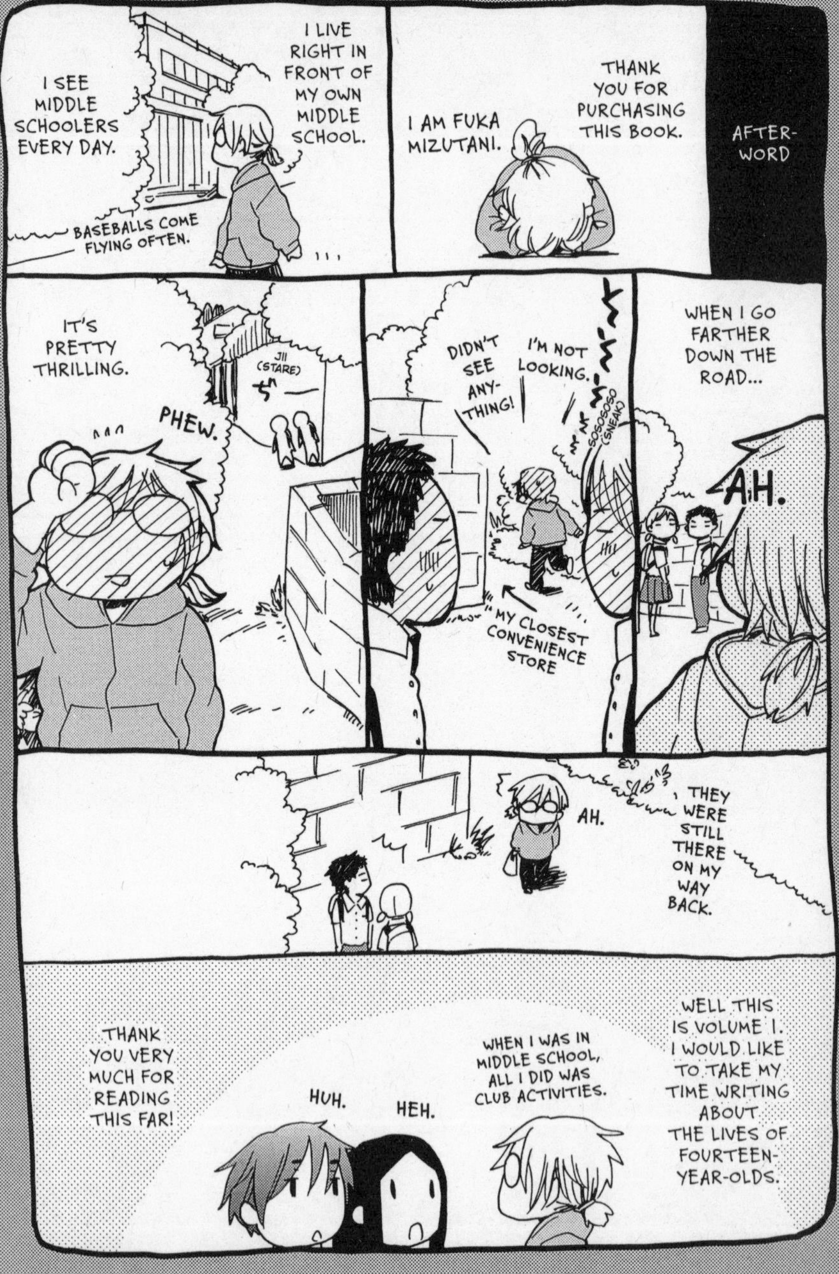
AFTER-WORD
THANK YOU FOR PURCHASING THIS BOOK.
I AM FUKA MIZUTANI.
I LIVE RIGHT IN FRONT OF MY OWN MIDDLE SCHOOL.
I SEE MIDDLE SCHOOLERS EVERY DAY.
BASEBALLS COME FLYING OFTEN.
WHEN I GO FARTHER DOWN THE ROAD...
AH.
SOSOSOSO (SNEAK)
I'M NOT LOOKING.
DIDN'T SEE ANY-THING!
MY CLOSEST CONVENIENCE STORE
IT'S PRETTY THRILLING.
JII (STARE)
PHEW.
THEY WERE STILL THERE ON MY WAY BACK.
AH.
WELL THIS IS VOLUME 1. I WOULD LIKE TO TAKE MY TIME WRITING ABOUT THE LIVES OF FOURTEEN-YEAR-OLDS.
WHEN I WAS IN MIDDLE SCHOOL, ALL I DID WAS CLUB ACTIVITIES.
HEH.
HUH.
THANK YOU VERY MUCH FOR READING THIS FAR!

Special Thanks

Iida-sama of Hakusensha
Kohei Nawata Design

My family
My great friends
Mitsuki-sama for CG assistance
Murata Sayo-chan

And all of you who are reading
this now.

Early summer 2011

水谷フーカ
Fuka Mizutani

TRANSLATION NOTES

COMMON HONORIFICS:

no honorific: Indicates familiarity or closeness; if used without permission or reason, addressing someone in this manner would constitute an insult.

-san: The Japanese equivalent of Mr./Mrs./Miss. If a situation calls for politeness, this is the fail-safe honorific.

-sama: Conveys great respect; may also indicate that the social status of the speaker is lower than that of the addressee.

-kun: Used most often when referring to boys, this indicates affection or familiarity. Occasionally used by older men among their peers, but it may also be used by anyone referring to a person of lower standing.

-chan: An affectionate honorific indicating familiarity used mostly in reference to girls; also used in reference to cute persons or animals of either gender.

-senpai: A suffix used to address upperclassmen or more experienced coworkers.

-sensei: A respectful term for teachers, artists, or high-level professionals.

PAGE 63
Obi: A sash worn with kimonos or martial arts uniforms.

PAGE 64
Zori: Japanese sandals that are similar to thonged flip-flops, often worn with kimonos.

Love at Fourteen

SEE YOU IN VOLUME 2!

LOVE AT FOURTEEN ①

FUKA MIZUTANI

Translation: Yoshito Hinton

Lettering: Lys Blakeslee

Love at Fourteen by Fuka Mizutani
© 2011 by Fuka Mizutani
All rights reserved.
First published in Japan in 2011 by HAKUSENSHA, Inc., Tokyo.
English translation rights in U.S.A., Canada, and U.K. arranged with HAKUSENSHA, Inc., through Tuttle-Mori Agency, Inc.

English Translation © 2014 by Hachette Book Group, Inc.

Yen Press
Hachette Book Group
1290 Avenue of the Americas
New York, NY 10104

www.HachetteBookGroup.com
www.YenPress.com

Yen Press is an imprint of Hachette Book Group, Inc.
The Yen Press name and logo are trademarks of Hachette Book Group, Inc.

First Yen Press Edition: December 2014

ISBN: 978-0-316-33665-9

10 9 8 7 6 5 4 3 2 1

BVG

Printed in the United States of America